The Postmodern Turn gathers together in one volume some of the most important statements of the postmodern approach to human studies. In emphasizing the social and rhetorical character of knowledge, this book advocates a concept of social knowledge that abandons the disciplinary boundaries separating the sciences and the humanities. This volume is the first collection of its kind, providing the classic essays of authors such as Lyotard, Haraway, Foucault, and Rorty. Contributors include well known theorists in the fields of sociology, anthropology, women's and gay studies, philosophy, and history. *The Postmodern Turn* will be indispensable to students and professors in all of these disciplines.

The postmodern turn

The postmodern turn
New perspectives on social theory

Edited by

Steven Seidman

CAMBRIDGE
UNIVERSITY PRESS

Published by the Press Syndicate of the University of Cambridge
The Pitt Building, Trumpington Street, Cambridge CB2 1RP
40 West 20th Street, New York, NY 10011-4211, USA
10 Stamford Road, Oakleigh, Melbourne 3166, Australia

First published 1994

Printed in the United States of America

Library of Congress Cataloging-in-Publication Data
The Postmodern turn : new perspectives on social theory / edited by
Steven Seidman.
p.   cm.
ISBN 0-521-45235-X. – ISBN 0-521-45879-X (pbk.)
1. Sociology – Philosophy.   2. Social sciences – Philosophy.
3. Postmodernism – Social aspects.   I. Seidman, Steven.
HM24.P663   1994
301′.01—dc20   93-48758
                                                          CIP
A catalog record for this book is available from the British Library.

ISBN 0-521-45235-X hardback
ISBN 0-521-45879-X paperback

Contents

v

vi   *Contents*

Introduction

Steven Seidman

Does postmodernism have a positive def. & agenda or does it conceive of itself only in terms of reaction to & transcendence of Enlightenment?

At the heart of the modern west is the culture of the Enlightenment. Assumptions regarding the unity of humanity, the individual as the creative force of society and history, the superiority of the west, the idea of science as Truth, and the belief in social progress, have been fundamental to Europe and the United States. This culture is now in a state of crisis. Signs of cultural turmoil are everywhere: in the resurgence of religious fundamentalism, in the declining authority of key social institutions, in the enfeeblement of western political ideologies and parties, and in the cultural wars over literary and aesthetic canons and paradigms of knowledge. A broad social and cultural shift is taking place in western societies. The concept of the "postmodern" captures at least certain aspects of this social change.

Modernity is not abruptly coming to an end. In most parts of the globe, modernization remains the chief social goal. Third World societies are absorbing modernizing technologies and ideologies. In societies characterized by agrarian economies, pluralistic local cultural traditions, and paternalistic rulers, promodernization elites often look favorably on the centralizing social dynamic and the universalistic moralities and knowledges of the west. In the west, modernity remains entrenched. The chief signs of modernity have not disappeared: for example, an industrial-based economy; a politics organized around unions, political parties, and interest groups; ideological debates centered on the relative merits of the market and state regulation to ensure economic growth, and the good society; institutional differentiation and role specialization and professionalism within institutions; knowledges divided into disciplines and organized around an ideology of scientific enlightenment and progress; the public celebration of a culture of self redemption and emancipatory hope. Modernity has not exhausted itself; it may be in crisis but it continues to shape the contours of our lives.

I am grateful to Chrys Ingraham and Linda Nicholson for their helpful comments on the Introduction.

1

If modernity has not come to an end, what sense, if any, does it make to speak of a "postmodern turn." In part, it makes no sense if we speak of the nonwest (e.g., Africa, China, or Islamic societies) and perhaps of many East European societies. Let me be absolutely clear. The discussion over postmodernity has to date transpired almost exclusively in the west, notably in France and the United States and to a lesser extent in Great Britain, Germany, and Australia. Indeed, the idea of a civilizational shift to postmodernity has been advanced largely by western, mostly academic intellectuals, many of whom are connected to the social rebellions of the sixties and seventies. In other words, the announcement of a postmodern turn needs to be registered as part of recent western history.

The assertion that the west is shifting to a postmodern terrain need not presuppose the end of modernity. The terms "modern" and "postmodern" refer to broad social and cultural patterns or sensibilities that can be analytically distinguished for the purpose of highlighting social trends. In the spheres of art and architecture, we can point to the surfacing of postmodern in styles, the collapse of the hierarchical distinction between high art and popular art, an eclectic mixing of aesthetic codes, a nostalgia for past and local traditions, and a playful and ironic attitude instead of the moral seriousness of the modern aesthetic. These aesthetic shifts have been interpreted by some social analysts as part of a more general social and cultural "postmodern turn" in western societies. Signs of postmodernity are visible in processes of "de-differentiation" (the breakdown of boundaries between social institutions and cultural spheres) and the "de-territorialization" of national economies and cultures.

Postmodern themes seem especially visible in the realm of knowledge. For example, disciplinary boundaries are blurring and new interdisciplinary, hybrid knowledges such as feminism, lesbian and gay studies, ethnic studies, urban studies, and cultural studies are moving into the center of the human studies. The lines between science, literature, and ideology, between literature and literary criticism, between philosophy and cultural criticism, and between high cultural criticism and popular criticism, have blurred considerably – much to the dismay of the defenders of the Enlightenment culture. As disciplinary boundaries and the line between science and nonscience blur, as claims to universal knowledge lack credibility, as knowledges are viewed as interlaced with rhetoric and power, the very meaning of knowledge is changing.

The Postmodern Turn presents statements which challenge the Enlightenment paradigm of social knowledge. Its purpose is to survey proposals to rethink the human studies. This "postmodern" knowledge contests disciplinary boundaries, the separation of science, literature, and ideology, and the division between knowledge and power.

The case for postmodernism as social theory

The human sciences were integral to the making of western modernity. Hobbes, Montesquieu, Condorcet, Hume, and Adam Smith did not simply reflect on modernization, but their theorizing was part of the making of modernity. For example, the new science of society articulated ideals of the new social order, designed maps for constructing institutions and cultures, provided legitimations of a centralized bureaucratic state and its aspiration to reorder the social world, techniques and skills to manage large shifts of population from the countryside to cities, and strategies of social control through defining identities and social norms.

Paralleling the conflicts involved in the making of the modern state, secular educational institutions, industrial capitalism, and the modern bureaucracy, the human sciences had to struggle for their place and legitimacy in the new world order that was taking shape. Defenders of the new sciences battled the church and humanistic elites who defended Christian, Aristotelian, or Platonic world views. They struggled against entrenched folk and elite cultures which viewed the social world as part of a fixed and hierarchical natural or sacred order.

Central to the struggles of the creators of the social sciences was the claim of the exclusive truth-producing capacity of science in contrast to religion, metaphysics, and folk traditions. The latter were defined as mere opinion, ideology, myth, or personal faith. Privileging science as truth had important social and political implications. In particular, it delegitimated the church whose authority rested upon a religious culture. The struggle over the legitimacy of science was a key political site of social conflict in the seventeenth and eighteenth centuries.

Two justificatory strategies were pivotal to the legitimation of the human sciences. First, a theory of the nature of knowledge was advanced which distinguished between knowledge and religion, opinion, ideology, or myth. Philosophy stepped forward as the discipline whose charge was to stipulate this line of demarcation. Despite disagreements among philosophers about the structure and conditions of knowledge, there was consensus that such a theory involved the distinction between mind and world and the view that language functioned as a neutral medium for the mind to mirror or represent the world. A second strategy to legitimate the social sciences involved sketching grand stories of human evolution which interpreted the rise of the human sciences as both a sign of social progress and a contributing cause.

The development of the social sciences in the nineteenth and twentieth centuries underwent many changes in their form and social role. Universities became the chief site for the production of such knowledges; the human sciences were organized along disciplinary lines (for example, sociology, anthropology, political science, economics); the boundaries between the human sciences and the humanities hardened; the human sciences underwent a process of mathematization and professionalization. In the course of the academic disciplining of social knowledge, the social sciences continued to rest on "foundational" justifications which took the form of a theory of knowledge and a theory of social evolution. To a significant degree, the human sciences derived their legitimacy from the twin claims of being true and contributing to human advancement.

The Enlightenment concept of the human sciences has not gone uncontested. Conservatives (for example, Bonald and Burke) and romantics (for example, Herder, Hegel, and Wordsworth) objected to the separation of reason from affect, imagination, and faith. They criticized the mechanistic world view of science as dehumanizing and protested the minimizing of moral freedom implied in a scientific culture. Speaking in broad terms, many conservative and romantic critics rejected the sciences as part of their overall opposition to modernization. In contrast to these critics who were often backward-looking and sweeping in their dismissal of science and modernity, postmodern critics in the main do not share this flight from the present. They have neither forsaken a secular culture nor necessarily abandoned the social hopes of the Enlightenment and the human sciences. Many postmodernists wish to preserve the chief values of the Enlightenment, for example autonomy, individualism, tolerance, pluralism, and democracy, but insist that this requires a reconfiguring of knowledge and society.

The case for a postmodern turn in the human sciences turns, in the first instance, on the history of failed efforts to provide "foundations" for the human sciences. The proliferation of theoretical proposals intended to establish a line of demarcation between science and nonscience have failed by their own standards. In addition, critics of the Enlightenment tradition have traced the entanglement of science in dynamics of social control and domination. Whether it is feminists who view science as implicated in male domination or poststructuralists analyzing the disciplining and normalizing role of scientific-medical discourses, the claim that a scientific culture necessarily advances the progress of humanity has lost considerable plausibility. If the link of science to social progress is in doubt, it is, in part, because changes in western societies have positioned science practically and politically in such a way that its entanglement in everyday relations of social control is becoming evident. In other words, the postmodern turn in the human studies is linked to the rise of a social condition of postmodernity. A postmodern reconfiguring of knowledge is thus crucial to understand the contemporary west and to preserve a con-

nection between the human studies and its emancipatory aims. Proposals
for a human studies that is deconstructive or genealogical and that imagines altered relations between knowledge and power and between knowledge producers and citizens are intended to preserve the critical spirit of
the Enlightenment in a postmodern culture.

Lyotard's *The Postmodern Condition* is a pivotal statement in the debate over knowledge. He announces a chief theme of the postmodern
turn: the decline of the legitimating power of "metanarratives" as distinctive of postmodern culture. Metanarratives refer to foundational theories (theories of knowledge, morality, or aesthetics) and grand stories of
social progress which have been central to the legitimation of modern
knowledge, culture, and social institutions. Lyotard argues that metanarratives such as the philosophical theories of knowledge in the tradition of
Locke, Kant, Husserl, and Bertrand Russell or the stories of social
progress related by Condorcet, Marx, or Parsons have lost their authority to justify modern social practices.

What form do social knowledges assume in a postmodern culture? Lyotard alludes to two possibilities. First, the human sciences may become
instruments of bureaucratic social control. In a universe increasingly perceived as unstable and unpredictable, however, it is more likely that the
limits, uncertainty, and incompleteness of knowledge will be underscored. In this regard, Lyotard describes the rise of a postmodern science.
Such knowledges abandon absolute standards, universal categories, and
grand theories; they favor local, historically contextualized, and pragmatic types of social inquiry. The value of postmodern knowledges lies in
making us aware of and tolerant toward social differences, ambiguity,
and conflict. *In what sense "science"? Or just "play"? Or simply paralysis?*

In the thesis of the decline of the metanarrative, Lyotard voices a major theme of the postmodern turn: the decentering of the subject and the
social world. Metanarratives presuppose an archimedian or ahistorical
standpoint from which to understand the human mind, knowledge, society, and history. Lyotard suggests that the decline of the legitimacy of
such narratives reflects, in part, a considerable doubt about the credibility of such an ahistorical standpoint and universally valid knowledge. The
shift from metanarratives to local narratives and from general theories to
pragmatic strategies suggests that in place of assuming a universal mind
or a rational knowing subject, we imagine multiple minds, subjects, and
knowledges reflecting different social locations and histories. A parallel
process of decentering is evident in the social world. Whether we speak
of the self or politics Lyotard insists that there is no center, no unifying
ground of order, coherence, and purpose. Postmodernity is characterized
by a loss of certainty and a "God's eye point of view" in the sphere of

But isn't a "local" narrative just a mini-meta-narrative? And what does "pragmatic" mean, then?

But doesn't this ultimately mean "one person—one mind" & solipsism? Like Protestant sectarians? And isn't all social scientific discourse then reduced to rhetoric? How can we justify speech at all?

knowledge, a loss of a central, organizing principle governing society and a unitary standard of cultural excellence or morality, and a decline in the belief in a unitary, coherent self.

The theme of a decentered world is pivotal to Foucault. For example, a chief claim of *The Order of Things* is that the concept of "man" is not the origin of the human sciences but its creation. Similarly, in the *History of Sexuality* he argues that the sexual subject is not the natural origin of sexual truths but that sexual knowledges (for example, sexology and psychiatry) help produce sexual subjects. Instead of viewing knowledge in terms of an ahistorical mind, and a language of truth and enlightenment, Foucault speaks of dominant and subjugated knowledges, multiple subjects or producers of knowledges, and the interconnection of knowledges to various axes of domination and resistance. Foucault urges that we abandon the Enlightenment quest for the foundations of knowledge and systems of knowledge as this conceals knowledge's entanglement in power. In place of science he favors "genealogies." These are historical-critical analyses tracing the making of identities, selves, social norms, and institutions which focus on the role of the medical and human sciences in the shaping of a "disciplinary" society.

From a less explicitly political standpoint, Richard Rorty sounds the same theme of the decentering of culture and society. His focus is the modern tradition of philosophy. In his *Philosophy and the Mirror of Nature*, Rorty perceives in modern philosophy a sustained quest to establish the foundations of knowledge. Philosophy assumed the role of legitimating science as knowledge. Toward this end, philosophy assumed a separation between the knowing mind and the world; language was viewed as a neutral medium of representation and knowledge was framed as a mirroring between word and world. Rorty disputes the credibility of this foundational project. Philosophical efforts to demarcate knowledge from illusion, science from nonscience, truth from error, and to articulate universal standards of truth, morality, and beauty, have been unable to avoid contradictions and metaphysical assertions. Whereas modern philosophy often posits a universal mind and universal truths, Rorty speaks of traditions and communities which produce multiple vocabularies of self and world. He highlights the pragmatic character of knowledge. Ideas are intended to do things – to promote certain interests and goals. In this regard, Rorty believes that many of the disagreements in the human sciences boil down to divergent social aims. For example, the debate between positivists who defend "explanation" and interpretive social analysts who legitimate "understanding" as the preferred logic of the social sciences is less a disagreement about the nature than about the purpose of knowledge. Instead of retreating from the moral character of knowledge, Rorty urges an approach to knowledge with an eye to its practical significance.

[handwritten marginalia, left margin: Who besides positivists ever held this? And so we are to try to distinguish truth from error?]

[handwritten note, bottom: The commitment to objectivity isn't a metaphysical or epistemological claim but a mentality that protects us from a descent into a purely partisan subjectivity & cynical rhetoric.]

He imagines social analysts as cultural critics and storytellers whose value lies in our commitment to a democratic public realm.

The social origins of the challenge to the Enlightenment paradigm of social knowledge by Lyotard and Foucault lie in the social rebellions of the sixties and seventies. In the student and labor protests, in the movements for prison and psychiatric reform, and in the feminist and gay movements, they perceive a far-reaching questioning of the culture of the Enlightenment. These rebellions broadened the focus of theory and politics from an exclusive concern with issues of labor, class, and political economy to issues related to the body, sexuality, gender, dynamics of discipline, normalization, administrative control, and consumerism. The social clashes of the sixties gave birth to new knowledges (for example, genealogies and local narratives) and the resurrection of discredited or silenced folk knowledges.

Reflecting a similar political viewpoint, Cornel West and Donna Haraway describe the social and political origins of the "postmodern turn." West sketches a broad genealogy of what he calls the "new cultural politics of difference." This refers to the challenges to a hegemonic Eurocentric, male dominated, heterosexist culture by marginalized, disempowered groups. He traces the declining authority of a European and Anglo-American social elite in the postwar west who managed to claim universality for their particular, ethnocentric culture and politics. The social rebellions associated with the counterculture, the New Left, feminism, lesbians and gay men, and ethnic and racial minorities, along with Third World rebellions against Western colonialism, criticized the Enlightenment culture for perpetuating inequality and oppression in the name of reason and social progress. In place of false claims to universality and truth, the new politics of difference asserts the value of individuality, difference, heterogeneity, locality, and pluralism. In place of the tradition of Western scientism, West advocates "prophetic criticism," a public-centered, moral, and political critical thinking.

As a feminist, Donna Haraway experienced the ways the Enlightenment tradition, despite its emancipatory ideology, functioned to oppress women. Science projected men as the norm of all humanity. This ignored women's lives which have historically differed in important ways from those of men. Western science contributed to the cultural invisibility and social subordination of women. Women's distinctive ways of knowing and living have been devalued or ignored in the traditions of western science. In place of one universal language of humanity, feminists have proposed that social analysts attend to the ways men and women vary in their ways of being and knowing. One prominent feminist perspective has claimed that men and women represent unitary, antithetical gender experiences and identities. Haraway defends the broad claim of the gen-

[handwritten marginal notes:]
But the critique was eminently rational, wasn't it?

→ What is that? And how does it stake a claim to public credibility?

But is this inherent in science or anti-scientific? Didn't these constitute a violation of scientific norms that can be... definitively refuted? science?

To say that scientific perspectives, especially science-based social perspectives, are never free of ideological prejudices is not the same as claiming that science is nothing but ideology with a different mask.

"Women's distinctive ways of knowing" — What does this mean?

dered texture of selves and society but criticizes the assertion of a universal gender dichotomy. Women and men vary in their experiences, interests,
and values according to their class, race, age, sexual, or national status.
Constructions asserting the unity of women exclude and silence some
women. Haraway proposes a decentered perspective of the self: Identities
are viewed as fractured, multiple, and protean. Asserting the unity of female identity may be legitimate but only as a rhetorical and political strategy. Haraway connects the decentering of social subjects and knowledges
to the new social movements and rebellions of the postwar period. Moreover, she links these social rebellions to more general social changes such
as the emergence of an information-based economy, the restructuring of
work and households, and the altered configurations of gender, sexuality, and race in a globalized world order.

Even if known to be false?

The culture of the Enlightenment is losing its capacity to legitimate
and give coherence and purpose to the lives of many of us in the west. Its
certainties and social goals are being contested and losing precious cultural capital.

As we move toward the end of the second millenium we in the west are
entering a postmodern cultural terrain. This is a culture in which knowledge becomes knowledges, identities are understood as fractured, plural,
and porous, and society and politics is without a fixed center. What will
social knowledge look like? What form will the disciplinary organization
of knowledge assume? In the next three sections of this introduction, I
survey some key statements of postmodernism as social theory.

Contesting foundations: The crisis of representation

Despite the diversity of social theories and research programs proliferating under the banner of the Enlightenment, there has been little or no disagreement that their legitimacy rests primarily on their claim to truth.
Moreover, truth has been imagined as liberating. Whereas myth and ideology promote ethnocentric interests masquerading as universal, science
uncovers truths which mark a path of enlightenment and social progress.
Demarcating truth from error and privileging science as knowledge has
assumed enormous social importance in western cultures. The task of authorizing this line of demarcation has been the charge of "foundational"
discourses or theories of knowledge.

A sign of the crisis of the culture of the Enlightenment is the growing
prominence of arguments challenging foundationalism. For example,
Derrida's "deconstructionist" critique of the "logocentrism" of western
philosophy proposes that the central binary oppositions which under-

pin western thought – speech/writing, presence/absence, meaning/form, mind/body, and literal/metaphorical – are arbitrary, unstable, and reversible. Derrida wishes to show that efforts to establish foundations conceal a will to power. Similarly, Rorty challenges many of the core assumptions of modern western philosophy, the subject-object dualism and the view of language as representation and truth as a mirroring between word and world. Rorty urges a pragmatic approach: knowledge as social practice, valued for its social role. The Enlightenment quest for an archimedian standpoint from which to pronounce on the nature of truth, morality, and beauty is today being widely contested. Central to the "postmodern turn" in the realm of knowledge is the shift from a language of subject-object dualism, objectivity, and truth, to a perspective which asserts the interconnection of knowledge and power and which troubles the boundaries between science, rhetoric and narrative.

[handwritten margin note: Isn't this a straw man?]

The challenge to foundational discourses is more than a local debate amongst philosophers. A widespread discontent with the Enlightenment paradigm of knowledge is evident across disciplinary knowledges. If a suspicion toward foundations and Enlightenment traditions of knowledge received a powerful expression in philosophy (for example, in the works of Derrida, Foucault, Rorty, Lyotard), parallel developments are visible in the more "specialized" knowledges, from feminism, Queer Theory to urban studies, anthropology, and history.

Foundational arguments are not confined to philosophical theories of knowledge in general, for example, Kant's *Critique of Pure Reason* or Husserl's *Ideas*. Foundational claims underpin specialized knowledges. In "The End of Sociological Theory," I argue that much of sociological theory is foundational; it aims to justify the most elementary premises and concepts recommended to guide social analysis.

Sociology is a discipline rife with interpretive disputes over social realities. Are the chief lines of stratification in contemporary societies around class, gender, race, or sexuality? Are contemporary western societies postindustrial or late capitalist? Where appeals to empirical criteria cannot resolve such interpretive conflicts, theorists propose theoretical standards. They reason that underlying interpretive disputes are differences in foundational assumptions. If consensus is possible around issues such as the nature of action, the relation between agency and structure, the micro and macro link, or the interconnection between social structure and culture, sociologists would have guidelines to assess and resolve interpretive disputes or narrow them to local empirical disagreements. Unfortunately, there has been little or no consensus about what standards should guide such metatheoretical decisions. The foundational turn in sociological theory has yielded neither a consensus nor an enriched interpretive debate, but a growing social insularity of theory. I urge a shift from sociological theory as a foundational practice to narrative knowledges which unite moral advocacy and social analysis.

Foundational arguments are losing their plausibility, at least in western cultures. One reason is that the premise of an ahistorical subject of knowledge – the sociologist or the social scientist – appears indefensible. The Enlightenment paradigm assumed that the scientific community, with its culture of objectivity, criticalness, and the reign of empiricism, would cleanse the individual scientist of all social particularities (for example, class, gender, and nationality) producing a rational mind interested only in truth. Such a position is inconsistent with the dominant logic of sociological knowledges and has been seriously challenged by various critics of science. One important movement of political criticism has been feminism.

A guiding assumption of western feminism has been the gendered character of social realities, including knowledge. Feminists arrived at a political view of knowledge from their social struggles for gender justice. They had to confront many scientific and medical knowledges (sociology, psychology, biology, medicine, and psychiatry, for instance) which constructed and positioned women as subordinate to men. Indeed, many feminists have criticized the Enlightenment paradigm of knowledge as favoring men's interests and values. For example, the emphasis in many theories of knowledge on the duality between the knowing subject and the world, the separation of cognition from affect and intuition, of fact and values, a logical, linear idea of knowledge, and the view of knowledge as promoting social control are said to express a male-centered standpoint. Despite the intention of Enlightenment traditions to advance human freedom, its concept of knowledge helped to perpetuate the dominance of men's interests and values. A feminist perspective views scientific knowledge as a social force, not necessarily beneficent to women.

Many feminists have defended some version of a "standpoint" theory of knowledge. This holds that knowledge is always produced from a specific social position exhibiting particular interests, values, and beliefs. Men and women are assumed to differ in some important respects in terms of their social locations and therefore their epistemological values. An example of standpoint theory might argue that men comprehend reality from their positions of power in the public sphere; by contrast, many women know the world from their primary location in the private sphere where their lack of economic independence leaves them subordinate to men. Thus, men's knowledges would focus on public institutions and dynamics whereas women's knowledges would be tailored to intimate and familial processes. Standpoint theory troubles dominant Enlightenment models of knowledge because it contests the presumption of an ahistorical, value-neutral, general knowing subject. Yet it remains tied to an Enlightenment paradigm to the extent that the appeal to a unitary concept of the knowing subject (for example, "woman") is said to serve as a foundation for objective knowledge.

The idea that women occupy a common ground of experience which makes feminist knowledge and politics possible has been contested. In the pathbreaking anthology *This Bridge Called My Back*, women of color criticized western feminism for its Eurocentric, middle-class, and heterosexist biases. The foundational category of feminism – "woman" – has often turned out to mean white, middle-class, European-centered, often academic women. The lives and interests of women of color were not given expression in much of western feminism. This is particularly the case for feminist theory and politics in the sixties and seventies.

The theoretical and political implications of this volume are developed by Norma Alarcón. She raises serious questions about the concept of the subject in western feminism. Many feminists, she argues, have uncritically absorbed the dominant male-centered Enlightenment view of the individual as a separate, autonomous, and unitary self. The authors of the *Bridge*, however, have suggested a different concept: a self who occupies simultaneous social axes of gender, class, race, and sexuality. Thus, Alarcón proposes that feminism should abandon speaking of women as if they share the same social location and interests in favor of describing women as occupying multiple social positions. Alarcón counsels a theoretical approach which locates the self in the intersection of the dynamics of gender, race, class, and sexuality.

If women differ along multiple social axes must feminists surrender a general warrant for feminism's knowledges and politics? Alarcón is insistent that feminists must give up appeals to a unitary idea of women because it inevitably excludes some women and impedes coalition building. She imagines the possibility of subjects who are aware of themselves as occupying multiple social junctures. Such subjects approach politics pragmatically. Which aspects of identity are highlighted and in what combinations (for example, black, working-class, lesbian) depends on theoretical and practical interests. "The multiple-voiced subjectivity is lived in resistance to competing notions for one's allegiance or self-identification. . . . The choice of one [I am a woman, for instance] or many themes [I am white, working-class woman, for instance] is both theoretical and a political decision." An infinite number of such locations?

Many feminists are uncomfortable with the abandonment of the category of woman as the foundation of feminism. If there are multiple, virtually infinite female subjects varying by race, class, sexuality, age, and so on, won't feminists dilute their political power by being fractured and divided into a multitude of groups and organizations? Without a foundation in the concept of women feminism would seem to surrender to relativism, a position thought to undermine its claims to political authority.

In "Contingent Foundations: Feminism and the Question of 'Postmodernism,'" Judith Butler tries to navigate around the seeming impasse between feminists who defend and oppose the idea that women's common gender identity is an essential foundation for feminist knowledge and politics. Critics object to standpoint theory for its exclusionary politics while defending a version of feminism which does not assume the identity or unity of women's experiences or interests. Butler tries to rearticulate the debate. She suggests that the issue is less the question of defending or abandoning foundations since all theories and politics make assumptions about the nature of social reality and knowledge. At stake is the way we think of foundations and the theoretical and political implications of foundational strategies. Instead of assuming an antifoundationalist pose, Butler proposes that we think of foundations as permanently contestable assumptions and take a pragmatic approach to them. In this regard, she does not wish to abandon the deployment of the category of woman but to approach it as a site of multiple and contested meanings. This approach has the advantage of allowing feminists both to rally behind broad appeals to women's empowerment and to sustain the many voices of women as part of the living culture of feminism.

The question of foundations is pivotal to the project of social analysis as critique. If general standards of truth and morality can be identified, they can serve as grounds for social criticism. What happens to social critique when secure foundations are abandoned? In "Subjectivity in Social Analysis," Renato Rosaldo addresses this issue in the context of engaging the debate about the relation between social analysis and moral advocacy. Rosaldo notes that the opposition between social science and social critique has been pivotal to the Enlightenment tradition. He recommends a position which turns away from the Enlightenment model of the detached observer objectively analyzing social reality in favor of a view of social knowledge as involving multiple standpoints and perspectives, the interconnection between social analyst and society, the role of interests and values in producing knowledge, and the interlacing of knowledge and power.

If there is no ahistorical, archimedian standpoint from which to criticize society, what is the moral basis of critique? Contrary to the fears of many critics, Rosaldo argues that abandoning the ideal of objectivity and the quest for foundations does not undermine the credibility of social criticism. He recommends that social critics draw on the cultural traditions and communities of which they are a part for their moral standards and visions. Critics are imagined as part of the communities they criticize; they should draw on the moral traditions of these communities for standards of critique and projects of social change. Critics aim to uncover inequality and oppression in order to awaken public perceptions of injustice and foster political activity. They not only draw from the moral languages of particular communities but address particular communities, for example scientific communities, policymakers, or citizen activists. Rosaldo favors a plurality of languages of critique anchored in specific local communities and traditions.

> The social analysts' multiple identities at once underscore the potential for uniting an analytical with an ethical project and render obsolete the view of the utterly detached observer who looks down from on high. In this respect, my argument parallels Walzer's discussion of the social critic who is connected to a community, not isolated and detached. . . . Social critics work outward from in-depth knowledge of a specific form of life. Informed by such conceptions as social justice, human dignity, and equality, they use their moral imagination to move from the world as it actually is to a locally persuasive vision of how it ought to be. Because different communities differ in their problems and possibilities, such visions must be more local than universal.

But we are in the midst of a dramatic process that is collapsing localities + producing emergent universal values.

Human studies as rhetoric, narrative, and critique

The Enlightenment tradition has organized knowledges around a series of major oppositions: science/rhetoric, science/politics, science/literature, and science/narrative. Science represented true knowledge; it was based on reason and fact. In contrast, the second term of the binary – rhetoric, politics, literature, and narrative – belonged in the realm of the imagination, feelings, and values. Science was defined by its exclusion of rhetoric and politics. It was not, however, that science lacked moral or political significance. From Adam Smith to Marx, W. E. B. DuBois, Margaret Mead, and Parsons, the promise of science was that its truths could deliver humankind closer to a state of freedom. The quest for true knowledge exacted a high price, however: a strict disciplinary regime of science which enjoined its practitioners to renounce rhetoric and politics.

The oppositions between science and rhetoric and science and politics were conjoined to a related series of binaries – theory/narrative, knowledge/literature, reason/affect, disinterested/interested, knowledge/ideology, masculine/feminine, and knowledge/power. In these contrasts, the first term is positioned as superior. Science is true, literal, rational, and useful; nonscience is fiction, figurative, subjective, and merely decorative.

Marx + DuBois renounced rhetoric + politics ?! There is no such dichotomy in Marxism with its insistence on the unity of theory + practice, of changing the world rather than merely understanding it.

These oppositions were not only characteristic of the positivist tradition but were no less central to Marxism and interpretive approaches to social science. For example, Marx located his social thought in the sphere of science and insisted that science was exclusive of rhetoric, narrative, and ideology. The politics of Marxism were authorized by an appeal to the real laws of history and society, not by an appeal to affect or imagination. Weber codified this binary culture of knowledge in the doctrine of value-neutrality and objectivity.

What?! Nonsense. He insisted that all science is the ideology of a class.

The Enlightenment culture of knowledge has been challenged. Critical theorists, feminists, reflexive sociologists, and normative political theorists have imagined social knowledges which unite science, critique, and politics. Yet most of these critics of scientism have not contested the central organizing binary oppositions of this culture, that of science/rhetoric, science/literature, and science/ideology.

To the extent that human studies makes the postmodern turn, these hierarchical oppositions are marginalized or displaced. A process of cultural de-differentiation and reconfiguration occurs. For example, in a postmodern culture, the boundaries between science/rhetoric and science/ideology blur or collapse; the hierarchies of fact/fiction, knowledge/prejudice, science/literature, literal/figurative, reason/intuition, and masculine/feminine are disturbed and left unstable. Postmodern social knowledge shifts to a new terrain where social analysis combines empiricism and moral advocacy, theory and narrative, analytical abstraction and intuitive rhetorical gestures. The marking of knowledge in these terms announces that we are leaving the epoch of the Enlightenment.

Very dangerous. See post-modernist fundamentalism.

Zygmunt Bauman sketches a shift from modernity to postmodernity. The former is characterized by the dominance of a culture of control. In the sphere of knowledge, a "legislative" reason intent on designing and imposing order through categorizing, classifying, and regulating nature and humanity prevails. This is an era organized around the search for general principles, laws of the mind, society, and history, and the quest for certainty and foundations. Postmodernity features a process of de-differentiation or the collapse of boundaries and a loss of an epistemic and social center. The social world is fragmented into a multitude of communities, cultural traditions, and knowledges. The language of the detached observer, objectivity, universality, and truth passes into a culture organized around the irreducible plurality of knowledges and standpoints and the intermingling of knowledge, rhetoric, and politics. Under conditions of postmodernity, Bauman urges that the social analyst will abandon a legislative role in favor of an "interpretive" role: the social analyst as mediator between different social worlds, as interpreter of alien cultures, and as advocate for particular moral visions.

Bauman imagines postmodern social analysis as a hermeneutic inquiry. Like the literary critic, the interpretive social analyst approaches communities as texts with the intention of translating the unfamiliar into the familiar. Interpretive knowledge is valued to the extent that it legitimates difference, expands tolerance, promotes diversity, and fosters understanding and communication between different groups. Human studies as a literary textual analysis resonates with the spirit of ambiguity, tolerance, playfulness, and diversity central to the postmodern sensibility.

If Bauman gestures toward a blending of science and literature, James Clifford and Richard Brown make the rhetorical and literary aspects of analysis pivotal to the human studies. They go beyond asserting a parallel between the literary interpretation of texts and an interpretive social analysis to collapsing the boundaries between science and literature.

James Clifford maintains that the science/literature binary cannot withstand serious scrutiny. The persuasiveness and coherence of the social sciences rely not only on a logic of evidence and reason but on metaphor and allegory. These literary techniques structure social analysis; they give coherence and meaning to conceptual and empirical statements. Science is said to exhibit a deeply rhetorical or literary character. The rhetorical structuring of scientific knowledge is particularly evident in ethnography. In "On Ethnographic Allegory," Clifford observes the widespread circulation in American ethnographies of "redemptive" allegories whose chief theme is "saving the vanishing primitive." Allegories provide a religious-moral framing of social reality. The allegorical ordering of ethnography contradicts the Enlightenment view of science as empirical or representational truth. It suggests that ethnographic texts exhibit multiple meanings, that they construct metanarratives, that they situate the reader in a unique world order and aim to persuade or propel action. Clifford is suggesting that, with respect to the structure of knowledge, there is little difference between ethnographic and literary texts. Instead of associating ethnography with the language of truth, he recommends that it be associated with a discourse at once involving understanding and moral persuasion, explanation, and social practice.

Arguably, ethnography might be thought of as peculiarly suspectible to literary or allegorical meanings. By contrast, sociology, with its culture of empiricism, quantification, methodological rigor, and positivist spirit, might present a more cogent case for the plausibility of the science/rhetoric binary.

In "Rhetoric, Textuality, and The Postmodern Turn in Sociological Theory," Richard Brown takes issue with realist or literalist views of sociology. He offers a textualist approach to society and sociology. "In this rhetorical view, reality and truth are formed through practices of representation and interpretation by rhetors and their publics." Knowledge is less a matter of correspondence of word and world than conformity to specific authorized practices of writing and reading. Similarly, society is imagined less as a material structure, organic order, or social system than

[marginal annotation, right side top:] And what's the foundation of these values rather than any other? Aren't they parasitic on previous foundationalist perspectives?

[marginal annotation, right side bottom:] science/literature or science/rhetoric

[handwritten note, bottom:] All of this critique only shows the pursuit of knowledge to be profoundly more elusive than we used to think. It should humble us, strip us of our pretensions to quasi-omniscience. But it is no justification for surrender, for throwing up our hands + abandoning the distinctions between

as a symbolic, meaning-produced construction rooted in historically spe-cific linguistic and discursive practices. Moreover, sociology and society are viewed as interconnected and mutually productive. To the extent that sociology carries moral and political meanings, it is implicated in the mak-ing of society. Brown envisions a sociology that is deliberately critical and politically engaged. *to what justifiable ends? on what grounds?*

In Richard Brown's postmodern sociology, the neat boundaries be-tween science and literature, explanation and narrative, knowledge and power collapse. This does not mean, though, that social knowledges are reduced to a metaphorical or fictional status. Brown imagines a critical social discourse that is empirical and analytical yet frankly moral and political. A similar effort to rearticulate human studies on a decidely postmodern terrain is offered by Nancy Fraser and Linda Nicholson. In "Criticism without Philosophy: An Encounter between Feminism and Postmodernism," they defend a postmodern feminism which would abandon foundationalism but not general theories or explanations. They insist that large-scale accounts of sexism are necessary to the extent that gender is a pervasive axis of social structure and domination. Postmod-ern explanations would be different in key respects, however, from stan-dard Enlightenment theories. Conceptual strategies would be historical and organized by a logic of social difference. They would be comparati-vist not universalistic and would dispense with the idea of a subject of history. Essentializing concepts of "woman" and "man" would give way to "plural and complexly constructed conceptions of social identity, treating gender as one relevant strand among others, attending also to class, race, ethnicity, age, and sexual orientation." A postmodern femi-nism would be pragmatic; its conceptual strategies would be tailored to specific social ends. It would embrace the permanence of a plurality of feminist voices and politics.

Postmodern social analysis: Empirical illustrations

How would postmodern empirical social analysis differ from the modern human sciences? What difference would the "postmodern turn" make for social analysts and critics?

Recall the guiding premises of the human sciences in the modern epoch. The disciplines have been organized around the following assumptions: the privileging of science as knowledge, the establishment of foundations, efforts to elaborate basic premises and concepts into general theories, laws, models, and explanations, the mathematization of knowledge, the separation of fact and values, the exclusion of the moral and political from science, the pursuit of scientific progress through instituting an austere culture of methodologcal rigor, empiricism, and conceptual justification based upon truth claims. *This is only one strand. C. Wright Mills is elsewhere.*

How would a postmodern culture alter the practice of human studies? Postmodern premises would change the focus of human studies. For example, a postmodern human studies would abandon arguments about the nature of knowledge and methatheoretical discussions over the nature of *From where does a postmodern pragmatism get its goals + values?* action, order, and change or the relation between materialism and idealism or agency and structure. In place of such foundational arguments, there would be pragmatic justificatory discourses. Theorists would shift their attention from the nature of knowledge to the pragmatics of knowledge. Instead of making a foundational move in the face of empirical or interpretive conflicts, a postmodernist would consider social, moral, and political consequences, the practical purposes of knowledges, and their situational impact. *that is, which perspective best serves my unexamined values?*

Insofar as postmodern knowledges assert the intermingling of the empirical, moral, and political, human studies would abandon the separation of the cognitive, normative, and aesthetic spheres and the division between fact and values or knowledge and politics. Reflecting general *But how w/o surrendering to an almost solipsistic subjectivism?* processes of differentiation characteristic of modernization, knowledges were not only distinguished by disciplines but the cognitive sphere of scientific knowledge was separated from the spheres of ethics, aesthetics, and politics. Reflecting a social process of de-differentiation characteristic of postmodernity, disciplinary boundaries blur and domains of knowledge (for example, the humanities and the social sciences), once separated, intermingle; the lines separating science, literature, and history are already loosening considerably. A postmodern human studies suggests the reorganization of the disciplinary organization of knowledge; it points to knowledges that are hybrid discourses, uniting the empirical and the rhetorical, the cognitive and the moral, the analytical and the practical, and the theoretical and the literary. Accordingly, in a postmodern culture, social analysts will need to develop new languages, conventions, and skills; we will have to learn to address the moral and political implications of our knowledges, to justify knowledges with an eye to situational and practical considerations. *But doesn't that depend on certain knowledge of consequences?*

I have been describing broad shifts in the frameworks of knowledge in a postmodern culture. Such shifts have significant impact on the shape of human studies, changes in the strategies of justification and in the very form and aims of social knowledge. Moreover, a shift to a postmodern culture would involve changes in conceptual strategies. For example, social analysis guided by postmodern premises would evolve a different language of the self and social order. Assuming a view of identities that are plural, unstable, situationally enacted, and sites of social contestation, we would need a postmodern language of the self and society. Thus, we might learn to speak of "composite" rather than unitary, additive identities, of selves simultaneously positioned along multiple social axes (gender, race, class, sexuality, and age). Instead of deploying concepts such as "men" and "women" we might be compelled to speak of twentieth-century, white, middle-class, heterosexual American men. Such composite formulations of identities are less susceptible of exclusionary effects, less silencing of differences, and make us more aware of the socially constructed, normative, and practical character of our knowledges. In a postmodern mode, the conceptual language chosen to speak of the self would be pragmatically guided, that is, with an eye to our aims or the effects of discourse. Aware of the constructed character of selves, a postmodern human studies would take as one of its purposes analysis of the making of identities or subjects. This is the Foucauldian project, the genealogical analysis of the social production of sexual, criminal, psychological, and deviant identities and their political effects.

It needs to be emphasized that there is no one conceptual strategy, approach, paradigm, or language that defines the postmodern turn. As should be clear already, the term "postmodern" as applied to the sphere of knowledge represents little more than a way of speaking of a very broad, heterogeneous shift now transpiring in the cultures of western knowledges. The ways in which these refigured premises get elaborated into paradigms of social analysis will vary immensely. Postmodern strains of social analysis are evident in the feminist critique of essentialism, in Queer Theory, Rorty's pragmatism, Foucault's genealogies, Lyotard's local narratives, and in the rhetorical turn in the social sciences.

One of the most productive points of departure for postmodern human studies has been poststructuralism. The product of French intellectuals aspiring to a post-Marxian critical approach, poststructuralism expresses the rebellious spirit of May 1968. Influenced by the linguistic turn in philosophical and social thought in the postwar west, poststructuralism emphasizes the role of language and discourse in shaping subjectivity, social institutions, and politics. Language is viewed as a system of signs or words whose meanings derive from relations of difference and contrast. In western societies, binary oppositions such as man/woman, body/mind, material/ideal, reason/intuition, and speech/writing have structured language and the broader cultural and institutional organization of society. Moreover, such binary oppositions have been productive of linguistic and social hierarchies. For example, the word "man" is defined in terms of what men are not – women. The very meaning of "man" excludes the "feminine" and vice versa. Moreover, the two terms of the binary are not equal. The first term – man – is superior. For example, "man" might be associated with reason, leadership, the public sphere, control, and au-

This leads to solipsism since each individual is ultimately unique. All of those categories can be further subdivided infinitely. Again from whence would these aims or effects of discourse be derived?

No. Women have been defined as not-man but not much the reverse.

thority. The hierarchical oppositions structuring linguistic and discursive meanings shape social practices as they become part of institutions, mass culture, therapeutic regimes, gender codes, and so on.

These linguistically organized subjective and social orders are never fixed or stable; meanings are always unstable, shifting, multivocal, and sites of contestation. For example, the coupling, man/woman, carries multiple, contradictory meanings subject to perpetual contestation. This is so because assigning meaning to the two terms simultaneously locates them in a normative social space. Defining men as rational, intellectual, and assertive positions them as psychologically fit for social roles of authority and leadership. By contrast, defining women as intuitive, emotional, and other-directed positions them as suited for domestic, child-rearing, or social service roles. Poststructuralism aims to disturb the dominant binary meanings that function to perpetuate social and political hierarchies. Deconstructionism is the method deployed. This involves unsettling and displacing the binary hierarchies. Deconstructionism un covers their historically contingent origin and their political role not with an eye to providing a better foundation for knowledge and society but in order to dislodge their dominance and to create a social space which is tolerant of difference, ambiguity, and playful innovation, and favors autonomy and democracy. *Where do these values come from + what justifies their priority?*

The three selections in this section of the anthology illustrate the value of a poststructuralist social analysis. In "Post-Structuralism and Sociology," Charles Lemert sketches a poststructural approach to the American involvement in Vietnam. By a poststructural human studies, Lemert intends a framing of social realities in textual or discursive terms; such an approach is attentive to a social logic of difference and the political effect of knowledge. He suggests a textualist reading of the American war policy toward Vietnam, a reality created and maintained through texts, readings, interpretations, and discursive constructions. Lemert imagines "Vietnam" as a network of texts rendered intelligent in their intertextuality. A textualist approach to Vietnam does not deny death and destruction but insists that such experiences are meaningful through readings, interpretations, and contestations. *And what insight does this produce?*

In "Deconstructing Equality-Versus-Difference: Or, the Uses of Poststructuralist Theory For Feminism," Joan Scott makes the case for the advantages of poststructuralism for feminism. She addresses a long-standing division between feminists who emphasize the equality of men and women in making demands for women's rights and those who stress their differences. The former suggest that women's skills and talents should be the only basis for consideration of social roles whereas the latter insist that discrimination and different patterns of gender socialization are relevant to considerations of women's employment and education. Scott claims that the equality/difference binary divides women and perpetuates their social subordination. She aims to contest and displace this opposition. Instead of viewing equality and difference as a fixed, universal opposition, she argues that they presuppose one another, are implicated in one another, and need not be posed as an immutable hierarchical binary.

> Placing equality and difference in antithetical relationship has, then, a double effect. It denies the way in which difference has long figured in political notions of equality and it suggests that sameness is the only ground on which equality can be claimed. It thus puts feminists in an impossible position for as long as we argue within the terms of a discourse set up by this opposition we grant the current conservative premise that because women cannot be identical to men in all respects, we cannot expect to be equal to them. The only alternative . . . is to refuse to oppose equality to difference and insist continually on differences – differences as the condition of individual and collective identities . . . [and] differences as the very meaning of equality itself.

See Todorov

Scott maintains that if equality and difference are imagined as mutually productive with difference serving as the central concept, feminists can simultaneously advocate equality and difference.

In a similarly deft effort to use a poststructuralist approach to social analysis, Lee Edelman deconstructs AIDS discourses. Although he positions himself as a literary theorist, his analysis of AIDS blurs, if not collapses, any meaningful distinction between literary and social analysis. Reflecting the textualist turn of poststructuralism, Edelman approaches AIDS in textual, rhetorical terms. Texts frame the reality of AIDS; it exists only through texts and readings. This textualist epistemology in no way denies that AIDS involves human suffering, death, and oppression. Texts and readings render such experiences meaningful and coherent.

No. It also exists through microbes & antibodies & physiological, objective processes that no reading of texts can alter.

Much of the discursive construction of AIDS asserts a literal reality to AIDS; readings and interpretations are conflated with reality. The figurative, metaphorical, and rhetorical character of these representations is concealed behind a fiercely literalist understanding. A discourse of the virtual, literal reality of AIDS dominates the public imagining of AIDS. This is true not only with regard to medical statements but also for the social and political statements about AIDS. For example, AIDS activists declare Silence equals Death as a way to dramatize the failure of society to respond to AIDS. This is paralleled by homophobic cultural activists who declare that Gay Rights equals AIDS. Edelman's point is that both camps of cultural activism make literal and real a figurative or symbolic reality; both camps are engaged in a rhetorical and political practice in their very discursive actions. Silence does not literally equal death any more than gay rights literally equals AIDS; both equations rely ironically upon the metaphorical or rhetorical trope of the equation. They both naturalize symbolic processes. Although the literalization of Silence equals Death has the ability to call attention to injustice and mobilize protest, this same literalization validates the homophobic Gay Rights equals AIDS. The literalization of AIDS constructions and politics conjoins opposites in a perpetual antagonism, a circle of advocacy and defense.

There is no one postmodern paradigm of social knowledge. Under the banner of the postmodern there are a plurality of approaches and conceptual strategies. All share a certain affinity or kinship with respect to abandoning certain key Enlightenment assumptions. They advocate broadly postfoundational, pragmatic premises and points of departure. If I choose to call these premises and conceptual strategies "postmodern" it is largely for rhetorical reasons. It reflects my sense that the creation of an alternative, post-Enlightenment culture of knowledge requires a certain level of social mobilization, a certain posturing as a crusade, a certain presumption of there being a movement – organized and sustained in aim. The term postmodern becomes the occasion for that effort at consolidation and mobilization, for the crystallization of the accumulated discontents that are surfacing in many contexts in the western organization of knowledge and culture.

[handwritten: Postmodernism seems to me to be parasitic on modernism + is in fact a particular manifestation of modernism, a reductio ad absurdum of modernism, rather than a transcendence of it. It is the ultimate, extreme expression of the rejection of the absolutes of a religious perspective, an unveiling of the relativistic implications of the Enlightenment, a demonstration of modernism's radical capacity for undermining its own foundations, which turn out to be unscientific, unobjective, unverifiable, unempirical, unjustifiable in any terms acceptable to science itself. It is reason devouring itself, which is why it always is forced to define itself in negative terms rather than by what it affirms. It is the death rattle of modernism, not its successor and, in the absence of a viable successor, ends up giving aid + comfort to all of modernism's reactionary enemies + their obsolete absolutisms. A disillusionment on the part of those who believed their own propaganda.]

A SHORT BIBLIOGRAPHY OF KEY WORKS IN POSTMODERN SOCIAL THEORY

Alcoff, Linda. "Cultural Feminism Versus Post-Structuralism: The Identity Crisis in Feminist Theory," *Signs* 13 (1988).

Anzaldúa, Gloria. *Borderlands/La Frontera* (San Francisco: Spinsters/Aunt Lute, 1987).

Aronowitz, Stanley, and Henry Giroux. *Postmodern Education* (Minneapolis: University of Minnesota Press, 1991).

Barrett, Michele, and Phillips, Anne. Eds. *Destabilizing Theory* (Stanford: Stanford University Press, 1992).

Baudrillard, Jean. *Simulations* (New York: Semiotext(e), 1983).

Bauman, Zygmunt. *Intimations of Postmodernity* (New York: Routledge, 1992). *Legislators and Interpreters* (Cambridge: Polity, 1987).

Best, Steven, and Douglas Kellner. *Postmodern Theory* (New York: Guilford, 1991).

Boyne, Roy, and Rattansi, Ali. Eds. *Postmodernism and Society* (New York: St. Martin's Press, 1990).

Brown, Richard. *Social Science as Civic Discourse* (Chicago: University of Chicago Press, 1989).

Butler, Judith, and Scott, Joan. Eds. *Feminists Theorize the Political* (New York: Routledge, 1992).

Clifford, James, and Marcus, George. Eds. *Writing Culture* (Berkeley: University of California Press, 1986).

Denzin, Norman, *Images of Postmodern Society* (Newbury Park, CA.: Sage, 1991).

Derrida, Jacques. *Writing and Difference* (Chicago: University of Chicago Press, 1978).

   "Structure, Sign, and Play in the Discourse of the Human Sciences." In Richard Macksey and Eugenio Donato, *The Languages of Criticism and the Sciences of Man* (Baltimore: Johns Hopkins University Press, 1970).

Eagleton, Terry. "Capitalism, Modernism and Postmodernism." In *Against the Grain: Essays 1975–1985* (London: Verso, 1986).

Foster, Hal. Ed. *Postmodern Culture* London: Pluto Press, 1985).

Foucault, Michel. *The Order of Things* (New York: Pantheon, 1972).

   The History of Sexuality, vol. 1: *An Introduction* (New York: Pantheon, 1978).

   Power/Knowledge (New York: Pantheon, 1980).

Fraser, Nancy. *Unruly Practices* (Minneapolis: University of Minnesota Press, 1989).

Fuss, Diana. Ed. *Inside/Out* (New York: Routledge, 1990).

Gates, Henry Louis. Ed. *"Race," Writing and Difference* (Chicago: University of Chicago Press, 1985).

Habermas, Jürgen, *The Philosophical Discourse of Modernity* (Cambridge, MA.: MIT Press, 1987).

Haraway, Donna. *Simians, Cyborgs, and Women* (New York: Routledge, 1991).

Harding, Sandra. *The Science Question in Feminism* (Ithaca, N.Y.: Cornell University Press, 1986).

Hooks, Bell. *Yearning* (Boston: South End Press, 1990).

Huyssen, Andreas. *After the Great Divide* (Bloomington: Indiana University Press, 1986).

Jameson, Fredric. *Postmodernism, or The Cultural Logic of Late Capitalism* (Durham, N.C.: Duke University Press, 1990).

Kaplan, Ann. Ed. *Postmodernism and Its Discontents* (London: Verso, 1988).

Kellner, Douglas, Ed. *Postmodernism/Jameson/Critique* (Washington, D.C.: Maisonneuve Press, 1989).

Lemert, Charles, Ed. *Social Theory* (Boulder, CO.: Westview Press, 1993).

Lash, Scott. *The Sociology of Postmodernism* (New York: Routledge, 1990).

Lyotard, Jean-François. *The Postmodern Condition* (Minneapolis: University of Minnesota Press, 1984).

Nelson, John, Allan Megill, and Donald McCloskey. Eds. *The Rhetoric of the Human Sciences* (Madison: University of Wisconsin Press, 1987).

Nicholson, Linda. Ed. *Feminism/Postmodernism* (New York: Routledge, 1990).

Rosaldo, Renato. *Culture and Truth* (Boston: Beacon Press, 1989).

Rorty, Richard. *Philosophy and the Mirror of Nature* (Princeton, N.J.: Princeton University Press, 1979).

   Consequences of Pragmatism (Minneapolis: University of Minnesota Press, 1982).

Ross, Andrew. Ed. *Universal Abandon?* (Minneapolis: University of Minnesota Press, 1988).

Seidman, Steven. *Contested Knowledge* (Oxford: Basil Blackwell, 1994).

Seidman, Steven, and Wagner, David. Eds. *Postmodernism and Social Theory* (Oxford: Basil Blackwell, 1991).

Smart, Barry. *Modern Conditions, Postmodern Controversies* London: Routledge, 1992).

Spivak, Gayatri. *In Other Worlds* (New York: Routledge, 1988).

Trinh, Minh-ha, T. *Woman, Native, Other* (Bloomington: IN: Indiana University Press, 1989).

Weedon, Chris. *Feminist Practice and Poststructuralist Theory* (Oxford: Basil Blackwell, 1987).

West, Cornel. "The New Cultural Politics of Difference." *October,* 53 (1990).

Young, Iris. *Justice and the Politics of Difference* (Princeton, N.J.: Princeton University Press, 1990).

Special issues of journals

Cultural Critique 5 (1987). Modernity and Modernism; Postmodernity and Postmodernism.

New German Critique 22 (1981). Habermas and Postmodernism.

Theory, Culture and Society, 5:2–3 (1988). Postmodernism.

Differences. 3 (Spring 1991). Politics/Power/Culture: Postmodernity and Feminist Political Theory.

Sociological Theory 8 (Fall 1990). Writing The Social Text.
  9 (Fall 1991). Symposium on Postmodernism.

THE CASE FOR POSTMODERNISM
AS SOCIAL THEORY

- Jean-François Lyotard, *The postmodern condition*
- Michel Foucault, *Genealogy and social criticism*
- Richard Rorty, *Method, social science, and social hope*
- Cornel West, *The new cultural politics of difference*
- Donna Haraway, *A manifesto for cyborgs: Science, technology, and socialist feminism in the 1980s*

1

The postmodern condition
Jean-François Lyotard

[handwritten margin note: But this is a purely negative reactive definition. What about a definition of what it is for? Is it capable of formulating a positive definition that is not derived from modernism?]

I define postmodern as incredulity toward metanarratives. This incredulity is undoubtedly a product of progress in the sciences: But that progress in turn presupposes it. To the obsolescence of the metanarrative apparatus of legitimation corresponds, most notably, the crisis of metaphysical philosophy and of the university institution which in the past relied on it. The narrative function is losing its functors, its great hero, its great dangers, its great voyages, its great goal. It is being dispersed in clouds of narrative language elements – narrative, but also denotative, prescriptive, descriptive, and so on. Conveyed within each cloud are pragmatic valencies specific to its kind. Each of us lives at the intersection of many of these. However, we do not necessarily establish stable language combinations, and the properties of the ones we do establish are not necessarily communicable.

Thus the society of the future falls less within the province of a Newtonian anthropology (such as structuralism or systems theory) than a pragmatics of language particles. There are many different language games – a heterogeneity of elements. They only give rise to institutions in patches – local determinism. *[handwritten: Why is "local" determinism any more plausible than universal determinism?]*

The decision makers, however, attempt to manage these clouds of sociality according to input/output matrices, following a logic which implies that their elements are commensurable and that the whole is determinable. They allocate our lives for the growth of power. In matters of social justice and of scientific truth alike, the legitimation of that power is based on its optimizing the system's performance – efficiency. The application of this criterion to all of our games necessarily entails a certain level of terror, whether soft or hard: be operational (that is, commensurable) or disappear.

The logic of maximum performance is no doubt inconsistent in many ways, particularly with respect to contradiction in the socio-economic

Excerpted from Lyotard, *The Postmodern Condition*. Minneapolis: University of Minnesota Press, 1984. Reprinted with permission.

field: It demands both less work (to lower production costs) and more (to lessen the social burden of the idle population). But our incredulity is now such that we no longer expect salvation to rise from these inconsistencies, as did Marx.

Still, the postmodern condition is as much a stranger to disenchantment as it is to the blind positivity of delegitimation. Where, after the metanarratives, can legitimacy reside? The operativity criterion is technological; it has no relevance for judging what is true or just. Is legitimacy to be found in consensus obtaining through discussion, as Jürgen Habermas thinks? Such consensus does violence to the heterogeneity of language games. And invention is always born of dissension. Postmodern knowledge is not simply a tool of the authorities; it refines our sensitivity to differences and reinforces our ability to tolerate the incommensurable. Its principle is not the expert's homology, but the inventor's paralogy. . . .

In contemporary society and culture – postindustrial society, postmodern culture – the question of the legitimation of knowledge is formulated in different terms. The grand narrative has lost its credibility, regardless of what mode of unification it uses, regardless of whether it is a speculative narrative or a narrative of emancipation.

The decline of narrative can be seen as an effect of the blossoming of techniques and technologies since the Second World War, which has shifted emphasis from the ends of action to its means; it can also be seen as an effect of the redeployment of advanced liberal capitalism after its retreat under the protection of Keynesianism during the period 1930–60, a renewal that has eliminated the communist alternative and valorized the individual enjoyment of goods and services.

Anytime we go searching for causes in this way we are bound to be disappointed. Even if we adopted one or the other of these hypotheses, we would still have to detail the correlation between the tendencies mentioned and the decline of the unifying and legitimating power of the grand narratives of speculation and emancipation.

It is, of course, understandable that both capitalist renewal and prosperity and the disorienting upsurge of technology would have an impact on the status of knowledge. But in order to understand how contemporary science could have been susceptible to those effects long before they took place, we must first locate the seeds of "delegitimation" and nihilism that were inherent in the grand narratives of the nineteenth century.

First of all, the speculative apparatus maintains an ambiguous relation to knowledge. It shows that knowledge is only worthy of that name to the extent that it reduplicates itself ("lifts itself up," *hebt sich auf;* is sublated) by citing its own statements in a second-level discourse (autonomy) that functions to legitimate them. This is as much as to say that, in its immediacy, denotative discourse bearing on a certain referent (a living organism, a chemical property, a physical phenomenon, etc.) does not really know what it thinks it knows. Positive science is not a form of knowledge. And speculation feeds on its suppression. The Hegelian speculative narrative thus harbors a certain skepticism toward positive learning, as Hegel himself admits.

A science that has not legitimated itself is not a true science; if the discourse that was meant to legitimate it seems to belong to a prescientific form of knowledge, like a "vulgar" narrative, it is demoted to the lowest rank, that of an ideology or instrument of power. And this always happens if the rules of the science game that discourse denounces as empirical are applied to science itself.

Take for example the speculative statement: "A scientific statement is knowledge if and only if it can take its place in a universal process of engendering." The question is: Is this statement knowledge as it itself defines it? Only if it can take its place in a universal process of engendering. Which it can. All it has to do is to presuppose that such a process exists (the Life of spirit) and that it is itself an expression of that process. This presupposition, in fact, is indispensable to the speculative language game. Without it, the language of legitimation would not be legitimate; it would accompany science in a nosedive into nonsense, at least if we take idealism's word for it.

But this presupposition can also be understood in a totally different sense, one which takes us in the direction of postmodern culture: We could say, in keeping with the perspective we adopted earlier, that this presupposition defines the set of rules one must accept in order to play the speculative game. Such an appraisal assumes first that we accept that the "positive" sciences represent the general mode of knowledge and second that we understand this language to imply certain formal and axiomatic presuppositions that it must always make explicit. This is exactly what Nietzsche is doing, though with a different terminology, when he shows that "European nihilism" resulted from the truth requirement of science being turned back against itself.

There thus arises an idea of perspective that is not far removed, at least in this respect, from the idea of language games. What we have here is a process of delegitimation fueled by the demand for legitimation itself. The "crisis" of scientific knowledge, signs of which have been accumulating since the end of the nineteenth century, is not born of a chance proliferation of sciences, itself an effect of progress in technology and the expansion of capitalism. It represents, rather, an internal erosion of the legitimacy principle of knowledge. There is erosion at work inside the speculative game, and by loosening the weave of the encyclopedic net in which each science was to find its place, it eventually sets them free.

The classical dividing lines between the various fields of science are thus called into question – disciplines disappear, overlappings occur at the borders between sciences, and from these new territories are born. The speculative hierarchy of learning gives way to an immanent and, as it were, "flat" network of areas of inquiry, the respective frontiers of which are in constant flux. The old "faculties" splinter into institutes and foundations of all kinds, and the universities lose their function of speculative legitimation. Stripped of the responsibility for research (which was stifled by the speculative narrative), they limit themselves to the transmission of what is judged to be established knowledge, and through didactics they guarantee the replication of teachers rather than the production of researchers. This is the state in which Nietzsche finds and condemns them.

The potential for erosion intrinsic to the other legitimation procedure, the emancipation apparatus flowing from the *Aufklarung,* is no less extensive than the one at work within speculative discourse. But it touches a different aspect. Its distinguishing characteristic is that it grounds the legitimation of science and truth in the autonomy of interlocutors involved in ethical, social, and political praxis. As we have seen, there are immediate problems with this form of legitimation: The difference between a denotative statement with cognitive value and a prescriptive statement with practice value is one of relevance, therefore of competence. There is nothing to prove that if a statement describing a real situation is true, it follows that a prescriptive statement based upon it (the effect of which will necessarily be a modification of that reality) will be just.

Take, for example, a closed door. Between "The door is closed" and "Open the door" there is no relation of consequence as defined in propositional logic. The two statements belong to two autonomous sets of rules defining different kinds of relevance, and therefore of competence. Here, the effect of dividing reason into cognitive or theoretical reason on the one hand, and practical reason on the other, is to attack the legitimacy of the discourse of science; not directly, but indirectly, by revealing that it is a language game with its own rules (of which the a priori conditions of knowledge in Kant provide a first glimpse) and that it has no special calling to supervise the game of praxis (nor the game of aesthetics, for that matter). The game of science is thus put on a par with the others.

If this "delegitimation" is pursued in the slightest and if its scope is widened (as Wittgenstein does in his own way, and thinkers such as Martin Buber and Emmanuel Levinas in theirs) the road is then open for an important current of postmodernity: Science plays its own game; it is incapable of legitimating the other language games. The game of prescription, for example, escapes it. But above all, it is incapable of legitimating itself, as speculation assumed it could.

The social subject itself seems to dissolve in this dissemination of language games. The social bond is linguistic, but is not woven with a single thread. It is a fabric formed by the intersection of at least two (and in reality an indeterminate number of) language games, obeying different rules. Wittgenstein writes: "Our language can be seen as an ancient city: a maze of little streets and squares, of old and new houses, and of houses with additions from various periods; and this surrounded by a multitude of new boroughs with straight regular streets and uniform houses." And to drive home that the principle of unitotality – or synthesis under the authority of a metadiscourse of knowledge – is inapplicable, he subjects the "town" of language to the old sorites paradox by asking: "how many houses or streets does it take before a town begins to be a town?"

New languages are added to the old ones, forming suburbs of the old town: "the symbolism of chemistry and the notation of the infinitesimal calculus." Thirty-five years later we can add to the list: machine languages, the matrices of game theory, new systems of musical notation, systems of notation for nondenotative forms of logic (temporal logics, deontic logics, modal logics), the language of the genetic code, graphs of phonological structures, and so on.

We may form a pessimistic impression of this splintering: Nobody speaks all of those languages, they have no universal metalanguage, the project of the system-subject is a failure, the goal of emancipation has nothing to do with science, we are all stuck in the positivism of this or that discipline of learning, the learned scholars have turned into scientists, the diminished tasks of research have become compartmentalized and no one can master them all. Speculative or humanistic philosophy is forced to relinquish its legitimation duties, which explains why philosophy is facing a crisis wherever it persists in arrogating such functions and is reduced to the study of systems of logic or the history of ideas where it has been realistic enough to surrender them.

Turn-of-the-century Vienna has weaned on this pessimism: not just artists such as Musil, Kraus, Hofmannsthal, Loos, Schonberg, and Broch, but also the philosophers Mach and Wittgenstein. They carried awareness of and theoretical and artistic responsibility for delegitimation as far as it could be taken. We can say today that the mourning process has been completed. There is not need to start all over again. Wittgenstein's strength is that he did not opt for the positivism that was being developed by the Vienna Circle, but outlined in his investigation of language games a kind of legitimation not based on performativity. This is what the postmodern world is all about. Most people have lost the nostalgia for the lost narrative. It in no way follows that they are reduced to barbarity. What saves them from it is their knowledge that legitimation can only spring from their own linguistic practice and communicational interaction. Science "smiling into its beard" at every other belief has taught them the harsh austerity of realism. ....

[margin annotations, handwritten: What sort of "legitimation" is this?]

[handwritten at bottom: Isn't "legitimation" itself the Emperor's new clothes? Once we see it is a game, how can we play it any more except as a joke among insiders or as a cynical manipulation wrt the still unenlightened? How is it possible that the abolitionists of metanarratives + foundationalism all seem so insufferably self-righteous about their moral certainties?]

Legitimation by paralogy

Let us say at this point that the facts we have presented concerning the problem of the legitimation of knowledge today are sufficient for our purposes. We no longer have recourse to the grand narratives – we can resort neither to the dialectic of Spirit nor even to the emancipation of humanity as a validation for postmodern scientific discourse. But as we have just seen, the little narrative [*petit recit*] remains the quintessential form of imaginative invention, most particularly in science. In addition, the principle of consensus as a criterion of validation seems to be inadequate. It has two formulations. In the first, consensus is an agreement between men, defined as knowing intellects and free wills, and is obtained through dialogue. This is the form elaborated by Habermas, but his conception is based on the validity of the narrative of emancipation. In the second, consensus is a component of the system, which manipulates it in order to maintain and improve its performance. It is the object of administrative procedures, in Luhmann's sense. In this case, its only validity is as an instrument to be used toward achieving the real goal, which is what legitimates the system – power.

The problem is therefore to determine whether it is possible to have a form of legitimation based solely on paralogy. Paralogy must be distinguished from innovation: The latter is under the command of the system, or at least used by it to improve its efficiency; the former is a move (the importance of which is often not recognized until later) played in the pragmatics of knowledge. The fact that it is in reality frequently, but not necessarily, the case that one is transformed into the other presents no difficulties for the hypothesis.

Returning to the description of scientific pragmatics . . . it is now dissension that must be emphasized. Consensus is a horizon that is never reached. Research that takes place under the aegis of a paradigm tends to stabilize; it is like the exploitation of a technological, economic, or artistic "idea." It cannot be discounted. But what is striking is that someone always comes along to disturb the order of "reason." It is necessary to posit the existence of a power that destabilizes the capacity for explanation, manifested in the promulgation of new norms for understanding or, if one prefers, in a proposal to establish new rules circumscribing a new field of research for the language of science. This, in the context of scientific discussion, is the same process Thom calls morphogenesis. It is not without rules (there are classes of catastrophes), but it is always locally determined. Applied to scientific discussion and placed in temporal framework, this property implies that "discoveries" are unpredictable. In terms of the idea of transparency, it is a factor that generates blind spots and defers consensus.

This summary makes it easy to see that systems theory and the kind of legitimation it proposes have no scientific basis whatsoever; science itself does not function according to this theory's paradigm of the system, and contemporary science excludes the possibility of using such a paradigm to describe society.

In this context, let us examine two important points in Luhmann's argument. On the one hand, the system can only function by reducing complexity, and on the other, it must induce the adaptation of individual aspirations to its own ends. The reduction in complexity is required to maintain the system's power capability. If all messages could circulate freely among all individuals, the quantity of the information that would have to be taken into account before making the correct choice would delay decisions considerably, thereby lowering performativity. Speed, in effect, is a power component of the system.

The objection will be made that these molecular opinions must indeed be taken into account if the risk of serious disturbances is to be avoided. Luhmann replies – and this is the second point – that it is possible to guide individual aspirations through a process of "quasi-apprenticeship," "free of all disturbance," in order to make them compatible with the system's decisions. The decisions do not have to respect individuals' aspirations: The aspirations have to aspire to the decisions, or at least to their effects. Administrative procedures should make individuals "want" what the system needs in order to perform well. It is easy to see what role telematics technology could play in this.

It cannot be denied that there is persuasive force in the idea that context control and domination are inherently better than their absence. The performativity criterion has its "advantages." It excludes in principle adherence to a metaphysical discourse; it requires the renunciation of fables; it demands clear minds and cold wills; it replaces the definition of essences with the calculation of interactions; it makes the "players" assume responsibility not only for the statements they propose, but also for the rules to which they submit those statements in order to render them acceptable. It brings the pragmatic functions of knowledge clearly to light, to the extent that they seem to relate to the criterion of efficiency: the pragmatics of argumentation, of the production of proof, of the transmission of learning, and of the apprenticeship of the imagination.

It also contributes to elevating all language games to self-knowledge, even those not within the realm of canonical knowledge. It tends to jolt everyday discourse into a kind of metadiscourse: Ordinary statements are now displaying a propensity for self-citation, and the various pragmatic posts are tending to make an indirect connection even to current messages concerning them. Finally, it suggests that the problems of internal communication experienced by the scientific community in the course of its work of dismantling and remounting its languages are comparable in nature to the problems experienced by the social collectivity when, deprived of its narrative culture, it must reexamine its own internal communication and in the process question the nature of the legitimacy of the decision made in its name.

At [the]risk of scandalizing the reader, I would also say that the system can count severity among its advantages. Within the framework of the power criterion, a request (that is, a form of prescription) gains nothing in legitimacy by virtue of being based on the hardship of an unmet need. Rights do not flow from hardship, but from the fact that the alleviation of hardship improves the system's performance. The needs of the most underprivileged should not be used as a system regulator as a matter of principle: Since the means of satisfying them is already known, their actual satisfaction will not improve the system's performance, but only increase its expenditures. The only counterindication is that not satisfying them can destablize the whole. It is against the nature of force to be ruled by weakness. But it is in its nature to induce new requests meant to lead to a redefinition of the norms of "life." In this sense, the system seems to be a vanguard machine dragging humanity after it, dehumanizing it in order to rehumanize it at a different level of normative capacity. The technocrats declare that they cannot trust what society designates as its needs; they "know" that society cannot know its own needs since they are not variables independent of the new technologies. Such is the arrogance of the decision makers – and their blindness.

What their "arrogance" means is that they identify themselves with the social system conceived as a totality in quest of its most performative unity possible. If we look at the pragmatics of science, we learn that such an identification is impossible: In principle, no scientist embodies knowledge or neglects the "needs" of a research project, or the aspirations of a researcher, on the pretext that they do not add to the performance of "science" as a whole. The response a researcher usually makes to a request is: "We'll have to see, tell me your story." In principle, he does not prejudge that a case has already been closed or that the power of "science" will suffer if it is reopened. In fact, the opposite is true.

Of course, it does not always happen like this in reality. Countless scientists have seen their "move" ignored or repressed, sometimes for decades, because it too abruptly destabilized the accepted positions, not only in the university and scientific hierarchy, but also in the problematic. The stronger the "move," the likely it is to be denied the minimum consensus, precisely because it changes the rules of the game upon which consensus had been based. But when the institution of knowledge functions in this manner, it is acting like an ordinary power center whose behavior is governed by a principle of homeostasis.

Such behavior is terrorist, as is the behavior of the system described by Luhmann. By terror I mean the efficiency gained by eliminating, or threatening to eliminate, a player from the language game one shares with him. He is silenced or consents, not because he has been refuted, but because his ability to participate has been threatened (there are many ways to prevent someone from playing). The decision makers' arrogance, which in principle has no equivalent in the sciences, consists in the exercise of terror. It says: "Adapt your aspirations to our ends – or else."

Even permissiveness toward the various games is made conditional on performativity. The redefinition of the norms of life consists in enhancing the system's competence for power. That this is the case is particularly evident in the introduction of telematics technology: The technocrats see in telematics a promise of liberalization and enrichment in the interactions between interlocutors; but what makes this process attractive for them is that it will result in new tensions in the system, and these will lead to an improvement in its performativity.

To the extent that science is differential, its pragmatics provides the antimodel of a stable system. A statement is deemed worth retaining the moment it marks a difference from what is already known, and after an argument and proof in support of it has been found. Science is a model of an "open system," in which a statement becomes relevant if it "generates ideas," that is, if it generates other statements and other game rules. Science possesses no general metalanguage into which all other languages can be transcribed and evaluated. This is what prevents its identification with the system and, all things considered, with terror. If the division between decision makers and executors exists in the scientific community (and it does), it is a fact of the socioeconomic system and not of the pragmatics of science itself. It is in fact one of the major obstacles to the imaginative development of knowledge.

The general question of legitimation becomes: What is the relationship between the antimodel of the pragmatics of science and society? Is it applicable to the vast clouds of language material constituting a society? Or is it limited to the game of learning? And if so, what role does it play with respect to the social bond? Is it an impossible ideal of an open community? Is it an essential component for the subset of decision makers, who force on society the performance criterion they reject for themselves? Or, conversely, is it a refusal to cooperate with the authorities, a move in the direction of counterculture, with the attendant risk that all possibility for research will be foreclosed due to lack of funding?

From the beginning of this study, I have emphasized the differences (not only formal, but also pragmatic) between the various language games, especially between denotative, or knowledge, games and prescriptive, or action, games. The pragmatics of science is centered on denotative utterances, which are the foundation upon which it builds institutions of learning (institutes, centers, universities, etc.). But its postmodern development brings a decisive "fact" to the fore: Even discussions of denotative statements need to have rules. Rules are not denotative but prescriptive utterances, which we are better off calling metaprescriptive utterances to avoid confusion (they prescribe what the moves of language games must be in order to be admissible). The function of the differential or imaginative or paralogical activity of the current pragmatics of science is to point out these metaprescriptives (science's "presuppositions") and to petition the players to accept different ones. The only legitimation that can make this kind of request admissible is that it will generate ideas, in other words, new statements.

Social pragmatics does not have the "simplicity" of scientific pragmatics. It is a monster formed by the interweaving of various networks of heteromorphous classes of utterances (denotative, prescriptive, performative, technical, evaluative, etc.). There is no reason to think that it would be possible to determine metaprescriptives common to all of these language games or that a revisable consensus like the one in force at a given moment in the scientific community could embrace the totality of metaprescriptions regulating the totality of statements circulating in the social collectivity. As a matter of fact, the contemporary decline of narratives of legitimation – be they traditional or "modern" (the emancipation of humanity, the realization of the Idea) – is tied to the abandonment of this belief. It is its absence for which the ideology of the "system," with its pretensions to totality, tries to compensate and which it expresses in the cynicism of its criterion of performance.

For this reason, it seems neither possible, nor even prudent, to follow Habermas in orienting our treatment of the problem of legitimation in the direction of a search for universal consensus through what he calls *Diskurs,* in other words, a dialogue of argumentation.

This would be to make two assumptions. The first is that it is possible for all speakers to come to agreement on which rules or metaprescriptions are universally valid for language games, when it is clear that language games are heteromorphous, subject to heterogenous sets of pragmatic rules.

The second assumption is that the goal of dialogue is consensus. But as I have shown in the analysis of the pragmatics of science, consensus is only a particular state of discussion, not its end. Its end, on the contrary, is paralogy. This double observation (the heterogeneity of the rules and the search for dissent) destroys a belief that still underlies Habermas's research, namely, that humanity as a collective (universal) subject seeks its common emancipation through the regularization of the "moves" permitted in all language games and that the legitimacy of any statement resides in its contributing to that emancipation.

It is easy to see what function this recourse plays in Habermas's argument against Luhmann. *Diskurs* is his ultimate weapon against the theory of the stable system. The cause is good, but the argument is not. Consensus has become an outmoded and suspect value. But justice as a value is neither outmoded nor suspect. We must thus arrive at an idea and practice of justice that is not linked to that of consensus.

A recognition of the hetermorphous nature of language games is a first step in that direction. This obviously implies a renunciation of terror, which assumes that they are isomorphic and tries to make them so. The second step is the principle that any consensus on the rules defining a game and the "moves" playable within it *must* be local, in other words, agreed on by its present players and subject to eventual cancellation. The orientation then favors a multiplicity and finite meta-arguments, by which I mean argumentation that concerns metaprescriptives and is limited in space and time.

This orientation corresponds to the course that the evolution of social interaction is currently taking; the temporary contract is in practice supplanting permanent institutions in the professional, emotional, sexual, cultural, family, and international domains, as well as in political affairs. This evolution is of course ambiguous: The temporary contract is favored by the system due to its greater flexibility, lower cost, and the creative turmoil of its accompanying motivations – all of these factors contribute to increased operativity. In any case, there is no question here of proposing a "pure" alternative to the system: We all now know, as the 1970s come to a close, that an attempt at an alternative of that kind would end up resembling the system it was meant to replace. We should be happy that the tendency toward the temporary contract is ambiguous: It is not totally subordinated to the goal of the system, yet the system tolerates it. This bears witness to the existence of another goal within the system: knowledge of language games as such and the decision to assume responsibility for their rules and effects. Their most significant effect is precisely what validates the adoption of rules – the quest for paralogy.

We are finally in a position to understand how the computerization of society affects this problematic. It could become the "dream" instrument for controlling and regulating the market system, extended to include knowledge itself and governed exclusively by the performativity principle. In that case, it would inevitably involve the use of terror. But it could also aid groups discussing metaprescriptives by supplying them with the information they usually lack for making knowledgeable decisions. The line to follow for computerization to take the second of these two paths is, in principle, quite simple: Give the public free access to the memory and data banks. Language games would then be games of perfect information at any given moment. But they would also be non-zero-sum games, and by virtue of that fact discussion would never risk fixating in a position of minimax equilibrium because it had exhausted its stakes. For the stakes would be knowledge (or information, if you will), and the reserve of knowledge – language's reserve of possible utterances – is inexhaustible. This sketches the outline of a politics that would respect both the desire for justice and the desire for the unknown.

2

Genealogy and Social Criticism
Michel Foucault

You will recall my work here, such as it has been: some brief notes on the history of penal procedure, a chapter or so on the evolution and institutionalisation of psychiatry in the nineteenth century, some observations on sophistry, on Greek money, on the medieval Inquisition. I have sketched a history of sexuality or at least a history of knowledge of sexuality on the basis of the confessional practice of the seventeenth century or the forms of control of infantile sexuality in the eighteenth to nineteenth century. I have sketched a genealogical history of the origins of a theory and a knowledge of anomaly and of the various techniques that relate to it. None of it does more than mark time. Repetitive and disconnected, it advances nowhere. Since indeed it never ceases to say the same thing, it perhaps says nothing. It is tangled up into an indecipherable, disorganised muddle. In a nutshell, it is inconclusive.

However, it is not simply a taste for such Freemasonry that has inspired my course of action. It seems to me that the work we have done could be justified by the claim that it is adequate to a restricted period, that of the last ten, fifteen, at most twenty years, a period notable for two events which for all they may not be really important are nonetheless to my mind quite interesting.

On the one hand, it has been a period characterised by what one might term the efficacy of dispersed and discontinuous offensives. There are a number of things I have in mind here. I am thinking, for example, where it was a case of undermining the function of psychiatric institutions, of that curious efficacy of localised anti-psychiatric discourses. These are discourses which you are well aware lacked and still lack any systematic principles of coordination of the kind that would have provided or might today provide a system of reference for them. I am thinking of the original reference towards existential analysis or of certain directions inspired in a general way by Marxism, such as Reichian theory. Again, I have in mind that strange efficacy of the attacks that have been directed against traditional morality and hierarchy, attacks which again have no reference except perhaps in a vague and fairly distant way to Reich and Marcuse. On the other hand there is also the efficacy of the attacks upon the legal and penal system, some of which had a very tenuous connection with the general and in any case pretty dubious notion of class justice, while others had a rather more precisely defined affinity with anarchist themes. Equally, I am thinking of the efficacy of a book such as *L'Anti-Oedipe*, which really has no other source of reference than its own prodigious theoretical inventiveness: a book, or rather a thing, an event, which has managed, even at the most mundane level of psychoanalytic practice, to introduce a note so long continued uninterrupted between couch and armchair.

I would say, then, that what has emerged in the course of the last ten or fifteen years is a sense of the increasing vulnerability to criticism of things, institutions, practices, discourses. A certain fragility has been discovered in the very bedrock of existence – even, and perhaps above all, in those aspects of it that are most familiar, most solid and most intimately related to our bodies and to our everyday behaviour. But together with this sense of instability and this amazing efficacy of discontinuous, particular and local criticism, one in fact also discovers something that perhaps was not initially foreseen, something one might describe as precisely the inhibiting effect of global, *totalitarian theories*. It is not that these global theories have not provided nor continue to provide in a fairly consistent fashion useful tools for local research: Marxism and psychoanalysis are proofs of this. But I believe these tools have only been provided on the condition that the theoretical unity of these discourses was in some sense put in abeyance, or at least curtailed, divided, overthrown, caricatured, theatricalised, or what you will. In each case, the attempt to think in terms of a totality has in fact proved a hindrance to research.

So, the main point to be gleaned from these events of the last fifteen years, their predominant feature, is the *local* character of criticism. That should not, I believe, be taken to mean that its qualities are those of an obtuse, naïve or primitive empiricism; nor is it soggy eclecticism, an opportunism that laps up any and every kind of theoretical approach; nor does it mean a self-imposed ascetism which taken by itself would reduce to the worst kind of theoretical impoverishment. I believe that what this essentially local character of criticism indicates in reality is an autonomous, non-centralised kind of theoretical production, one that is to say whose validity is not dependent on the approval of the established régimes of thought.

It is here that we touch upon another feature of these events that has been manifest for some time now: it seems to me that this local criticism has proceeded by means of what one might term 'a return of knowledge'. What I mean by that phrase is this: it is a fact that we have repeatedly encountered, at least at a superficial level, in the course of most recent times, an entire thematic to the effect that it is not theory but life that matters, not knowledge but reality, not books but money etc.; but it also seems to me that over and above, and arising out of this thematic, there is something else to which we are witness, and which we might describe as an *insurrection of subjugated knowledges*.

By subjugated knowledges I mean two things: on the one hand, I am referring to the historical contents that have been buried and disguised in a functionalist coherence or formal systemisation. Concretely, it is not a semiology of the life of the asylum, it is not even a sociology of delinquency, that has made it possible to produce an effective criticism of the asylum and likewise of the prison, but rather the immediate emergence of historical contents. And this is simply because only the historical contents allow us to rediscover the ruptural effects of conflict and struggle that the order imposed by functionalist or systematising thought is designed to mask. Subjugated knowledges are thus those blocs of historical knowledge which were present but disguised within the body of functionalist and systematising theory and which criticism – which obviously draws upon scholarship – has been able to reveal.

On the other hand, I believe that by subjugated knowledges one should understand something else, something which in a sense is altogether different, namely, a whole set of knowledges that have been disqualified as inadequate to their task or insufficiently elaborated: naive knowledges, located low down on the hierarchy, beneath the required level of cognition or scientificity. I also believe that it is through the re-emergence of these low-ranking knowledges, these unqualified, even directly disqualified knowledges (such as that of the psychiatric patient, of the ill person, of the nurse, of the doctor – parallel and marginal as they are to the knowledge of medicine – that of the delinquent etc.), and which involve what I would call a popular knowledge (*le savoir des gens*) though it is far from being a general commonsense knowledge, but is on the contrary a particular, local, regional knowledge, a differential knowledge incapable of unanimity and which owes its force only to the harshness with which it is opposed by everything surrounding it – that it is through the re-appearance of this knowledge, of these local popular knowledges, these disqualified knowledges, that criticism performs its work.

However, there is a strange kind of paradox in the desire to assign to this same category of subjugated knowledges what are on the one hand the products of meticulous, erudite, exact historical knowledge, and on the other hand local and specific knowledges which have no common meaning and which are in some fashion allowed to fall into disuse whenever they are not effectively and explicitly maintained in themselves. Well, it seems to me that our critical discourses of the last fifteen years have in effect discovered their essential force in this association between the buried knowledges of erudition and those disqualified from the hierarchy of knowledges and sciences.

In the two cases – in the case of the erudite as in that of the disqualified knowledges – with what in fact were these buried, subjugated knowledges really concerned? They were concerned with a *historical knowledge of struggles*. In the specialised areas of erudition as in the disqualified, popular knowledge there lay the memory of hostile encounters which even up to this day have been confined to the margins of knowledge.

What emerges out of this is something one might call a genealogy, or rather a multiplicity of genealogical researches, a painstaking rediscovery of struggles together with the rude memory of their conflicts. And these genealogies, that are the combined product of an erudite knowledge and a popular knowledge, were not possible and could not even have been attempted except on one condition, namely that the tyranny of globalising discourses with their hierarchy and all their privileges of a theoretical *avant-garde* was eliminated.

Let us give the term *genealogy* to the union of erudite knowledge and local memories which allows us to establish a historical knowledge of struggles and to make use of this knowledge tactically today. This then will be a provisional definition of the genealogies which I have attempted to compile with you over the last few years.

You are well aware that this research activity, which one can thus call genealogical, has nothing at all to do with an opposition between the abstract unity of theory and the concrete multiplicity of facts. It has nothing at all to do with a disqualification of the speculative dimension which opposes to it, in the name of some kind of scientism, the rigour of well established knowledges. It is not therefore via an empiricism that the genealogical project unfolds, nor even via a positivism in the ordinary sense of that term. What it really does is to entertain the claims to attention of local, discontinuous, disqualified, illegitimate knowledges against the claims of a unitary body of theory which would filter, hierarchise and order them in the name of some true knowledge and some arbitrary idea of what constitutes a science and its objects. Genealogies are therefore not positivistic returns to a more careful or exact form of science. They are precisely anti-sciences. Not that they vindicate a lyrical right to ignorance or non-knowledge: it is not that they are concerned to deny knowledge or that they esteem the virtues of direct cognition and base their practice upon an immediate experience that escapes encapsulation in knowledge.

It is not that with which we are concerned. We are concerned, rather, with the insurrection of knowledges that are opposed primarily not to the contents, methods or concepts of a science, but to the affects of the centralising powers which are linked to the institution and functioning of an organised scientific discourse within a society such as ours. Nor does it basically matter all that much that this institutionalisation of scientific discourse is embodied in a university, or, more generally, in an educational apparatus, in a theoretical-commercial institution such as psychoanalysis or within the framework of reference that is provided by a political system such as Marxism; for it is really against the effects of the power of a discourse that is considered to be scientific that the genealogy must wage its struggle.

To be more precise, I would remind you how numerous have been those who for many years now, probably for more than half a century, have questioned whether Marxism was, or was not, a science. One might say that the same issue has been posed, and continues to be posed, in the case of psychoanalysis, or even worse, in that of the semiology of literary texts. But to all these demands of: 'Is it or is it not a science?', the genealogies or the genealogist would reply: 'If you really want to know, the fault lies in your very determination to make a science out of Marxism or psychoanalysis or this or that study'. If we have any objection against Marxism, it lies in the fact that it could effectively be a science. In more detailed terms, I would say that even before we can know the extent to which something such as Marxism or psychoanalysis can be compared to a scientific practice in its everyday functioning, its rules of construction, its working concepts, that even before we can pose the question of a formal and structural analogy between Marxist or psychoanalytic discourse, it is surely necessary to question ourselves about our aspirations to the kind of power that is presumed to accompany such a science. It is surely the following kinds of questions that would need to be posed: What types of knowledge do you want to disqualify in the very instant of your demand: 'Is it a science'? Which speaking, discoursing subjects – which subjects of experience and knowledge – do you then want to 'diminish' when you say: 'I who conduct this discourse am conducting a scientific discourse, and I am a scientist'? Which theoretical-political *avant garde* do you want to enthrone in order to isolate it from all the discontinuous forms of knowledge that circulate about it? When I see you straining to establish the scientificity of Marxism I do not really think that you are demonstrating once and for all that Marxism has a rational structure and that therefore its propositions are the outcome of verifiable procedures; for me you are doing something altogether different, you are investing Marxist discourses and those who uphold them with the effects of a power which the West since Medieval times has attributed to science and has reserved for those engaged in scientific discourse.

By comparison, then, and in contrast to the various projects which aim to inscribe knowledges in the hierarchical order of power associated with science, a genealogy should be seen as a kind of attempt to emancipate historical knowledges from that subjection, to render them, that is, capable of opposition and of struggle against the coercion of a theoretical, unitary, formal and scientific discourse. It is based on a reactivation of local knowledges – of minor knowledges, as Deleuze might call them – in opposition to the scientific hierarchisation of knowledges and the effects intrinsic to their power: this, then, is the project of these disordered and fragmentary genealogies. If we were to characterise it in two terms, then 'archaeology' would be the appropriate methodology of this analysis of local discursivities, and 'genealogy' would be the tactics whereby, on the basis of the descriptions of these local discursivities, the subjected knowledges which were thus released would be brought into play.

So much can be said by way of establishing the nature of the project as a whole. I would have you consider all these fragments of research, all these discourses, which are simultaneously both superimposed and discontinuous, which I have continued obstinately to pursue for some four or five years now, as elements of these genealogies which have been composed – and by no means by myself alone – in the course of the last fifteen years. At this point, however, a problem arises, and a question: why not continue to pursue a theory which in its discontinuity is so attractive and plausible, albeit so little verifiable? Why not continue to settle upon some aspect of psychiatry or of the theory of sexuality etc.? It is true, one could continue (and in a certain sense I shall try to do so) if it were not for a certain number of changes in the current situation. By this I mean that it could be that in the course of the last five, ten or even fifteen years, things have assumed a different complexion – the contest could be said to present a different complexion – the contest could be said to present a different physiognomy. Is the relation of forces today still such as to allow these disinterred knowledges some kind of autonomous life? Can they be isolated by these means from every subjugating relationship? What force do they have taken in themselves? And, after all, is it not perhaps the case that these fragments of genealogies are no sooner brought to light, that the particular elements of the knowledge that one seeks to disinter are no sooner accredited and put into circulation, than they run the risk of re-codification, re-colonisation? In fact, those unitary discourses, which first disqualified and then ignored them when they made their appearance, are, it seems, quite ready now to annex them, to take them back within the fold of their own discourse and to invest them with everything this implies in terms of their effects of knowledge and power. And if we want to protect these only lately liberated fragments are we not in danger of ourselves constructing, with our own hands, that unitary discourse to which we are invited, perhaps to lure us into a trap, by those who say to us: 'All this is fine, but where are you heading? What kind of unity are you after?' The temptation, up to a certain point, is to reply: 'Well, we just go on, in a cumulative fashion; after all, the moment at which we risk colonisation has not yet arrived'. One could even attempt to throw out a challenge: 'Just try to colonise us then!' Or one might say, for example, 'Has there been, from the time when anti-psychiatry or the genealogy of psychiatric institutions were launched – and it is now a good fifteen years ago – a single Marxist, or a single psychiatrist, who has gone over the same ground in his own terms and shown that these genealogies that we produced were false, inadequately elaborated, poorly articulated and ill-founded?' In fact, as things stand in reality, these collected fragments of a genealogy remain as they have always been, surrounded by a prudent silence. At most, the only arguments that we have heard against them have been of the kind I believe were voiced by Monsieur Juquin: 'All this is all very well, but Soviet psychiatry nonetheless remains the foremost in the world'. To which I would reply: 'How right you are; Soviet psychiatry is indeed the foremost in the world and it is precisely that which one would hold against it'.

The silence, or rather the prudence, with which the unitary theories avoid the genealogy of knowledges might therefore be a good reason to continue to pursue it. Then at least one could proceed to multiply the genealogical fragments in the form of so many traps, demands, challenges, what you will. But in the long run, it is probably over-optimistic, if we are thinking in terms of a contest – that of knowledge against the effects of the power of scientific discourse – to regard the silence of one's adversaries as indicative of a fear we have inspired in them. For perhaps the silence of the enemy – and here at the very least we have a methodological or tactical principle that it is always useful to bear in mind – can also be the index of our failure to produce any such fear at all. At all events, we must proceed just as if we had not alarmed them at all, in which case it will be no part of our concern to provide a solid and homogeneous theoretical terrain for all these dispersed genealogies, nor to descend upon them from on high with some kind of halo of theory that would unite them. Our task, on the contrary, will be to expose and specify the issue at stake in this opposition, this struggle, this insurrection of knowledges against the institutions and against effects of the knowledge and power that invests scientific discourse.

Isn't post-modernism in fact a rejuvenation of the modernist, Enlightenment claim that it most affects to reject – the emancipatory power of knowledge as embodied in systems of language + reason? That the truth (the real truth, to be sure, the deconstructed, desanitized, engaged truth) can set us free, can liberate us from the tyrannies of a technological establishment that has taken the place of the theological establishment it professed to despise? Isn't this just a replay of the arrogant presumption of the Enlightenment a new call to ecraser l'infame (or épeter le bourgeois).

Isn't this just a new call to a revolution that will liberate humanity once again?

3

Method, social science, and social hope
Richard Rorty

I. Science without method

Galileo and his followers discovered, and subsequent centuries have amply confirmed, that you get much better predictions by thinking of things as masses of particles blindly bumping each other than by thinking of them as Aristotle thought of them – animistically, teleologically, anthromorphically. They also discovered that you get a better handle on the universe by thinking of it as infinite and cold and comfortless than by thinking of it as finite, homey, planned, and relevant to human concerns. Finally, they discovered that if you view planets or missiles or corpuscles as point-masses, you can get nice simple predictive laws by looking for nice simple mathematical ratios. These discoveries are the basis of modern technological civilization. We can hardly be too grateful for them. But they do not, *pace* Descartes and Kant, point any epistemological moral. They do not tell us anything about the nature of science or rationality. In particular, they were not due to the use of, nor do they exemplify, something called 'the scientific method.'

The tradition we call 'modern philosophy' asked itself 'How is it that science has had so much success? What is the secret of this success?' The various bad answers to these bad questions have been variations on a single charming but uncashable metaphor: viz. the New Science discovered the language which nature itself uses. When Galileo said that the book of nature was written in the language of mathematics he meant that his new

This paper is a revision of one called 'Method and Morality' which was delivered at a conference in Berkeley in march of 1980, and was read to a meeting of the Western Canadian Philosophical Association at the University of Regina in October of that year. The earlier version will appear in N. Hamn, R. Bellah, and P. Rabinow, eds. *Values and the Social Sciences*. Reprinted with permission of the *Canadian Journal of Philosophy*, University of Calgary Press, the University of Calgary.

reductionistic, mathematical, vocabulary didn't just *happen* to work, but that it worked *because* that was the way things *really were*. He meant that that vocabulary worked because it fitted the universe as a key fits a lock. Ever since, philosophers have been trying, and failing, to give sense to these notions of 'working *because*,' and 'things as they *really are*.'

Descartes explicated these notions in terms of the natural clarity and distinctness of Galilean ideas – ideas which, for some reason, had been foolishly overlooked by Aristotle. Locke, struck by the indistinctness of this notion of 'clarity,' thought he might do better with a program of reducing complex to simple ideas. To make this program relevant to current science, he used an *ad hoc* distinction between ideas which resembled their objects and those which do not. This distinction was so dubious as to lead us, via Berkeley and Hume, to Kant's rather desperate suggestion that the key only worked because we had, behind our own backs, constructed the lock it was to fit. In retrospect, we have come to see Kant's suggestion as giving the game away. For his transcendental idealism opened the back door to all the teleological, animistic, Aristotelian notions which the intellectuals had repressed for fear of being old-fashioned. The speculative idealists who succeeded Kant dropped the notion of finding Nature's secrets. They substituted the notion of making worlds by creating vocabularies, a notion echoed in our century by maverick philosophers of science like Cassirer and Goodman.

In an effort to avoid these so-called 'excesses of German idealism' a host of philosophers – roughly classifiable as 'positivist' – have spent the last hundred years trying to use notions like 'objectivity,' 'rigor,' and 'method' to isolate science form non-science. They have done this because they thought that the idea that we can explain scientific success in terms of discovering Nature's Own Language must, *somehow*, be right – even if the metaphor could *not* be cashed, even if neither realism nor idealism could explain just what the imagined 'correspondence' between nature's language and current scientific jargon was supposed to consist in. Very few thinkers have suggested that maybe science doesn't *have* a secret of success – that there is *no* metaphysical or epistemological or transcendental explanation of why Galileo's vocabulary has worked so well so far, any more than there is an explanation of why the vocabulary of liberal democracy has worked so well so far. Very few have been willing to abjure the notions that 'the mind' or 'reason' has a nature of its own, that discovery of this nature will give us a 'method,' and that following that method will enable us to penetrate beneath the appearances and see nature 'in its own terms.'

The importance of Kuhn seems to me to be that, like Dewey, he is one of these few. Kuhn and Dewey suggest we give up the notion of science traveling towards an end called 'correspondence with reality' and instead

[handwritten margin note: Just chance then or what? exactly.]

say *merely* that a given vocabulary works better than another for a given purpose. If we accept their suggestion, we shall not be inclined to ask 'What method do scientists use?' Or, more precisely, we shall say that within what Kuhn calls 'normal science' – puzzlesolving – they use the same banal and obvious methods all of us use in every human activity. They check off examples against criteria; they fudge the counter-examples enough to avoid the need for new models; they try out various guesses, formulated within the current jargon, in the hope of coming up with something which will cover the unfudgeable cases. We shall not think there is or could be an epistemologically pregnant answer to the question 'What did Galileo do right that Aristotle did wrong?,' any more than we should expect such an answer to the questions 'What did Plato do right that Xenophon did wrong?' or 'What did Mirabeau do right that Louis XVI did wrong?' We shall just say that Galileo had a good idea, and Aristotle a less good idea; Galileo was using some terminology which helped, and Aristotle wasn't. Galileo's terminology was the *only* 'secret' he had – he didn't pick that terminology because it was 'clear' or 'natural,' or 'simple,' or in line with the categories of the pure understanding. He just lucked out. *But why does his language "help? Isn't that still impt..?*

[margin: !]

   The moral seventeenth-century philosophers *should* have drawn from Galileo's success was a Whewellian and Kuhnian one: viz., that scientific breakthroughs are not so much a matter of deciding which of various alternative hypotheses are true, but of finding the right jargon in which to frame hypotheses in the first place. But, instead, as I have said, they drew the moral that the new vocabulary was the one nature had always *wanted* to be described in. I think they drew this moral for two reasons. First they thought that the fact that Galileo's vocabulary was devoid of metaphysical comfort, moral significance, and human interest was a reason why it worked. They vaguely thought that it was *because* the Galilean scientist was able to face up to the frightening abysses of infinite space that he was being so successful. They identified his distance from common sense and from religious feeling – his distance from decisions about how men should live – as part of the secret of his success. So, they said, the more metaphysically comfortless and morally insignificant our vocabulary, the likelier we are to be 'in touch with reality' or to be 'scientific,' or to describe reality as it wants to be described and thereby get it under control. Second, they thought the only way to eliminate 'subjective' notions – those expressible in *our* vocabulary but not in Nature's – was to eschew terms which could not be definitionally linked to those in Galileo's and Newton's vocabularies, terms denoting 'primary qualities.'

[margin: Is this fair at all?]

   These intertwined mistakes – the notion that a term is more likely to 'refer to the real' if it is morally insignificant and if it occurs in true, predictively useful, generalizations – give substance to the idea of 'scientific method' as (in Bernard Williams' phrase)[1] the 'search for an absolute conception of reality.' This is reality conceived as somehow represented by representations which are not merely ours but its own, as it looks to itself, as it would describe itself if it could. Williams, and others who take Cartesianism seriously, think this notion not only unconfused but one of our intuitions about the nature of knowledge. On my account, by contrast, it is merely one of our intuitions about what counts as being philosophical. It is the Cartesian form of the archetypal philosophical fantasy – first spun by Plato – of cutting through all description, all representation, to a state of consciousness which, *per impossibile*, combines the best features of inarticulate confrontation with the best features of linguistic formulation. This fantasy of discovering, and somehow *knowing* that one has discovered, Nature's Own Vocabulary *seemed* to become more concrete when Galileo and Newton formulated a comprehensive set of predictively useful universal generalizations, written in suitably 'cold,' 'inhuman,' mathematical terms. From their time to the present, the notions of 'rationality,' 'method,' and 'science' were inextricably bound up with the search for such generalizations.

Without this model to go on, the notion of 'a scientific method,' in its modern sense, could not have been taken seriously. The term would have retained the sense it had in the period prior to the New Science, for people like Ramus and Bacon. In that sense, to have a method was simply to have a good comprehensive list of topics or headings – to have, so to speak, an efficient filing system. In its post-Cartesian philosophical sense, however, it does not mean simply ordering one's thoughts, but *filtering* them in order to eliminate 'subjective' or 'noncognitive' or 'confused' elements, leaving only the thoughts which are Nature's Own. This distinction between the parts of one's mind which do and don't correspond to reality is, in the epistemological tradition, confused with the distinction between rational and irrational ways of doing science. If 'scientific method' means merely being rational in some given area of inquiry, then it has a perfectly reasonable 'Kuhnian' sense – it means obeying the normal conventions of your discipline, not fudging the data *too* much, not letting your hopes and fears influence your conclusions unless those hopes and fears are shared by all those who are in the same line of work, being open to refutation by experiences, not blocking the road of inquiry. In this sense, 'method' and 'rationality' are names for a suitable balance between respect for the opinions of one's fellows and respect for the stubbornness of sensation. But epistemologically centered philosophy has wanted notions of 'method' and 'rationality' which signify more than good epis-

1. Cf. Bernard Williams, *Descartes: The Project of Pure Enquiry* (London and New York: Penguin, 1978), 64ff.

temic manners, notions which describe the way in which the mind is naturally fitted to learn Nature's Own Language.

If one believes, as I do, that the traditional ideas of 'an absolute ("objective") conception of reality' and of 'scientific method' are neither clear nor useful, then one will see the interlocked questions 'What should be the method of the social sciences?' and 'What are the criteria of an objective moral theory?' as badly posed. In the remainder of this paper, I want to say in detail why I think these are bad questions, and to recommend a Deweyan approach to both social science and morality, one which emphasizes the utility of narratives and vocabularies rather than the objectivity of laws and theories.

II. 'Value-free' social science and 'hermeneutic' social science

There has recently been a reaction against the idea that students of man and society will be 'scientific' only if they remain faithful to the Galilean model – if they find 'value-neutral,' purely descriptive, terms in which to state their predictive generalizations, leaving evaluation to 'policy-makers.' This has led to a revival of Dilthey's notion that to understand human beings 'scientifically' we must apply non-Galilean, 'hermeneutic' methods. From the point of view I wish to suggest, the whole idea of 'being scientific' or of choosing between 'methods' is confused. Consequently the question about whether social scientists should seek value-neutrality along Galilean lines, or rather should try for something more cosy, Aristotelian, and 'softer' – a distinctive 'method of the human sciences' – seems to me misguided.

One reason this quarrel has developed is that it has become obvious that *whatever* terms are used to describe human beings *become* 'evaluative' terms. The suggestion that we segregate the 'evaluative' terms in a language and use their absence as one criterion for the 'scientific' character of a discipline or a theory cannot be carried out. For there is no way to prevent anybody using *any* term 'evaluatively.' If you ask somebody whether he is using 'repression' or 'primitive' or 'working class' normatively or descriptively, he might be able to answer in the case of a given statement, made on a given occasion. But if you ask him whether he uses the term only when he is describing, only when he is engaging in moral reflection, or both, the answer is almost always going to be 'both.' Further, and this is the crucial point, unless the answer *is* 'both' it is just not the sort of term which will do us much good in social science. Predictions will do 'policy-making' no good if they are not phrased in the terms in which policy can be formulated.

Suppose we picture the 'value-free' social scientist walking up to the divide between 'fact' and 'value' and handing his predictions to the policy-makers who live on the other side. They will not be of much use unless they contain some of the terms which the policy-makers use among themselves. What the policy-makers would like, presumably, are rich juicy predictions like 'If basic industry is socialized, the standard of living will (or won't) decline.' 'If literacy is more widespread, more (or fewer) honest people will be elected to office,' and so on. They would like hypothetical sentences whose consequents are phrased in terms which might occur in morally urgent recommendations. When they get predictions phrased in the sterile jargon of 'quantified' social sciences ('maximizes satisfaction,' 'increases conflict,' etc.) they either tune out, or, more dangerously, begin to use the jargon in moral deliberation. The desire for a new, 'interpretative,' social science seems to me best understood as a reaction against the temptation to formulate social policies in terms so thin as barely to count as 'moral' at all – terms which never stray far from definitional links with 'pleasure,' 'pain' and 'power.'

The issue between those who hanker after 'objective,' 'value-free,' 'truly scientific,' social sciences and those who think this should be replaced with something more hermeneutical is misdescribed as a quarrel about 'method.' A quarrel about method presupposes a common goal and disagreement about the means for reaching it. But the two sides to this quarrel are not disagreeing about how to get more accurate predictions of what will happen if certain policies are adopted. Neither side is very good at making such predictions, and if anybody ever did find a way of making them both sides would be equally eager to incorporate this strategy in their view. The nature of the quarrel is better, but still misleadingly, seen as one between the competing goals of 'explanation' and 'understanding.' As this contrast has developed in the recent literature, it is a contrast between the sort of jargon which permits Galilean-style generalizations and Hempelian specification of confirming and disconfirming instances of such generalizations, and the sort which sacrifices this virtue for the sake of describing in roughly the same vocabulary as one evaluates (a 'teleological' vocabulary, crudely speaking).

This contrast is real enough. But it is not an issue to be resolved, only a difference to be lived with. The idea that explanation and understanding are opposed ways of doing social science is as misguided as the notion that microscopic and macroscopic descriptions of organisms are opposed ways of doing biology. There are lots of things you want to do with bacteria and cows for which it is very useful to have biochemical descriptions of them; there are lots of things you want to do with them for which such descriptions would be merely a nuisance. Similarly, there are lots of things you want to do with human beings for which descriptions of them in non-evaluative, 'inhuman,' terms is very useful; there are others (e.g., thinking of them as your fellow-citizens) in which they are not. 'Explanation' is merely the sort of understanding one looks for when one wants to predict and control. It does not contrast with something else called 'understanding' as the abstract contrasts with the concrete, or the artificial with the natural, or the 'repressive' with the 'liberating.' To say that something is better 'understood' in one vocabulary than another is always an ellipsis for the claim that a description in the preferred vocabulary is most useful for a certain purpose. If the purpose is prediction, then one will want one sort of vocabulary. If it is evaluation, one may or may not want a different sort of vocabulary. (In the case of evaluating artillery fire, for example, the predictive vocabulary of ballistics will do nicely. In the case of evaluating human character, the vocabulary of stimulus and response is beside the point.)

To sum up this point: there are two distinct desiderata for the vocabulary of the social sciences:

(1) It should contain descriptions which permit prediction and control.
(2) It should contain descriptions which help one decide what to do.

Value-free social science assumed that a thin 'behavioristic' vocabulary would be useful for predicting human behavior. This suggestion has not panned out very well; the last fifty years of social-science research have not notably increased our predictive abilities. But even if it *had* succeeded in offering predictions this would not *necessarily* have made it useful in deciding what to do. The debate between friends of value-freedom and friends of hermeneutics has often taken for granted that neither desideratum can be satisfied unless the other is also. Friends of hermeneutics have protested that behaviorese was inappropriate for 'understanding' people – meaning that it could not catch what they were 'really' doing. But this is a misleading way of saying it is not a good vocabulary for moral reflection. We just don't want to be the sort of policy-makers who use those terms for deciding what to do to our fellow-humans. Conversely, friends of value-freedom, insisting that as soon as social science finds its Galileo (who is somehow known in advance to be a behaviorist) the first requirement will be satisfied, have argued that it is our duty to start making policy decisions in suitably thin terms – so that our 'ethics' may be 'objective' and 'scientifically based.' For only in that way will we be able to make maximal use of all those splendid predictions which will shortly be coming our way. Both sides make the same mistake in thinking that there is some intrinsic connection between the two requirements. It is a mistake to think that when we know how to deal justly and honorably with a person or a society we *thereby* know how to predict and control him or her or it, and a mistake to think that ability to predict and control is *necessarily* an aid to such dealing.

To be told that only a certain vocabulary is *suited* to human beings or human societies, that only *that* vocabulary permits us to 'understand' it, is the seventeenth-century myth of Nature's Own Vocabulary all over again. If, with Dewey, one sees vocabularies as instruments for coping with things rather than representations of their intrinsic natures, then one will not think that there is an intrinsic connection, or an intrinsic *lack* of connection, between 'explanation' and 'understanding' – between being able to predict and control people of a certain sort and being able to sympathize and associate with them, to view them as fellow citizens. One will not think that there are two 'methods' – one for explaining somebody's behavior and another for understanding his nature.

III. Epistemic and moral privilege

The current movement to make the social sciences 'hermeneutical' rather than Galilean makes a reasonable, Deweyan, point if it is taken as saying: narratives as well as laws, redescriptions as well as predictions, serve a useful purpose in helping us deal with the problems of society. In this sense, the movement is a useful protest against the fetishism of old-fashioned 'behaviorist' social scientists who worry about whether they are being 'scientific.' But this protest goes too far when it waxes philosophical and begins to draw a principled distinction between man and nature, announcing that the ontological difference dictates a methodological difference. Thus for example, when it is said that 'interpretation begins from the postulate that the web of meaning constitutes human existence,'[2] this suggests that fossils (for example) might get constituted *without* a web of meanings. But once the relevant sense of 'constitution' is distinguished from the physical sense (in which houses are 'constituted out of' bricks), to claim that 'X constitutes Y' reduces to the claim that you can't know anything about Y without knowing a lot about X. To say that human beings wouldn't be human, would be merely animal, unless they talked a lot is true enough. If you can't figure out the relation between a person, the noises he makes, and other persons, then you won't know much about him. But one could equally well say that fossils wouldn't be fossils, would be merely rocks, if we couldn't grasp their relations to lots of other fossils. Fossils are constituted as fossils by a web of relationships to other fossils and to the speech of the paleontologists who describe such rela-

2. Paul Rabinow and William M. Sullivan, 'The Interpretive Turn: Emergence of an Approach' in P. Rabinow and W. M. Sullivan, eds., *Interpretive Social Science* (Berkeley: U. of California Press, 1979), 5.

tionships. If you can't grasp some of these relationships the fossil will remain, to you, a mere rock. *Anything* is, for purposes of being inquired into, 'constituted' by a web of meanings.

To put this another way: if we think of the distribution of fossil records as a text, then we can say that paleontology, in its early stages, followed 'interpretive' methods. That is, it cast around for some way of making sense of what was happening by looking for a vocabulary in which the puzzling object could be related to other, more familiar objects, so as to become intelligible. Before the discipline became 'normalized,' nobody had any clear idea of what sort of thing might be relevant to predicting where similar fossils might be found. To say that 'paleontology is now a science' means something like 'Nobody has any doubts what sorts of questions you are supposed to ask, and what sort of hypotheses you can advance, when confronted with a puzzling fossil.' On my view, being 'interpretive' or 'hermeneutical' is not having a special method but simply casting about for a vocabulary which might help. When Galileo came up with his mathematicized vocabulary, he was successfully concluding an inquiry which was, in the only sense I can give the term, hermeneutical. The same goes for Darwin. I do not see any interesting differences between what they were doing and what Biblical exegetes, literary critics, or historians of culture do. So I think that it would do no harm to adopt the term 'hermeneutics' for the sort of by-guess-and-by-God hunt for new terminology which characterizes the initial stages of any new line of inquiry.

But although this would do no harm, it also would do no particular good. It is no more useful to think of people or fossils on the model of texts than to think of texts on the model of people or of fossils. It only appears more useful if we think that there is something *special* about texts – e.g., that they are 'intentional' or 'intelligible only holistically.' But I do not think (*pace,* e.g., Searle's notion of 'intrinsic intentionality') that 'possessing intentionality' means more than 'suitable to be described anthropomorphically, as if it were a language-user.'[3] The relations, on my view, between actions and movements, noises and assertions, is that each is the other described in an alternative jargon. Nor do I see that explanation of fossils is less holistic than explanations of texts – in both cases one needs to bring the object into relation with many other different sorts of objects in order to tell a coherent narrative which will incorporate the initial object.

Given this attitude, it behooves me to offer an explanation of why some people *do* think that texts are very different from fossils. I have suggested

3. See the discussion of Searle's 'Minds, Brains, and Programs,' in *The Behavioral and Brain Sciences* 3 (1980) 417–57, especially my 'Searle and the Secret Powers of the Brain' at pp. 445–6 and Searle's 'Intrinsic Intentionality' at pp. 450–6.

elsewhere, in arguing against Charles Taylor,[4] that such people make the mistaken assumption that somebody's *own* vocabulary is always the best vocabulary for understanding what he is doing, that his own explanation of what's going on is the one we want. This mistake seems to me a special case of the confused notion that science tries to learn the vocabulary which the universe uses to explain itself to itself. In both cases, we are thinking of our explanandum as if it were our epistemic equal or superior. But this is not always correct in the case of our fellow-humans, and is merely a relic of pre-Galilean anthropomorphism in the case of nature. There are, after all, cases in which the other person's, or culture's, explanation of what it's up to is so primitive or so nutty that we brush it aside. The only general hermeneutical rule is that it's always wise to ask what the subject *thinks* it's up to before formulating our own hypotheses. But this is an effort at saving time, not a search for the 'true meaning' of the behavior. If the explanandum can come up with a good vocabulary for explaining its own behavior, this saves us the trouble of casting about for one ourselves. From this point of view, the only difference between an inscription which is a gloss on the first, whereas the relation between the first fossil and the one next door, though perhaps equally illuminating, will be described in a non-intentional vocabulary.

In addition to the mistake of thinking that a subject's own vocabulary is always relevant to explaining him, philosophers who make a sharp distinction between man and nature are, like the positivists, bewitched by the notion that irreducibility of one vocabulary to another implies something ontological. Yet the discovery that we can or cannot reduce a language containing terms like 'is about,' 'is true of,' 'refers to,' etc., or one which contains 'believes' or 'intends,' to a language which is extensional and 'empiricist' would show us nothing at all about how to predict, or deal with, language-users or intenders. Defenders of Dilthey make a simple inversion of the mistake made, e.g., by Quine, who thinks there can be no 'fact of the matter' about intentional states of affairs because different such states can be attributed without making a difference to the elementary particles. Quine thinks that if a sentence can't be paraphrased in the sort of vocabulary which Locke and Boyle would have liked it doesn't stand for anything real. Diltheyans who exaggerate the difference between the *Geistes-* and the *Naturwissenschaften* think that the fact that it can't be paraphrased is a hint about a distinctive metaphysical or epistemic status, or the need for a distinctive methodological strategy. But surely all that such irreducibility shows is that one particular vocabulary (Locke's and Boyle's) is not going to be helpful for certain things we want to do with certain explananda (e.g., people and cultures). This shows as

4. 'Reply to Dreyfus and Taylor,' *Review of Metaphysics* 34 (1980) 39–46.

little, to use Hilary Putnam's analogy, as the fact that if you want to know why a square peg doesn't fit into a round hole you had better not describe the peg in terms of the positions of its constituent elementary particles.

The reason definitional irreducibility acquires this illusory importance, it seems to me, is that it *is* important to make a *moral* distinction between the brutes and ourselves. So, looking about for relevantly distinct behavior, we have traditionally picked our ability to *know*. In previous centuries, we made the mistake of hypostatizing cognitive behavior as the possession of 'mind' or 'consciousness' or 'ideas' and then insisting on the irreducibility of mental representations to their physiological correlates. When this became *vieux jeu,* we switched from mental representations to linguistic representations. We switched from Mind to Language as the name of a quasi-substance or quasi-power which made us morally different. So recent defenders of human dignity have been busy proving the irreducibility of the semantic instead of the irreducibility of the psychical. But all the Ryle-Wittgenstein sorts of arguments against the ghost in the machine work equally well against the ghost between the lines – the notion that having been penned by a human hand imparts a special something, textuality, to inscriptions, something which fossils can never have.

As long as we think of knowledge as representing reality rather than coping with it, mind or language will continue to seem numinous, and 'materialism,' 'behaviorism' and the Galilean style will seem morally dubious. We shall be stuck with this notion of 'representing' or 'corresponding to' reality as long as we think that there is some analogy between calling things by their 'right' – i.e., their conventional – names and finding the 'right' – i.e., Nature's Own – way of describing them. But if we could abandon this metaphor, and the vocabulary of representation which goes with it – as Kuhn and Dewey suggest we might – then we would not find language or mind mysterious, nor 'materialism' or 'behaviorism' particularly dangerous. If the line I am taking is right, we need to think of our distinctive moral status as just *that,* rather than 'grounded' on our possession of mind, language, culture, feeling, intentionality, textuality, or anything else. All these numinous notions are just expressions of our awareness that we are members of a moral community, phrased in one or another pseudo-explanatory jargon. This awareness is something which cannot be further 'grounded' – it is simply taking a certain point of view on our fellow-humans. The question of whether it is an 'objective' pint of view is not to any point.

This can be made a bit more concrete as follows. I said that, *pace* Taylor, it was a mistake to think of somebody's own account of his behavior or culture as epistemically privileged. He might have a good account of what he's doing or he might not. But it is *not* a mistake to think of it as morally privileged. We have a duty to listen to his account, not because he has privileged access to his own motives but because he is a human being like ourselves. Taylor's claim that we need to look for *internal* explanations of people or cultures or texts takes civility as a methodological strategy. But civility is not a method, it is simply a virtue. The reason why we invite the moronic psychopath to address the court before being sentenced is not that we hope for better explanations than expert psychiatric testimony has offered. We do so because he is, after all, one of us. By asking for his own account in his own words, we hope to decrease our chances of acting badly. What we hope form the social sciences is that they will act as interpreters for those how to talk to whom we are not sure. This is the same thing we hope for from our poets and dramatists and novelists.

Just as I argued in the previous section of this paper that it is a mistake to think that there is a principled distinction between explanation and understanding, or between two methods, one appropriate for nature and the other for man, I have been arguing in this section that the notion that we know *a priori* that nature and man are distinct sorts of objects is a mistake. It is a confusion between ontology and morals. There are lots of useful vocabularies which ignore the nonhuman-human or thing-person distinctions. There is at least one vocabulary – the moral – and possibly many more, for which these distinctions are basic. Human beings are no more 'really' described in the latter sort of vocabulary than in the former. Objects are not 'more objectively' described in any vocabulary that in any other. Vocabularies are useful or useless, good or bad, helpful or misleading, sensitive or coarse, and so on; but they are not 'more objective' or 'less objective' nor more or less 'scientific.'

IV. Ungrounded hope: Dewey vs. Foucault

The burden of my argument so far has been that if we get rid of traditional notions of 'objectivity' and 'scientific method' we shall be able to see the social sciences as continuous with literature – as interpreting other people to us, and thus enlarging and deepening our sense of community. We shall see the anthropologists and historians as having made it possible fur us – us educated, leisured, policy-makers of the West – to see exotic specimens of humanity as also 'one of us,' the sociologists as having done the same for the poor (and various sorts of nearby outsiders), the psychologists having done the same for the eccentric and the insane. This is not all that the social sciences have done, but it is perhaps the most important thing. If we emphasize this side of their achievement, then we shall not object to their sharing a narrative and anecdotal style with the novelist and the journalist. We shall not worry about how this style is related to the 'Galilean' style which 'quantified behavioral science' has tried to emulate. We shall not think either style particularly appropriate or inappropriate to the study of man. For we shall not think that 'the study of man' or 'the human sciences' have a nature, anymore than we think that Man does. When the notion of knowledge as representation goes, then the notion of inquiry as split into discrete sectors with discrete subject matters goes. The lines between novels, newspaper articles, and sociological research get blurred. The lines between subject-matters are drawn by reference to current practical concerns, rather than putative ontological status.

Once this pragmatist line is adopted, however, there are still two ways to go. One can emphasize, as Dewey did, the moral importance of the social sciences – their role in widening and deepening our sense of community and of the possibilities open to this community. Or one can emphasize, as Michel Foucault does, the way in which the social sciences have served as instruments of 'the disciplinary society.' That is to emphasize the connection between knowledge and power rather than that between knowledge and human solidarity. Much present-day concern about the status and the role of the social sciences comes out of the realization that in addition to broadening the sympathies of the educated classes, the social sciences have also helped them manipulate all the other classes (not to mention, so to speak, helping them manipulate themselves). Foucault's is the best account of this dark side of the social sciences. Admirers of Habermas and of Foucault join in thinking of the 'interpretative turn' in the social sciences as a turn against their use as 'instruments of domination,' as tools for what Dewey called 'social engineering.' This has resulted in a confusing quasi-politicization of what was already a factitious 'methodological' issue. In this final section of my paper, I want to argue that one should not attribute undue importance to the 'Galilean-vs.-hermeneutic' or 'explanation-vs.-understanding' contrasts by seeing them as parallel with the contrast between 'domination' and 'emancipation.' We should see Dewey and Foucault as differing not over a theoretical issue, but about what we may hope.

Dewey and Foucault make exactly the same criticism of the tradition. They agree, right down the line, about the need to abandon traditional notions of rationality, objectivity, method and truth. They are both, so to speak, 'beyond method.' They agree that rationality is what history and society make it – that there is no over-arching ahistorical structure (the Nature of Man, the laws of human behavior, the Moral Law, the Nature of Society) to be discovered. They share the Whewellian and Kuhnian notion of Galilean Science – as illustrating the power of new vocabularies rather than the secret of scientific success. But Dewey emphasizes that this move 'beyond method' gives mankind an opportunity to grow up, to be free to make itself, rather than seeking direction from some imagined outside source (one of the ahistorical structures mentioned above). His experimentalism asks us to see knowledge-claims as proposals about what actions to try out next:

> The elaborate systems of science are born not of reason but of impulses at first slight and flickering; impulses to handle, move about, to hunt, to uncover, to mix things separated and divide things combined, to talk and to listen. Method is their effectual organization into continuous dispositions of inquiry, development, and testing. . . . Reason, the rational attitude, is the resulting disposition. . . . [5]

Foucault also moves beyond the traditional ideals of method and rationality as antecedent constraints upon inquiry, but he views this move as the Nietzschean realization that all knowledge-claims are moves in a power-game. 'We are subject to the production of truth through power, and we cannot exercise power except through the production of truth.'[6]

Here I think we have two philosophers saying the same thing but putting a different spin on it. The same phenomenon is found in their respective predecessors. James and Nietzsche (as Arthur Danto has pointed out[7]) developed the same criticisms of traditional notions of truth, and the same 'pragmatic' (or 'perspectivalist') alternative. James jovially says that 'ideas become true just insofar as they help us to get into satisfactory relation with other parts of our experience,'[8] and Dewey follows this up when he says that 'rationality is the attainment of a working harmony among diverse desires.'[9] Nietzsche says that 'the criterion of truth resides in the enhancement of the feeling of power'[10] and that

> The mistake of philosophy is that, instead of seeing logic and the categories of reasons as means for fixing up the world for utilitarian ends . . . one thinks that they give one a criterion of truth about *reality*.[11]

Foucault follows this up by saying that 'we should not imagine that the world presents us with a legible face . . . we must conceive discourse as a

5. John Dewey, *Human Nature and Conduct* (New York: Modern Library, 1930), 196.
6. Michel Foucault, *Power/Knowledge* (Brighton: Harverster Books, 1980), 93.
7. Arthur Danto, *Nietzsche as Philosopher* (New York: Macmillan, 1965), chapter 3.
8. William James, *Pragmatism* (New York: Longmans Green, 1947), 58.
9. Dewey, 196.
10. Friedrich Nietzsche, *The Will to Power*, trans. W. Kaufmann (New York: Random House, 1967), 290.
11. Friedrich Nietzsche, *Werke*, ed. Schlechta, Ill, 726 (Kaufmann, 314).

violence that we do to things.'[12] The arguments which James and Dewey on the one hand, and Nietzsche and Foucault on the other, present for these identical views are as similar as the tone is different. Neither pair has any arguments except the usual 'idealist' ones, familiar since Kant, against the notion of knowledge as correspondence to nonrepresentations (rather than coherence among representations). These are the arguments in whose direction I gestured in the first section of this paper when I said that all attempts to cash Galileo's metaphor of Nature's Own Language had failed. Since the cash-value of a philosophical conclusion is the pattern of argument around it, I do not think that we are going to find any *theoretical* differences which divide these two pairs of philosophers from each other.

Is the difference then merely one of tone – an ingenuous Anglo-Saxon pose as opposed to self-dramatizing Continental one? The difference could be better put in terms of something like 'moral outlook.' One is reminded of the famous passage in Wittgenstein:

> If good or bad willing changes the world, it can only change the limits of the worked, not the facts; not the things that can be expressed in language. In brief, the world must thereby become quite another. It must so to speak wax or wane as a whole. The world of the happy is quite another than that of the happy.[13]

But, again, 'good and bad willing,' 'happy and unhappy' are not right for the opposition we are trying to describe. 'Hopeful' and 'hopeless' are a bit better. Ian Hacking winds up a discussion of Foucault by saying

> 'What is Man,' asked Kant. 'Nothing,' says Foucault. 'For what then may we hope?' asks Kant. Does Foucault give the same *nothing* in reply? To think so is to misunderstand Foucault's reply to the question about Man. Foucault said that the concept Man is a fraud, not that you and I are as nothing. Likewise the concept Hope is all wrong. The hopes attributed to Marx and Rousseau are perhaps part of that very concept Man, and they are a sorry basis for optimism. Optimism, pessimism, nihilism and the like are all concepts that make sense only within the idea of a transcendental or enduring subject. Foucault is not in the least incoherent about all this. If we're not satisfied, it should not be because he is pessimistic. It is because he has given no surrogate for whatever it is that springs eternal in the human breast.[14]

12. Michel Foucault, *The Archeology of Knowledge* (New York: Harper & Row, 1972), 229.
13. Ludwig Wittgenstein, *Tractatus Logico-Philosophicus* 6.42.
14. Ian Hacking, review of Foucault's *Power/Knowledge, New York Review of Books*, April 1981.

What Foucault doesn't give us is what Dewey wanted to give us – a kind of hope which doesn't *need* reinforcement from 'the idea of a transcendental or enduring subject.' Dewey offered ways of using words like 'truth,' 'rationality,' 'progress,' 'freedom,' 'democracy,' 'culture,' 'art' and the like which presupposed neither the ability to use the familiar vocabulary of what Foucault calls 'the classic age,' nor that of the nineteenth-century French intellectuals (the vocabulary of 'man and his doubles').

Foucault sees no middle ground, in thinking about the social sciences, between the 'classic' Galilean conception of 'behavioral sciences' and the French notion of 'sciences de l'homme.' It was just such a middle ground that Dewey proposed, and which inspired the social sciences in America before the failure of nerve which turned them 'behavioral.' More generally, the recent reaction in favor of hermeneutical social sciences which I discussed earlier has taken for granted that if we don't want something like Parsons we have to take something like Foucault – that overcoming the deficiencies of Weberian *Zweckrationalität* requires going all the way, repudiating the 'will to truth.' What Dewey suggested was that we keep the will to truth and the optimism that goes with it, but free them from the behaviorist notion that behaviorese is Nature's Own Language *and* from the notion of Man as 'transcendental or enduring subject.' For, in Dewey's hands, the will to truth is not the urge to dominate but the urge to create, to 'attain working harmony among diverse desires.'

This may sound too pat, too good to be true. I suggest that the reason we find it so is that we are convinced that liberalism requires the notion of a common human nature, or a common set of moral principles which binds us all, or some other descendent of the Christian notion of the Brotherhood of Man. So we have come to see liberal social hope – such as Dewey's – as inherently self-deceptive and philosophically naive. We think that once we have freed ourselves from the various illusions which Nietzsche diagnosed we *must* find ourselves all alone: without the sense of community which liberalism requires. Perhaps, as Hacking says, Nietzsche and Foucault are not saying that you and I are as nothing, but they do seem to hint that you and I together, as *we,* aren't much – that human solidarity ages when God and his doubles go. Man as Hegel thought of him, as the Incarnation of the Idea, doubtless does have to go. The proletariat as the Redeemed Form of Man has to go too. But there seems no particular reason why, after dumping Marx, we have to keep on repeating all the nasty things about bourgeois liberalism which he taught us to say. There is no inferential connection between the disappearance of the transcendental subject – of man as something which has a nature which society can repress or understand – and the disappearance of human solidarity. Bourgeois liberalism seems to me the best example of this solidarity we have yet achieved, and Deweyan pragmatism the best articulation of it.[15]

The burden of my argument here is that we should see Dewey as having already gone the route Foucault is traveling, and as having arrived at the point Foucault is still trying to reach – the point at which we can make philosophical and historical ('genealogical') reflection useful to those, in Foucault's phrase, 'whose fight is located in the fine meshes of the webs of power.' Dewey spent his life trying to lend a hand in these little fights, and in the course of doing so he worked out the vocabulary and rhetoric of American 'pluralism.' This rhetoric made the first generation of American social scientists think of themselves as apostles of a new form of social life. Foucault does not, as far as I can see, do more than update Dewey by warn-

15. Dewey seems to me the twentieth-century counterpart of John Stuart Mill, whose attempt to synthesize Coleridge with Bentham is paralleled by Dewey's attempt to synthesize Hegel with Mill himself. In a brilliant critique of liberalism, John Dunn describes Mill as attempting to combine the 'two possible radical intellectual strategies open to those who aspire to rescue liberalism as a coherent political option:

> One is to shrink liberalism to a more or less pragmatic and sociological doctrine about the relations between types of political and social order and the enjoyment of political liberties. The version of liberalism which embraces this option is usually today termed 'pluralism,' a conception . . . which is still in effect the official intellectual ideology of American society. The second possible radical strategy is simply to repudiate the claims of sociology, to take an epistemological position of such stark scepticisms that the somewhat over-rated causal status of sociology can safely be viewed with limited scorn. (*Western Political Values in the Face of the Future* (Cambridge: Cambridge U.P. 1979) 47–8.)

Dunn thinks Mill's attempt to "integrate intellectual traditions so deeply and explicitly inimical to one another" failed, and that modern pluralism fails also:

> Modern pluralism is thus at least sufficiently sociologically self-aware not to blanch from the insight that a liberal polity is the political form of bourgeois capitalist society. But the price which it has paid, so far pretty willingly, for this self-awareness, is the surrender of any plausible overall intellectual frame, uniting epistemology, psychology and political theory, which explains and celebrates the force of such political commitment. (*Ibid.*, 49)

My view is that such an overall intellectual frame was exactly what Dewey gave us, and that he did so precisely by carrying out Mill's combination of strategies. [For some links between Rawls (who is Dunn's favorite example of modern pluralism) and Dewey, see Rawls' Dewey Lectures, 'Kantian Constructivism in Moral Theory' (*Journal of Philosophy* 77 (1980), 515–72]. Note especially p. 542, on

ing that the social scientists have often been, and are always likely to be, co-opted by the bad guys. Reading Foucault reinforces the disillusion which American intellectuals have suffered during the last few decades of watching the 'behavioralized' social sciences team up with the state.

The reason why it may appear that Foucault has something new and distinctive to add to Dewey is that he is riding the crest of a powerful but vaguely defined movement which I have elsewhere[16] described as 'textualism' – the movement which suggests, as Foucault puts it at the end of the *The Order of Things*, that 'Man is in the process of perishing as the being of language continues to shine ever brighter upon our horizon.'[17] Another reason is that Foucault is attempting to transform political discourse by seeing 'power' as not intrinsically repressive – because, roughly, there is no naturally good self to repress. But Dewey, it seems to me, had already grasped both points. Foucault's vision of discourse as a network of power-relations isn't very different from Dewey's vision of it as instrumental, as one element in the arsenal of tools people use for gratifying, synthesizing and harmonizing their desires. Dewey had learned form Hegel what Foucault learns form Nietzsche – that there is nothing much to 'man' except one more animal, until culture, the meshes of power, begin to shape him not something else. For Dewey too there is nothing Rousseauian to be 'repressed' – 'repression' and 'liberation' are just names for the sides we like and the sides we don't like of the structures of power. Once 'power' is freed from its connotation of 'repression,' then Foucault's 'structures of power' don't seem much different from Dewey's 'structures of culture.' 'Power' and 'culture' are equipollent indications of the social forces which make us more than animals and which can, when the bad guys take over, turn us into something worse and more miserable than animals.

These remarks are not meant to down-grade Foucault – who seems to me one of the most interesting philosophers alive – but just to insist that

a conception of justice which swings free of 'religious, philosophical or moral doctrines,' and *Weltnaschaungen* generally. See also p. 519 for Rawls' repudiation of an 'epistemological problem,' and his doctrine of 'moral facts' as 'constructed.' Dunn seems to me right in saying that liberalism has little useful to say about contemporary global politics, but wrong in pinning the blame for this on its lack of a philosophical synthesis of the old, Kantian, unpragmatic sort. On my view, we should be more willing than we are to celebrate bourgeois capitalist society as the best polity actualized so far, while regretting that it is irrelevant to most of the problems of most of the population of the planet.

16. 'Nineteenth-Century Idealism and Twentieth-Century Textualism,' *The Monist*, 64.2 (1981).
17. Michel Foucault, *The Order of Things* (New York: Random House, 1973), 386.

we go slow about assuming that the discovery of things like 'discourse,' 'textuality,' 'speech-acts' and the like have radically changed the philosophical scene. The current vogue of 'hermeneutics' is going to end soon and badly if we advertise these new notions as more than they are – namely, one more jargon which tries to get out form under some of the mistakes of the past. Dewey had his own jargon – popular at the time, but now a bit musty – for the same purpose. The difference in jargon should not obscure the common aim. This is the attempt to free mankind from Nietzsche's 'longest lie,' the notion that outside the haphazard and perilous experiments we perform there lies something (God, Science, Knowledge, Rationality, or Truth) which will, if only we perform the correct rituals, step in to save us. Although Foucault and Dewey are trying to do the same thing, Dewey seems to me to have done it better, simply because his vocabulary allows room for unjustifiable hope, and an ungroundable but vital sense of human solidarity.

4

The new cultural politics of difference
Cornel West

In these last few years of the 20th century, there is emerging a significant shift in the sensibilities and outlooks of critics and artists. In fact, I would go so far as to claim that a new kind of cultural worker is in the making, associated with a new politics of difference. These new forms of intellectual consciousness advance reconceptions of the vocation of critic and artist, attempting to undermine the prevailing disciplinary divisions of labor in the academy, museum, mass media and gallery networks, while preserving modes of critique within the ubiquitous commodification of culture in the global village. Distinctive features of the new cultural politics of difference are to trash the monolithic and homogeneous in the name of diversity, multiplicity and heterogeneity; to reject the abstract, general and universal in light of the concrete, specific and particular; and to historicize, contextualize and pluralize by highlighting the contingent, provisional, variable, tentative, shifting and changing. Needless to say, these gestures are not new in the history of criticism or art, yet what makes them novel – along with the cultural politics they produce – is how and what constitutes difference, the weight and gravity it is given in representation and the way in which highlighting issues like exterminism, empire, class, race, gender, sexual orientation, age, nation, nature, and region at this historical moment acknowledges some discontinuity and disruption from previous forms of cultural critique. To put it bluntly, the new cultural politics of difference consists of creative responses to the precise circumstances of our present moment – especially those of marginalized First World agents who shun degraded self-representations, articulating instead their sense of the flow of history in light of the contemporary terrors, anxieties and fears of highly commercialized North Atlantic capitalist cultures (with their escalating xenophobias against people of color, Jews, women, gays, lesbians and the elderly). The thawing, yet still rigid, Second World ex-communist cultures (with increasing nationalist revolts against the legacy of hegemonic party henchmen), and the diverse cultures of the majority of inhabitants on the globe smothered by international communication cartels and repressive postcolonial elites (sometimes in the name of communism, as in Ethiopia) or starved by austere World Bank and IMF policies that subordinate them to the North (as in free-market capitalism in Chile) also locate vital areas of analysis in this new cultural terrain.

The new cultural politics of difference are neither simply oppositional in contesting the mainstream (or *male*stream) for inclusion, nor transgressive in the avant-gardist sense of shocking conventional bourgeois audiences. Rather, they are distinct articulations of talented (and usually privileged) contributors to culture who desire to align themselves with demoralized, demobilized, depoliticized and disorganized people in order to empower and enable social action and, if possible, to enlist collective insurgency for the expansion of freedom, democracy and individuality. This perspective impels these cultural critics and artists to reveal, as an integral component of their production, the very operations of power within their immediate work contexts (i.e., academy, museum, gallery, mass media). This strategy, however, also puts them in an inescapable double bind – while linking their activities to the fundamental, structural overhaul of these institutions, they often remain financially dependent on them (so much for "independent" creation). For these critics of culture, theirs is a gesture that is simultaneously progressive *and* co-opted. Yet without social movement or political pressure from outside these institutions (extra-parliamentary and extra-curricular actions like the social movements of the recent past), transformation degenerates into mere accommodation or sheer stagnation, and the role of the "co-opted progressive" – no matter how fervent one's subversive rhetoric – is rendered more difficult. There can be no artistic breakthrough or social progress without some form of crisis in civilization – a crisis usually generated by organizations or collectivities that convince ordinary people to put their bodies and lives on the line. There is, of course, no guarantee that such pressure will yield the result one wants, but there is a guarantee that the status quo will remain or regress if no pressure is applied at all.

The new cultural politics of difference faces three basic challenges – intellectual, existential and political. The intellectual challenge – usually cast as methodological debate in these days in which academicist forms of expression have a monopoly on intellectual life – is how to think about representational practices in terms of history, culture and society. How does one understand, analyze and enact such practices today? An adequate answer to this question can be attempted only after one comes to terms with the insights and blindnesses of earlier attempts to grapple with the question in light of the evolving crisis in different histories, cultures and societies. I shall sketch a brief genealogy – a history that highlights the contingent origins and often ignoble outcomes – of exemplary critical responses to the question. This genealogy sets forth a historical framework that characterizes the rich yet deeply flawed Eurocentric traditions which the new cultural politics of difference build upon yet go beyond.

The intellectual challenge

The post-World War II era in the USA, or the first decades of what Henry Luce envisioned as "The American Century," was not only a period of incredible economic expansion but of active cultural ferment. In the classical Fordist formula, mass production required mass consumption. With unchallenged hegemony in the capitalist world, the USA took economic growth for granted. Next to exercising its crude, anti-communist, McCarthyist obsessions, buying commodities became the primary act of civic virtue for many American citizens at this time. The creation of a mass middle class – a prosperous working class with a bourgeois identity – was countered by the first major emergence of subcultures of American non-WASP intellectuals: the so-called New York intellectuals in criticism, the Abstract Expressionists in painting and the BeBop artists in jazz music. This emergence signaled a vital challenge to an American male WASP elite loyal to an older and eroding European culture.

The first significant blow was dealt when assimilated Jewish Americans entered the higher echelons of the cultural apparatuses (academy, museums, galleries, mass media). Lionel Trilling is an emblematic figure. This Jewish entree into the anti-Semitic and patriarchal critical discourse of the exclusivistic institutions of American culture initiated the slow but sure undoing of the male WASP cultural hegemony and homogeneity. Lionel Trilling's project was to appropriate Matthew Arnold for his own political and cultural purposes – thereby unraveling the old male WASP consensus, while erecting a new post-World War II liberal academic consensus around cold war, anti-communist renditions of the values of complexity, difficulty, variousness and modulation. In addition, the post-war boom laid the basis for intense professionalization and specialization in expanding institutions of higher education – especially in the natural sciences that were compelled to somehow respond to Russia's successful ventures in space. Humanistic scholars found themselves searching for new methodologies that could buttress self-images of rigor and scientific seriousness. For example, the close reading techniques of New Criticism (severed from their conservative, organicist, anti-industrialist ideological roots), the logical precision of reasoning in analytic philosophy and the jargon of Parsonian structural-functionalism in sociology helped create such self-images. Yet towering cultural critics like C. Wright Mills,

W. E. B. DuBois, Richard Hofstadter, Margaret Mead and Dwight Mac-Donald bucked the tide. This suspicion of the academicization of knowledge is expressed in Trilling's well-known essay "On the Teaching of Modern Literature"

> [c]an we not say that, when modern literature is brought into the classroom, the subject being taught is betrayed by the pedagogy of the subject? We have to ask ourselves whether in our day too much does not come within the purview of the academy. More and more, as the universities liberalize themselves, turn their beneficent imperialistic gaze upon what is called life itself, the feeling grows among our educated classes that little can be experienced unless it is validated by some established intellectual discipline.

Trilling laments the fact that university instruction often quiets and domesticates radical and subversive works of art, turning them into objects "of merely habitual regard." This process of "the socialization of the anti-social, or the acculturation of the anti-cultural, or the legitimization of the subversive" leads Trilling to "question whether in our culture the study of literature is any longer a suitable means for developing and refining the intelligence." Trilling asks this question not in the spirit of denigrating and devaluing the academy but rather in the spirit of highlighting the possible failure of an Arnoldian conception of culture to contain what he perceives as the philistine and anarchic alternatives becoming more and more available to students of the 60's – namely, mass culture and radical politics.

This threat is partly associated with the third historical coordinate of my genealogy – the decolonization of the Third World. It is crucial to recognize the importance of this world-historical process if one wants to grasp the significance of the end of the Age of Europe and the emergence of the USA as a world power. With the first defeat of a western nation by a non-western nation – in Japan's victory over Russia (1905), revolutions in Persia (1905), Turkey (1908), China (1912), Mexico (1911–12) and much later the independence of India (1947) and China (1948) and the triumph of Ghana (1957) – the actuality of a decolonized globe loomed large. Born of violent struggle, consciousness-raising and the reconstruction of identities, decolonization simultaneously brings with it new perspectives on that long festering underside of the Age of Europe (of which colonial domination represents the *costs* of "progress," "order" and "culture"), as well as requiring new readings of the economic boom in the USA (wherein the Black, Brown, Yellow, Red, female, elderly, gay, lesbian and White working class live the same *costs* as cheap labor at home as well as in US-dominated Latin American and Pacific rim markets).

The impetuous ferocity and moral outrage the motors the decolonization process is best captured by Frantz Fanon in *The Wretched of the Earth* (1961).

> Decolonization, which sets out to change the order of the world, is obviously, a program of complete disorder . . . Decolonization is the meeting of two forces, opposed to each other by their very nature, which in fact owe their originality to that sort of substantification which results from and is nourished by the situation in the colonies. Their first encounter was marked by violence and their existence together – that is to say the exploitation of the native by the settler – was carried on by dint of a great array of bayonets and cannons . . .

> In decolonization, there is therefore the need of a complete calling in question of the colonial situation. If we wish to describe it precisely, we might find it in the well-known words: "The last shall be first and the first last." Decolonization is the putting into practice of this sentence.

> The naked truth of decolonization evokes for us the searing bullets and bloodstained knives which emanate from it. For if the last shall be first, this will only come to pass after a murderous and decisive struggle between the two protagonists.

Fanon's strong words, though excessively Manichean, still describe the feelings and thoughts between the occupying British Army and colonized Irish in Northern Ireland, the occupying Israeli Army and subjugated Palestinians on the West Bank and Gaza Strip, the South African Army and oppressed Black South Africans in the townships, the Japanese Police and Koreans living in Japan, the Russian Army and subordinated Armenians and others in the Southern and Eastern USSR. His words also partly invoke the sense many Black Americans have toward police departments in urban centers. In other words, Fanon is articulating century-long heartfelt human responses to being degraded and despised, hated and hunted, oppressed and exploited, marginalized and dehumanized at the hands of powerful xenophobic European, American, Russian and Japanese imperial countries.

During the late '50s, '60s and early '70s in the USA, these decolonized sensibilities fanned and fueled the Civil Rights and Black Power movements, as well as the student anti-war, feminist, gray, brown, gay, and lesbian movements. In this period we witnessed the shattering of male WASP cultural homogeneity and the collapse of the short-lived liberal consensus. The inclusion of African Americans, Latino/a Americans, Asian Americans, Native Americans and American women into the culture of critical discourse yielded intense intellectual polemics and inescapable ideological polarization that focused principally on the exclusions, silences and blindness of male WASP cultural homogeneity and its concomitant Arnoldian notions of the canon.

In addition, these critiques promoted three crucial processes that affected intellectual life in the country. First is the appropriation of the theories of post-war Europe – especially the work of the Frankfurt school (Marcuse, Adorno, Horkheimer), French/Italian Marxisms (Sartre, Althusser, Lefebvre, Gramsci), structuralisms (Lévi-Strauss, Todorov) and post-structuralisms (Deleuze, Derrida, Foucault). These diverse and disparate theories – all preoccupied with keeping alive radical projects after the end of the Age of Europe – tend to fuse versions of transgressive European modernisms with Marxist or post-Marxist left politics and unanimously shun the term "post-modernism." Second, there is the recovery and revisioning of American history in light of the struggles of white male workers, women, African Americans, Native Americans, Latino/a Americans, gays and lesbians. Third is the impact of forms of popular culture such as television, film, music videos and even sports, on highbrow literate culture. The Black-based hip-hop culture of youth around the world is one grand example.

After 1973, with the crisis in the international world economy, America's slump in productivity, the challenge of OPEC nations to the North Atlantic monopoly of oil production, the increasing competition in hi-tech sectors of the economy from Japan and West Germany and the growing fragility of the international debt structure, the USA entered a period of waning self-confidence (compounded by Watergate) and a nearly contracting economy. As the standards of living for the middle classes declined, owing to runaway inflation, and the quality of living fell for most, due to escalating unemployment, underemployment and crime, religious and secular neo-conservatism emerged with power and potency. This fusion of fervent neo-nationalism, traditional cultural values and "free market" policies served as the ground work for the Reagan-Bush era.

The ambiguous legacies of the European Age, American preeminence and decolonization continue to haunt our postmodern moment as we come to terms with both the European, American, Japanese, Soviet, and Third World *crimes against* and *contributions to* humanity. The plight of Africans in the New World can be instructive in this regard.

By 1914 European maritime empires had dominion over more than half of the land and a third of the peoples in the world – almost 72 million square kilometers of territory and more than 560 million people under colonial rule. Needless to say, this European control included brutal enslavement, institutional terrorism and cultural degradation of Black diaspora people. The death of roughly seventy-five million Africans during the centuries-long transatlantic slave trade is but one reminder, among others, of the assault on Black humanity. The Black diaspora condition of New World servitude – in which they were viewed as mere commodities with production value, who had no proper legal status, social standing or public worth – can be characterized as, following Orlando Patterson, natal alienation. This state of perpetual and inheritable domination that diaspora Africans had at birth produced the *modern Black diaspora problematic of invisibility and namelessness.* White supremacist practices – enacted under the auspices of the prestigious cultural authorities of the churches, printed media and scientific academics – promoted Black inferiority and constituted the European background against which Black diaspora struggles for identity, dignity (self-confidence, self-respect, self-esteem) and material resources took place.

An inescapable aspect of this struggle was that the Black diaspora peoples' quest for validation and recognition occurred on the ideological, social and cultural terrains of other non-Black peoples. White supremacist assaults on Black intelligence, ability, beauty and character required persistent Black efforts to hold self-doubt, self-contempt and even self-hatred at bay. Selective appropriation, incorporation and re-articulation of European ideologies, cultures and institutions alongside an African heritage – a heritage more or less confined to linguistic innovation in rhetorical practices, stylizations of the body in forms of occupying an alien social space (hair styles, ways of walking, standing, hand expressions, talking) and means of constituting and sustaining comraderie and community (e.g. antiphonal, call-and-response styles, rhythmic repetition, risk-ridden syncopation in spectacular modes in musical and rhetorical expressions) – were some of the strategies employed.

The modern Black diaspora problematic of invisibility and namelessness can be understood as the condition of *relative lack of Black power to represent themselves to themselves and others as complex human beings, and thereby to contest the bombardment of negative, degrading stereotypes put forward by White supremacist ideologies.* The initial Black response to being caught in this whirlwind of Europeanization was to resist the misrepresentation and caricature of the terms set by uncontested non-Black norms and models and fight for self-representation and recognition. Every modern Black person, especially cultural disseminators, encounters this problematic of invisibility and namelessness. The initial Black diaspora response was a mode of resistance that was *moralistic in content* and *communal in character.* That is, the fight for representation and recognition highlighted moral judgments regarding Black "positive" images over and against White supremacist stereotypes. These images "re-presented" monolithic and homogeneous Black communities, in a way that could displace past misrepresentations of these communities. Stuart Hall has talked about these responses as attempts to change "the relations of representation."

These courageous yet limited Black efforts to combat racist cultural practices uncritically accepted non-Black conventions and standards in two ways. First, they proceeded in an *assimilationist manner* that set out to show that Black people were really like White people – thereby eliding differences (in history, culture) between Whites and Blacks. Black specificity and particularity was thus banished in order to gain White acceptance and approval. Second, these Black responses rested upon a *homogenizing impulse* that assumed that all Black people were really alike – hence obliterating differences (class, gender, region, sexual orientation) between Black peoples. I submit that there are elements of truth in both claims, yet the conclusions are unwarranted owing to the basic fact that non-Black paradigms set the terms of the replies.

The insight in the first claim is that Blacks and Whites are in some important sense alike – i.e., in their positive capacities for human sympathy, moral sacrifice, service to others, intelligence and beauty, or negatively, in their capacity for cruelty. Yet the common humanity they share is jettisoned when the claim is cast in an assimilationist manner that subordinates Black particularity to a false universalism, i.e., non-Black rubrics or prototypes. Similarly, the insight in the second claim is that all Blacks are in some significant sense "in the same boat" – that is, subject to White supremacist abuse. Yet this common condition is stretched too far when viewed in a *homogenizing* way that overlooks how racist treatment vastly differs owing to class, gender, sexual orientation, nation, region, hue and age.

The moralistic and communal aspects of the initial Black diaspora responses to social and psychic erasure were not simply cast into simplistic binary oppositions of positive/negative, good/bad images that privileged the first term in light of a White norm so that Black efforts remained inscribed within the very logic that dehumanized them. They were further complicated by the fact that these responses were also advanced principally by anxiety-ridden, middle-class Black intellectuals, (predominantly male and heterosexual) grappling with their sense of double-consciousness – namely their own crisis of identity, agency and audience – caught between a quest for White approval and acceptance and an endeavor to overcome the internalized association of Blackness with inferiority. And I suggest that these complex anxieties of modern Black diaspora intellectuals partly motivate the two major arguments that ground the assimilationist moralism and homogeneous communalism just outlined.

Kobena Mercer has talked about these two arguments as the *reflectionist* and the *social engineering* arguments. The reflectionist argument holds that the fight for Black representation and recognition must reflect or mirror the real Black community, not simply the negative and depressing representations of it. The social engineering argument claims that since any form of representation is constructed – i.e., selective in light of broader aims – Black representation (especially given the difficulty of Blacks gaining access to positions of power to produce any Black imagery) should offer positive images of themselves in order to inspire achievement among young Black people, thereby countering racist stereotypes. The hidden assumption of both arguments is that we have unmediated access to what the "real Black community" is and what "positive images" are. In short, these arguments presuppose the very phenomena to be interrogated, and thereby foreclose the very issues that should serve as the subject matter to be investigated.

Any notions of "the real Black community" and "positive images" are value-laden, socially-loaded and ideologically-charged. To pursue this discussion is to call into question the possibility of such an uncontested consensus regarding them. Stuart Hall has rightly called this encounter "the end of innocence or the end of the innocent notion of the essential Black subject . . . the recognition that 'Black' is essentially a politically and culturally *constructed* category." This recognition – more and more pervasive among the postmodern Black diaspora intelligentsia – is facilitated in part by the slow but sure dissolution of the European Age's maritime empires, and the unleashing of new political possibilities and cultural articulations among ex-colonialized peoples across the globe.

One crucial lesson of this decolonization process remains the manner in which most Third World authoritarian bureaucratic elites deploy essentialist rhetorics about "homogeneous national communities" and "positive images" in order to repress and regiment their diverse and heterogeneous populations. Yet in the diaspora, especially among First World countries, this critique has emerged not so much from the Black male component of the left but rather from the Black women's movement. The decisive push of postmodern Black intellectuals toward a new cultural politics of difference has been made by the powerful critiques and constructive explorations of Black diaspora women (e.g. Toni Morrison). The coffin used to bury the innocent notion of the essential Black subject was nailed shut with the termination of the Black male monopoly on the construction of the Black subject. In this regard, the Black diaspora womanist critique has had a greater impact than the critiques that highlight exclusively class, empire, age, sexual orientation or nature.

This decisive push toward the end of Black innocence – though prefigured in various degrees in the best moments of W. E. B. DuBois, Anna Cooper, C. L. R. James, James Baldwin, Claudia Jones, the later Malcolm X, Frantz Fanon, Amiri Baraka and others – forces Black diaspora cultural workers to encounter what Hall has called the "politics of representation." The main aim now is not simply access to representation in order to produce positive images of homogeneous communities – though broader access remains a practical and political problem. Nor is the primary goal here that of contesting stereotypes – though contestation remains a significant though limited venture. Following the model of the Black diaspora traditions of music, athletics and rhetoric, Black cultural workers must constitute and sustain discursive and institutional networks that deconstruct earlier modern Black strategies for identity-formation, demystify power relations that incorporate class, patriarchal and homophobic biases, and construct more multi-valent and multi-dimensional responses that articulate the complexity and diversity of Black practices in the modern and postmodern world.

Furthermore, Black cultural workers must investigate and interrogate the other of Blackness–Whiteness. One cannot deconstruct the binary oppositional logic of images of Blackness without extending it to the contrary condition of Blackness/Whiteness itself. However, a mere dismantling will not do – for the very notion of a deconstructive social theory is oxymoronic. Yet social theory is what is needed to examine and *explain* the historically specific ways in which "Whiteness" is a politically constructed category parasitic on "Blackness," and thereby to conceive of the profoundly hybrid character of what we mean by "race," "ethnicity," and "nationality." For instance, European immigrants arrived on American shores perceiving themselves as "Irish," "Sicilian," "Lithuanian," etc. They had to learn that they were "White" principally by adopting an American discourse of positively-valued Whiteness and negatively-charged Blackness. This process by which people define themselves physically, socially, sexually and even politically in terms of Whiteness or Blackness has much bearing not only on constructed notions of race and ethnicity but also on how we understand the changing character of U.S. nationalities. And given the Americanization of the world, especially in the sphere of mass culture, such inquiries – encouraged by the new cultural politics of difference – raise critical issues of "hybridity," "exilic status" and "identity" on an international scale. Needless to say, these inquiries must traverse those of "male/female," "colonizer/colonized," "heterosexual/homosexual," et al., as well.

In light of this brief sketch of the emergence of our present crisis – and the turn toward history and difference in cultural work – four major historicist forms of theoretical activity provide resources for how we understand, analyze and enact our representational practices: Heideggerian *destruction* of the western metaphysical tradition, Derridean *deconstruction* of the western philosophical tradition, Rortian *demythologization* of the western intellectual tradition and Marxist, Foucaultian, feminist, antiracist or anti-homophobic *demystification* of western cultural and artistic conventions.

Despite his abominable association with the Nazis, Martin Heidegger's project is useful in that it discloses the suppression of temporality and historicity in the dominant metaphysical system of the West from Plato to Rudolph Carnap. This is noteworthy in that it forces one to understand philosophy's representational discourses as thoroughly historical phenomena. Hence, they should be viewed with skepticism as they are often flights from the specific, concrete, practical and particular. The major problem with Heidegger's project – as noted by his neo-Marxist student, Herbert Marcuse – is that he views history in terms of fate, heritage and destiny. He dramatizes the past and present as if it were a Greek tragedy with no tools of social analyses to relate cultural work to institutions and structures or antecedent forms and styles.

Jacques Derrida's version of deconstruction is one of the most influential schools of thought among young academic critics. It is salutary in that it focuses on the political power of rhetorical operations – of tropes and metaphors in binary oppositions like white/black, good/bad, male/female, machine/nature, ruler/ruled, reality/appearance – showing how these operations sustain hierarchal world views by devaluing the second terms as something subsumed under the first. Most of the controversy about Derrida's project revolves around this austere epistemic doubt that unsettles binary oppositions while undermining any determinate meaning of a text, i.e., book, art-object, performance, building. Yet, his views about skepticism are no more alarming than those of David Hume, Ludwig Wittgenstein or Stanley Cavell. He simply revels in it for transgressive purposes, whereas others provide us with ways to dissolve, sidestep or cope with skepticism. None, however, slide down the slippery, crypto-Nietzschean slope of sophomoric relativism as alleged by old-style humanists, be they Platonists, Kantians or Arnoldians.

The major shortcoming of Derrida's deconstructive project is that it puts a premium on a sophisticated ironic consciousness that tends to preclude and foreclose analyses that guide action with purpose. And given Derrida's own status as an Algerian-born, Jewish leftist marginalized by a hostile French academic establishment (quite different from his reception by the youth in the American academic establishment), the sense of political impotence and hesitation regarding the efficacy of moral action is understandable – but not justifiable. His works and those of his followers too often become rather monotonous, Johnny-one-note rhetorical readings that disassemble texts with little attention to the effects and consequences these dismantlings have in relation to the operations of military, economic and social powers.

Richard Rorty's neo-pragmatic of demythologization is insightful in that it provides descriptive mappings of the transient metaphors – especially the ocular and specular ones – that regulate some of the fundamental dynamics in the construction of self-descriptions dominant in high-brow European and American philosophy. His perspective is instructive because it discloses the crucial role of narrative as the background for rational exchange and critical conversation. To put it crudely, Rorty shows why we should speak not of History, but histories, not of Reason, but historically constituted forms of rationality, not of Criticism or Art, but of socially constructed notions of criticism and art – all linked but not reducible to political purposes, material interests and cultural prejudices.

Rorty's project nonetheless leaves one wanting owing to its distrust of social analytical explanation. Similar to the dazzling new historicism of Stephen Greenblatt, Louis Montrose and Catherine Gallagher – inspired by the subtle symbolic-cum-textual anthropology of Clifford Geertz and the powerful discursive materialism of Michel Foucault – Rorty gives us mappings and descriptions with no explanatory accounts for change and conflict. In this way, it gives us an aestheticized version of historicism in which the provisional and variable are celebrated at the expense of highlighting who gains, loses or bears what costs.

Demystification is the most illuminating mode of theoretical inquiry for those who promote the new cultural politics of difference. Social structural analyses of empire, exterminism, class, race, gender, nature, age, sexual orientation, nation and region are the springboards – though not landing grounds – for the most desirable forms of critical practice that take history (and herstory) seriously. Demystification tries to keep track of the complex dynamics of institutional and other related power structures in order to disclose options and alternatives for transformative praxis; it also attempts to grasp the way in which representational strategies are creative responses to novel circumstances and conditions. In this way, the central role of human agency (always enacted under circumstances not of one's choosing) – be it in the critic, artist or constituency and audience – is accented.

I call demystificatory criticism "prophetic criticism" – the approach appropriate for the new cultural politics of difference – because while it begins with social structural analyses it also makes explicit its moral and political aims. It is partisan, partial, engaged and crisis-centered, yet always keeps open a skeptical eye to avoid dogmatic traps, premature closures, formulaic formulations or rigid conclusions. In addition to social structural analyses, moral and political judgments, and sheer critical consciousness, there indeed is evaluation. Yet the aim of this evaluation is neither to pit art-objects against one another like racehorses nor to create eternal canons that dull, discourage or even dwarf contemporary achievements. We listen to Ludwig Beethoven, Charlie Parker, Luciano Pavarotti, Laurie Anderson, Sarah Vaughan, Stevie Wonder or Kathleen Battle, read William Shakespeare, Anton Chekhov, Ralph Ellison, Doris Lessing,

Thomas Pynchon, Toni Morrison or Gabriel García Márquez, see works of Pablo Picasso, Ingmar Bergman, Le Corbusier, Martin Puryear, Barbara Kruger, Spike Lee, Frank Gehry or Howardena Pindell – not in order to undergird bureaucratic assents or enliven cocktail party conversations, but rather to be summoned by the styles they deploy for their profound insight, pleasures and challenges. Yet all evaluation – including a delight in Eliot's poetry despite his reactionary politics, or a love of Zora Neale Hurston's novels despite her Republican party affiliations – is inseparable from, though not identical or reducible to, social structural analyses, moral and political judgments and the workings of a curious critical consciousness.

The deadly traps of demystification – and any form of prophetic criticism – are those of reductionism, be it of the sociological, psychological, or historical sort. By reductionism I mean either one factor analyses (i.e., crude Marxisms, feminisms, racialisms, etc.) that yield a one-dimensional functionalism, or a hyper-subtle analytical perspective that loses touch with the specificity of an art work's form and the context of its reception. Few cultural workers of whatever stripe can walk the tightrope between the Scylla of reductionism and the Charybdis of aestheticism – yet demystificatory (or prophetic) critics must.

The political challenge

Adequate rejoinders to intellectual and existential challenges equip the practitioners of the new cultural politics of difference to meet the political ones. This challenge principally consists of forging solid and reliable alliances of people of color and white progressives guided by a moral and political vision of greater democracy and individual freedom in communities, states and transnational enterprises, e.g. corporations, information and communications conglomerates.

Jesse Jackson's Rainbow Coalition is a gallant yet flawed effort in this regard – gallant due to the tremendous energy, vision and courage of its leader and followers, yet flawed because of its failure to take seriously critical and democratic sensibilities within its own operations. In fact, Jackson's attempt to gain power at the national level is a symptom of the weakness of U.S. progressive politics, and a sign that the capacity to generate extra-parliamentary social motion or movements has waned. Yet given the present organizational weakness and intellectual timidity of left politics in the USA, the major option is that of multi-racial grass-roots citizens' participation in credible projects in which people see that their efforts can make a difference. The salutary revolutionary developments in Eastern Europe are encouraging and inspiring in this regard. Ordinary people organized can change societies.

The most significant theme of the new cultural politics of difference is the agency, capacity and ability of human beings who have been culturally degraded, politically oppressed and economically exploited by bourgeois liberal and communist illiberal status quos. This theme neither romanticizes nor idealizes marginalized peoples. Rather it accentuates their humanity and tries to attenuate the institutional constraints on their life-chances for surviving and thriving. In this way, the new cultural politics of difference shuns narrow particularisms, parochialisms and separatisms, just as it rejects false universalisms and homogeneous totalisms. Instead, the new cultural politics of difference affirms the perennial quest for the precious ideals of individuality and democracy by digging deep in the depths of human particularities and social specificities in order to construct new kinds of connections, affinities and communities across empire, nation, region, race, gender, age and sexual orientation.

The major impediments of the radical libertarian and democratic projects of the new cultural politics are threefold: the pervasive processes of objectification, rationalization and commodification throughout the world. The first process – best highlighted in Georg Simmel's *The Philosophy of Money* (1900) – consists of transforming human beings into manipulable objects. It promotes the notion that people's actions have no impact on the world, that we are but spectators not participants in making and remaking ourselves and the larger society. The second process – initially examined in the seminal works of Max Weber – expands bureaucratic hierarchies that impose impersonal rules and regulations in order to increase efficiency, be they defined in terms of better service or better surveillance. This process leads not only to disenchantment with past mythologies but also to deadening, flat, banal ways of life. The third and most important process – best examined in the works of Karl Marx, Georg Lukács and Walter Benjamin – augments market forces in the form of oligopolies and monopolies that centralize resources and powers and promote cultures of consumption that view people as mere spectatorial consumers and passive citizens.

These processes cannot be eliminated, but their pernicious effects can be substantially alleviated. The audacious attempt to lessen their impact – to preserve people's agency, increase the scope of their freedom and expand the operations of democracy – is the fundamental aim of the new cultural politics of difference. This is why the crucial questions become: What is the moral content of one's cultural identity? And what are the political consequences of this moral content and cultural identity?

In the recent past, the dominant cultural identities have been circumscribed by immoral patriarchal, imperial, jingoistic and xenophobic constraints. The political consequences have been principally a public sphere regulated by and for well-to-do White males in the name of freedom and democracy. The new cultural criticism exposes and explodes the exclusions, blindnesses and silences of this past, calling from it radical libertarian and democratic projects that will create a better present and future. The new cultural politics of difference is neither an ahistorical Jacobin program that discards tradition and ushers in new self-righteous authoritarianisms nor a guilt-ridden leveling anti-imperialist liberalism that celebrates token pluralism for smooth inclusion. Rather, it acknowledges the uphill struggle of fundamentally transforming highly objectified, rationalized and commodified societies and cultures in the name of individuality and democracy. This means locating the structural causes of unnecessary forms of social misery (without reducing all such human suffering to historical causes), depicting the plight and predicaments of demoralized and depoliticized citizens caught in market-driven cycles of therapeutic release – drugs, alcoholism, consumerism – and projecting alternative visions, analyses and actions that proceed from particularities and arrive at moral and political connectedness. This connectedness does not signal a homogeneous unity or monolithic totality but rather a contingent, fragile coalition building in an effort to pursue common radical libertarian and democratic goals that overlap.

In a world in which most of the resources, wealth and power are centered in huge corporations and supportive political elites, the new cultural politics of difference may appear to be solely visionary, utopian and fanciful. The recent cutbacks of social service programs, business takebacks at the negotiation tables of workers and management, speedups at the workplace and buildups of military budgets reinforce this perception. And surely the growing disintegration and decomposition of civil society – of shattered families, neighborhoods and schools – adds to this perception. Can a civilization that evolves more and more around market activity, more and more around the buying and selling of commodities, expand the scope of freedom and democracy? Can we simply bear witness to its slow decay and doom – a painful denouncement prefigured already in many poor black and brown communities and rapidly embracing all of us? These haunting questions remain unanswered yet the challenge they pose must not remain unmet. The new cultural politics of difference tries to confront these enormous and urgent challenges. It will require all the imagination, intelligence, courage, sacrifice, care and laughter we can muster.

The time has come for critics and artists of the new cultural politics of difference to cast their nets widely, flex their muscles broadly and thereby refuse to limit their visions, analyses and praxis to their particular terrains. The aim is to dare to recast, redefine and revise, the very notions of "modernity," "mainstream," "margins," "difference," "otherness." We have now reached a new stage in the perennial struggle for freedom and

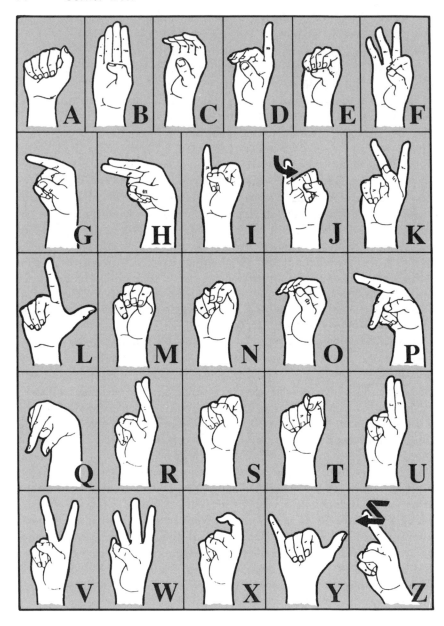

dignity. And while much of the First World intelligentsia adopts retrospective and conservative outlooks that defend the crisis-ridden present, we promote a prospective and prophetic vision with a sense of possibility and potential, especially for those who bear the social costs of the present. We look to the past for strength, not solace; we look at the present and see people perishing, not profits mounting; we look toward the future and vow to make if different and better.

To put it boldly, the new kind of critic and artist associated with the new cultural politics of difference consists of an energetic breed of New World *bricoleurs* with improvisational and flexible sensibilities that sidestep mere opportunism and mindless eclecticism; persons from all countries, cultures, genders, sexual orientations, ages and regions with protean identities who avoid ethnic chauvinism and faceless universalism; intellectual and political freedom-fighters with partisan passion, international perspectives, and, thank God, a sense of humor that combats the ever-present absurdity that forever threatens our democratic and libertarian projects and dampens the fire that fuels our will to struggle. Yet we will struggle and stay, as those brothers and sisters on the block say, "out there" – with intellectual rigor, existential dignity, moral vision, political courage and soulful style.

5

A manifesto for cyborgs: Science, technology, and socialist feminism in the 1980s
Donna Haraway

An ironic dream of a common language for women in the integrated circuit

This chapter is an effort to build an ironic political myth faithful to feminism, socialism, and materialism. Perhaps more faithful as blasphemy is faithful, than as reverent worship and identification. Blasphemy has always seemed to require taking things very seriously. I know no better stance to adopt from within the secular-religious, evangelical traditions of U.S. politics, including the politics of socialist feminism. Blasphemy protects one from the Moral Majority within, while still insisting on the need for community. Blasphemy is not apostasy. Irony is about contradictions that do not resolve into larger wholes, even dialectically, about the tension of holding incompatible things together because both or all are necessary and true. Irony is about humor and serious play. It is also a rhetorical strategy and a political method, one I would like to see more

This article was first published in *Socialist Review*, No. 80, 1985. The essay originated as a response to a call for political thinking about the 1980s from socialist-feminist points of view, in hopes of deepening our political and cultural debates in order to renew commitments to fundamental social change in the face of the Reagan years. The cyborg manifesto tried to find a feminist place for connected thinking and acting in profoundly contradictory worlds. Since its publication, this bit of cyborgian writing has had a surprising half life. It has proved impossible to rewrite the cyborg. Cyborg's daughter will have to find its own matrix in another essay, starting from the proposition that the immune system is the biotechnical body's chief system of differences in late capitalism, where feminists might find provocative extraterrestrial maps of the networks of embodied power marked by race, sex, and class. This chapter is substantially the same as the 1985 version, with minor revisions and correction of notes. Donna Haraway, "A Manifesto for Cyborgs," *Socialist Review*, 80. Copyright 1985 by Duke University Press. Reprinted by permission.

honored within socialist feminism. At the center of my ironic faith, my blasphemy, is the image of the cyborg.

A cyborg is a cybernetic organism, a hybrid of machine and organism, a creature of social reality as well as a creature of fiction. Social reality is lived social relations, our most important political construction, a world-changing fiction. The international women's movements have constructed "women's experience," as well as uncovered or discovered this crucial collective object. This experience is a fiction and fact of the most crucial, political kind. Liberation rests on the construction of the consciousness, the imaginative apprehension, of oppression, and so of possibility. The cyborg is a matter of fiction and lived experience that changes what counts as women's experience in the late twentieth century. This is a struggle over life and death, but the boundary between science fiction and social reality is an optical illusion.

Contemporary science fiction is full of cyborgs – creatures simultaneously animal and machine, who populate worlds ambiguously natural and crafted. Modern medicine is also full of cyborgs, of couplings between organism and machine, each conceived as coded devices, in an intimacy and with a power that was not generated in the history of sexuality. Cyborg "sex" restores some of the lovely replicative baroque of ferns and invertebrates (such nice organic prophylactics against heterosexism). Cyborg replication is uncoupled from organic reproduction. Modern production seems like a dream of cyborg colonization of work, a dream that makes the nightmare of Taylorism seem idyllic. Modern war is a cyborg orgy, coded by C^3I, command-control-communication-intelligence, an $84 billion item in 1984's U.S. defense budget. I am making an argument for the cyborg as a fiction mapping our social and bodily reality and as an imaginative resource suggesting some very fruitful couplings. Foucault's biopolitics is a flaccid premonition of cyborg politics, a very open field.

By the late twentieth century, our time, a mythic time, we are all chimeras, theorized and fabricated hybrids of machine and organism; in short, we are cyborgs. The cyborg is our ontology; it gives us our politics. The cyborg is a condensed image of both imagination and material reality, the two joined centers structuring any possibility of historical transformation. In the traditions of Western science and politics – the tradition of racist, male-dominant capitalism; the tradition of progress; the tradition of the appropriation of nature as resource for the productions of culture; the tradition of reproduction of the self from the reflections of the other – the relation between organism and machine has been a border war. The stakes in the border war have been the territories of production, reproduction, and imagination. This chapter is an argument for pleasure in the confusion of boundaries and for responsibility in their construction.

It is also an effort to contribute to socialist-feminist culture and theory in a postmodernist, nonnaturalist mode and in the utopian tradition of imagining a world without gender, which is perhaps a world without genesis, but maybe also a world without end. The cyborg incarnation is outside salvation history. Nor does it mark time on an Oedipal calendar, attempting to heal the terrible cleavages of gender in oral symbiotic utopia or post-Oedipal apocalypse. As Zoe Sofoulis argues in her unpublished manuscript on Lacan, Klein, and nuclear culture, *Lacklein,* the most terrible and perhaps the most promising monsters in cyborg worlds are embodied in non-Oedipal narratives with a different logic of repression, which we need to understand for our survival.

The cyborg is a creature in a postgender world; it has no truck with bisexuality, pre-Oedipal symbiosis, unalienated labor, or other seductions to organic wholeness through a final appropriation of all the powers of the parts into a higher unity. In a sense, the cyborg has no origin story in the Western sense; a "final" irony since the cyborg is also the awful apocalyptic telos of the West's escalating dominations of abstract individuation, an ultimate self untied at last from all dependency, a man in space. An origin story in the Western humanist sense depends on the myth of original unity, fullness, bliss, and terror, represented by the phallic mother from whom all humans must separate, the task of individual development and of history, the twin potent myths inscribed most powerfully for us in psychoanalysis and Marxism. Hilary Klein has argued that both Marxism and psychoanalysis, in their concepts of labor and of individuation and gender formation, depend on the plot of original unity out of which difference must be produced and enlisted in a drama of escalating domination of woman/nature. The cyborg skips the step of original unity, of identification with nature in the Western sense. This is its illegitimate promise that might lead to subversion of its teleology as Star Wars.

The cyborg is resolutely committed to partiality, irony, intimacy, and perversity. It is oppositional, utopian, and completely without innocence. No longer structured by the polarity of public and private, the cyborg defines a technological polis based partly on a revolution of social relations in the oikos, the household. Nature and culture are reworked; the one can no longer be the resource for appropriation or incorporation by the other. The relationships for forming wholes from parts, including those of polarity and hierarchical domination, are at issue in the cyborg world. Unlike the hopes of Frankenstein's monster, the cyborg does not expect its father to save it through a restoration of the garden, that is, through the fabrication of a heterosexual mate, through its completion in a finished whole, a city and cosmos. The cyborg does not dream of community on the model of the organic family, this time without the Oedipal project. The cyborg would not recognize the Garden of Eden; it is not made of mud and cannot dream of returning to dust. Perhaps that is why I want to see if cyborgs can subvert the apocalypse of returning to nuclear dust in the manic compulsion to name the Enemy. Cyborgs are not reverent; they do not remember the cosmos. They are wary of holism, but needy for connection – they seem to have a natural feel for united front politics, but without the vanguard party. The main trouble with cyborgs, of course, is that they are the illegitimate offspring of militarism and patriarchal capitalism, not to mention state socialism. But illegitimate offspring are often exceedingly unfaithful to their origins. Their fathers, after all, are inessential.

I will return to the science fiction of cyborgs at the end of the chapter, but now I want to signal three crucial boundary breakdowns that make the following political fictional (political scientific) analysis possible. By the late twentieth century in United States, scientific culture, the boundary between human and animal, is thoroughly breached. The last beachheads of uniqueness have been polluted, if not turned into amusement parks – language, tool use, social behavior, mental events. Nothing really convincingly settles the separation of human and animal. Many people no longer feel the need of such a separation; indeed, many branches of feminist culture affirm the pleasure of connection with human and other living creatures. Movements for animal rights are not irrational denials of human uniqueness; they are clear-sighted recognition of connection across the discredited breach of nature and culture. Biology and evolutionary theory over the last two centuries have simultaneously produced modern organisms as objects of knowledge and reduced the line between humans and animals to a faint trace re-etched in ideological struggle or professional disputes between life and social sciences. Within this framework, teaching modern Christian creationism should be fought as a form of child abuse.

Biological-determinist ideology is only one position opened up in scientific culture for arguing the meanings of human animality. There is much room for radical political people to contest for the meanings of the breached boundary.[1] The cyborg appears in myth precisely where the

---

1. Useful references to left and/or feminist radical science movements and theory and to biological/biotechnological issues include Ruth Bleier, *Science and Gender: A Critique of Biology and Its Themes on Women* (New York: Pergamon, 1984); Ruth Bleier, ed., *Feminist Approaches to Science* (New York: Pergamon, 1986); Sandra Harding, *The Science Question in Feminism* (Ithaca, NY: Cornell University Press, 1986); Anne Fausto-Sterling, *Myths of Gender* (New York: Basic Books, 1985): Stephen J. Gould, *Mismeasure of Man* (New York: Norton, 1981); Ruth Hubbard, Mary Sue Henifin, Barbara Fried, eds., *Biological Woman, the Convenient Myth* (Cambridge, MA: Schenkman, 1982); Evelyn Fox Keller, *Reflections on Gender and Science*

boundary between human and animal is transgressed. Far from signaling a walling off of people from other living things, cyborgs signal disturbingly and pleasurably tight coupling. Bestiality has a new status in this cycle of marriage exchange.

The second leaky distinction is between animal-human (organism) and machine. Pre-cybernetic machines could be haunted; there was always the specter of the ghost in the machine. This dualism structured the dialogue between materialism and idealism that was settled by a dialectical progeny called spirit or history, according to taste. But basically machines were not self-moving, self-designing, autonomous. They could not achieve man's dream, only mock it. They were not man, an author of himself, but only a caricature of that masculinist reproductive dream. To think they were otherwise was paranoid. Now we are not so sure. Late twentieth-century machines have made thoroughly ambiguous the difference between natural and artificial, mind and body, self-developing and externally designed, and many other distinctions that used to apply to organisms and machines. Our machines are disturbingly lively, and we ourselves frighteningly inert.

Technological determinism is only one ideological space opened up by the reconceptions of machine and organism as coded texts through which we engage in the play of writing and reading the world.[2] "Textualization"

(New Haven, CT: Yale University Press, 1985); R. C. Lewontin, Steve Rose, and Leon Kamin, *Not in Our Genes* (New York: Pantheon, 1984); *Radical Science Journal* (from 1987, *Science as Culture*), 26 Freegrove Road, London N7 9RQ; *Science for the People*, 897 Main St., Cambridge, MA 02139.

2. Starting points for left and/or feminist approaches to technology and politics include Ruth Schwartz Cowan, *More Work for Mother: The Ironies of Household Technology from the Open Hearth to the Microwave* (New York: Basic Books, 1983); Joan Rothschild, *Machina ex Dea: Feminist Perspectives on Technology* (New York: Pergamon, 1983); Sharon Traweek, *Beantimes and Lifetimes: The World of High Energy Physics* (Cambridge, MA: Harvard University Press, 1988); R. M. Young and Les Levidov, eds., *Science, Technology, and the Labour Process,* Vols. 1–3 (London: CSE Books); Joseph Weizenbaum, *Computer Power and Human Reason* (San Francisco: Freeman, 1976); Langdon Winner, *Autonomous Technology: Technics Out of Control as a Theme in Political Thought* (Cambridge, MA: MIT Press, 1977); Langdon Winner, *The Whale and the Reactor* (Chicago: Chicago University Press, 1986); Jan Zimmerman, ed., *The Technological Woman: Interfacing with Tomorrow* (New York: Praeger, 1983); Tom Athanasiou, "High-tech Politics. The Case of Artificial Intelligence," *Socialist Review,* No. 92, 1987, pp. 7–35; Carol Cohn, "Nuclear Language and How We Learned to Pat the Bomb," *Bulletin of Atomic Scientists,* June 1987, pp. 17–24; Terry Winograd and Fernando Flores, *Understanding Computers and Cognition: A New Foundation for Design* (New Jersey: Ablex, 1986); Paul Edwards, "Border

of everything in poststructuralist, postmodernist theory has been damned by Marxists and socialist feminists for its utopian disregard for lived relations of domination that ground the "play" of arbitrary reading.[3]* It is certainly true that postmodernist strategies, like my cyborg myth, subvert

Wars: The Politics of Artificial Intelligence," *Radical America,* Vol. 19, No. 6, 1985, pp. 39–52; *Global Electronics Newsletter,* 867 West Dana St., #204, Mountain View, CA 94041; *Processed World,* 55 Sutter St., San Francisco, CA 94104; *ISIS,* Women's International Information and Communication Service, P.O. Box 50 (Cornavin), 1211 Geneva 2, Switzerland, and Via Santa Maria dell'Anima 30, 00186 Rome, Italy. Fundamental approaches to modern social studies of science that do not continue the liberal mystification that it all started with Thomas Kuhn, include: Karin Knorr-Cetina, *The Manufacture of Knowledge* (Oxford: Pergamon, 1981); K. D. Knorr-Cetina and Michael Mulkay, eds., *Science Observed: Perspectives on the Social Study of Science* (Beverly Hills, CA: Sage, 1983); Bruno Latour and Steve Woolgar, *Laboratory Life: The Social Construction of Scientific Facts* (Beverly Hills, CA: Sage, 1979); Robert M. Young, "Interpreting the Production of Science," *New Scientist,* Vol. 29, March 1979, pp. 1026–1028. More is claimed than is known about room for contesting productions of science in the mythic/material space of "the laboratory"; the 1984 Directory of the Network for the Ethnographic Study of Science, Technology, and Organizations lists a wide range of people and projects crucial to better radical analysis; available from NESSTO, P.O. Box 11442, Stanford, CA 94305.

3. Fredric Jameson, "Post Modernism, or the Cultural Logic of Late Capitalism," *New Left Review,* July/August 1984, pp. 53–94. See Marjorie Perloff, "'Dirty' Language and Scramble Systems," *Sulfur* Vol 2, 1984, pp. 178–183; Kathleen Fraser, *Something (Even Human Voices) in the Foreground, a Lake* (Berkeley, CA: Kelsey St. Press, 1984). For feminist modernist/postmodernist cyborg writing, see *How(ever),* 871 Corbett Ave., San Francisco, CA 94131.

* A provocative, comprehensive argument about the politics and theories of postmodernism is made by Fredric Jameson, who argues that postmodernism is not an option, a style among others, but a cultural dominant requiring radical reinvention of left politics from within; there is no longer any place from without that gives meaning to the comforting fiction of critical distance. Jameson also makes clear why one cannot be for or against postmodernism, an essentially moralist move. My position is that feminists (and others) need continuous cultural reinvention, postmodernist critique, and historical materialism; only a cyborg would have a chance. The old dominations of white capitalist patriarchy seem nostagically innocent now: They normalized heterogeneity, e.g., into man and woman, white and black. "Advanced capitalism" and postmodernism release heterogeneity without a norm, and we are flattened, without subjectivity, which requires depth, even unfriendly and drowning depths. It is time to write *The Death of the Clinic.* The clinic's methods required bodies and works; we have texts and surfaces. Our dominations don't work by medicalization and normalization anymore; they work by networking, communications redesign, stress management.

myriad organic wholes (e.g., the poem, the primitive culture, the biological organism). In short, the certainty of what counts as nature – a source of insight and a promise of innocence – is undermined, probably fatally. The transcendent authorization of interpretation is lost and with it the ontology grounding Western epistemology. But the alternative is not cynicism or faithlessness, that is, some version of abstract existence, like the accounts of technological determinism destroying "man" by the "machine" or "meaningful political action" by the "text." Who cyborgs will be is a radical question; the answers are a matter of survival. Both chimpanzees and artifacts have politics, so why shouldn't we?[4]

The third distinction is a subset of the second: The boundary between physical and nonphysical is very imprecise for us. Pop physics books on the consequences of quantum theory and the indeterminacy principle are a kind of popular scientific equivalent to the Harlequin romances as a marker of radical change in American white heterosexuality: They get it wrong, but they are on the right subject. Modern machines are quintessentially microelectronic devices: They are everywhere and they are invisible. Modern machinery is an irreverent upstart god, mocking the Father's ubiquity and spirituality. The silicon chip is a surface for writing; it is etched in molecular scales disturbed only by atomic noise, the ultimate interference for nuclear scores. Writing, power, and technology are old partners in Western stories of the origin of civilization, but miniaturization has changed our experience of mechanism. Miniaturization has turned out to be about power; small is not so much beautiful as preeminently dangerous, as in Cruise missiles. Contrast the TV sets of the 1950s or the news cameras of the 1970s with the TV wristbands or hand-sized video cameras now advertised. Our best machines are made of sunshine; they are all light and clean because they are nothing but signals, electromagnetic waves, a section of a spectrum. These machines are eminently

Normalization gives way to automation, utter redundancy. Michel Foucault's *Birth of the Clinic, History and Sexuality,* and *Discipline and Punish* name of form of power at its moment of implosion. The discourse of biopolitics gives way to technobabble, the language of the spliced substantive; no noun is left whole by the multinationals. These are their names, listed from one issue of *Science:* Tech-Knowledge, Genentech, Allergen, Hybritech, Compupro, Genen-cor, Syntex, Allelix, Agrigenetics Corp., Syntro, Codon, Repligen; Micro-Angelo from Scion Corp., Percom Data, Inter Systems, Cyborg Corp., Statcom Corp., Intertec. If we are imprisoned by language, then escape from that prison-house requires language poets, a kind of cultural restriction enzyme to cut the code; cyborg heteroglossia is one form of radical culture politics.

4. Frans de Waal, *Chimpanzee Politics: Power and Sex among the Apes* (New York: Harper & Row, 1982); Langdon Winner, "Do artifacts have politics?" *Daedalus* (Winter 1980): 121–136.

portable, mobile – a matter of immense human pain in Detroit and Singapore. People are nowhere near so fluid, being both material and opaque. Cyborgs are ether, quintessence.

The ubiquity and invisibility of cyborgs is precisely why these Sunshine Belt machines are so deadly. They are as hard to see politically as materially. They are about consciousness – or its simulation.⁵ They are floating signifiers moving in pickup trucks across Europe, blocked more effectively by the witch-weavings of the displaced and so unnatural Greenham women, who read the cyborg webs of power very well, than by the militant labor of older masculinist politics, whose natural constituency needs defense jobs. Ultimately, the "hardest" science is about the realm of greatest boundary confusion, the realm of pure number, pure spirit, C³I, cryptography, and the preservation of potent secrets. The new machines are so clean and light. Their engineers are sun worshipers mediating a new scientific revolution associated with the night dream of post industrial society. The diseases evoked by these clean machines are "no more" than the minuscule coding changes of an antigen in the immune system, "no more" than the experience of stress. The "nimble" fingers of "Oriental" women, the old fascination of little Anglo-Saxon Victorian girls with dollhouses, and women's enforced attention to the small take on quite new dimensions in this world. There might be a cyborg Alice taking account of these new dimensions. Ironically, it might be the unnatural cyborg women making chips in Asia and spiral dancing in Santa Rita jail after an antinuclear action whose constructed unities will guide effective oppositional strategies.

So my cyborg myth is about transgressed boundaries, potent fusions, and dangerous possibilities which progressive people might explore as one part of needed political work. One of my premises is that most American socialists and feminists see deepened dualisms of mind and body, animal and machine, idealism and materialism in the social practices, symbolic formulations, and physical artifacts associated with high technology and scientific culture. From *One-Dimensional Man* to *The Death of Nature*,⁶ the analytic resources developed by progressives have insisted on the necessary domination of technics and recalled us to an imagined organic body to integrate our resistance. Another of my premises is that

5. Jean Baudrillard, *Simulations,* trans. P. Foss, P. Patton, P. Beitchman (New York: Semiotext(e), 1983). Jameson ("Postmodernism," p. 66) points out that Plato's definition of the simulacrum is the copy for which there is no original, i.e., the world of advanced capitalism, of pure exchange. See *Discourse 9*, Spring/Summer 1987, for a special issue on technology (Cybernetics, Ecology, and the Postmodern Imagination).

6. Herbert Marcuse, *One-Dimensional Man* (Boston: Beacon Press, 1964); Carolyn Merchant, *Death of Nature* (San Francisco: Harper & Row, 1980).

the need for unity of people trying to resist worldwide intensification of domination has never been more acute. But a slightly perverse shift of perspective might better enable us to contest for meanings, as well as for other forms of power and pleasure in technologically mediated societies.

From one perspective, a cyborg world is about the final imposition of a grid of control on the planet, about the final abstraction embodied in a Star Wars apocalypse waged in the name of defense, about the final appropriation of women's bodies in a masculinist orgy of war.[7] From another perspective, a cyborg world might be about lived social and bodily realities in which people are not afraid of their joint kinship with animals and machines, not afraid of permanently partial identities and contradictory standpoints. The political struggle is to see from both perspectives at once because each reveals both dominations and possibilities unimaginable from the other vantage point. Single vision produces worse illusions than double vision or many-headed monsters. Cyborg unities are monstrous and illegitimate; in our present political circumstances, we could hardly hope for more potent myths for resistance and recoupling. I like to imagine the Livermore Action Group, LAG, as a kind of cyborg society, dedicated to realistically converting the laboratories that most fiercely embody and spew out the tools of technological apocalypse, and committed to building a political form that actually manages to hold together witches, engineers, elders, perverts, Christians, mothers, and Leninists long enough to disarm the state. Fission Impossible is the name of the affinity group in my town. (Affinity: related not by blood but by choice, the appeal of one chemical nuclear group for another, avidity.)[8]

7. Zoe Sofia, "Exterminating Fetuses," *Diacritics,* Vol. 14, No. 2, Summer 1984, pp. 47–59, and "Jupiter Space" (Pomona, CA: American Studies Association, 1984).

8. For ethnographic accounts and political evaluations, see Barbara Epstein, "The Politics of Prefigurative Community: The Non-Violent Direction Action Movement," *The Year Left,* forthcoming, and Noel Sturgeon, qualifying essay on feminism, anarchism, and nonviolent direct-action politics, University of California, Santa Cruz, 1986. Without explicit irony, adopting the spaceship earth/whole earth logo of the planet photographed from space, set off by the slogan "Love Your Mother," the May 1987 Mothers and Others Day action at the nuclear weapons testing facility in Nevada nonetheless took account of the tragic contradictions of views of the earth. Demonstrators applied for official permits to be on the land from officers of the Western Shoshone tribe, whose territory was invaded by the U.S. government when it built the nuclear weapons test ground in the 1950s. Arrested for trespassing, the demonstrators argued that the police and weapons facility personnel, without authorization from the proper officials, were the trespassers. One affinity group at the women's action called themselves the Surrogate Others, and in solidarity with the creatures forced to tunnel in the same ground with

Fractured identities

It has become difficult to name one's feminism by a single adjective – or even to insist in every circumstance upon the noun. Consciousness of exclusion through naming is acute. Identities seem contradictory, partial, and strategic. With the hard-won recognition of their social and historical constitution, gender, race, and class cannot provide the basis for belief in "essential" unity. There is nothing about being "female" that naturally binds women. There is not even such a state as "being" female, itself a highly complex category constructed in contested sexual scientific discourses and other social practices. Gender, race, or class consciousness is an achievement forced on us by the terrible historical experience of the contradictory social realities of patriarchy, colonialism, racism and capitalism. Who counts as "us" in my own rhetoric? Which identities are available to ground such a potent political myth called "us," and what could motivate enlistment in this collectivity? Painful fragmentation among feminists (not to mention among women) along every possible fault line has made the concept of woman elusive, an excuse for the matrix of women's dominations of each other. For me – and for many who share a similar historical location in white, professional, middle-class, female, radical, North American, mid-adult bodies – the sources of a crisis in political identity are legion. The recent history for much of the U.S. Left and the U.S. feminism has been a response to this kind of crisis by endless splitting and searches for a new essential unity. But there has also been a growing recognition of another response through coalition – affinity, not identity.[9]

Chela Sandoval, from a consideration of specific historical moments in the formation of the new political voice called women of color, has theorized a hopeful model of political identity called "oppositional consciousness," born of the skills for reading webs of power by those refused

the bomb, they enacted a cyborgian emergence from the constructed body of a large, nonheterosexual desert worm.
9. Powerful developments of coalition politics emerge from "third world" speakers, speaking from nowhere, the displaced center of the universe, earth: "We live on the third planet from the sun" – *Sun Poem* by Jamaican writer Edward Kamau Braithwaite, review by Nathaniel Mackey, *Sulfur*, Vol. 2, 1984, pp. 200–205. *Home Girls*, ed. Barbara Smith (New York: Kitchen Table Women of Color Press, 1983), ironically subverts naturalized identities precisely while constructing a place from which to speak called home. See Bernice Reagan, "Coalition Politics, Turning the Century," pp. 356–368. Trinh T. Minh-ha, ed., "She, the Inappropriate/d Other," *Discourse*, Vol. 8, Fall/Winter 1986–1987.

stable membership in the social categories of race, sex, or class.[10] "Women of color," a name contested at its origins by those whom it would incorporate, as well as a historical consciousness marking systematic breakdown of all the signs of Man in Western traditions, constructs a king of postmodernist identity out of otherness, difference, and specificity. This postmodernist identity is fully political, whatever might be said about other possible postmodernisms. Sandoval's oppositional consciousness is about contradictory locations and heterochronic calendars, not about relativisms and pluralisms.

Sandoval emphasizes the lack of any essential criterion for identifying who is a woman of color. She notes that the definition of the group has been by conscious appropriation of negation. For example, a chicana or a U.S. black woman has not been able to speak as a woman or as a black person or as a chicano. Thus, she was at the bottom of a cascade of negative identities, left out of even the "privileged" oppressed authorial categories called "women and blacks," who claimed to make the important revolutions. The category "woman" negated all nonwhite women; "black" negated all nonblack people, as well as all black women. But there was also no "she," no singularity, but a sea of differences among U.S. women who have affirmed their historical identity as U.S. women of color. This identity marks out a self-consciously constructed space that cannot affirm the capacity to act on the basis of natural identification, but only on the basis of conscious coalition, of affinity, of political kinship.[11] Unlike the "woman" of some streams of the white women's movement in the United States, there is no naturalization of the matrix, or at least this is what Sandoval argues is uniquely available through the power of oppositional consciousness.

Sandoval's argument has to be seen as one potent formulation for feminists out of the worldwide development of anti-colonialist discourse, that is, discourse dissolving the West and its highest product –

---

10. Chela Sandoval, "Dis-Illusion and the Poetry of the Future: The Making of Oppositional Consciousness," Ph.D. qualifying essay, University of California, Santa Cruz, 1984.
11. Bell Hooks, *Ain't I a Woman?* (Boston: South End Press, 1981); Bell Hooks, *Feminist Theory: From Margin to Center* (Boston: South End Press, 1984); Gloria Hull, Patricia Bell Scott, and Barbara Smith, eds., *All the Women Are White, All the Men Are Black, But Some of Us Are Brave: Black Women's Studies* (Old Westbury, NY: Feminist Press, 1982). Toni Cade Bambara, *The Salt Eaters* (New York: Vintage/Random House, 1981), writes an extraordinary postmodernist novel, in which the women of color theater group, The Seven Sisters, explores a form of unity. Elliott Butler-Evans, *Race, Gender, and Desire: Narrative Strategies and the Production of Ideology in the Fiction of Toni Cade Bambara, Toni Morrison and Alice Walker*, Ph.D. Dissertation, University of California, Santa Cruz, 1987.

the one who is not animal, barbarian, or woman: that is, man, the author of a cosmos called history. As Orientalism is deconstructed politically and semiotically, the identities of the Occident destabilize, including those of its feminists.[12] Sandoval argues that "women of color" have a chance to build an effective unity that does not replicate the imperializing, totalizing revolutionary subjects of previous Marxisms and feminisms which had not faced the consequences of the disorderly polyphony emerging from decolonization.

Katie King has emphasized the limits of identification and the political/poetic mechanics of identification built into reading "the poem," that generative core of cultural feminism. King criticizes the persistent tendency among contemporary feminists from different "moments" or "conversations" in feminist practice to taxonomize the women's movement to make one's own political tendencies appear to be the telos of the whole. These taxonomies tend to remake feminist history to appear to be an ideological struggle among coherent types persisting over time, especially those typical units called radical, liberal, and socialist feminism. Literally, all other feminisms are either incorporated or marginalized, usually by building an explicit ontology and epistemology.[13] Taxonomies of feminism produce epistemologies to police deviation from official women's experience. Of course, "women's culture," like women of color, is consciously created by mechanisms inducing affinity. The rituals of poetry, music, and certain forms of academic practice have been preeminent. The politics of race and culture in the U.S. women's movements are intimately interwoven. The common achievement of King and Sandoval is learning how to craft a poetic/political unity without relying on a logic of appropriation, incorporation, and taxonomic identification.

12. On Orientalism in feminist works and elsewhere, see Lisa Lowe, "Orientation: Representations of Cultural and Sexual 'Others,'" Ph.D. thesis, University of California, Santa Cruz; Edward Said, *Orientalism* (New York: Pantheon, 1978). Chandra Talpade Mohanty, "Under Western Eyes: Feminist Scholarship and Colonial Discourse," *Boundary,* Vol. 2, No. 12, and Vol 3, No. 13, 1984, pp. 333–357; "Many Voices, One Chant: Black Feminist Perspectives," *Feminist Review,* Vol. 17, Autumn 1984.

13. Katie King has developed a theoretically sensitive treatment of the workings of feminist taxonomies as genealogies of power in feminist ideology and polemic: Katie King, "Canons without Innocence," Ph.D. thesis, University of California, Santa Cruz, 1987, and "The Situation of Lesbianism as Feminism's Magical Sign: Contests for Meaning in the U.S. Women's Movement, 1968–72," *Communication,* Vol. 9, No. 1, 1985, pp. 65–91. King examines an intelligent, problematic example of taxonomizing feminisms to make a little machine producing the desired final position; Alison Jaggar, *Feminist Politics and Human Nature* (Totowa, NJ: Rowman & Allanheld, 1983). My caricature here of socialist and radical feminism is also an example.

The theoretical and practical struggle against unity-through-domination or unity-through-incorporation ironically not only undermines the justifications for patriarchy, colonialism, humanism, positivism, essentialism, scientism, and other unlamented -isms, but all claims for an organic or natural standpoint. I think that radical and socialist/Marxist feminisms have also undermined their/our own epistemological strategies and that this is a crucially valuable step in imagining possible unities. It remains to be seen whether all epistemologies as Western political people have known them fail us in the task to build effective affinities.

It is important to note that the effort to construct revolutionary standpoints, epistemologies as achievements of people committed to changing the world, has been part of the process showing the limits of identification. The acid tools of postmodernist theory and the constructive tools of ontological discourse about revolutionary subjects might be seen as ironic allies in dissolving Western selves in the interests of survival. We are excruciatingly conscious of what it means to have a historically constituted body. But with the loss of innocence in our origin, there is no expulsion from the Garden either. Our politics lose the indulgence of guilt with the *naïveté* of innocence. But what would another political myth for socialist feminism look like? What kind of politics could embrace partial, contradictory, permanently unclosed constructions of personal and collective selves and still be faithful, effective – and, ironically, socialist feminist?

I do not know of any other time in history when there was greater need for political unity to confront effectively the dominations of race, gender, sexuality, and class. I also do not know of any other time when the kind of unity we might help build could have been possible. None of "us" have any longer the symbolic or material capability of dictating the shape of reality to any of "them." Or at least "we" cannot claim innocence from practicing such dominations. White women, including Euroamerican socialist feminists, discovered (i.e., were forced kicking and screaming to notice) the noninnocence of the category "woman." That consciousness changes the configuration of all previous categories; it denatures them as heat denatures a fragile protein. Cyborg feminists have to argue that "we" do not want any more natural matrix of unity and that no construction is whole. Innocence, and the corollary insistence on victimhood as the only ground for insight, has done enough damage. But the constructed revolutionary subject must give late twentieth-century people pause as well. In the fraying of identities and in the reflexive strategies for constructing them, the possibility opens up for weaving something other than a shroud for the day after the apocalypse that so prophetically ends salvation history.

But Marxist/socialist feminisms and radical feminisms have simultaneously naturalized and denatured the category "woman" and consciousness of the social lives of "women." Perhaps a schematic caricature can highlight both kinds of moves. Marxian socialism is rooted in an analysis of wage labor which reveals class structure. The consequence of the wage relationship is systematic alienation, as the worker is dissociated from his [sic] product. Abstraction and illusion rule in knowledge; domination rules in practice. Labor is the preeminently privileged category enabling the Marxist to overcome illusion and find that point of view which is necessary for changing the world. Labor is the humanizing activity that makes man; labor is an ontological category permitting the knowledge of a subject, and so the knowledge of subjugation and alienation.

In faithful filiation, socialist feminism advanced by allying itself with the basic analytic strategies of this Marxism. The main achievement of both Marxist feminists and socialist feminists was to expand the category of labor to accommodate what (some) women did, even when the wage relation was subordinated to a more comprehensive view of labor under capitalist patriarchy. In particular, women's labor in the household and women's activity as mothers generally, that is, reproduction in the socialist feminist sense, entered theory on the authority of analogy to the Marxian concept of labor. The unity of women here rests on an epistemology based on the ontological structure of "labor." Marxist/socialist feminism does not "naturalize" unity; it is a possible achievement based on a possible standpoint rooted in social relations. The essentializing move is in the ontological structure of labor or of its analogue, women's activity.[14]* The inheritance of Marxian humanism, with its preeminently

14. The feminist standpoint argument has been developed by Jane Flax, "Political Philosophy and the Patriarchal Unconsciousness," *Discovering Reality,* ed. Sandra Harding and Merill Hintikka (Dordrecht: Reidel, 1983); Sandra Harding, "The Contradictions and Ambivalence of a Feminist Science," ms.; Harding and Hintikka, *Discovering Reality;* Nancy Hartsock, *Money, Sex and Power* (New York: Longman, 1983) and "The Feminist Standpoint: Developing the Ground for a Specifically Feminist Historical Materialism," *Discovering Reality,* ed. S. Harding and M. Hintikka; Mary O'Brien, *The Politics of Reproduction* (New York: Routledge & Kegan Paul, 1981); Hilary Rose, "Hand, Brain, and Heart: A Feminist Epistemology for the Natural Sciences," *Signs,* Vol. 9, No. 1, 1983, pp. 73–90; Dorothy Smith, "Women's Perspective as a Radical Critique of Sociology," *Sociological Inquiry,* Vol. 44, 1974, and "A Sociology of Women," *The Prism of Sex,* ed. J. Sherman and E. T. Beck, Madison, WI: University of Wisconsin Press, 1979)

For rethinking theories of feminist materialism and feminist standpoint in response to criticism, see Chapter 7 in Harding, *The Science Question in Feminism,* op. cit. (note 1); Nancy Hartsock, "Rethinking Modernism: Minority vs. Majority Theories," *Cultural Critique* 7 (1987): 187–206; Hilary Rose, "Women's Work: Women's Knowledge," *What is Feminism? A Re-examination,* ed. Juliet Mitchell and Ann Oakley (New York: Pantheon, 1986), pp. 161–183.

* The central role of object-relations versions of psychoanalysis and related

Western self, is the difficulty for me. The contribution from these formulations has been the emphasis on the daily responsibility of real women to *build* unities, rather than to naturalize them.

Catherine MacKinnon's version of radical feminism is itself a caricature of the appropriating, incorporating, totalizing tendencies of Western theories of identity grounding action.[15] It is factually and politically wrong to assimilate all of the diverse "moments" or "conversations" in recent women's politics named radical feminism to MacKinnon's version. But the teleological logic of her theory shows how an epistemology and ontology – including their negations – erase or police difference. Only one of the effects of MacKinnon's theory is the rewriting of the history of the polymorphous field called radical feminism. The major effect is the production of a theory of experience, of women's identity, that is a kind of apocalypse for all revolutionary standpoints. That is, the totalization built into this tale of radical feminism achieves its end – the unity of women – by enforcing the experience of and testimony to radical nonbeing. As for the Marxist/socialist feminist, consciousness is an achievement, not a nat-

strong universalizing moves in discussing reproduction, caring work, and mothering in many approaches to epistemology underline their authors' resistance to what I am calling postmodernism. For me, both the universalizing moves and these versions of psychoanalysis make analysis of "women's place in the integrated circuit" difficult and lead to systematic difficulties in accounting for or even seeing major aspects of the construction of gender and gendered social life.

15. Catherine MacKinnon, "Feminism, Marxism, Method, and the State: An Agenda for Theory," *Signs*, Vo 7, No. 3, Spring 1982, pp. 515–544. See also MacKinnon, *Feminism Unmodified* (Cambridge, MA: Harvard University Press, 1987). I make a category error in "modifying" MacKinnon's positions with the qualifier "radical," thereby generating my own reductive critique of extremely heterogeneous writing, which does explicitly use that label, by my taxonomically interested argument about writing which does not use the modifier and which brooks no limits and thereby adds to the various dreams of a common, in the sense of univocal, language for feminism. My category error was occasioned by an assignment to write from a particular taxonomic position which itself has a heterogeneous history, socialist feminism, for *Socialist Review*. A critique indebted to MacKinnon, but without the reductionism and with an elegant feminist account of Foucault's paradoxical conservatism on sexual violence (rape), is Teresa de Lauretis, "The Violence of Rhetoric: Considerations on Representation and Gender," *Semiotica*, Vol. 54, 1985, pp. 11–31, and Teresa de Lauretis, ed., *Feminist Studies/Critical Studies* (Bloomington: Indiana University Press, 1986). A theoretically elegant feminist social-historical examination of family violence, that insists on women's, men's, and children's complex agency without losing sight of the material structures of male domination, race, and class, is Linda Gordon, *Heroes of their own Lives* (New York: Viking, 1988).

ural fact. MacKinnon's theory eliminates some of the difficulties built into humanist revolutionary subjects, but at the cost of radical reductionism.

MacKinnon argues that feminism necessarily adopted a different analytical strategy from Marxism, looking first not at the structure of class, but at the structure of sex/gender and its generative relationship, men's constitution and appropriation of women sexually. Ironically, MacKinnon's "ontology" constructs a nonsubject, a nonbeing. Another's desire, not the self's labor, is the origin of "woman." She therefore develops a theory of consciousness that enforces what can count as "women's" experience – anything that names sexual violation, indeed, sex itself as far as "women" can be concerned. Feminist practice is the construction of this form of consciousness; that is, the self-knowledge of a self-who-is-not.

Perversely, sexual appropriation in this feminism still has the epistemological status of labor, that is, the point from which analysis able to contribute to changing the world must flow. But sexual objectification, not alienation, is the consequence of the structure of sex/gender. In the realm of knowledge, the result of sexual objectification is illusion and abstraction. However, a woman is not simply alienated from her product, but in a deep sense she does not exist as a subject, or even potential subject, since she owes her existence as a woman to sexual appropriation. To be constituted by another's desire is not the same thing as to be alienated in the violent separation of the laborer from his product.

MacKinnon's radical theory of experience is totalizing in the extreme; it does not so much marginalize as obliterate the authority of any other women's political speech and action. It is a totalization producing what Western patriarchy itself never succeeded in doing – feminists' consciousness of the nonexistence of women, except as products of men's desire. I think MacKinnon correctly argues that no Marxian version of identity can firmly ground women's unity. But in solving the problem of the contradictions of any Western revolutionary subject for feminist purposes, she develops an even more authoritarian doctrine of experience. If my complaint about socialist/Marxian standpoints is their unintended erasure of polyvocal, unassimilable, radical difference made visible in anti-colonial discourse and practice, MacKinnon's intentional erasure of all difference through the device of the "essential" nonexistence of women is not reassuring.

In my taxonomy, which like any other taxonomy is a reinscription of history, radical feminism can accommodate all the activities of women named by socialist feminists as forms of labor only if the activity can somehow be sexualized. Reproduction had different tones of meanings for the two tendencies, one rooted in labor, one in sex, both calling the consequences of domination and ignorance of social and personal reality "false consciousness."

Beyond either the difficulties or the contributions in the argument of any one author, neither Marxist nor radical-feminist points of view have tended to embrace the status of a partial explanation; both were regularly constituted as totalities. Western explanation has demanded as much; how else could the Western author incorporate its others? Each tried to annex other forms of domination by expanding its basic categories through analogy, simple listing, or addition. Embarrassed silence about race among white radical and socialist feminists was one major, devastating political consequence. History and polyvocality disappear into political taxonomies that try to establish genealogies. There was no structural room for race (or for much else) in theory claiming to reveal the construction of the category "woman" and social group "women" as a unified or totalizable whole. The structure of my caricature looks like this:

> Socialist Feminism –
> structure of class//wage labor//alienation
> labor, by analogy reproduction, by extension sex, by addition race
> Radical Feminism –
> structure of gender//sexual appropriation//objectification
> sex, by analogy labor, by extension reproduction, by addition race

In another context, the French theorist Julia Kristeva claimed women appeared as a historical group after World War II, along with groups like youth. Her dates are doubtful, but we are now accustomed to remembering that as objects of knowledge and as historical actors, "race" did not always exist, "class" has a historical genesis, and "homosexuals" are quite junior. It is no accident that the symbolic system of the family of man – and so the essence of woman – breaks up at the same moment that networks of connection among people on the planet are unprecedentedly multiple, pregnant, and complex. "Advanced capitalism" is inadequate to convey the structure of this historical moment. In the Western sense, the end of man is at stake. It is no accident that woman disintegrates into women in our time. Perhaps socialist feminists were not substantially guilty of producing essentialist theory that suppressed women's particularity and contradictory interests. I think we have been, at least through unreflective participation in the logics, languages, and practices of white humanism and through searching for a single ground of domination to secure our revolutionary voice. Now we have less excuse. But in the consciousness of our failures, we risk lapsing into boundless difference and giving up on the confusing task of making partial, real connection. Some differences are playful; some are poles of world historical systems of domination. Epistemology is about knowing the difference.

The informatics of domination

In this attempt at an epistemological and political position, I would like to sketch a picture of possible unity, a picture indebted to socialist and feminist principles of design. The frame for my sketch is set by the extent and importance of rearrangements in worldwide social relations tied to science and technology. I argue for a politics rooted in claims about fundamental changes in the nature of class, race, and gender in an emerging system of world order analogous in its novelty and scope to that created by industrial capitalism; we are living through a movement from an organic, industrial society to a polymorphous, information system – from all work to all play, a deadly game. Simultaneously material and ideological, the dichotomies may be expressed in the following chart of transitions from the comfortable old hierarchical dominations to the scary new networks I have called the informatics of domination:

Representation	Simulation
Bourgeois novel, realism	Science fiction, postmodernism
Organism	Biotic component
Depth, integrity	Surface, boundary
Heat	Noise
Biology as clinical practice	Biology as inscription
Physiology	Communications engineering
Small group	Subsystem
Perfection	Optimization
Eugenics	Population Control
Decadence, *Magic Mountain*	Obsolescence, *Future Shock*
Hygiene	Stress management
Microbiology, tuberculosis	Immunology, AIDS
Organic division of labor	Ergonomics/cybernetics of labor
Functional specialization	Modular construction
Reproduction	Replication
Organic sex role specialization	Optimal genetic strategies
Biological determinism	Evolutionary inertia, constraints
Community ecology	Ecosystem
Racial chain of being	Neo-imperialism, United Nations humanism
Scientific management in home/factory	Global factory/electronic cottage
Family/market/factory	Women in the integrated circuit
Family wage	Comparable worth

Public/private	Cyborg citizenship
Nature/culture	Fields of difference
Cooperation	Communications enhancement
Freud	Lacan
Sex	Genetic engineering
Labor	Robotics
Mind	Artificial intelligence
World War II	Star Wars
White capitalist patriarchy	Informatics of domination

This list suggests several interesting things.[16] First, the objects on the right-hand side cannot be coded as "natural," a realization that subverts naturalistic coding for the left-hand side as well. We cannot go back ideologically or materially. It's not just that "god" is dead; so is the "goddess." Or both are revivified in the worlds charged with microelectronic and biotechnological politics. In relation to objects like biotic components, one must think not in terms of essential properties, but in terms of design, boundary constraints, rates of flows, systems logics, costs of lowering constraints. Sexual reproduction is one kind of reproductive strategy among many, with costs and benefits function of the system environment. Ideologies of sexual reproduction can no longer reasonably call on notions of sex and sex role as organic aspects in natural objects like organisms and families. Such reasoning will be unmasked as irrational, and ironically corporate executives reading *Playboy* and antiporn radical feminists will make strange bedfellows in jointly unmasking the irrationalism.

Likewise for race, racist and anti-racist ideologies about human diversity have to be formulated in terms of frequencies of parameters. It is "irrational" to invoke concepts like primitive and civilized. For liberals and radicals, the search for integrated social systems gives way to a new practice called "experimental ethnography" in which an organic object dissipates in attention to the play of writing. At the level of ideology, we see translations of racism and colonialism into languages of development

16. My previous efforts to understand biology as a cybernetic command-control discourse and organisms as "natural-technical objects of knowledge" are "The High Cost of Information in Post-World War II Evolutionary Biology," *Philosophical Forum,* Vol. 13, Nos. 2–3, 1979, pp. 206–237; "Signs of Dominance: From a Physiology to a Cybernetics of Primate Society," *Studies in History of Biology,* Vol. 6, 1983, pp. 129–219; "Class, Race, Sex, Scientific Objects of Knowledge: A Socialist-Feminist Perspective on the Social Construction of Productive Knowledge and Some Political Consequences," *Women in Scientific and Engineering Professions,* ed. Violet Haas and Carolyn Perucci (Ann Arbor, MI: University of Michigan Press, 1984), pp. 212–229.

and underdevelopment, rates and constraints of modernization. Any objects or persons can be "reasonably" thought of in terms of disassembly and reassembly; no "natural" architectures constrain system design. The financial districts in all the world's cities, as well as the export-processing and free-trade zones, proclaim this elementary fact of "late capitalism." The entire universe of objects that can be known scientifically must be formulated as problems in communications engineering (for the managers) or theories of the text (for those who would resist). Both are cyborg semiologies.

One should expect control strategies to concentrate on boundary conditions and interfaces, on rates of flow across boundaries – and not on the integrity of natural objects. "Integrity" or "sincerity" of the Western self gives way to decision procedures and expert systems. For example, control strategies applied to women's capacities to give birth to new human beings will be developed in the languages of population control and maximization of goal achievement for individual decisionmakers. Control strategies will be formulated in terms of rates, costs of constraints, degrees of freedom. Human beings, like any other component or subsystem, must be localized in a system architecture whose basic modes of operation are probabilistic, statistical. No objects, spaces, or bodies are sacred in themselves; any component can be interfaced with any other if the proper standard, the proper code, can be constructed for processing signals in a common language. Exchange in this world transcends the universal translation effected by capitalist markets that Marx analyzed so well. The privileged pathology affecting all kinds of components in this universe is stress – communications breakdown.[17] The cyborg is not subject to Foucault's biopolitics; the cyborg simulates politics, a much more potent field of operations. Discursive constructions are no joke.

This kind of analysis of scientific and cultural objects of knowledge which have appeared historically since World War II prepares us to notice some important inadequacies in feminist analysis which has proceeded as if the organic, hierarchical dualism ordering discourse in the West since Aristotle still ruled. They have been cannibalized, or as Zoe Sofia (Sofoulis) might have put it, they have been "techno-digested." The dichotomies between mind and body, animal and human, organism and machine, public and private, nature and culture, men and women, primitive and civilized are all in question ideologically. The actual situation of women is their integration/exploitation into a world system of production/reproduction and communication called the informatics of domination. The home, work place, market, public arena, the body itself – all can

17. E. Rusten Hogness, "Why Stress? A Look at the Making of Stress, 1936–1956," available from the author, 4437 Mill Creek Rd., Healdsburg, CA 95448.

be dispersed and interfaced in nearly infinite, polymorphous ways, with large consequences for women and others – consequences that themselves are very different for different people and which make potent opposi-tional international movements difficult to imagine and essential for sur-vival. One important route for reconstructing socialist-feminist politics is through theory and practice addressed to the social relations of science and technology, including crucially the systems of myth and meanings structuring our imaginations. The cyborg is a kind of disassembled and reassembled, postmodern collective and personal self. This is the self fem-inists must code.

Communications technologies and biotechnologies are the crucial tools recrafting our bodies. These tools embody and enforce new social relations for women worldwide. Technologies and scientific discourses can be par-tially understood as formalizations, that is, as frozen moments, of the fluid social interactions constituting them, but they should also be viewed as in-struments for enforcing meanings. The boundary is permeable between tool and myth, instrument and concept, historical systems of social rela-tions and historical anatomies of possible bodies, including objects of knowledge. Indeed, myth and tool mutually constitute each other.

Furthermore, communications sciences and modern biologies are con-structed by a common move – the translation of the world into a prob-lem of coding, a search for a common language in which all resistance to instrumental control disappears and all heterogeneity can be submitted to disassembly, reassembly, investment, and exchange.

In communications sciences, the translation of the world into a prob-lem in coding can be illustrated by looking at cybernetic (feedback con-trolled) systems theories applied to telephone technology, computer design, weapons deployment, or data-base construction and mainte-nance. In each case, solution to the key questions rests on a theory of lan-guage and control; the key operation is determining the rates, directions, and probabilities of flow of a quantity called information. The world is subdivided by boundaries differentially permeable to information. Infor-mation is just that kind of quantifiable element (unit, basis of unity) which allows universal translation and so unhindered instrumental power (called effective communication). The biggest threat to such power is in-terruption of communication. Any system breakdown is a function of stress. The fundamentals of this technology can be condensed into the metaphor C^3I, command-control-communication-intelligence, the mili-tary's symbol for its operations theory.

In modern biologies, the translation of the world into a problem in cod-ing can be illustrated by molecular genetics, ecology, sociobiological evo-lutionary theory, and immunobiology. The organism has been translated into problems of genetic coding and read-out. Biotechnology, a writing technology, informs research broadly.[18] In a sense, organisms have ceased to exist as objects of knowledge, giving way to biotic components, that is, special kinds of information-processing devices. The analogous moves in ecology could be examined by probing the history and utility of the concept of the ecosystem. Immunobiology and associated medical practices are rich exemplars of the privilege of coding and recognition systems as objects of knowledge, as constructions of bodily reality for us. Biology here is a king of cryptography. Research is necessarily a kind of intelligence activity. Ironies abound. A stressed system goes awry; its communication processes break down; it fails to recognize the difference between self and other. Human babies with baboon hearts evoke national ethical perplexity – for animal-rights activists at least as much as for the guardians of human purity. In the United States gay men and intravenous drug users are the most "privileged" victims of an awful immune-system disease that marks (inscribes on the body) confusion of boundaries and moral pollution.[19]

But these excursions into communications sciences and biology have been at a rarefied level; there is a mundane, largely economic reality to support my claim that these sciences and technologies indicate fundamental transformations in the structure of the world for us. Communications technologies depend on electronics. Modern states, multinational corporations, military power, welfare-state apparatuses, satellite systems, political processes, fabrication of our imaginations, labor-control systems, medical constructions of our bodies, commercial pornography, the international division of labor, and religious evangelism depend intimately upon electronics. Microelectronics is the technical basis of simulacra, that is, of copies without originals.

Microelectronics mediates the translations of labor into robotics and word processing, sex into genetic engineering and reproductive technologies, and mind into artificial intelligence and decision procedures. The new biotechnologies concern more than human reproduction. Biology as a powerful engineering science for redesigning materials and processes has revolutionary implications for industry, perhaps most obvious today in areas of fermentation, agriculture, and energy. Com-

18. A left entry to the biotechnology debate: *Genewatch,* a Bulletin of the Committee for Responsible Genetics, 5 Doane St., 4th floor, Boston, MA 02109; Susan Wright, "Recombinant DNA Technology and Its Social Transformation, 1972–82," *Osiris,* 2nd series, Vol. 2, 1986, pp. 303–360 and "Recombinant DNA: The Status of Hazards and Controls," *Environment,* July/August 1982; Edward Yoxen, *The Gene Business* (New York: Harper & Row, 1983).
19. Paula Treichler, "AIDS, Homophobia, and Biomedical Discourse: An Epidemic of Signification," forthcoming in *Cultural Studies.*

munications sciences and biology are constructions of natural-technical objects of knowledge in which the difference between machine and organism is thoroughly blurred; mind, body, and tool are on very intimate terms. The "multinational" material organization of the production and reproduction of daily life and the symbolic organization of the production and reproduction of culture and imagination seem equally implicated. The boundary-maintaining images of base and superstructure, public and private, or material and ideal never seemed more feeble.

I have used Rachel Grossman's image of women in the integrated circuit to name the situation of women in a world so intimately restructured through the social relations of science and technology.[20] I use the odd circumlocution, "the social relations of science and technology," to indicate that we are not dealing with a technological determinism, but with a historical system depending upon structured relations among people. But the phrase should also indicate that science and technology provide fresh sources of power, that we need fresh sources of analysis and political action.[21] Some of the rearrangements of race, sex, and class rooted in high-tech-facilitated social relations can make socialist feminism more relevant to effective progressive politics.

The homework economy

The "New Industrial Revolution" is producing a new worldwide working class, as well as new sexualities and ethnicities. The extreme mobility of capital and the emerging international division of labor are intertwined

20. Starting references for "women in the integrated circuit": *Scientific-Technological Change and the Role of Women in Development,* ed. Pamela D'Onofrio-Flores and Sheila M. Pfafflin (Boulder, CO: Westview Press, 1982); Maria Patricia Fernandez-Kelly, *For We Are Sold, I and My People* (Albany, NY: SUNY Press, 1983); Annette Fuentes and Barbara Ehrenreich, *Women in the Global Factory* (Boston: South End Press, 1983), with an especially useful list of resources and organizations; Rachael Grossman, "Women's Place in the Integrated Circuit," *Radical America,* Vol. 14, No. I, 1980, pp. 29–50; *Women and Men and the International Division of Labor,* ed. June Nash and M. P. Fernandez-Kelly (Albany, NY: SUNY Press, 1983); Aihwa Ong, "Japanese Factories, Malay Workers: Industrialization and the Cultural Construction of Gender in West Malaysia, *Power and Difference,* ed. Shelly Errington and Jane Atkinson (Palo Alto, CA: Stanford University Press, forthcoming); Aihwa Ong, *Spirits of Resistance and Capitalist Discipline: Factory Workers in Malaysia* (Albany, SUNY Press, 1987); *Science Policy Research Unity, Microelectronics and Women's Employment in Britain* (University of Sussex, 1982).
21. The best example is Bruno Latour, *Les Microbes: Guerre et Paix, suivi de Irréductions* (Paris: Métailié, 1984).

with the emergence of new collectivities and the weakening of familiar groupings. These developments are neither gender- nor race-neutral. White men in advanced industrial societies have become newly vulnerable to permanent job loss, and women are not disappearing from the job rolls at the same rates as men. It is not simply that women in third-world countries are the preferred labor force for the science-based multinationals in the export-processing sectors, particularly in electronics. The picture is more systematic and involves reproduction, sexuality, culture, consumption, and production. In the prototypical Silicon Valley, many women's lives have been structured around employment in electronics-dependent jobs, and their intimate realities include serial heterosexual monogamy, negotiating child care, distance from extended kin or most other forms of traditional community, a high likelihood of loneliness and extreme economic vulnerability as they age. The ethnic and racial diversity of women in Silicon Valley structures a microcosm of conflicting differences in culture, family, religion, education, and language.

Richard Gordon has called this new situation the homework economy.[22] Although he includes the phenomenon of literal homework emerging in connection with electronics assembly, Gordon intends "homework economy" to name a restructuring of work that broadly has the characteristics formerly ascribed to female jobs, jobs literally done only by

22. For the homework economy and some related arguments: Richard Gordon, "The Computerization of Daily Life, the Sexual Division of Labor, and the Homework Economy," paper delivered at the Silicon Valley Workshop Group conference, 1983; Richard Gordon and Linda Kimball, "High-Technology, Employment and the Challenges of Education," *SVRG Working Paper*, No. 1, July 1985; Judith Stacey, "Sexism by a Subtler Name? Postindustrial Conditions and Postfeminist Consciousness in the Silicon Valley," *Socialist Review*, no. 96, 1987, pp. 7–30; Women's Work, Men's Work, ed. Barbara F. Reskin and Heidi Hartmann (Washington, DC: National Academy of Sciences Press, 1986); *Signs*, Vol. 10, No. 2, 1984, special issue on women and poverty; Stephen Rose, *The American Profile Poster: Who Owns What, Who Makes How Much, Who Works Where, and Who Lives With Whom?* (New York: Pantheon, 1986); Patricia Hill Collins, "Third World Women in America," and Sara G. Burr, "Women and Work," ed. Barbara K. Haber, *The Women's Annual*, 1981 (Boston: G. K. Hall, 1982); Judith Gregory and Karen Nussbaum, "Race against Time: Automation of the Office," *Office: Technology and People*, Vol. 1, 1982, pp. 197–236; Frances Fox Piven and Richard Cloward, *The New Class War: Reagan's Attack on the Welfare State and Its Consequences* (New York: Pantheon, 1982); Microelectronics Group, *Microelectronics: Capitalist Technology and the Working Class* (London: CSE, 1980); Karin Stallard, Barbara Ehrenreich, and Holly Sklar, *Poverty in the American Dream* (Boston: South End Press, 1983) including a useful organization and resource list.

women. Work is being redefined as both literally female and feminized, whether performed by men or women. To be feminized means to be made extremely vulnerable; able to be disassembled, reassembled, exploited as a reserve labor force; seen less as workers than as servers; subjected to time arrangements on and off the paid job that make a mockery of a limited work day; leading an existence that always borders on being obscene, out of place, and reducible to sex. De-skilling is an old strategy newly applicable to formerly privileged workers. However, the homework economy does not refer only to large-scale de-skilling, nor does it deny that new areas of high skill are emerging, even for women and men previously excluded from skilled employment. Rather, the concept indicates that factory, home, and market are integrated on a new scale and that the places of women are crucial – and need to be analyzed for differences among women and for meanings for relations between men and women in various situations.

The homework economy as a world capitalist organizational structure is made possible by (not caused by) the new technologies. The success of the attack on relatively privileged, mostly white men's unionized jobs is tied to the power of the new communications technologies to integrate and control labor despite extensive dispersion and decentralization. The consequences of the new technologies are felt by women both in the loss of the family (male) wage (if they ever had access to this white privilege) and in the character of their own jobs, which are becoming capital-intensive, for example, office work and nursing.

The new economic and technological arrangements are also related to the collapsing welfare state and the ensuing intensification of demands on women to sustain daily life for themselves as well as for men, children, and old people. The feminization of poverty – generated by dismantling the welfare state, by the homework economy where stable jobs become the exception, and sustained by the expectation that women's wage will not be matched by a male income for the support of children – has become an urgent focus. The causes of various women-headed households are a function of race, class, or sexuality; but their increasing generality is a ground for coalitions of women on many issues. That women regularly sustain daily life partly as a function of their enforced status as mothers is hardly new; the kind of integration with the overall capitalist and progressively war-based economy is new. The particular pressure, for example, on U.S. black women, who have achieved an escape from (barely) paid domestic service and who now hold clerical and similar jobs in large numbers, has large implications for continued enforced black poverty with employment. Teenage women in industrializing areas of the third world increasingly find themselves the sole or major source of a cash wage for their families, while access to land is ever more problematic. These developments must have major consequences in the psychodynamics and politics of gender and race.

Within the narrative framework of three major stages of capitalism (commercial/early industrial, monopoly, multinational) – tied to nationalism, imperialism, and multinationalism, and related to Jameson's three dominant aesthetic periods of realism, modernism, and postmodernism – I would argue that specific forms of families dialectically relate to forms of capital and to its political and cultural concomitants. Although lived problematically and unequally, ideal forms of these families might be schematized as (1) the patriarchal nuclear family, structured by the dichotomy between public and private and accompanied by the white bourgeois ideology of separate spheres and nineteenth-century Anglo-American bourgeois feminism; (2) the modern family mediated (or enforced) by the welfare state and institutions like the family wage, with a flowering of afeminist heterosexual ideologies, including their radical versions represented in Greenwich Village around World War I; and (3) the "family" of the homework economy with its oxymoronic structure of women-headed households and its explosion of feminisms and the paradoxical intensification and erosion of gender itself.

This is the context in which the projections for worldwide structural unemployment stemming from the new technologies are part of the picture of the homework economy. As robotics and related technologies put men out of work in "developed" countries and exacerbate failure to generate male jobs in third-world "development" and as the automated office becomes the rule even in labor-surplus countries, the feminization of work intensifies. Black women in the United States have long known what it looks like to face the structural underemployment ("feminization") of black men, as well as their own highly vulnerable position in the wage economy. It is no longer a secret that sexuality, reproduction, family, and community life are interwoven with this economic structure in myriad ways which have also differentiated the situations of white and black women. Many more women and men will contend with similar situations, which will make cross-gender and race alliances on issues of basic life support (with or without jobs) necessary, not just nice.

The new technologies also have a profound effect on hunger and on food production for subsistence worldwide. Rae Lessor Blumberg estimates that women produce about 50 percent of the world's subsistence food.[23] Women are excluded generally from benefiting from the increased

23. Rae Lessor Blumberg, "A General Theory of Sex Stratification and Its Application to the Position of Women in Today's World Economy," paper delivered to Sociology Board, University of California, Santa Cruz, February 1983. Also R. L. Blumberg, *Stratification: Socioeconomic and Sexual Inequality* (Boston: Brown, 1981). See also Sally Hacker, "Doing It the Hard

high-tech commodification of food and energy crops, their days are made more arduous because their responsibilities to provide food do not diminish, and their reproductive situations are made more complex. Green Revolution technologies interact with other high-tech industrial production to alter gender divisions of labor and differential gender migration patterns.

The new technologies seem deeply involved in the forms of "privatization" that Ros Petchesky has analyzed, in which militarization, right-wing family ideologies and policies, and intensified definitions of corporate (and state) property as private synergistically interact.[24] The new communications technologies are fundamental to the eradication of "public life" for everyone. This facilitates the mushrooming of a permanent high-tech military establishment at the cultural and economic expense of most people, but especially of women. Technologies like video games and highly miniaturized television seem crucial to production of modern

Way: Ethnographic Studies in the Agribusiness and Engineering Classroom," California American Studies Association, Pomona, 1984, forthcoming in *Humanity and Society;* S. Hacker and Lisa Bovit, "Agriculture to Agribusiness: Technical Imperatives and Changing Roles," *Proceedings of the Society for the History of Technology, Milwaukee,* 1981; Lawrence Busch and William Lacy, *Science, Agriculture, and the Politics of Research* (Boulder, CO: Westview Press, 1983); Denis Wilfred, "Capital and Agriculture, a Review of Marxian Problematics," *Studies in Political Economy,* No. 7, 1982, pp. 127–154; Carolyn Sachs, *The Invisible Farmers: Women in Agricultural Production* (Totowa, NJ: Rowman & Allanheld, 1983). International Fund for Agricultural Development, IFAD Experience Relating to Rural Women, 1977–84 (Rome: IFAD, 1985), 37 pp. Thanks to Elizabeth Bird, "Green Revolution Imperialism," I & II, ms. University of California, Santa Cruz, 1984.

* The conjunction of the Green Revolution's social relations with biotechnologies like plant genetic engineering makes the pressures on the land in the third world increasingly intense. The Agency for International Development's estimates (*New York Times* October 14, 1984) used at the 1984 World Food Day are that in Africa, women produce about 90 percent of rural food supplies, about 60 to 80 percent in Asia, and provide 40 percent of agricultural labor in the Near East and Latin America. Blumberg charges that world organizations'agricultural politics, as well as those of multinationals and national governments in the third world, generally ignore fundamental issues in the sexual division of labor. The present tragedy of famine in Africa might owe as much to male supremacy as to capitalism, colonialism, and rain patterns. More accurately, capitalism and racism are usually structurally male dominant.

24. Cynthia Enloe, "Women Textile Workers in the Militarization of Southeast Asia," *Women and Men,* ed. Nash and Fernandez-Kelly; Rosalind Petchesky, "Abortion, Anti-Feminism, and the Rise of the New Right," *Feminist Studies,* Vol. 7, No. 2, 1981. Cynthia Enloe, *Does Khaki Become You? The Militarization of Women's Lives* (Boston: South End Press, 1983).

forms of "private life." The culture of video games is heavily oriented to individual competition and extraterrestrial warfare. High-tech, gendered imaginations are produced here, imaginations that can contemplate destruction of the planet and a sci-fi escape from its consequences. More than our imaginations is militarized, and the other realities of electronic and nuclear warfare are inescapable. These are the technologies that promise ultimate mobility and perfect exchange – and incidentally enable tourism, that perfect practice of mobility and exchange, to emerge as one of the world's largest single industries.

The new technologies affect the social relations of both sexuality and reproduction, and not always in the same ways. The close ties of sexuality and instrumentality, of views of the body as a kind of private satisfaction- and utility-maximizing machine, are described nicely in sociobiological origin stories that stress a genetic calculus and explain the inevitable dialectic of domination of male and female gender roles.[25] These sociobiological stories depend on a high-tech view of the body as a biotic component or cybernetic communications system. Among the many transformations of reproductive situations is the medical one, where women's bodies have boundaries newly permeable to both "visualization" and "intervention." Of course, who controls the interpretation of bodily boundaries in medical hermeneutics is a major feminist issue. The speculum served as an icon of women's claiming their bodies in the 1970s; that handcrafted tool is inadequate to express our needed body politics in the negotiation of reality in the practices of cyborg reproduction. Self-help is not enough. The technologies of visualization recall the important cultural practice of hunting with the camera and the deeply predatory nature of a photographic consciousness.[26] Sex, sexuality, and

25. For a feminist version of this logic, see Sarah Blaffer Hrdy, *The Woman That Never Evolved* (Cambridge, MA: Harvard University Press, 1981). For an analysis of scientific women's story-telling practices, especially in relation to sociobiology, in evolutionary debates around child abuse and infanticide, see Donna Haraway, "The Contest for Primate Nature: Daughters of Man the Hunter in the Field, 1960–80," *The Future of American Democracy,* ed. Mark Kann (Philadelphia: Temple University Press, 1983), pp. 175–208. See also D. Haraway, *Primate Visions: Gender, Race, and Nature in the World of Modern Science* (New York: Routledge, 1989).

26. For the moment of transition of hunting with guns to hunting with cameras in the construction of popular meanings of nature for an American urban immigrant public, see Donna Haraway, "Teddy Bear Patriarchy," *Social Text,* No. 11, Winter 1984–1985, pp. 20–64; Roderick Nash, "The Exporting and Importing of Nature: Nature-Appreciation as a Commodity, 1850–1980," *Perspectives in American History,* Vol. 3, 1979, pp. 517–560; Susan Sontag, *On Photography* (New York: Dell, 1977); and Douglas Preston, "Shooting in Paradise," *Natural History,* Vol. 93, No. 12, December 1984, pp. 14–19.

reproduction are central actors in high-tech myth systems structuring our imaginations of personal and social possibility.

Another critical aspect of the social relations of the new technologies is the reformulation of expectations, culture, work, and reproduction for the large scientific and technical work force. A major social and political danger is the formation of a strongly bimodal social structure, with masses of women and men of all ethnic groups, but especially people of color, confined to a homework economy, illiteracy of several varieties, and general redundancy and impotence, controlled by high-tech repressive apparatuses ranging from entertainment to surveillance and disappearance. An adequate socialist-feminist politics should address women in the privileged occupational categories and particularly in the production of science and technology that constructs scientific-technical discourse, processes, and objects.[27]

This issue is only one aspect of inquiry into the possibility of a feminist science, but it is important. What kind of constitutive role in the production of knowledge, imagination, and practice can new groups doing science have? How can these groups be allied with progressive social and political movements? What kind of political accountability can be constructed to tie women together across the scientific-technical hierarchies separating us? Might there be ways of developing feminist science/technology politics in alliance with anti-military science facility conversion action groups? Many scientific and technical workers in Silicon Valley, the high-tech cowboys included, do not want to work on military science.[28] Can these personal preferences and cultural tendencies be welded into progressive politics among this professional middle class in which women, including women of color, are coming to be fairly numerous?

27. For crucial guidance for thinking about the political/cultural implications of the history of women doing science in the United States see *Women in Scientific and Engineering Professions*, ed. Violet Haas and Carolyn Perucci (Ann Arbor, MI: University of Michigan Press, 1984); Sally Hacker, "The Culture of Engineering: Women, Workplace, and Machine," *Women's Studies International Quarterly*, Vol. 4, No. 3, 1981, pp. 341–353; Evelyn Fox Keller, *A Feeling for the Organism* (San Francisco: Freeman, 1983); National Science Foundation, *Women and Minorities in Science and Engineering* (Washington, DC: NSF, 1988); Margaret Rossiter, *Women Scientists in America* (Baltimore, MD: Johns Hopkins University Press, 1982); Londa Schiebinger, "The History and Philosophy of Women in Science: A Review Essay," *Signs*, Vol. 12, No. 2, 1987, pp. 305–332.
28. John Markoff and Lenny Siegel, "Military Micros," University of California, Santa Cruz, Silicon Valley Research Project conference, 1983. High Technology Professionals for Peace and Computer Professionals for Social Responsibility are promising organizations.

Women in the integrated circuit

Let me summarize the picture of women's historical locations in advanced industrial societies, as these positions have been restructured partly through the social relations of science and technology. If it was ever possible ideologically to characterize women's lives by the distinction of public and private domains – suggested by images of the division of working-class life into factory and home, of bourgeois life into market and home, and of gender existence into personal and political realms – it is now a totally misleading ideology, even to show how both terms of these dichotomies construct each other in practice and in theory. I prefer a network ideological image, suggesting the profusion of spaces and identities and the permeability of boundaries in the personal body and in the body politic. "Networking" is both a feminist practice and a multinational corporate strategy – weaving is for oppositional cyborgs.

So let me return to the earlier image of the informatics of domination and trace one vision of women's "place" in the integrated circuit, touching only a few idealized social locations seen primarily from the point of view of advanced capitalist societies: Home, Market, Paid Work Place, State, School, Clinic-Hospital, and Church. Each of these idealized spaces is logically and practically implied in every other locus, perhaps analogous to a holographic photograph. I want to suggest the impact of the social relations mediated and enforced by the new technologies in order to help formulate needed analysis and practical work. However, there is no "place" for women in these networks, only geometries of difference and contradiction crucial to women's cyborg identities. If we learn how to read these webs of power and social life, we might learn new couplings, new coalitions. There is no way to read the following list from a standpoint of "identification," of a unitary self. The issue is dispersion. The task is to survive in diaspora.

Home: Women-headed households, serial monogamy, flight of men, old women alone, technology of domestic work, paid home work, reemergence of home sweatshops, home-based businesses and telecommuting, electronic cottage, urban homelessness, migration, module architecture, reinforced (simulated) nuclear family, intense domestic violence.

Market: Women's continuing consumption work, newly targeted to buy the profusion of new production from the new technologies (especially as the competitive race among industrialized and industrializing nations to avoid dangerous mass unemployment necessitates finding ever bigger new markets for ever less clearly needed commodities); bimodal buying power, coupled with advertising targeting of the numerous affluent groups and neglect of the previous mass markets; growing importance of informal markets in labor and commodities parallel to high-tech, affluent market structures; surveillance systems through electronic funds transfer; intensified market abstraction (commodification) of experience, resulting in ineffective utopian or equivalent cynical theories of community; extreme mobility (abstraction) of marketing/financing systems; interpenetration of sexual and labor markets; intensified sexualization of abstracted and alienated consumption.

Paid Work Place: Continued intense sexual and racial division of labor, but considerable growth of membership in privileged occupational categories for many white women and people of color; impact of new technologies on women's work in clerical, service, manufacturing (especially textiles), agriculture, electronics; international restructuring of the working classes; development of new time arrangements to facilitate the homework economy (flex time, part time, overtime, no time); homework and out work; increased pressures for two-tiered wage structures; significant numbers of people in cash-dependent populations worldwide with no experience or no further hope of stable employment; most labor "marginal" or "feminized."

State: Continued erosion of the welfare state; decentralizations with increased surveillance and control; citizenship by telematics; imperialism and political power broadly in the form of information-rich/information-poor differentiation; increased high-tech militarization increasingly opposed by many social groups; reduction of civil service jobs as a result of the growing capital intensification of office work, with implications for occupational mobility for women of color; growing privatization of material and ideological life and culture; close integration of privatization and militarization, the high-tech forms of bourgeois capitalist personal and public life; invisibility of different social groups to each other, linked to psychological mechanisms of belief in abstract enemies.

School: Deepening coupling of high-tech capital needs and public education at all levels, differentiated by race, class, and gender; managerial classes involved in educational reform and refunding at the cost of remaining progressive educational democratic structures for children and teachers; education for mass ignorance and repression in technocratic and militarized culture; growing anti-science mystery cults in dissenting and radical political movements; continued relative scientific illiteracy among white women and people of color; growing industrial direction of education (especially higher education) by science-based multinationals (particularly in electronics- and biotechnology-dependent companies); highly educated, numerous elites in a progressively bimodal society.

Clinic–Hospital: Intensified machine-body relations; renegotiations of public metaphors which channel personal experience of the body, particularly in relation to reproduction, immune system functions, and "stress" phenomena; intensification of reproductive politics in response to world historical implications of women's unrealized, potential control of their relation to reproduction; emergence of new historically specific diseases; struggles over meanings and means of health in environments pervaded by high-technology products and processes; continuing feminization of health work; intensified struggle over state responsibility for health; continued ideological role of popular health movements as a major form of American politics.

Church: Electronic fundamentalist "super-saver" preachers solemnizing the union of electronic capital and automated fetish gods; intensified importance of churches in resisting the militarized state; central struggle over women's meanings and authority in religion; continued relevance of spirituality, intertwined with sex and health, in political struggle.

The only way to characterize the informatics of domination is as a massive intensification of insecurity and cultural impoverishment, with common failure of subsistence networks for the most vulnerable. Since much of this picture interweaves with the social relations of science and technology, the urgency of a socialist-feminist politics addressed to science and technology is plain. There is much now being done, and the grounds for political work are rich. For example, the efforts to develop forms of collective struggle for women in paid work, like District 925 of the SEIU (Service Employees International Union) should be a high priority for all of us. These efforts are profoundly tied to technical restructuring of labor processes and reformations of working classes. These efforts also are providing understanding of a more comprehensive kind of labor organization, involving community, sexuality, and family issues never privileged in the largely white male industrial unions.

The structural rearrangements related to the social relations of science and technology evoke strong ambivalence. But it is not necessary to be ultimately depressed by the implications of late twentieth-century women's relation to all aspects of work, culture, production of knowledge, sexuality, and reproduction. For excellent reasons, most Marxisms see domination best and have trouble understanding what can only look like false consciousness and people's complicity in their own domination in late capitalism. It is crucial to remember that what is lost, perhaps especially from women's points of view, is often virulent forms of oppression, nostalgically naturalized in the face of current violation. Ambivalence toward the disrupted unities mediated by high-tech culture requires not sorting consciousness into categories of "clear-sighted critique grounding a solid political epistemology" versus "manipulated false consciousness," but subtle understanding of emerging pleasures, experiences, and powers with serious potential for changing the rules of the game.

There are grounds for hope in the emerging bases for new kinds of unity across race, gender, and class, as these elementary units of socialist-feminist analysis themselves suffer protean transformations. Intensifications of hardship experienced worldwide in connection with the social relations of science and technology are severe. But what people are experiencing is not transparently clear, and we lack sufficiently subtle connections for collectively building effective theories of experience. Present efforts – Marxist, psychoanalytic, feminist, anthropological – to clarify even "our" experience are rudimentary.

I am conscious of the odd perspective provided by my historical position – a Ph.D. in biology for an Irish Catholic girl was made possible by Sputnik's impact on U.S. national science-education policy. I have a body and mind as much constructed by the post–World War II arms race and cold war as by the women's movements. There are more grounds for hope by focusing on the contradictory effects of politics designed to produce loyal American technocrats, which as well produced large numbers of dissidents, rather than by focusing on the present defeats.

The permanent partiality of feminist points of view has consequences for our expectations of forms of political organization and participation. We do not need a totality in order to work well. The feminist dream of a common language, like all dreams for a perfectly true language, of a perfectly faithful naming of experience, is a totalizing and imperialist one. In that sense, dialectics too is a dream language, longing to resolve contradiction. Perhaps, ironically, we can learn from our fusions with animals and machines how not to be Man, the embodiment of Western logos. From the point of view of pleasure in these potent and taboo fusions, made inevitable by the social relations of science and technology, there might indeed be a feminist science.

Acknowledgments

Research was funded by an Academic Senate Faculty Research Grant from the University of California, Santa Cruz. An earlier version of this chapter, on genetic engineering, appeared as "Lieber Kyborg als Göttin: Für eine sozialistisch-feministische Unterwanderung der Gentechnologie," in Bernd-Peter Lange and Anna Marie Stuby, eds. (Berlin: Argument-Sonderband 105, 1984), pp. 66–84. The cyborg manifesto grew from "New Machines, New Bodies, New Communities: Political Dilemmas of a Cyborg Feminist," The Scholar and the Feminist X: The Question of Technology Conference, April 1983.

The people associated with the History of Consciousness Board of University of California, Santa Cruz, have had an enormous influence on this essay, so that it feels collectively authored more than most, although those I cite may not recognize their ideas. In particular, members of graduate and undergraduate feminist theory, science and politics, and theory and methods courses have contributed to the cyborg manifesto. Particular debts here are due Hilary Klein ("Marxism, Psychoanalysis, and Mother Nature"); Paul Edwards ("Border Wars: The Science and Politics of Artificial Intelligence"); Lisa Lowe ("Julia Kristeva's *Des Chinoises:* Representing Cultural and Sexual Others"); Jim Clifford, "On Ethnographic Allegory," in James Clifford and George E. Marcus, eds., *Writing Culture, the Poetics and Politics of Ethnography* (University of California Press, 1985), pp. 98–121.

Parts of the chapter were my contribution to a collectively developed session, Poetic Tools and Political Bodies: Feminist Approaches to High Technology Culture, 1984 California American Studies Association, with History of Consciousness graduate students Zoe Soufoulis, "Jupiter Space"; Katie King, "The Pleasures of Repetition and the Limits of Identification in Feminist Science Fiction: Reimaginations of the Body after the Cyborg"; and Chela Sandoval, "The Construction of Subjectivity and Oppositional Consciousness in Feminist Film and Video." Sandoval's theory of oppositional consciousness was published as "Women Respond to Racism: A Report on the National Women's Studies Association Conference," Center for Third World Organizing, Oakland, California, n.d. For Sofoulis's semiotic–psychoanalytic readings of nuclear culture, see Z. Sofia, "Exterminating Fetuses: Abortion, Disarmament and the Sexo-Semiotics of Extraterrestrialism," Nuclear Criticism issue, *Diacritics,* Vol 14, No. 2, 1984, pp. 47–59. King's manuscripts ("Questioning Tradition: Canon Formation and the Veiling of Power"; "Gender and Genre: Reading the Science Fiction of Joanna Russ"; "Varley's Titan and Wizard: Feminist Parodies of Nature, Culture, and Hardware") deeply inform the cyborg manifesto.

Barbara Epstein, Jeff Escoffier, Rusten Hogness, and Jaye Miler gave extensive discussion and editorial help. Members of the Silicon Valley Research Project of the University of California, Santa Cruz and participants in conferences and workshops sponsored by SVRP (Silicon Valley Research Project) have been very important, especially Rick Gordon, Linda Kimball, Nancy Snyder, Langdon Winner, Judith Stacey, Linda Lim, Patricia Fernandez-Kelly, and Judith Gregory. Finally, I want to thank Nancy Hartsock for years of friendship and discussion on feminist theory and feminist science fiction. I also thank Elizabeth Bird for my favorite political button: Cyborgs for Earthly Survival.

CONTESTING FOUNDATIONS:
THE CRISIS OF REPRESENTATION

- Steven Seidman, *The end of sociological theory*
- Norma Alarcón, *The theoretical subjects(s) of* This Bridge Called My Back *and Anglo-American feminism*
- Judith Butler, *Contingent foundations: Feminism and the question of postmodernism*
- Renato Rosaldo, *Subjectivity in social analysis*

6

The end of sociological theory
Steven Seidman

Sociological theory has gone astray. It has lost most of its social and intellectual importance; it is disengaged from the conflicts and public debates that have nourished it in the past; it has turned inward and is largely self-referential. Sociological theory today is produced and consumed almost exclusively by sociological theorists.[1] Its social and intellectual insularity accounts for the almost permanent sense of crisis and malaise that surrounds contemporary sociological theory. This distressing condition originates, in part, from its central project: the quest for foundations and for a totalizing theory of society.[2]

To revitalize sociological theory requires that we renounce scientism – that is, the increasingly absurd claim to speak the Truth, to be an epistemically privileged discourse. We must relinquish our quest for foundations or the search for the one correct or grounded set of premises, conceptual strategy, and explanation. Sociological theory will be revitalized if and when it becomes "social theory." My critique of sociological theory and advocacy of social theory as a social narrative with a moral intent will be advanced from the standpoint of postmodernism.[3]

Anticipating the end of sociological theory entails renouncing the millennial social hopes that have been at the center of modernist sociological theory.[4] Postmodernism carries no promise of liberation – of a society

Reprinted with permission of the American Sociological Association.
1. Discontent about the state of sociological theory is becoming more and more evident. See, for example, Geertz (1983), Sica (1989), Skocpol (1986), and Turner and Wardell (1986).
2. For an argument exploring the institutional sources or intellectual distress among the disciplines, see Jacoby (1987).
3. For useful discussions of postmodernism, especially as it pertains to social theory, see Bauman (1988), Brown (1990), Kellner (1988), Kroker and Cook (1986), Lash (1985, 1988), Lemert (1991), Nicholson (1990), and Seidman and Wagner (1991).
4. This antimillennial theme is prominent in Baudrillard (1975, 1981), Foucault (1978, 1980), and Lyotard (1984).

free of domination. Postmodernism gives up the modernist idol of human emancipation in favor of deconstructing false closure, prying open present and future social possibilities, detecting fluidity and porousness in forms of life where hegemonic discourses posit closure and a frozen order. The hope of a great transformation is replaced by the more modest aspiration of a relentless defense of immediate, local pleasures and struggles for justice. Postmodernism offers the possibility of a social analysis that takes seriously the history of cruelty and constraint in Western modernity without surrendering to the retreat from criticalness that characterizes much current conservative and liberal social thought.

Sociological theory/social theory: A difference that matters

I'd like to posit a distinction between social theory and sociological theory. Social theories typically take the form of broad social narratives. They relate stories of origin and development, tales of crisis, decline, or progress. Social theories are typically closely connected to contemporary social conflicts and public debates. These narratives aim not only to clarify an event or a social configuration but also to shape its outcome – perhaps by legitimating one outcome or imbuing certain actors, actions, and institutions with historical importance while attributing to other social forces malicious, demonic qualities. Social theory relates moral tales that have practical significance; they embody the will to shape history. Marx wrote *The Communist Manifesto* and the successive drafts of his critique of political economy in response to current social conflicts, as a practical intervention for the purpose of effecting change – to wit, contributing to the transformation of wage labor into the proletariat (i.e., into self-identified members of the working class antagonistic to capitalism). Weber wrote the *The Protestant Ethic and the Spirit of Capitalism* in part to stimulate the building of a politicized German middle class willing to seize power. Durkheim wrote *The Division of Labor in Society* in order to legitimate and shape the Third Republic against attacks from the right and the left. Social theories might be written to represent the truth of social matters, but they arise out of ongoing contemporary conflicts and aim to affect them. Their moral intent is never far from the surface. They are typically evaluated in terms of their moral, social, and political significance.

Sociological theory, by contrast, intends to uncover a logic of society; it aims to discover the one true vocabulary that mirrors the social universe. Sociological theorists typically claim that their ideas arise out of humanity's self-reflection as social beings. They position theory in relation to a legacy of social discourse, as if theorizing were simply humanity's continuous dialogue on "the social." Sociological theorists aim to abstract from current social conflicts to reflect on the conditions of society everywhere, to articulate the language of social action, conflict, and change in general. They seek to find a universal language, a conceptual casuistry that can assess the truth of all social languages. Sociological theory aims to denude itself of its contextual embeddedness; to articulate humanity's universal condition. Insofar as sociological theory speaks the language of particularity, it is said to have failed. It must elevate itself to the universal, to the level of theoretical logics or central problems or to the study of social laws or the structure of social action. The intent of sociological theorists is to add to the stock of human knowledge in the hope that this will bring enlightenment and social progress.

The story I wish to tell is not that of a movement from social theory to sociological theory. Social theory and sociological theory, at least since the eighteenth century, have lived side by side and frequently have been intertwined. Marx wrote social theory but also sociological theory; Weber may have penned *The Protestant Ethic,* but he also wrote methodological essays that attempted to offer ultimate grounds for his conceptual strategies. Durkheim wrote *The Division of Labor in Society* but also *The Rules of Sociological Method,* which set out a logic of sociology; Parsons wrote *The Structure of Social Action* but also *The American University.* Although sociological and social theory intermingle in the history of social thought, I want to suggest that within the discipline of sociology, especially since the post–World War II period, the emphasis has been on sociological theory. Indeed, social theory is often devalued; it is described as ideological. Sociological theorists are encouraged to do sociological theory, not social theory. In the discipline of sociology, sociological theorists stake their claim to prestige and privilege on their ability to produce new analytic approaches to supposedly universal problems. I want to claim further that the hegemony of sociological theory within sociology has contributed to rendering sociological theorists insular and making their products – theories – socially and intellectually obscure and irrelevant to virtually everyone except other theorists. As sociological theorists have moved away from social theory, they have contributed to the enfeeblement of public moral and political debate.

A critique of sociological theory as a foundationalist discourse

Many sociological theorists have accepted a concept of theory as a foundational discourse (Seidman 1989, 1990, 1991a, 1991b). We have come to define our principal task as providing foundations for sociology. This entails giving ultimate reasons why sociology should adopt a specific conceptual strategy. We have assigned ourselves the task of defining and defending the basic premises, concepts, and explanatory models of sociology. We have assumed the role of resolving disciplinary disputes and conceptual conflicts by presuming to be able to discover a universal epistemic rationale that provides objective, value-neutral standards of conflict resolution. Sociological theorists have stepped forward as the virtual police of the sociological mind. In the guise of maintaining rationality and safeguarding intellectual and social progress, we have proposed to legislate codes of disciplinary order by providing a kind of epistemological casuistry that can serve as a general guide to conceptual decision making.

The quest for foundations has rendered sociological theory a metatheoretical discourse. Its disputes are increasingly self-referential and epistemological. Theory discussions have little bearing on major social conflicts and political struggles or on important public debates over current social affairs. Sociological theory has diminished impact on crucial public texts of social commentary, criticism, and analysis. And if I'm not mistaken, sociological theory functions as little more than a legitimating rhetoric for ongoing research programs and empirical analyses. Theory texts and conferences are preoccupied with foundational disputes regarding the logic of the social sciences, the respective merits of a conflict versus an order paradigm, the nature of social action and order, the conceptual link between agency and structure or a micro and macro level of analysis, the problem of integrating structural with cultural analysis, and so on. These discussions are rehearsed endlessly and use a short list of rhetorical tropes, such as the appeal to classic texts or to the higher values of humanism or scientism, to legitimate a favored vocabulary or conceptual strategy.

Has this discursive proliferation produced a centered, evolving vital theoretical tradition? No. Instead of a concentrated, productive discourse focused on a limited set of problems that exhibits sustained elaboration, we find a dispersed, discursive clamoring that covers a wide assortment of ever-changing issues in a dazzling diversity of languages. These vocabularies of social discourse typically imply divergent (if not incommensurable) philosophical, moral, and ideological standpoints. In this discursive clamor there is virtually no standardization of language, no agreement on what are central problems or standards of evaluation. There is a virtual babble of different vocabularies addressing a heterogeneous cluster of changing disputes. Indeed, a good deal of this discourse involves struggles to authorize a particular dispute or a particular conceptual vocabulary or a specific justificatory rationale (e.g., empirical adequacy or explanatory comprehensiveness). Typically, a text backed by a social network briefly captures the attention of some of the principal players in the field. A discussion ensues; local skirmishes break out in journals, books, and conferences; a particular vocabulary may acquire salience among sociological theorists. Such coherence, however, is typically short-lived because the field is always divided, and rival theorists with their own agendas and networks clamor for recognition and reward. This metatheoretical proliferation has yielded little, if any, conceptual order or progress.

Foundational disputes to date have admitted of little, if any, consensus. Why? Because the criteria that guide conceptual decisions seem, in the end, local, heterogeneous, and perhaps ultimately incommensurable. How do "we" judge or prioritize epistemic standards that include empirical adequacy, explanatory comprehensiveness, quantitative precision, empirical predictability, logical coherence, conceptual economy, aesthetic appeal, practical efficacy, and moral acceptability? And how do "we" agree on what theoretical foundations might look like? What would need to be included (or excluded, for that matter)? What would closure or totalization or comprehensiveness look like (Turner 1991)? And what, after all, should serve here as a standard of validity? Finally, who is to make these decisions? Who, in other words, is the "we" that legislates justificatory strategies?

If one conclusion to date seems painstakingly clear, even if resisted equally painstakingly, it is that metatheoretical disputes do not appear to be resolvable by appeals to abstract or formal reason. Rival ontological and epistemological claims seem meaningful only insofar as they are tied to practical interests or specific forms of life. Yet if this is true – and I am claiming only that from my historical and social vantage point this point seems compelling – then foundational discourses can hardly escape being local and ethnocentric. This point suggests that the search for ultimate or universal grounds for our conceptual strategies should be abandoned in favor of local, pragmatic justifications.

The notion that foundational discourses cannot avoid being local and ethnocentric is pivotal to what has come to be called postmodernism (Rorty 1979, 1982, 1991). Postmodernists have evoked the suspicion that the products of the human studies – concepts, explanations, theories – bear the imprint of the particular prejudices and interests of their creators. This suspicion may be posed as follows: How can a knowing subject, who has particular interests and prejudices by virtue of living in a specific society at a particular historical juncture and occupying a specific social position defined by his or her class, gender, race, sexual orientation, and ethnic and religious status, produce concepts, explanations, and standards of validity that are universally valid? How can we both assert that humans are constituted by their particular sociohistorical circumstances and also claim that they can escape their embeddedness by creating non-local, universally valid concepts and standards? How can we escape the suspicion that every move by culturally bound agents to generalize their conceptual strategy is not simply an effort to impose particular, local prejudices on others?

Postmodernism elicits the suspicion that science is tied to the project of Western modernity and to a multiplicity of more local, more specific struggles around class, status, gender, sexuality, race, and so on. Thus feminists have not only documented the androcentric bias of sociology but have analyzed critically the politics of science in its normative constructions of femininity and womanhood (e.g., Andersen 1983; Harding 1986; Harding and Hintikka 1983; Jagger and Bordo 1989; Keller 1985; Millman and Kanter 1975; Smith 1979, 1989; Westcott 1979). Because this relentless epistemological suspicion is turned against disciplinary discourses by, say, feminists, and because the same trope is rehearsed among African-Americans, gay men and lesbians, Latinos, Asians, the differently abled and so on, no social discourse can escape the doubt that its claims to truth are tied to and yet mask an ongoing social interest to shape the course of history. Once the veil of epistemic privilege is torn away by postmodernists, science appears as a social force enmeshed in particular cultural and power struggles. The claim to truth, as Foucault has proposed, is inextricably an act of power – a will to form humanity.

This epistemic suspicion is at the core of postmodernism. Postmodernists challenge the charge of theory as a foundational discourse. The postmodern critique does not deny the possibility of success in the quest for foundations. I urge only that from the standpoint of the history of such foundational efforts, and from the vantage point of modern consciousness, which itself has generated this relentless epistemic doubt, this project does not seem compelling or credible.

Aside from this epistemic doubt, there are practical and moral reasons to consider in assessing the value of the foundational project. Postmodernists view such discourses as exhibiting a bad faith: concealed in the will to truth is a will to power. To claim that there are universal and objective reasons to warrant a social discourse, to claim that a discourse speaks the language of truth, is to privilege that discourse, its carriers, and its social agenda. Insofar as we believe that social discourses are social practices which, like other social forces, shape social life and history, privileging a discourse as true authorizes its social values and agenda (Brown 1990).

Social discourses, especially the broad social narratives of development produced by sociological theorists, but also the specialized discourses produced by demographers, criminologists, organizational sociologists, and so on, shape the social world by creating normative frameworks of racial, gender, sexual, national, and other types of identity, social order, and institutional functioning that carry the intellectual and social authority of science. A discourse that bears the stamp of scientific knowledge gives its normative concepts of identity and order an authority while discrediting the social agendas produced by other (scientific and nonscientific) discourses. To claim to have discovered the true language of society delegitimates rival paradigms – now described as merely ideological or, at best, as precursors – and their social agendas and carriers. It entails a demand to marginalize or withdraw privilege and its rewards from these rivals. Indeed, to claim epistemic privilege for a social discourse is to demand social authority not only for its social agenda but also for its producers and carriers. To assert that a social discourse speaks a universally valid language of truth confers legitimacy on its social values and its carriers. In a word, the politics of epistemology is bound up with social struggles to shape history.

When one appeals solely to the truth of a discourse to authorize it intellectually and socially, one represses reflection on its practical-moral meaning and its social consequences. A discourse that justifies itself solely by epistemic appeals will not be compelled to defend its conceptual decisions on moral and political grounds. The practical and moral significance of the discourse will go unattended or else will be considered only in the most cursory way. On the other hand, if theorists – as postmodernists – believe that all appeals to universal standards or justificatory strategies are not ultimately compelling, they will be forced to offer "local" moral, social, and political reasons for their conceptual decisions. Disputes between rival theories or conceptual strategies would not concern epistemic first principles – e.g., individualism versus holism, materialism versus idealism, micro-versus macro-level analysis, instrumental versus normative concepts of action and order. Instead theorists would argue about the intellectual, social, moral, and political consequences of choosing one conceptual strategy or another.

A pragmatic turn has distinct advantages. It expands the number of parties who may participate more or less as equals in a debate about society. Where a discourse is redeemed ultimately by metatheoretical appeals, experts step forward as the authorities. This situation contributes to the enfeeblement of a vital public realm of moral and political debate because social questions are deemed the domain of experts. By contrast, when a discourse is judged by its practical consequences or its moral implications, more citizens are qualified to assess it by considering its social and moral implications. A pragmatic move, in principle, implies an active, politically engaged citizenry participating in a democratic public realm.

Postmodernism contests a representational concept of science whose legitimacy hinges on an increasingly cynical belief in science's enlightening and empowering role. This Enlightenment legitimation obscures the social entanglement of the disciplines and permits them to abandon moral responsibility for their own social efficacy. Postmodernism underscores the practical and moral character of science. It sees the disciplines as implicated in heterogeneous struggles around gender, race, sexuality, the body, and the mind, to shape humanity.

The postmodern alternative: Social narrative with a moral intent

Foundational theorizing is by no means a product of the social scientific disciplines. The attempt to resolve conceptual disputes or to authorize a particular conceptual strategy by appealing to some presumably universal or objective justification has accompanied modern social thought. Yet the institutionalization of social science and the phenomenal growth of the disciplines in the twentieth century has contributed greatly to the rise of theory specialists whose expertise revolves around metatheoretical or foundational concerns. Although foundational discourses may play a beneficial role at certain sociohistorical junctures (e.g., during periods of epochal transition, such as the 18th century), my view is that today they contribute to the social and intellectual insularity and irrelevance of much sociological theory. Moreover, I have voiced an epistemological doubt about the likely success of the foundational project. This suspicion has been a systematic feature of modern Western social consciousness at least since Marx's time. Postmodernism evokes this suspicion as current.

From a postmodern perspective, justifications of conceptual strategies appear to be unable to avoid a local, ethnocentric character. This is not an argument denying the possibility of foundations; I offer no proof of the impossibility of achieving a grounded social discourse. My epistemic doubt is local, if you will. It stems from my reflection on the historical failure of foundational efforts; it reflects a sympathy for the relentless epistemic doubt generated by modernist social science itself. If a genius comes along tomorrow and proves to the satisfaction of the social scientific community that he or she has succeeded in providing foundations, I will relinquish my standpoint. Until then, however, I propose that we renounce the quest for foundations in favor of local rationales for our conceptual strategies. Instead of appealing to absolutist justifications, instead of constructing theoretical logics and epistemic casuistries to justify a conceptual strategy, to lift them out of contextual embeddedness and elevate them to the realm of universal truths, I propose that we be satisfied with local, pragmatic rationales for our conceptual approaches. Instead of asking what is the nature of reality or knowledge in the face of conflicting conceptual strategies – and therefore going metatheoretical – I suggest we evaluate conflicting perspectives by asking what are their intellectual, social, moral, and political consequences. Does a conceptual strategy promote precision or conceptual economy? Does it enhance empirical predictability? What social values or forms of life does it promote? Does it lead to relevant policy-related information? Postmodern justifications shift the debate from that of Truth and abstract rationality to that of social and intellectual consequences.

The quest for foundations has been connected intimately to the project of creating a general theory (Seidman and Wagner 1991). Many modern social theorists have sought to elaborate an overarching totalizing conceptual framework that would be true for all times and all places. The search for the one right vocabulary or language that would mirror the social world, that would uncover the essential structures and dynamics or laws of society, has been integral to sociological theory. In *The German Ideology,* Marx and Engels believed that they had uncovered a universally valid language of history and society. In their view, the categories of labor, mode of production, class, and class conflict crystallized what they considered to be a general theory that captured the essential structure and dynamics of history. Durkheim proposed in *The Division of Labor in Society* and in *The Rules of the Sociological Method* the dual categories of collective representations and social morphology as the conceptual basis for a universal theory of society; Parsons wrote *The Structure of Social Action* and *The Social System* to reveal a universal set of premises and concepts that would unify and guide all social inquiry. This quest to discover the one true language of the social world, to uncover its laws, general structure, and universal logic, has been an abiding aim of sociological theory.

The quest for a totalizing general theory, in my view, is misguided. My reasoning parallels my reservations about foundationalism. General theories have not succeeded; their basic premises, concepts, and explanatory models, along with their metatheoretical rationales, consistently have been shown to be local, ethnocentric projections (Turner and Wardell 1986). The project of general theory has pushed theorists into the realm of metatheory as theorists attempt to specify an epistemic rationale to resolve conceptual or paradigm disputes; it has isolated theorists from vital ongoing research programs and empirical analyses; the quest for foundations and for a totalizing theory has marginalized theorists in regard to the major social events and public debates of the times. Moreover, when concepts are stretched to cover all times and places or to be socially inclusive, they become so contentless as to lose whatever explanatory value they have. These flat, contentless general categories seem inevitably to ignore or repress social differences (Nicholson 1991). For example, the categories of labor, mode of production, or class conflict may be useful in explaining nineteenth-century England, but are much less so, I think, in explaining nineteenth-century France or Germany or the United States and are virtually irrelevant for societies that are more kinship-centered or politically centered (e.g., Balbus 1982; Baudrillard 1975; Habermas 1977, 1984, 1987; Nicholson 1986; Rubin 1975).

If social theorists renounce the project of foundationalism and the quest for general theories, as I am recommending, what's left for us? Undoubtedly some theorists will want to argue that a more modest version of the project of general theory is still feasible, such as Merton's middle range theories or some variant, say, in the mold of Skocpol's *States and Social Revolution*. I won't dispute here the value of these alternatives, although I believe that they remain tied too closely to scientism and the modernist ideology of enlightenment and progress that have been suspect for decades. Instead I wish to propose that when theorists abandon the foundationalist project in the broad sense – elaborating general theories and principles of justification – what they have left is social theory as social narrative. When we strip away the foundationalist aspects of Marx's texts, what remain are stories of social development and crisis; when we purge Durkheim's *Division of Labor in Society* of its foundationalist claims, we have a tale of the development of Western modernity. The same applies to Parsons, Luhmann, Munch, or Habermas. I am not recommending that we simply return to the grand stories of social evolution from Condorcet to Habermas. If social theory is to return to its function as social narrative, I believe it must be a narrative of a different sort than those of the great modernists. In the remainder of this section, I will outline briefly one version of a postmodern social narrative.[5]

The postmodern social narrative I advocate is event-based and therefore careful about its temporal and spatial boundaries. By event-based, I mean that the primary reference points of postmodern narratives are major social conflicts or developments. As event-based narratives, postmodern social analyses also would be densely contextual. Social events always occur in a particular time and place, related to both contemporary and past developments in a specific social space.

The grand narratives of the great modernist social theorists responded to the major events of the day but typically disregarded their temporal and spatial settings. Instead of locating events in their specific sociohistorical setting, these grand narratives framed events as world historical and evolved stories of the course of Western, if not human, history. Instead of

5. Although I focus on postmodern assumptions about agency, history, and freedom that I believe strongly should guide social narratives, my understanding of narrative has profited from the works of Gennette (1980), Mink (1978), Ricoeur (1984), and White (1973).

telling the story of capitalism or secularization in, say, England or Italy, they analyzed these events as part of a sketch of "Western" or human development. Thus, instead of analyzing the unique industrial development of England or Germany, which had "capitalistic" aspects, by being attentive to their dramatic differences and singular histories, Marx proposed a theory of capitalism that purported to uncover essential, uniform processes in all "capitalist" social formations. His "theory of capitalism" outlined a history of Western and ultimately human development that disregarded the specificity of particular "Western" and non-Western societies. To be sure, Marx counseled that the uniform operation of capitalism would vary in different societies even if the essential dynamics and direction of history were set by the "laws of capitalism." Marx assumed that the fact that different societies have divergent national traditions, geopolitical positions, and political, cultural, familial-kinship, gender, racial, and ethnic structures would not seriously challenge the utility of his model of capitalism as setting out the essential dynamics and direction of human history.

In my view, this was a serious mistake. Even if one takes Marx's model of capitalism to be of some utility for analyzing nineteenth-century dynamics of socioeconomic change, I believe that the immense sociohistorical differences among European and Anglo-American societies and between them and non-Western societies would affect seriously the form and functioning of industrializing dynamics. Individual societies evolve their own unique configurations and historical trajectories, which are best analyzed historically, not from the heights of general theory.

The Eurocentrism of these grand narratives has been exposed thoroughly (e.g., Baudrillard 1975). Human history in these modernist tales really meant Western history. Non-Western societies were relegated to a marginal position in past, present, and future history; their fate was presumed to be tied to that of Europe and the United States. The West, in these stories, was the principal agent of history; it showed the future to all of humanity. Behind this conceit was the arrogance of the western theorists, with their claim that the western breakthrough to "modernity" carried world historical significance. The great modernists claimed not only that Western modernity unleashed processes which would have world impact, but also that modernization contained universally valid forms of life (e.g., science, bureaucracy, socialism, organic solidarity, secularism). Not much effort is required to see that behind the aggrandizing intellectualism of the modernists were the expansionist politics of the age of colonialism.

These grand narratives seem to bear the mark of their own national origin. They contain an element of national chauvinism. Modernists projected their own nations' unique development and conflicts onto the globe as if their particular pattern were of world historical importance. These totalizing conceptual strategies that attempted to sketch a world historical story seem today extremely naive and misguided. The grand narratives of industrialization, modernization, secularization, democratization, these sweeping stories that presume to uncover a uniform social process in a multitude of different societies, these stories with their simplistic binary schemes (e.g., Tonnies's *Gemeinschaft* to *Gesellschaft,* Durkheim's mechanical to organic solidarity) which purport to relate a story of change over hundreds of years, should be abandoned. They repress important differences between societies; they perpetuate Western-world hegemonic aspirations and national chauvinistic wishes; they are, in short, little more than myths that aim to authorize certain social patterns.

Although I believe we should abandon the great modernist narratives, general stories are still needed. This is so because in all societies there occur certain events and developments that prompt highly charged social, moral, and political conflicts. The various parties to these conflicts frequently place them in broad conceptual or narrative frameworks. In order to imbue an event with national moral and political significance or to legitimate a specific social agenda, advocates elaborate social narratives that link the event to the larger history and fate of their society or humanity. This process is clear, for example, in the case of the AIDS epidemic: the spread of HIV in the United States occasioned social discourses that relate a fairly broad story of the failure of the "sexual revolution" or, indeed, the failure of a liberal, permissive society (Seidman 1988; Sontag 1988; Watney 1987). The construction of broad social narratives by theorists still has an important role.

These narratives offer alternative images of the past, present, and future; they can present critical alternatives to current dominant images; they can provide symbolic cultural resources on which groups can draw in order to redefine themselves, their social situation, and their possible future. I consider paradigmatic, for example, texts such as Linda Gordon's (1977) *Woman's Body, Woman's Right,* which offered a novel feminist interpretation of the conflict over birth control; Jeffrey Weeks's (1977) *Coming Out: Homosexual Politics in Great Britain,* which proposed a new social and historical reading of homosexuality; Barbara Ehrenreich's and Deirdre English's *For Her Own Good* (1979) or Robert Bellah's *The Broken Covenant* (1975). These texts offer redescriptions of the present that open up new ways of defining the present and the future (Seidman 1991b). Broad social narratives that cover large chunks of time and space are still important.

Postmodern social narratives will depart from those of the great modernists in an additional way: such narratives abandon the centrality of the ideas of progress or decadence that have served as the unifying themes of modernist social thought. From *philosophes* like Condorcet or Turgot to Comte, Marx, Durkheim, and Parsons, these stories of social development are little more than variations of the motif of human advancement. They amount to millennial, salvationist tales. In reaction to the stories of the enlighteners, there appeared the great tales of lament or decadence by Rousseau, Bonald, Schiller, Weber, Simmel, Spengler, Adorno, and Horkheimer. Both the great modernist narratives of progress and the counterenlightenment motif of decadence are decidedly Eurocentric. In all cases the site of the fateful struggles of humanity is the West. Indeed, national histories are important in these grand narratives only insofar as they exhibit a pattern of progress or decadence. These stories typically disregard the enormous social complexities and heterogeneous struggles and strains within a specific society at a specific time. They have one story to tell, which they rehearse relentlessly on a national and world historical scale. They utterly fail to grasp the multisided, heterogeneous, morally ambiguous social currents and strains that make up the life of any society. In the end they amount to little more than rhetorics of national and Eurocentric chauvinism or rhetorics of world rejection.

The great modernist stories of progress or decadence almost always operate with one-dimensional notions of domination and liberation. Ignoring complex conflicts and power dynamics with their ambiguous calculus of gains and losses, benefits and costs, pleasure and pain, these grand narratives frame history and social conflicts in grossly simplifying millennial or apocalyptic images. For these modernists, the dynamics of domination are merely a matter of freedom lost or gained; whole strata, indeed whole epochs, are described as unfree, alienated, or repressed; large chunks of time are regarded as periods of darkness or light, freedom or tyranny. History is thought to play out a unidimensional human drama revolving around the human quest for liberation against the forces of domination.

These images of liberation and domination are often tied to essentialist concepts of the human subject.[6] The modernists presuppose a notion of humanity as having a fixed, unchanging identity and dynamic regardless of historical variation and social considerations such as gender, race, ethnicity, class, or sexual orientation. This unified human subject is thought to be in a constant struggle for freedom. The forces of oppression, in this tale, aim to deny humanity's quest for liberation. Human freedom is identified with the realization of human nature. Most modernist social narratives are underpinned by these notions of progress, liberation, domination, the human subject who is oppressed and striving for emancipation. As an obvious example, in the *1844 Manuscripts* Marx relates

6. The discussion of essentialism is especially vigorous among feminists and gay intellectuals. See, for example, Butler (1990), Epstein (1987), Foucault (1978), Katz (1983), Spelman (1989), Weeks (1985), Vance (1984), and Young (1991).

a story of the struggle of humanity to actualize its full nature by over-coming an alienated human condition. Although this tale of humanity's struggle for self-realization is later transfigured into the struggle of the working class to overcome capitalist oppression, there is no change in the focus on a grand world historical drama in which "humanity" – now in the guise of the working class – resists oppression to achieve a state of freedom. The same symbolic configuration reappears in the more con-temporary social discourses of the black liberationist, women's, and gay movements. In all these movements, a world historical drama is depicted, involving humanity's struggle to overcome a state of domination to achieve liberation.

The problem with this discursive strategy relates not only to the short-comings of the categories of progress, to the flattened-out concepts of domination and liberation, as I've stated already, but also to the concept of the human subject that is built into these discourses. Although Marx-ists, feminists, or gay liberationists may have abandoned the essentialist strategy of speaking of humanity as if "humanity" referred to a fixed, un-changing essence across all times and places, they continue to appeal to the agency of women, blacks, homosexuals, or the working class. Yet these categories are no more fixed or uniform in their meaning than the concept of humanity. Without rehearsing an argument that is now being played out with a vengeance among people of color, feminists, and gay and lesbian intellectuals, I believe that the language of agency, whether that of womanhood or of the working class, is viewed by many parties to these debates as normative (e.g., Spelman 1988).

For example, postmodern feminists have criticized the essentialist dis-course of gender – both androcentric and gynocentric – that posits a bipolar gender order composed of a fixed, universal "man" and "woman." According to these postmodernists, such agentic concepts are understood as social constructions in which the discourse of gender, in-cluding the feminist discourse, is itself a part of the will to shape a gen-dered human order. The discourse of gender is tied to ongoing struggles to assign gender identities and social roles to human bodies. Womanhood and manhood are seen as neither a natural fact – nor a settled social fact but as part of a ceaseless, contested struggle among various groups to es-tablish a gender ordering of human affairs.7 Therefore those who appeal to the agency of women or homosexuals or African-Americans intend to become part of the clamor of voices and interests struggling to shape a system of identity, normative order, and power. Discourses that use cat-

7. Regarding the claim that gender is a site of normative conflict among feminists, see Butler (1990) and the essays collected in Nicholson (1990). A construc-tionist notion of gender underlies a good deal of the new feminist social his-tory. See, for example, Cott (1977), Ryan (1979), and Smith-Rosenberg (1985).

egories such as woman, man, gay, black American, and white American need to be seen as social forces embodying the will to shape a gender, racial, and sexual order; they seek to inscribe in our bodies specific desires, needs, expectations, and social identities.

My point is not that such categories of agency should not be used but that we need, first of all, to recognize their socially efficacious character. Although they are attached to a discourse of truth, they are inextricably entangled in the very constitution of identities, normative orders, and power relations. Second, we must be sharply aware that just as there is no "humanity" which acts as an agent (because humans exist always as particular national or tribal, gendered or aged, religious or ethnic beings), the same is true with respect to "women" or "blacks" or "homosexuals." These categories do not have a uniform meaning and social import across different societies or even within any given society. For example, same-sex intimacies do not carry an essentially fixed and common meaning across different histories. As many historians have argued compellingly, the concept of homosexuality and the homosexual exhibit historically and culturally specific meanings that cannot be applied to all experiences of same-sex intimacies (e.g., Katz 1983; Seidman 1991b; Weeks 1977; Williams 1986). Moreover, even within a given society at a specific historical juncture, these categories of identity and agency (woman, man, homosexual, black American) not only acquire diverse meanings but do so, in part, because categories of identity are always multiple and intersect in highly idiosyncratic and diverse ways. Just as individuals are not simply instances of the abstraction "humanity," we are not embodiments of the abstractions of woman or man. Even within the contemporary United States, "woman" does not have a uniform meaning. It varies by ethnic, racial, religious, or class status as well as by factors relating to sexual orientation, age, or geographical/regional characteristics. There is no reason to believe that a middle-class southern heterosexual Methodist woman will share a common experience or even common gender interests with a northern working-class Jewish lesbian. It is equally naive to assume that whatever gender commonalities they do share will override their divergent interests and values.

This argument suggests, of course, that the experience of oppression and liberation is not flat or unidimensional. Individuals are not simply oppressed or liberated. Just as an individual's identity mix is varied in innumerable ways, his or her experience of self as empowered or dis-empowered will be similarly varied and multidimensional. We need to shift from an essentialist language of self and agency to conceiving of the self as having multiple and contradictory identities, community affiliations, and social interests. Our social narratives should be attentive to this concept of multiple identities; our stories should replace the flat, unidimensional language of domination and liberation with the multivocal notion of multiple, local heterogeneous struggles and a many-sided experience of empowerment and disempowerment.

Insofar as postmodern social discourses are seen simply as narratives with all the rhetorical, aesthetic, moral, ideological, and philosophical aspects characteristic of all storytelling, their social role would have to be acknowledged explicitly. Postmodern social analyses amount to stories about society that carry moral, social, ideological, and perhaps directly political significance.

Postmodern social narratives would do more than acknowledge their moral and social character; they would take this moral dimension as a site for a more elaborated analysis. I believe that there are fruitful possibilities here for sociological theorists to shift their reflexive analytical focus from metatheoretical foundational concerns to practical-moral ones (cf. Bellah *et al.* 1985; Rosaldo 1989). In other words, I am urging that the effort which theorists have invested in foundational, general theorizing, an effort that has yielded so little and has cost us so dearly, be shifted in part to moral analysis.

Needless to say, I am not counseling a shift to foundational moral theory or to the search for universal values or standards of justification I wish to endorse a pragmatic, socially informed moral analysis (e.g., Seidman, 1992). From a postmodern pragmatic standpoint, it would not be sufficient simply to invoke general values (e.g., freedom, democracy, solidarity, order, material comfort, pleasure) or moral imperatives (e.g., that individuals should be treated with respect or dignity or should be treated as ends) either to justify or to criticize current social arrangements or to recommend changes. Social criticism must go beyond pointing to the deficiencies of current social realities from some general moral standpoint. It would be compelled to argue out its standpoint through an analysis that is socially informed and pragmatic. The social critic has a responsibility, it seems to me, not only to say what is wrong with current realities in some broad, abstract way but also to make his or her critique as specific as possible so as to make it socially relevant. Similarly, the critic should be compelled at least to outline in some detail the social changes desired and the consequences that would follow for the individual and society. Again, this process forces social criticism to be potentially socially useful to (say) policy makers, activists, and legislators. It also makes theorists more accountable for their criticisms.

Finally, insofar as the social critic cannot appeal to transcendent or universal moral standards to justify his or her moral standpoint, the critique must be justified by an appeal to local values or traditions. Lacking a transcendental move, the postmodern critic must be satisfied with local justifications of those social forms of life which he or she advocates. The justification perhaps will take the form of endorsing a specific social arrangement because it promotes particular social values that are held by specific communities. This kind of pragmatic moral argumentation must be informed by a sociological understanding that allows one to analyze the impact of proposed changes on individuals and society. For example, a postmodern feminist critique of gender arrangements should do more than document and criticize general inequalities and discrimination against women from a moral standpoint that values freedom and equality. It also should show what a gender order of equality in specific social domains would be like and what social impact such changes towards gender equality would have. In addition, feminist critique in a postmodern mode would appeal to local traditions, practices, and values to justify these changes.

Recognizing that all social narratives have a socially effective character, we would not try to purge them of this character but would try to acknowledge it and, indeed, to seize it as a fruitful source of an elaborated social reason. How so? Not, as I've said, by simply offering a general criticism or defense of social forms from the high ground of some abstract moral values or standpoint. And certainly not by trying to ground one's moral standpoint in an appeal to some objective universal element (e.g., nature, God, natural law). Rather, I have recommended a pragmatic, socially informed moral analysis in which the critic is compelled to defend social arrangements by analyzing their individual and social consequences in light of local traditions, values, and practices. The values of the community of which the critic is a part stand as the "ultimate" realm of moral appeal.

Theorists would become advocates. We would be advocates, however, of a slightly different sort from (say) public officials or social activists. Unlike the advocacy of these partisans, which typically might take the form of rhetorical, moral, or national appeals, the presentation of documents or data, or appeals to particular social interests, the advocacy of theorists would take the form of elaborated social and moral argumentation about consequences and social values. Like other partisans, we would be advocates for a way of life, but unlike them, we would be compelled to produce elaborated social and moral discourses. As theorists we would be in a role of encouraging moral public discussion; we would be catalysts for public moral and social debate. We would be advocates, but not narrow partisans or politicos. Our value would be both in providing socially informed analyses that would be useful to partisans and in promoting an uncoerced public moral discussion in the face of various partisans who repeatedly act to restrict such elaborated discourse. We would become defenders of an elaborated reason against the partisans of closure and orthodoxy, and of all those who try to circumvent open public moral debate by partisan or foundational appeals.

Conclusion

Sociological theory, in my view, has become insular and irrelevant to all but theory specialists. At least in part, this insularity is connected to a foundationalist project that has been at the center of modernist social thought. Ironically, the institutional successes of sociology have been accompanied by the growing obtuseness of sociological theory. Today, sociological theorists are largely entangled in metatheoretical disputes revolving around the search for a general, universal grounded science of society.

I have suggested some reasons why there is little likelihood of escaping this morass. Moreover, although the foundationist project may have had beneficial practical significance from the eighteenth century through the latter part of the nineteenth century in Europe and the United States, which was linked to legitimating "modernity" against its critics, it has lost most of its social benefits, at least in the contemporary United States and perhaps in many western European nations. The argument that the foundational project is important for the defense of certain desirable social arrangements can hardly be entertained seriously in view of the social and intellectual insularity of disciplinary theory. I don't doubt that the foundational, totalizing theoretical project might still be valuable for promoting a reflexive, critical reason. Yet the same intellectual and social values can be cultivated just as easily in the postmodern project.

Under the banner of postmodernism, I have pressed for a major reorientation of sociological theory. To be revitalized, theory must be reconnected in integral ways to ongoing national public moral and political debates and social conflicts. This vital tie between theorizing and public life accounts for the continuing attractiveness of classical social theory, but that connection has been broken. To reestablish that tie I have urged that sociological theory reaffirm a core concept of itself as a broad, synthetic narrative. I have proposed, however, that a postmodern social narrative should depart in certain important ways from those of the great modernists. Postmodernist narratives would be well advised to discard the configuration of core modernist concepts such as progress, domination, liberation, and humanity. The basic postmodern concepts will revolve around the notion of a self with multiple identities and group affiliations, which is entangled in heterogeneous struggles with multiple possibilities for empowerment.

Finally, postmodern narratives would acknowledge their practical-moral significance. Moral analysis would become a part of an elaborated social reason. Theorists would become advocates, abandoning the increasingly cynical, unbelievable guise of objective, value-neutral scientists. We would become advocates but not narrow partisans or activists. Our broader social significance would lie in encouraging unencumbered open public moral and social debate and in deepening the notion of public discourse. We would be a catalyst for the public to think seriously about moral and social concerns.

REFERENCES

Andersen, Margaret. 1983. *Thinking about Women.* New York: Macmillan.

Balbus, Isaac. 1982. *Marxism and Domination.* Princeton: Princeton University Press.

Baudrillard, Jean. 1975. *The Mirror of Production.* St. Louis: Telos.

 1981. *For a Critique of the Political Economy of the Sign.* St. Louis: Telos.

Bauman, Zygmunt. 1988. "Is There a Postmodern Sociology?" *Theory, Culture & Society* 5: 217–38.

Bellah, Robert. 1975. *The Broken Covenant.* New York: Seabury.

Bellah, Robert, Richard Madsen, William Sullivan, Ann Swidler, Steven Tipton. 1985. *Habits of the Heart.* Berkeley: University of California Press.

Brown, Richard. 1990. "Rhetoric, Textuality, and the Postmodern Turn." *Sociological Theory* 8 (Fall): 188–98.

Butler, Judith. 1990. *Gender Trouble.* New York: Routledge.

Cott, Nancy. 1977. *The Bonds of Womanhood.* New Haven: Yale University Press.

Ehrenreich, Barbara and Deidre English. 1979. *For Her Own Good.* New York: Doubleday.

Epstein, Steven. 1987. "Gay Politics, Ethnic Identity: The Limits of Social Constructionism." *Socialist Review* 17 (May-August): 9–54.

Foucault, Michel. 1978. *The History of Sexuality: An Introduction.* New York: Pantheon.

 1980. *Power/Knowledge.* New York: Pantheon.

Fraser, Nancy and Linda Nicholson. 1990. "Social Criticism without Philosophy: An Encounter between Feminism and Postmodernism." Pp. 19–38 in *Feminism/Postmodernism,* edited by Linda Nicholson. New York: Routledge.

Fuss, Diana. 1989. *Essentially Speaking.* New York: Routledge.

Geertz, Clifford. 1983. *Local Knowledge.* New York: Basic Books.

Gennette, Gerard. 1980. *Narrative Discourse.* Ithaca: Cornell University Press.

Gordon, Linda. 1977. *Woman's Body, Woman's Right.* New York: Penguin.

Habermas, Jürgen. 1977. *Communication and the Evolution of Society.* Boston: Beacon.

 1984. *The Theory of Communicative Action,* Vol. 1. Boston: Beacon.

 1987. *The Theory of Communicative Action,* Vol. 2. Boston: Beacon.

Harding, Sandra. 1986. *The Science Question in Feminism.* Ithaca: Cornell University Press.

Harding, Sandra and Merrill Hintikka (eds.). 1983. *Discovering Reality.* London: D. Reidel.

Jacoby, Russell. 1987. *The Last Intellectuals*. New York: Basic Books.

Jagger, Alison and Susan Bordo (eds.). 1989. *Gender/Body/Knowledge*. New Brunswick: Rutgers University Press.

Katz, Jonathan. 1983. *Gay/Lesbian Almanac*. New York: Harper & Row.

Keller, Evelyn Fox. 1985. *Science and Gender*. New Haven: Yale University Press.

Kellner, Douglas. 1988. "Postmodernism as Social Theory: Some Challenges and Problems." *Theory, Culture & Society* 5: 239–69.

Kroker, Arthur and David Cook. 1986. *The Postmodern Scene*. New York: St. Martin's.

Lash, Scott. 1985. "Postmodernity and Desire." *Theory & Society* 14: 1–33.

    1988. "Discourse or Figure? Postmodernism as a Regime of Signification." *Theory, Culture & Society* 5: 311–36.

Lemert, Charles. 1991. "Social Theory? Theoretical Play after Difference." Pp. 17–46 in *Postmodernism and Social Theory*, edited by Steven Seidman and David Wagner. Cambridge: Blackwell.

Lyotard, Jean-Francois. 1984. *The Postmodern Condition*. Minneapolis: University of Minnesota Press.

Millman, Marcia and Rosabeth Moss Kanter (eds.). 1975. *Another Voice*. New York: Anchor.

Mink, Louis. 1978. "Narrative Form as a Cognitive Instrument." Pp. 129–49 in *The Writing of History: Literary Form and Historical Understanding*, edited by Robert Canary and Henry Kozicki. Madison: University of Wisconsin Press.

Nicholson, Linda. 1986. *Gender and History*. New York: Columbia University Press.

    (ed.) 1990. *Feminism/Postmodernism*. New York: Routledge.

    1991. "On the Postmodern Barricades: Feminism, Politics and Theory." Pp. 82–100 in *Postmodernism & Social Theory*, edited by Steven Seidman and David Wagner. Cambridge: Blackwell.

Ricoeur, Paul. *Time and Narrative*. 1984. Chicago: University of Chicago Press. Vol. 1.

Riley, Denise. 1988. *Am I That Name? Feminism and the Category of Women in History*. New York: Macmillan.

Rorty, Richard. 1979. *Philosophy and the Mirror of Nature*. Princeton: Princeton University Press.

    1982. *Consequences of Pragmatism*. Minneapolis: University of Minnesota Press.

    1991. *Objectivity, Relativism, and Truth*. Cambridge: Cambridge University Press.

Rosaldo, Renato. 1989. *Culture and Truth*. Boston: Beacon.

Rubin, Gayle. 1975. "The Traffic in Women." Pp. 157–210 in *Towards an Anthropology of Women*, edited by Rayna Reiter. New York: Monthly Review.

Ryan, Mary. 1979. *Womanhood in America*. 2d ed. New York: New Viewpoints.

Scott, Joan, 1988. *Gender and the Politics of History*. New York: Columbia University Press.

Seidman, Steven. 1988. "Transfiguring Sexual Identity: AIDS & the Contemporary Construction of Homosexuality." *Social Text* 19/20 (Fall)): 187–205.

1989. "The Tedium of General Theory." *Contemporary Sociology* 18:.92–4.

1990. "Against Theory as a Foundationalist Discourse." *Perspectives* (Spring): pp. 1–3.

1991. "Theory as Social Narrative with a Moral Intent: A Postmodern Intervention." Pp. 47–81 in *Postmodernism & Social Theory,* edited by Steven Seidman and David Wagner. New York: Blackwell.

1991b. *Romantic Longings: Love in America, 1830–1980.* New York: Routledge.

1992. *Embattled Eros: Sexual Politics and Ethics in Contemporary America.* New York: Routledge.

Seidman, Steven and David Wagner (eds.). 1991. *Postmodernism, & Social Theory.* New York: Blackwell.

Sica, Alan. 1989. "Social Theory's Constituents." *The American Sociologist* 20: 227–41.

Skocpol, Theda. 1986. "The Dead End of Metatheory." *Contemporary Sociology* 16: 10–12.

Smith, Dorothy. 1979. "A Sociology for Women." Pp. 135–87 in *The Prism of Sex,* edited by Julia Sherman and Evelyn Torton. Madison: University of Wisconsin Press.

1989. "Sociological Theory: Methods of Writing Patriarchy." Pp. 34–64 in *Feminism and Sociological Theory,* edited by Ruth Wallace. Newbury Park, CA: Sage.

Smith-Rosenberg. Carroll. 1985. *Disorderly Conduct.* New York: Oxford University Press.

Sontag, Susan. 1988. *AIDS and Its Metaphors.* New York: Farrar, Straus, & Giroux.

Spelman, Elizabeth. 1989. *Inessential Women.* Boston: Beacon.

Turner, Stephen. 1981. "The Strange Life and Hard Times of the Concept of General Theory in Sociology: A Short History of Hope." Pp. 101–33 in *Postmodernism and Social Theory,* edited by Steven Seidman and David Wagner. New York: Blackwell.

Turner, Stephen and Mark Wardell, eds. 1986. *The Transition in Sociological Theory.* Boston: Allen & Unwin.

Vance, Carole (ed.). 1984. *Pleasure and Danger.* New York: Routledge.

Watney, Simon. 1987. *Policing Desire.* Minneapolis: University of Minnesota Press.

Weeks, Jeffrey. 1977. *Coming Out: Homosexual Politics in Britain, From the Nineteenth Century to the Present.* London: Quartet.

1985. *Sexuality and Its Discontents.* London: Routledge & Kegan Paul.

Westcott, Marcia. 1979. "Feminist Criticism of the Social Sciences." *Harvard Educational Review.* 49: pp. 422–30.

White, Hayden. 1973. *Metahistory.* Baltimore: Johns Hopkins University Press.

Williams, Walter. 1986. *The Spirit and the Flesh.* Boston: Beacon.

Young, Iris. 1991. *Justice and the Politics of Difference.* Princeton: Princeton University Press.

7

The theoretical subject(s) of This Bridge Called My Back *and Anglo-American feminism*

Norma Alarcón

This Bridge Called My Back: Writings by Radical Women of Color,
edited by Chicana writers Cherríe Moraga and Gloria Anzaldúa,* was intended as a collection of essays, poems, tales and testimonials that would
give voice to the contradictory experiences of "women of color." In fact,
the editors state:

> We are the colored in a white feminist movement.
> We are the feminists among the people of our culture.
> We are often the lesbians among the straight.[1]

By giving voice to such experiences, each according to her style, the editors and contributors believed they were developing a theory of subjectivity and culture that would demonstrate the considerable differences
between them and Anglo-American women, as well as between them and
Anglo-European men and men of their own culture. As speaking subjects
of a new discursive formation, many of *Bridge*'s writers were aware of the
displacement of their subjectivity across a multiplicity of discourses: fem-
inist/lesbian, nationalist, racial, socioeconomic, historical, etc. The pecu-
liarity of their displacement implies a multiplicity of positions from which
they are driven to grasp or understand themselves and their relations with
the real, in the Althusserian sense of the word.[2] *Bridge* writers, in part,
were aware that these positions are often incompatible or contradictory,
and others did not have access to the maze of discourses competing for
their body and voice. The self-conscious effort to reflect on their "flesh

---

* Hereafter cited as *Bridge,* the book has two editions. I use the second edition
published by Kitchen Table Press, 1983. The first edition was published by Persephone Press, 1981. Reprinted with permission of Aunt Lute Books.
1. Moraga and Anzaldúa, 23.
2. Louis Althusser, *Lenin and Philosophy and Other Essays,* Ben Brewster, tr.
(London: New Left Books, 1971).

140

and blood experiences to concretize a vision that can begin to heal our 'wounded knee' "[3] led many *Bridge* speakers to take a position in conflict with multiple intercultural and intracultural discursive interpretations in an effort to come to grips with "the many-headed demon of oppression."[4]

Since its publication in 1981, *Bridge* has had a diverse impact on Anglo-American feminist writings in the United States. Teresa de Lauretis, for example, claims that *Bridge* has contributed to a "shift in feminist consciousness,"[5] yet her explanation fails to clarify what the shift consists of and for whom. There is little doubt, however, that *Bridge,* along with the 1980s writings by many women of color in the United States, has problematized many a version of Anglo-American feminism, and has helped open the way for alternative feminist discourses and theories. Presently, however the impact among most Anglo-American theorists appears to be more cosmetic than not because, as Jane Flax has recently noted, "The modal 'person' in feminist theory still appears to be a self-sufficient individual adult."[6] This particular "modal person" corresponds to the female subject most admired in literature which Gayatri Chakravorty Spivak had characterized as one who "articulates herself in shifting relationship to . . . the constitution and 'interpellation' of the subject not only as individual but as 'individualist.' "[7] Consequently, the "native female" or "woman of color" can be excluded from the discourse of feminist theory. The "native female" – object of colonialism and racism – is excluded because, in Flax's terms, white feminists have not "explored how our understanding of gender relations, self, and theory are partially constituted in and through experiences of living in a culture in which asymmetric race relations are a central organizing principle of society."[8] Thus, the most popular subject of Anglo-American feminist is an autonomous, self-making, self-determining subject who first proceeds according to the *logic of identification* with regard to the subject of consciousness, a notion usually viewed as the purview of man, but now claimed for women.[9] Believing that in this respect she is the same as man, she now claims the right to pursue her own identity, to name herself, to

3. Moraga and Anzaldúa, 23

4. Moraga and Anzaldúa, 195.

5. Teresa de Lauretis, *Technologies of Gender* (Bloomington: Indiana University Press, 1987), 10.

6. Jane Flax, "Postmodernism and Gender Relations in Feminist Theory," *Signs* 12:4 (Summer 1987), 640.

7. Gayatri Chakravorty Spivak, "Three Women's Texts and a Critique of Imperialism," *Critical Inquiry* 12:1 (Autumn 1985), 243–44.

8. Flax, 640.

9. Julia Kristeva, "Women's Time," *Signs* 7:1 (Autumn 1981), 19.

pursue self-knowledge, and, in the words of Adrienne Rich, to effect "a change in the concept of sexual identity."[10]

Though feminism has problematized gender relations, indeed, as Flax observes, gender is "the single most important advance in feminist theory,"[11] it has not problematized the subject of knowledge and her complicity with the notion of consciousness as "synthetic unificatory power, the centre and active point of organization of representations determining their concatenation."[12] The subject (and object) of knowledge is now a woman, but the inherited view of consciousness has not been questioned at all. As a result, some Anglo-American feminist subjects of consciousness have tended to become a parody of the masculine subject of consciousness, thus revealing their ethnocentric liberal underpinnings. In 1982, Jean Bethke Elshtain had noted the "masculine cast" of radical feminist language, for example, noting the terms of "raw power, brute force, martial discipline, law and order with a feminist face – and voice."[13] Also in critiquing liberal feminism and its language, she notes that "no vision of the political community that might serve as the groundwork of a life in common is possible within a political life dominated by a self-interested, predatory individualism."[14] Althusser argues that this tradition "has privileged the category of the 'subject' as Origin, Essence and Cause, responsible in its internality for all determinations of the external object. In other words, this tradition has promoted Man, in his ideas and experience, as the source of knowledge, morals and history."[15] By identifying in this way with this tradition standpoint epistemologists have substituted, ironically, woman for man. This 'logic of identification' as a first step in constructing the theoretical subject of feminism is often veiled from standpoint epistemologists because greater attention is given to naming female identity, and describing women's ways of knowing as being considerably different than men's.[16] By emphasizing 'sexual difference,' the second step

10. Adrienne Rich, *On Lies, Secrets and Silence* (New York: W. W. Norton, 1979), 35.
11. Flax, 627.
12. Michel Pecheux, *Language, Semantics and Ideology* (New York: St. Martin's Press, 1982), 122.
13. Jean Bethke Elshtain, "Feminist Discourse and Its Discontents: Language, Power, and Meaning," *Signs* 7:3 (Spring 1981), 611.
14. Elshtain, 617.
15. Diane Macdonell, *Theories of Discourses: An Introduction* (New York: Basil Blackwell, 1986), 76.
16. For an intriguing demonstration of these operations, see Seyla Benhabib, "The Generalized and the Concrete Other: The Kohlberg-Gilligan Controversy and Feminist Theory" in Seyla Benhabib and Drucilla Cornell, *Feminism as Critique* (Minneapolis: University of Minnesota Press, 1987), 77–95.

takes place, often called oppositional thinking (counteridentifying). However, this gendered standpoint epistemology leads to feminism's bizarre position with regard to other liberation movements, working inherently against the interests of non-white women and no one else. For example, Sandra Harding argues that oppositional thinking (counteridentification) with white men should be retained even though "[t]here are suggestions in the literature of Native Americans, Africans, and Asians that what feminists call feminine versus masculine personalities, ontologies, ethics, epistemologies, and world views may be what these other liberation movements call Non-Western versus Western personalities and world views. . . . I set aside the crucial and fatal complication for this way of thinking – the fact that one half of these people are women and that most women are not Western."[17] She further suggests that feminists respond by relinquishing the totalizing "master theory" character of our theory-making: "This response to the issue [will manage] to retain the categories of feminist theory . . . and simply set them alongside the categories of the theory making of other subjugated groups. . . . Of course, it leaves bifurcated (and perhaps even more finely divided) the identities of all except ruling-class white Western women."[18] The apperception of this situation is precisely what led to the choice of title for the book *All The Women Are White, All The Blacks Are Men, But Some of Us Are Brave*, edited by Gloria T. Hull, Patricia Bell Scott and Barbara Smith.[19]

Notwithstanding the power of *Bridge* to affect the personal lives of its readers, *Bridge*'s challenge to the Anglo-American subject of feminism has yet to effect a newer discourse. Women of color often recognize themselves in the pages of *Bridge,* and write to say, "The women writers seemed to be speaking to me, and they actually understood what I was going through. Many of you put into words feelings I have had that I had no way of expressing. . . . The writings justified some of my thoughts telling me I had a right to feel as I did."[20] On the other hand, Anglo feminist readers of *Bridge* tend to appropriate it, cite it as an instance of difference between women, and proceed to negate that difference by subsuming women of color into the unitary category of woman/women. The latter is often viewed as the "common denominator" in an oppositional (counteridentifying) discourse with some white men, that leaves us unable to explore relationships among women.

17. Sandra Harding, "The Instability of the Analytical Categories of Feminist Theory," *Signs* 11:4 (Summer 1986), 659.
18. Harding, 660.
19. Gloria T. Hull, Patricia B, Scott and Barbara Smith, eds., *All The Women Are White, All The Blacks Are Men, But Some of Us Are Brave* (Westbury, N.Y.: Feminist Press, 1982).
20. Moraga and Anzaldúa, Foreword to the Second Edition, n.p.

Bridge's writers did not see the so-called "common denominator" as the solution for the construction of the theoretical feminist subject. In the call for submissions the editors clearly stated: "We want to express to all women – especially to white middle class women – the experiences which divide us as feminists; we want to explore the causes, and sources of, and solutions to these divisions. We want to create a definition that expands what 'feminist' means to us."[21] Thus, the female subject of *Bridge* is highly complex. She is and has been constructed in a crisis of meaning situation which includes racial and cultural divisions and conflicts. The psychic and material violence that gives shape to that subjectivity cannot be underestimated nor passed over lightly. The fact that not all of this violence comes from men in general but also from women renders the notion of "common denominator" problematic.

It is clear, however, that even as *Bridge* becomes a resource for the Anglo-American feminist theory classroom and syllabus, there's a tendency to deny differences if those differences pose a threat to the "common denominator" category. That is, unity would be purchased with silence, putting aside the conflictive history of groups' interrelations and interdependence. In the words of Paula Treichler, "[h]ow do we address the issues and concerns raised by women of color, who may themselves be even more excluded from theoretical feminist discourse than from the women's studies curriculum? . . . Can we explore our 'common differences' without overemphasizing the division that currently seems to characterize the feminism of the United States and the world?"[22] Clearly, this exploration appears impossible without a reconfiguration of the subject of feminist theory, and her relational position to a multiplicity of others, not just white men.

Some recent critics of the "exclusionary practices in Women's Studies" have noted that its gender standpoint epistemology leads to a 'tacking on' of "material about minority women" without any note of its "significance for feminist knowledge."[23] The common approaches noted were the tendency to 1) treat race and class as secondary features in social organization (as well as representation) with primacy given to female subordination; 2) acknowledge that inequalities of race, class and gender generate different experiences and then set race and class inequalities aside on the grounds that information was lacking to allow incorporation into an analysis; 3) focus on descriptive aspects of the ways of life, values, cus-

21. Moraga and Anzaldúa, Introduction to the First Edition, xxiii.
22. Paula Treichler, "Teaching Feminist Theory," *Theory in the Classroom*, Cary Nelsen, ed. (Urbana: University of Illinois Press, 1986), 79.
23. Maxine Baca Zinn, Lynn Weber Cannon, Elizabeth Higginbotham and Bonnie Thornton Dill, "The Cost of Exclusionary Practices in Women's Studies," *Signs* 11:4 (Summer 1986), 296.

toms and problems of women in subordinate race and class categories with little attempt to explain their source or their broader meaning. In fact, it may be impossible for gender standpoint epistemology to ever do more than a "pretheoretical presentation of concrete problems."[24] Since the subject of feminist theory and its single theme – gender – go largely unquestioned, its point of view tends to suppress and repress voices that question its authority, and as Jane Flax remarks, "The suppression of these voices seems to be a necessary condition for the (apparent) authority, coherence, and universality of our own."[25] This may account for the inability to include the voices of "women of color" into feminist discourse, though they are not necessarily under-represented in the reading list.

For the standpoint epistemologists, the desire to construct a feminist theory based solely on gender, on the one hand, and the knowledge or implicit recognition that such an account might distort the representation of many women and/or correspond to that of some men, on the other, gives rise to anxiety and ambivalence with respect to the future of that feminism, especially in Anglo-America. At the core of that attitude is the often unstated recognition that if the pervasiveness of women's oppression is virtually 'universal' on some level, it is also highly diverse from group to group and that women themselves may become complicitous with that oppression. "Complicity arises," says Macdonell, "where through lack of a positive starting point either a practice is driven to make use of prevailing values or a critique becomes the basis for a new theory."[26] Standpoint epistemologists have made use of the now gendered and feminist notion of consciousness, without too much question. (This notion, of course, represents the highest value of European culture since the Enlightenment.) The inclusion of other analytical categories such as race and class becomes impossible for a subject whose consciousness refuses to acknowledge that "one becomes a woman" in ways that are much more complex than in a simple opposition to men. In cultures in which "asymmetric race and class relations are a central organizing principle of society," one may also "become a woman" in opposition to other women. In other words, the whole category of woman may also need to be problematized, a point that I shall take up later. In any case, one should not step into that category nor that of man that easily or simply.

Simone de Beauvoir and her key work *The Second Sex* have been most influential in the development of feminist standpoint epistemology. She may even be responsible for the creation of Anglo-American feminist theory's "episteme": a highly self-conscious ruling class white Western fe-

24. Baca Zinn *et al.*, 296–97.
25. Flax, 633.
26. Macdonell, 62.

male subject locked in a struggle to the death with "Man." De Beauvoir has shaken the world of women, most especially with the ramification of her phrase, "One is not born, but rather becomes, a woman."[27] For over 400 pages of text after that statement, de Beauvoir demonstrates how a female is constituted as a "woman" by society as her freedom is curtailed from childhood. The curtailment of freedom incapacitates her from affirming "herself as a subject."[28] Very few women, indeed, can escape the cycle of indoctrination except perhaps the writer/intellectual because "[s]he knows that she is a conscious being, a subject."[29] This particular kind of woman can perhaps make of her gender a project and transform her sexual identity.[30] But what of those women who are not so privileged, who neither have the political freedom nor the education? Do they now, then, occupy the place of the Other (the 'Brave') while some women become subjects? Or do we have to make a subject of the whole world?

Regardless of our point of view in this matter, the way to becoming a female subject has been effected through consciousness-raising. In 1982, in a major theoretical essay, "Feminism, Method and the State: An Agenda for Theory," Catharine A. MacKinnon cited *Bridge* as a book that explored the relationship between sex and race and argued that "consciousness-raising" was *the* feminist method.[31] The reference to *Bridge* was brief. It served as an example, along with other texts, of the challenge that race and nationalism have posed for Marxism. According to her, Marxism has been unable to account for the appearance of these emancipatory discourses nor has it been able to assimilate them. Nevertheless, MacKinnon's major point was to demonstrate the epistemological challenge that feminism and its primary method, "consciousness-raising," posed for Marxism. Within Marxism, class as method of analysis has failed to reckon with the historical force of sexism. Through "consciousness-raising" (from women's point of view), women are led to know the world in a different way. Women's experience of politics, of life as sex objects, gives rise to its own method of appropriating that reality: feminist method. It challenges the objectivity of the "empirical gaze" and "rejects the distinction between knowing subject and known object."[32] By having women be the subject of knowledge, the so-called "objectivity" of

27. Simone de Beauvoir, *The Second Sex* (New York: Vintage Books, 1974), 301.
28. de Beauvoir, 316.
29. de Beauvoir, 761.
30. For a detailed discussion of this theme, see Judith Butler, "Variations on Sex and Gender: Beauvoir, Wittig, and Foucault" in Benhabib and Cornell, 128–42.
31. Catharine MacKinnon, "Feminism, Marxism, Method and the State: An Agenda for Theory," *Signs* 7:3 (Spring 1982), 536–38.
32. MacKinnon, 536.

men is brought into question. Often, this leads to privileging women's way of knowing in opposition to men's way of knowing, thus sustaining the very binary opposition that feminism would like to change or transform. Admittedly, this is only one of the many paradoxical procedures in feminist thinking, as Nancy Cott confirms: "It acknowledges diversity among women while positing that women recognize their unity. It requires gender consciousness for its basis, yet calls for the elimination of prescribed gender roles."[33]

However, I suspect that these contradictions or paradoxes have more profound implications than is readily apparent. Part of the problem may be that as feminist practice and theory recuperate their sexual differential, through "consciousness-raising," women reinscribe such a differential as feminist epistemology or theory. With gender as the central concept in feminist thinking, epistemology is flattened out in such a way that we lose sight of the complex and multiple ways in which the subject and object of possible experience are constituted. The flattening effect is multiplied when one considers that gender is often solely related to white men. There's no inquiry into the knowing subject beyond the fact of being a "woman." But what is a "woman," or a "man" for that matter? If we refuse to define either term according to some "essence," then we are left with having to specify their conventional significance in time and space, which is liable to change as knowledge increases or interests change. The fact that Anglo-American feminism has appropriated the generic term for itself leaves many a woman in this country having to call herself otherwise, i.e., "woman of color," which is equally "meaningless" without further specification. It also gives rise to the tautology "Chicana women." Needless to say, the requirement of gender consciousness only in relationship to man leaves us in the dark about a good many things, including interracial and intercultural relations. It may be that the only purpose this type of differential has is as a political strategy. It does not help us envision a world beyond binary restrictions, nor does it help us to reconfigure feminist theory to include the "native female." It does, however, help us grasp the paradox that within this cultural context one cannot be a feminist without becoming a gendered subject of knowledge, which makes it very difficult to transcend gender at all and to imagine relations between women.

In *Feminist Politics and Human Nature,* Alison M. Jaggar, speaking as a socialist feminist, refers repeatedly to *Bridge* and other works by women of color. In that work, Jaggar states that subordinated women are unrepresented in feminist theory. Jaggar claims that socialist feminism is in-

33. Nancy F. Cott, "Feminist Theory and Feminist Movements: The Past Before Us," *What Is Feminism: A Re-Examination,* Juliet Mitchell and Ann Oakley, eds. (New York: Pantheon Books, 1986), 49.

spired by Marxist and radical feminist politics though the latter has failed to be scientific about its insights. *Bridge* is cited various times to counter the racist and classist position of radical feminists.[34] Jaggar charges that "[r]adical feminism has encouraged women to name their own experience but it has not recognized explicitly that this experience must be analyzed, explained and theoretically transcended."[35] In a sense, Jaggar's charge amounts to the notion that radical feminists were flattening out their knowledge by an inadequate methodology, i.e. gender consciousness-raising. Many of Jaggar's observations are a restatement of *Bridge*'s challenge to Anglo-American feminists of all persuasions, be it Liberal, Radical, Marxist, and Socialist, the types sketched out by Jaggar. For example, "[a] representation of reality from the standpoint of women must draw on the variety of all women's experience"[36] may be compared to Barbara Smith's view in *Bridge* that "Feminism is the political theory and practice to free *all* women: women of color, working-class women, poor women, physically challenged women, lesbians, old women, as well as white economically privileged heterosexual women."[37] Jaggar continues, "Since historically diverse groups of women, such as working-class women, women of color, and others have been excluded from intellectual work, they somehow must be enabled to participate as subjects as well as objects of feminist theorizing."[38] Writers in *Bridge* did appear to think that "consciousness-raising" and the naming of one's experience would deliver some theory and yield a notion of "what 'feminist' means to us."[39] Except for Smith's statement, there is no overarching view that would guide us as to "what 'feminist' means to us." Though there is a tacit political identity – gender/class/race-encapsulated in the phrase "women of color" that connects the pieces – they tend to split apart into "vertical relations" between the culture of resistance and the culture resisted or from which excluded. Thus, the binary restrictions become as prevalent between race/ethnicity of oppressed versus oppressor as between the sexes. The problems inherent in Anglo-American feminism and race relations are so locked into the "Self/Other" theme that it is no surprise that *Bridge*'s co-editor Moraga would remark, "In the last three years I have learned that Third World feminism does not provide the kind of easy political framework that women of color are running to in droves. The *idea* of Third World feminism has proved to be much easier between

34. Alison M. Jaggar, *Feminist Politics and Human Nature* (Totowa, N.J.: Rowman & Allanheld, 1983), 249–50; 295–96.
35. Jaggar, 381.
36. Jaggar, 386.
37. Moraga and Anzaldúa, 61.
38. Jaggar, 386.
39. Moraga and Anzaldúa, Introduction, xxiii.

the covers of a book than between real live women."[40] She refers to the United States, of course, because feminism is alive and well throughout the Third World largely within the purview of women's rights, or as a class struggle.[41]

The appropriation of *Bridge*'s observations in Jaggar's work differs slightly from the others in its view of linguistic use, implying to a limited extent that language is also reflective of material existence. The crucial question is how, indeed, can women of color be subjects as well as objects of feminist theorizing? Jaggar cites María Lugones' doubts: "We cannot talk to you in our language because you do not understand it. . . . The power of white Anglo women vis-à-vis Hispanas and Black women is in inverse proportion to their working knowledge of each other. . . . Because of their ignorance, white Anglo women who try to do theory with women of color inevitably disrupt the dialogue. Before they can contribute to collective dialogue, they need to 'know the text,' to have become familiar with an alternative way of viewing the world. . . . You need to learn to become unintrusive, unimportant, patient to the point of tears, while at the same time open to learning any possible lessons. You will have to come to terms with the sense of alienation, of not belonging, of having your world thoroughly disrupted, having it criticized and scrutinized from the point of view of those who have been harmed by it, having important concepts central to it dismissed, being viewed with mistrust."[42] One of *Bridge*'s breaks with prevailing conventions is linguistic. Lugones' advice to Anglo women to listen was post-*Bridge*. If prevailing conventions of speaking/writing had been observed, many a contributor would have been censored or silenced. So would have many a major document or writing of minorities. *Bridge* leads us to understand that the silence and silencing of people begins with the dominating enforcement of linguistic conventions, the resistance to relational dialogues, as well as the disenablement of peoples by outlawing their forms of speech. Anglo-American feminist theory assumes a speaking subject who is an autonomous, self-conscious individual woman. Such theory does not discuss the linguistic status of the person. It takes for granted the linguistic status which founds subjectivity. In this way it appropriates woman/women for itself, and turns its work into a theoretical project within which the rest of us are compelled to 'fit.' By 'forgetting' or refusing to take into account that we are culturally constituted in and through language in complex ways and not just engendered in a homogeneous situation, the Anglo-American subject of consciousness cannot come to terms with her (his) own class-biased ethnocentrism. She is blinded to her own construction not just as a woman

40. Moraga and Anzaldúa, Foreword to the Second Edition, n.p.
41. Miranda Davies, *Third World: Second Sex* (London: Zed Books, 1987).
42. Jaggar, 386.

but as an Anglo-American one. Such a subject creates a theoretical subject that could not possibly include all women just because we are women. It is against this feminist backdrop that many "women of color" have struggled to give voice to their subjectivity and which effected the publication of the writings collected in *Bridge.* However, the freedom of women of color to posit themselves as multiple-voiced subjects is constantly in peril of repression precisely at that point where our constituted contradictions put us at odds with women different from ourselves.

The pursuit of a "politics of unity" solely based on gender forecloses the "pursuit of solidarity" through different political formations and the exploration of alternative theories of the subject of consciousness. There is a tendency in more sophisticated and elaborate gender standpoint epistemologists to affirm "an identity made up of heterogeneous and heteronomous representations of gender, race, and class, and often indeed across languages and cultures"[43] with one breath, and with the next to refuse to explore how that identity may be theorized or analyzed, by reconfirming a unified subjectivity or "shared consciousness" through gender. The difference is handed over with one hand and taken away with the other. If it be true, as Teresa de Lauretis has observed, that "[s]elf and identity . . . are always grasped and understood within particular discursive configurations,"[44] it does not necessarily follow that one can easily and self-consciously decide "to reclaim [an identity] from a history of multiple assimilations,"[45] and still retain a "shared consciousness." Such a practice goes counter to the homogenizing tendency of the subject of consciousness in the United States. To be oppressed means to be disenabled not only from grasping an "identity," but also from reclaiming it. In this culture, to grasp or reclaim an identity means always already to have become a subject of consciousness. The theory of the subject of consciousness as a unitary and synthesizing agent of knowledge is always already a posture of domination. One only has to think of Gloria Anzaldúa's essay in *Bridge,* "Speaking in Tongues: A Letter to Third World Women Writers."[46] Though de Lauretis concedes that a racial "shared consciousness" may have prior claims than gender, she still insists on unity through gender: "the female subject is always constructed and defined in gender, starting from gender."[47] One is interested in having more than an account of gender, there are other relations to be accounted for. De Lauretis insists, in most of her work, that "the differences

43. Teresa de Lauretis, "Feminist Studies/Critical Studies: Issues, Terms, and Contexts," *Feminist Studies/Critical Studies,* Teresa de Lauretis, ed. (Bloomington: Indiana University Press 1986), 9.
44. de Lauretis, *Feminist Studies,* 8.
45. de Lauretis, *Feminist Studies,* 9.
46. Moraga and Anzaldúa, 165–74.
47. de Lauretis, *Feminist Studies,* 14.

among women may be better understood as differences within women."[48] This position returns us all to our solitary, though different, consciousness, without noting that some differences are (have been) a result of relations of domination of women by women; that differences may be purposefully constituted for the purpose of domination or exclusion, especially in oppositional thinking. Difference, whether it be sexual, racial, social, has to be conceptualized within a political and ideological domain.[49] In *Bridge,* for example, Mirtha Quintanales points out that "in this country, in this world, racism is used *both* to create false differences among us *and* to mask very significant ones – cultural, economic, political."[50]

One of the most remarkable tendencies in the work reviewed is the implicit or explicit acknowledgement that women of color are excluded from feminist theory, on the one hand, and on the other the reminder that though excluded from theory, their books are read in the classroom and/or duly footnoted. It is clear that some of the writers in *Bridge* thought at some point in the seventies that feminism could be the ideal answer to their hope for liberation. Chrystos, for example, states her disillusionment as follows: "I no longer believe that feminism is a tool which can eliminate racism or even promote better understanding between different races and kinds of women."[51] The disillusionment is eloquently reformulated in the theme poem by Donna Kate Ruchin, "The Bridge Poem."[52] The dream of helping the people who surround her to reach an interconnectedness that would change society is given up in favor of self-translation into a "true self." In my view, the speaker's refusal to play "bridge," an enablement to others as well as self, is the acceptance of defeat at the hands of political groups whose self-definition follows the view of self as unitary, capable of being defined by a single "theme." The speaker's perception that the "self" is multiple ("I'm sick of mediating with your worst self/on behalf of your better selves,"[53]) and its reduction harmful, gives emphasis to the relationality between one's selves and those of others as an ongoing process of struggle, effort and tension. Indeed, in this poem the better "bridging self" of the speaker is defeated by the overriding notion of the unitary subject of knowledge and consciousness so prevalent in Anglo-American culture. Consciousness as a site of multiple voicings is the theoretical subject, par excellence, of *Bridge.* Con-

48. de Lauretis, *Feminist Studies,* 14.
49. Monique Wittig, cited in Elizabeth Meese, *Crossing the Double-Cross: The Practice of Feminist Criticism* (Chapel Hill: University of North Carolina Press, 1986), 74.
50. Moraga and Anzaldúa, 153.
51. Moraga and Anzaldúa, 69.
52. Moraga and Anzaldúa, xxi–xxii.
53. Moraga and Anzaldúa, xxii.

comitantly, these voicings (or thematic threads) are not viewed as necessarily originating with the subject, but as discourses that transverse consciousness and which the subject must struggle with constantly. Rosario Morales, for example, says "I want to be whole. I want to claim myself to be puertorican, and U.S. American, working class and middle class, housewife and intellectual, feminist, marxist and anti-imperialist."[54] Gloria Anzaldúa observes, "What am I? *A third world lesbian feminist with Marxist and mystic leanings.* They would chop me up into little fragments and tag each piece with a label."[55] The need to assign multiple registers of existence is an effect of the belief that knowledge of one's subjectivity cannot be arrived at through a single discursive "theme." Indeed, the multiple-voiced subjectivity is lived in resistance to competing notions for one's allegiance or self-identification. It is a process of disidentification[56] with prevalent formulations of the most forcefully theoretical subject of feminism. The choice of one or many themes is both theoretical and a political decision. Like gender epistemologists and other emancipatory movements, the theoretical subject of *Bridge* gives credit to the subject of consciousness as the site of knowledge but problematizes it by representing it as a weave. In Anzaldúa's terms, the woman of color has a "plural personality." Speaking of the new mestiza in *Borderlands/ La Frontera,* she says, "[s]he learns to juggle cultures. . . . [the] juncture where the mestiza stands is where phenomena tend to collide."[57] As an object of multiple indoctrinations that heretofore have collided upon her, their new recognition as products of the oppositional thinking of others can help her come to terms with the politics of varied discourses and their antagonistic relations.

Thus, current political practices in the United States make it almost impossible to go beyond an oppositional theory of the subject, which is the prevailing feminist strategy and that of others; however, it is not the theory that will help us grasp the subjectivity of women of color. Socially and historically, women of color have been now central, now outside antagonistic relations between races, classes, and gender(s); this struggle of multiple antagonisms, almost always in relation to culturally different groups and not just genders, gives configuration to the theoretical subject of *Bridge.* It must be noted, however, that each woman of color cited here, even in her positing of a "plurality of self," is already privileged enough to reach the moment of cognition of a situation for herself. This should suggest that to privilege the subject, even if multiple-voiced, is not enough.

54. Moraga and Anzaldúa, 91.
55. Moraga and Anzaldúa, 205.
56. Pecheux, 158–59.
57. Gloria Anzaldúa, *Borderlands/La Frontera: The New Mestiza* (San Francisco: Spinsters/Aunt Lute, 1987), 79.

8

Contingent foundations: Feminism and the question of 'postmodernism'
Judith Butler

The question of postmodernism is surely a question, for is there, after all, something called postmodernism? Is it an historical characterization, a certain kind of theoretical position, and what does it mean for a term that has described a certain aesthetic practice now to apply to social theory and to feminist social and political theory in particular? Who are these postmodernists? Is this a name that one takes on for oneself, or is it more often a name that one is called if and when one offers a critique of the subject, a discursive analysis, or questions the integrity or coherence of totalizing social descriptions?

I know the term from the way it is used, and it usually appears on my horizon embedded in the following critical formulations: "if discourse is all there is, . . . ," or "if everything is a text . . . " or "if the subject is dead . . . " or "if real bodies do not exist . . . ?" The sentence begins as a warning against an impending nihilism, for if the conjured content of these series of conditional clauses proves to be true, then, and there is always a then, some set of dangerous consequences will surely follow. So 'postmodernism' appears to be articulated in the form of a fearful conditional or sometimes in the form of paternalistic disdain toward that which is youthful and irrational. Against this postmodernism, there is an effort to shore up the primary premises, to establish in advance that any theory of politics requires a subject, needs from the start to presume its subject, the referentiality of language, the integrity of the institutional descriptions it provides. For politics is unthinkable without a foundation, without these premises. But do these claims seek to secure a contingent formation of politics that requires that these notions remain unproblematized features of its own definition? Is in the case that all politics, and feminist politics in particular, is unthinkable without these prized premises? Or is it

This paper was first presented in a different version as "Feminism and the Question of Postmodernism" at the Greater Philadelphia Philosophy Consortium in September, 1990. Reprinted with permission of Blackwell publishers.

rather that a specific version of politics is shown in its contingency once those premises are problematically thematized?

To claim that politics requires a stable subject is to claim that there can be no *political* opposition to that claim. Indeed, that claim implies that a critique of the subject cannot be a politically informed critique but, rather, an act which puts into jeopardy politics as such. To require the subject means to foreclose the domain of the political, and that foreclosure, installed analytically as an essential feature of the political, enforces the boundaries of the domain of the political in such a way that enforcement is protected from political scrutiny. The act which unilaterally establishes the domain of the political functions, then, as an authoritarian ruse by which political contest over the status of the subject is summarily silenced.[1]

To refuse to assume or to require a notion of the subject from the start is not the same as negating or dispensing with such a notion altogether; on the contrary, it is to ask after the process of its construction and the political meaning and consequentiality of taking the subject as a requirement or presupposition of theory. But have we arrived yet at a notion of postmodernism?

1. Here it is worth noting that in some recent political theory, notably in the writings of Ernesto Laclau, Chantal Mouffe (*Hegemony and Socialist Strategy*, London: Verso, 1986) William Connolly (*Politics and Ambiguity*, Madison: Univ. of Wisconsin, 1987) (*Identity/Difference: Democratic Negotiations of Political Paradox*, Cornell University Press, 1991), Jean-Luc Nancy and Philippe Lacoue-Labarthe ('Le "retrait" du politique' in *Le retrait du politique*, eds. Lacoue-Labarthe, Nancy, Paris: Editions galilée, 1983), there is an insistence that the political field is of necessity constructed through the production of a domain of essential exclusion. In other words, the very domain of politics constitutes itself through the production and naturalization of the "pre-" or "non-" political. In Derridean terms, this is the production of a "constitutive outside." Here I would like to suggest a distinction between the constitution of a political field that produces *and naturalizes* that constitutive outside and a political field that produces and *renders contingent* the specific parameters of that constitutive outside. Although I do not think that the differential relations through which the political field itself is constituted can ever be fully elaborated (precisely because the status of that elaboration would have to be elaborated as well *ad infinitum*), I do not find useful William Connolly's notion of constitutive antagonisms, a notion that finds a parallel expression in Laclau and Mouffe, which suggests a form of political struggle which puts the parameters of the political itself into question. This is especially important for feminist concerns insofar as the grounds of politics ('universality,' 'equality,' 'the subject of rights' have been constructed through unmarked racial and gender exclusions and by a conflation of politics with public life that renders the private (reproduction, domains of femininity') pre-political.

A number of positions are ascribed to postmodernism, as if it were the kind of thing that could be the bearer of a set of positions: discourse is all there is, as if discourse were some kind of monistic stuff out of which all things are composed; the subject is dead, I can never say 'I' again; there is no reality, only representations. These characterizations are variously imputed to postmodernism or poststructuralism, which are conflated with each other and sometimes conflated with deconstruction, and sometimes understood as an indiscriminate assemblage of French Feminism, deconstruction, Lacanian psychoanalysis, Foucaultian analysis, Rorty's conversationalism and cultural studies. On this side of the Atlantic and in recent discourse the terms "postmodernism" or "poststructuralism" settle the differences among those positions in a single stroke, providing a substantive, a noun, that includes those positions as so many of its modalities or permutations. It may come as a surprise to some purveyors of the continental scene to learn that Lacanian psychoanalysis in France positions itself officially against poststructuralism, that Kristeva denounces postmodernism,[2] that Foucaultians rarely relate to Derrideans, that Cixous and Irigaray are fundamentally opposed, and that the only tenuous connection between French Feminism and deconstruction exists between Cixous and Derrida, although a certain affinity in textual practices is to be found between Derrida and Irigaray. Biddy Martin is also right to point out that almost all of French Feminism adheres to a notion of high modernism and the avante-garde, which throws some question on whether these theories or writings can be grouped simply under the category of postmodernism.

I propose that the question of postmodernism be read not merely as the question that postmodernism poses for feminism, but as the question, what is postmodernism, what kind of existence does it have? Lyotard champions the term, but he cannot be made into the example of what all the rest of the purported postmodernists are doing.[3] Lyotard's work is, for instance, seriously at odds with that of Derrida, who does not affirm the notion of "the postmodern," and with others for whom Lyotard is made to stand. Is he paradigmatic? Do all these theories have the same structure (a comforting notion to the critic who would dispense with them all at once)? Is the effort to colonize and domesticate these theories under the sign of the same, to group them synthetically and masterfully under a

2. Julia Kristeva, *Black Sun: Depression and Melancholy,* New York: Columbia University Press, 1989, pp. 258–259.
3. The conflation of Lyotard with the array of thinkers summarily positioned under the rubric of "postmodernism" is performed by the title and essay by Seyla Benhabib: "Epistemologies of Postmodernism: A Rejoinder to Jean-François Lyotard," in *Feminism/Postmodernism,* ed. Linda Nicholson, New York: Routledge, 1989.

single rubric, a simple refusal to grant the specificity of these positions, an excuse not to read, and not to read closely? For if Lyotard uses the term, and if he can be conveniently grouped with a set of writers, and if some problematic quotation can be found in his work, then can that quotation serve as an "example" of postmodernism, symptomatic of the whole?

But if I understand part of the project of postmodernism, it is to call into question the ways in which such "examples" and "paradigms" serve to subordinate and erase that which they seek to explain. The "whole," the field of postmodernism in its supposed breadth, is effectively produced by the example which is made to stand as a symptom and exemplar of the whole. In effect, if in the example of Lyotard we think we have a representation of postmodernism, we have then forced a substitution of the example for the entire field, to effect a violent reduction of the field to the one piece of text the critic is willing to read, a piece which, conveniently, uses the term "postmodern."

In a sense, this gesture of conceptual mastery that groups together a set of positions under the postmodern, that makes the postmodern into an epoch or a synthetic whole, and that claims that the part can stand for this artificially constructed whole, enacts a certain self-congratulatory ruse of power. It is paradoxical, at best, that the act of conceptual mastery that effects this dismissive grouping of positions under the postmodern wants to ward off the peril of political authoritarianism. For the assumption is that some piece of the text is representational, that it stands for the phenomenon, and that the structure of "these" positions can be properly and economically discerned in the structure of the one. What authorizes such an assumption from the start? From the start we must believe that theories offer themselves in bundles or in organized totalities, and that historically a set of theories which are structurally similar emerge as the articulation of an historically specific condition of human reflection. This Hegelian trope, which continues through Adorno, assumes from the start that these theories can be substituted for one another because they variously symptomatize a common structural preoccupation. And yet, that presumption can no longer be made, for the Hegelian presumption that a synthesis is available from the start is precisely what has come under contest in various ways by some of the positions happily unified under the sign of the postmodern. One might argue that if, and to the extent that, the postmodern functions as such a unifying sign, then it is a decidedly "modern" sign, which is why there is some question whether one can debate for or against this postmodernism. To install the term as that which can be only affirmed or negated is to force it to occupy one position within a binary, and so to affirm a logic of non-contradiction over and against some more generative scheme.

Perhaps the reason for this unification of positions is occasioned by the very unruliness of the field, by the way in which the differences among these positions cannot be rendered symptomatic, exemplary, or representative of each other and of some common structure called postmodernism. If postmodernism as a term has some force or meaning within social theory, or feminist social theory in particular, perhaps it can be found in the critical exercise that seeks to show how theory, how philosophy, is always implicated in power, and perhaps that is precisely what is symptomatically at work in the effort to domesticate and refuse a set of powerful criticisms under the rubric of postmodernism. That the philosophical apparatus in its various conceptual refinements is always engaged in exercising power is not a new insight, but then again the postmodern ought not be confused with the new; after all, the pursuit of the "new" is the preoccupation of high modernism; if anything, the postmodern casts doubt upon the possibility of a "new" that is not in some way already implicated in the "old."

But the point articulated forcefully by some recent critics of normative political philosophy is that the recourse to a position, hypothetical, counterfactual, or imaginary, that places itself beyond the play of power, and which seeks to establish the meta-political basis for a negotiation of power-relations, is perhaps the most insidious ruse of power. That this position beyond power lays claim to its legitimacy through recourse to a prior and implicitly universal agreement does not in any way circumvent the charge, for what rationalist project will designate in advance what counts as agreement? What form of insidious cultural imperialism here legislates itself under the sign of the universal?[4]

I don't know about the term "postmodern," but if there is a point, and a fine point, to what I perhaps better understand as poststructuralism, it is that power pervades the very conceptual apparatus that seeks to negotiate its terms, including the subject-position of the critic; and further, that this implication of the terms of criticism in the field of power is *not* the advent of a nihilistic relativism incapable of furnishing norms, but, rather, the very precondition of a politically engaged critique. To establish a set of norms that are beyond power or force is itself a powerful and forceful

---

4. This is abundantly clear in feminist criticism of Jürgen Habermas as well as Catherine MacKinnon. See Iris Young, "Impartiality and the Civic Public: Some Implication of Feminist Criticisms of Modern Political Theory" in Seyla Benhabib and Drucilla Cornell, eds., *Feminism as Critique: Essays on the Politics of Gender in Late-Capitalism*, Basil Blackwell, 1987; Nancy Fraser, *Unruly Practices: Power and Gender in Contemporary Social Theory*, especially "What's Critical about Critical Theory: The Case of Habermas and Gender, Minneapolis, University of Minnesota Press, 1989. Wendy Brown, "Razing Consciousness," *The Nation*, 250: #2, January 8/15, 1990.

conceptual practice that sublimates disguises and extends its own power-play through recourse to tropes of normative universality. And the point is not to do away with foundations, or even to champion a position that goes under the name of anti-foundationalism. Both of those positions belong together as different versions of foundationalism and the skeptical problematic it engenders. Rather, the task is to interrogate what the theoretical move that establishes foundations *authorizes,* and what precisely it excludes or forecloses.

It seems that theory posits foundations incessantly, and forms implicit metaphysical commitments as a matter of course, even when it seeks to guard against it; foundations function as the unquestioned and the unquestionable within any theory. And yet are these "foundations," i.e. those premises that function as authorizing grounds, are they themselves not constituted through exclusions which, taken into account, expose the foundational premise as a contingent and contestable presumption? Even when we claim that there is some implied universal basis for a given foundation, that implication and that universality simply constitute new dimensions of unquestionability.

How is it that we might ground a theory or politics in a speech situation or subject position which is "universal" when the very category of the universal has only begun to be exposed for its own highly ethnocentric biases? How many 'universalities' are there?[5] And to what extent is cultural conflict understandable as the clashing of a set of presumed and intransigent 'universalities', a conflict which cannot be negotiated through recourse to a culturally imperialist notion of the 'universal' or, rather, will be solved through such recourse only at the cost of violence. We have, I think, witnessed the conceptual and material violence of this practice in the US war against Iraq in which the Arab "other" is understood to be radically "outside" the universal structures of reason and democracy and, hence, calls to be brought forcibly within. Significantly, the US had to abrogate the democratic principles of political sovereignty and free speech, among others, to effect this forcible return of Iraq to the "democratic" fold, and this violent move reveals, among other things, that such notions of universality are installed through the abrogation of the very universal principles to be implemented. Within the political context of contemporary postcoloniality more generally, it is perhaps especially urgent to underscore the very category of the "universal" as a site of insistent contest and resignification.[6] Given the contested character of the term, to assume from the start a procedural or substantive notion of

5. See Ashis Nandy on the notion of alternative universalities in the preface to *The Intimate Enemy: Loss and Recovery of Self under Colonialism* (New Delhi: Oxford University Press, 1983).
6. Homi Babha's notion of "hybridity" is important to consider in this context.

the universal is of necessity to impose a culturally hegemonic notion on the social field. To herald that notion then as the philosophical instrument that will negotiate between conflicts of power is precisely to safeguard and reproduce a position of hegemonic power by installing it in the meta-political site of ultimate normativity.

It may at first seem that I am simply calling for a more concrete and internally diverse 'universality', a more synthetic and inclusive notion of the universal, and in that way committed to the very foundational notion that I seek to undermine. But my task is, I think, significantly different from that which would articulate a comprehensive universality. In the first place, such a totalizing notion could only be achieved at the cost of producing new and further exclusions. The term "universality" would have to be left permanently open, permanently contested, permanently contingent, in order not to foreclose in advance future claims for inclusion. Indeed, from my position and from any historically constrained perspective, any totalizing concept of the universal will shut down rather than authorize the unanticipated and unanticipatable claims that will be made under the sign of 'the universal.' In this sense. I am not doing away with the category, but trying to relieve the category of its foundationalist weight in order to render it as a site of permanent political contest.

A social theory committed to democratic contestation within a postcolonial horizon needs to find a way to bring into question the foundations it is compelled to lay down. It is this movement of interrogating that ruse of authority that seeks to close itself off from contest that is, in my view, at the heart of any radical political project. Inasmuch as poststructuralism offers a mode of critique that effects this contestation of the foundationalist move, it can be used as a part of such a radical agenda. Note that I have said, "it can be used": I think there are no necessary political consequences for such a theory, but only a possible political deployment.

If one of the points associated with postmodernism is that the epistemological point of departure in philosophy is inadequate, then it ought not to be a question of subjects who claim to know and theorize under the sign of the postmodern pitted against other subjects who claim to know and theorize under the sign of the modern. Indeed, it is that very way of framing debate that is being contested by the suggestion that the position articulated by the subject is always in some way constituted by what must be displaced for that position to take hold, and that the subject who theorizes is constituted as a 'theorizing subject' by a set of exclusionary and selective procedures. For, indeed, who is it that gets constituted as the feminist theorist whose framing of the debate will get publicity? Is it not always the case that power operates in advance, in the very procedures that establish who will be the subject who speaks in the name of feminism, and to whom? And is it not also clear that a process of subjection is presupposed in the subjectivating process that produces before you one speaking subject of feminist debate? What speaks when "I" speak to you? What are the institutional histories of subjection and subjectivation that "position" me here now? If there is something called "Butler's position," is this one that I devise, publish, and defend, that belongs to me as a kind of academic property? Or is there a grammar of the subject that merely encourages us to position me as the proprietor of those theories?

Indeed, how is it that a position becomes a position, for clearly not every utterance qualifies as such? It is clearly a matter for certain authorizing power, and that clearly does not emanate from the position itself. My position is mine to the extent that "I" – and I do not shrink from the pronoun – replay and resignify the theoretical positions that have constituted me, working the possibilities of their convergence, and trying to take account of the possibilities that they systematically exclude. But it is clearly not the case that "I" preside over the positions that have constituted me, shuffling through them instrumentally, casting some aside, incorporating others, although some of my activity may take that form. The "I" who would select between them is always already constituted by them. The "I" is the transfer point of that replay, but it is simply not a strong enough claim to say that the "I" is situated; the "I," this "I," is *constituted* by these positions, and these 'positions' are not merely theoretical products, but fully embedded organizing principles of material practices and institutional arrangements, that matrix of power and discourse that produces me as a viable "subject." Indeed, this "I" would not be a thinking, speaking "I" if it were not for the very positions that I oppose, for those positions, the ones that claim that the subject must be given in advance, that discourse is an instrument of reflection of that subject, are already part of what constitutes me.

No subject is its own point of departure, and the fantasy that it is one can disavow its constitutive relations only by recasting them as the domain of a countervailing externality. Indeed, one might consider Luce Irigaray's claim that the subject, understood as a fantasy of autogenesis, is always already masculine. Psychoanalytically, that version of the subject is constituted through a kind of disavowal or through the primary repression of its dependency on the maternal. And to become a *subject* on this model is surely not a feminist goal.

The critique of the subject is not a negation or repudiation of the subject, but, rather, a way of interrogating its construction as a pregiven or foundationalist premise. At the outset of the war Iraq, we almost all saw strategists who placed before us maps of the Middle East, objects of analysis and targets of instrumental military action. Retired and active generals were called up by the networks to stand in for the generals on the field whose intentions would be invariably realized in the destruction of various Iraqi military bases. The various affirmations of the early success of these operations were delivered with great enthusiasm, and it seemed that it was this hitting of the goal, this apparently seamless realization of intention through an instrumental action without much resistance or hindrance that was the occasion, not merely to destroy Iraqi military installations, but also to champion a masculinized subject whose will immediately translates into a deed, whose utterance or order materializes in an action which would destroy the very possibility of a reverse-strike, and whose obliterating power at once confirms the impenetrable contours of its own subjecthood.

It is perhaps interesting to remember at this juncture that Foucault linked the displacement of the intentional subject with modern power-relations that he himself associated with war.[7] What he meant, I think is that subjects who institute actions are themselves instituted effects of prior actions, and that the horizon in which we act is there as a constitutive possibility of our very capacity to act, not merely or exclusively as an exterior field or theatre of operations. But perhaps more significantly, the actions instituted via that subject are part of a chain of actions that can no longer be understood as unilinear in direction or predictable in their outcomes. And yet, the instrumental military subject appears at first to utter words that materialize directly into destructive deeds. And throughout the war, it was as if the masculine Western subject preempted the divine power to translate words into deeds; the newscasters were almost all full of giddy happiness as they demonstrated, watched, vicariously enacted the exactitude of destructiveness. As the war began, the word one would hear on television was "euphoria," and one newscaster remarked that US weapons were instruments of "terrible beauty" (CBS).

But the consequentiality of this act cannot be foreseen by the instrumental actor who currently celebrates the effectivity of its own intentions. What Foucault suggested was that this subject is itself the effect of a genealogy which is erased at the moment that the subject takes itself as the single origin of its action, and that the effects of an action always supersede the stated intention or purpose of the act. Indeed, the effects of the instrumental action always have the power to proliferate beyond the subject's control, indeed, to challenge the rational transparency of that subject's intentionality, and so to subvert the very definition of the subject itself. I suggest that we are in the midst of a celebration on the part of the U.S. government and some of its allies of the phantasmatic subject, the

---

7. Michel Foucault, *The History of Sexuality, Vol. 1: An Introduction,* tr. Robert Hurley (New York: Random House, 1980), p. 102.

one who determines its world unilaterally, and which is in some measure typified by the looming heads of retired generals framed against the map of the Middle East, where the speaking head of this subject is shown to be the same size as, or larger than, the area it seeks to dominate. This is, in a sense, the graphics of the imperialist subject, a visual allegory of the action itself.

But here you think that I have made a distinction between the action itself and something like a representation, but I want to make a stronger point. You will perhaps have noticed that Colin Powell, the general of the Joint Chiefs of Staff, invokes what is, I think, a new military convention of calling the sending of missiles "the delivery of an ordinance." The phrase is significant, I think; it figures an act of violence as an act of law, and so wraps the destruction in the appearance of orderliness; but in addition, it figures the missile as a kind of command, an order to obey, and is thus a certain act of speech which not only delivers a message, i.e. get out of Kuwait, but effectively enforces that message through the threat of death and through death itself. Of course, this is a message that can never be received, for it kills its addressee, and so it is not an ordinance at all, but the failure of all ordinances, the refusal of a communication. And for those who remain to read the message, they will not read what is sometimes quite literally written on the missile. The demi-god of a military subject which euphorically engaged the fantasy that it has with ease achieved its aims still fails to understand that its actions will produce effects that will far exceed its phantasmatic purview; it thinks that its goals were achieved in a matter of weeks, but the effects of its actions will inaugurate violence in places and in ways that it itself cannot possibly foresee, and which will produce a massive and violent contestation of that very pretension.

If I can, then, I'll try to return to the subject at hand. In a sense, the subject is constituted through an exclusion and differentiation, perhaps a repression, that is subsequently concealed, covered over, by the effect of autonomy. In this sense, autonomy is the logical consequence of a disavowed dependency, which is to say that the autonomous subject can maintain the illusion of its autonomy insofar as it covers over the break out of which it is constituted. This dependency and this break are already social relations, ones which precede and condition the formation of the subject. As a result, this is not a relation in which the subject finds itself, as one of the relations that forms its situation. The subject is constructed through acts of differentiation that distinguish the subject from its constitutive outside, a domain of abjected alterity conventionally associated with the feminine, but clearly not exclusively. Precisely in this recent war, we saw "the Arab" figured as the abjected other as well as a site of homophobic fantasy, made clear in the abundance of bad jokes grounded in the linguistic sliding from Saddam to Sodom. There is no ontologically intact reflexivity to the subject which is then placed within a cultural context; that cultural context, as it were, is already there as the disarticulated process of the subject's production, one that is concealed by the frame that would situate a ready-made subject in an external web of cultural relations.

We may be tempted to think that to assume the subject in advance is necessary in order to safeguard the *agency* of the subject. But to claim that the subject is constituted is not to claim that it is determined; on the contrary, the constituted character of the subject is the very precondition of its agency. For what is it that enables a purposive and significant reconfiguration of social relations? Do we need to assume theoretically from the start that there is a subject with agency before we can articulate the terms of a significant social and political task of transformation, resistance, radical democratization? If we do not offer in advance the theoretical guarantee of that agent, are we doomed to give up transformation and meaningful political practice? My suggestion is that agency belongs to a way of thinking about persons as instrumental actors who confront an external political field. But politics and power exist already at the level at which the subject and its agency are articulated and made possible. Consider that 'agency' has no formal existence, or if it does, it has no bearing on the question at hand. In a sense, the epistemological model that offers us a pregiven subject or agent is one that refuses to acknowledge that *agency is always and only a political prerogative.* As such, it seems crucial to question the conditions of its possibility, not to take it for granted as an a priori guarantee. We need instead to ask, what possibilities of mobilization are produced on the basis of existing configurations of discourse and power? Where are the possibilities of reworking that very matrix of power by which we are constituted, of reconstituting the legacy of that constitution, and of working against each other processes of regulation that can destabilize existing power regimes? For if the subject is constituted by power, that power does not cease at the moment the subject is constituted, for that subject is never fully constituted, but is subjected and produced time and again. That subject is neither a ground nor a product, but the permanent possibility of a certain resignifying process, one which gets detoured and stalled through other mechanisms of power, but which is power's own possibility of being reworked. It is not enough to say that the subject is invariably engaged in a political field; that phenomenological phrasing misses the point that the subject is an accomplishment regulated and produced in advance. And is as such fully political; indeed, perhaps *most* political at the point in which it is claimed to be prior to politics itself. To perform this kind of Foucaultian critique of the subject is not to do away with the subject or pronounce its death, but merely to claim that certain versions of the subject are politically insidious.

For the subject to be a pregiven point of departure for politics is to defer the question of the political construction and regulation of the subject itself; for it is important to remember that subjects are constituted through exclusion, that is, through the creation of a domain of deauthorized subjects, pre-subjects, figures of abjection, populations erased from view. This becomes clear, for instance, within the law when certain qualifications must first be met in order to be, quite literally, a claimant in sex discrimination or rape cases. Here it becomes quite urgent to ask, who qualifies as a "who," what systematic structures of disempowerment make it impossible for certain injured parties to invoke the "I" effectively within a court of law? Or less overtly, in a social theory like Albert Memmi's *The Colonizer and the Colonized,* an otherwise compelling call for radical enfranchisement, the category of women falls into neither category, the oppressor or the oppressed. How do we theorize the exclusion of women from the category of the oppressed? Here the construction of subject-positions works to exclude women from the description of oppression, and this constitutes a different kind of oppression, one that is effected by the very *erasure* that grounds the articulation of the emancipatory subject. As Joan Scott makes clear in *Gender and the Politics of History,* once it is understood that subjects are formed through exclusionary operations, it becomes politically necessary to trace the operations of that construction and erasure.[8]

The above sketches in part a Foucaultian reinscription of the subject, an effort to resignify the subject as a site of resignification. As a result, it

8. At the Philadelphia Consortium in which this paper was presented with that of Seyla Benhabib, the following paragraph was inserted in the text: And what of the subject who theorizes, here and now? To claim that this is *my* position, then, and to affix my name to it is not to say that it comes from me; paradoxically, it comes from Seyla, who was authorized to train me, and if I have become derailed, that is surely not her fault, for the process of becoming constituted as a subject cannot be explained through recourse to a single origin. But if there is an "I" who speaks and speaks differently now, the agency of that "I" is derived from its opposition, among other formations, and the process of replaying and reconstituting the scenes of that "I's" construction is all there is to that "I:" the "I" would be nowhere, would not qualify as an "I," were it not for the positions that now oppose it. In a sense, the "I" who offers now a notion of the subject as a legacy of indebtedness, and a site of resignification can only be this "I" that it describes by virtue of the one it appears in one respect to oppose. A peculiar dependency, I'm sure, but it serves to make my point that the subject is always already subjected, before its positions are overtly articulated or opposed, and that this subjection is at the same time a subjectivation, a scene of enablement; power is not only a relation between subjects, but the principle and possibility of their formation, reformation or, perhaps in my case, deformation.

is not a 'bidding farewell' to the subject per se, but rather, a call to rework that notion outside the terms of an epistemological given. But perhaps Foucault is not really postmodern; after all, his is an analytics of *modern* power. There is, of course, talk about the death of the subject, but *which* subject is that? And what is the status of the utterance that announces its passing? What speaks now that that subject is dead? That there is a speaking seems clear, for how else could the utterance be heard? So clearly, the death of the subject is not the end of agency, speech or of political debate. There is the refrain, just now, when women are beginning to assume that the subject is dead (there is a difference between positions of poststructuralism which claim that the subject *never* existed, and postmodern positions which claim that the subject *once* had integrity, but no longer does). Some see this as a conspiracy against women and other disenfranchised groups who are now only beginning to speak on their own behalf. But what precisely is meant by this, and how do we account for the very strong criticisms of the subject as an instrument of western imperialist hegemony theorized by Gloria Anzaldua, Gayatri Spivak and various the orists of postcoloniality? Surely there is a caution offered here, that in the very struggle toward enfranchisement and democratization, we might adopt the very models of domination by which we were oppressed, not realizing that one way that domination works is through the regulation and production of subjects. Through what exclusions has the feminist subject been constructed, and how do those excluded domains return to haunt the "integrity" and "unity" of the feminist "we?" And how is it that the very category, the subject, the "we," that is supposed to be presumed for the purpose of solidarity, produces the very factionalization it is supposed to quell? Do women want to become subjects on the model which requires and produces an anterior region of abjection, or must feminism become a process which is self-critical about the processes that produce and destabilize identity categories? To take the construction of the subject as a political problematic is not the same as doing away with the subject. To deconstruct the subject is not to negate or throw away the concept; on the contrary, deconstruction implies only that we suspend all commitments to that to which the term, "the subject," refers, and that we consider the linguistic functions it serves in the consolidation and concealment of authority. To deconstruct is not to negate or to dismiss, but to call into question and, perhaps most important, to open up a term, like "the subject," to a reusage or redeployment that previously has not been authorized.

Within feminism, it seems as if there is some political necessity to speak as for *women*, and I would not contest that necessity. Surely, that is the way in which representational politics operates, and in this country, lobbying efforts are virtually impossible without recourse to identity politics.

So we agree that demonstrations and legislative efforts and radical movements need to claims in the name of women.

But this necessity needs to be reconciled with another. When the category of women is invoked as *describing* the constituency for which feminism speaks, an internal debate invariably begins over what the descriptive content of that term will be. There are those who would claim that there is an ontological specificity to women as child-bearers that forms the basis of a specific legal and political interest in representation, and then there are others who understand maternity to be a social relation that is, under current social circumstances, the specific and cross-cultural situation of women. And there are those who seek recourse to Gilligan and others to establish a feminine specificity that makes itself clear in women's communities or ways of knowing. But every time that specificity is articulated, there is resistance and factionalization within the very constituency that is supposed to be *unified* by the articulation of its common element. In the early eighties, the feminist "we" rightly came under attack by women of color who claimed that the "we" was invariably white, and that that "we" that was meant to solidify the movement was the very source of a painful factionalization. The effort to characterize a feminine specificity through recourse to maternity, whether biological or social, produced a similar factionalization and even a disavowal of feminism altogether. For surely all women are not mothers; some cannot be, some are too young or too old to be, some choose not to be, and for some who are mothers, that is not necessarily the rallying point of their politicization in feminism.

I would argue that any effort to give universal or specific content to the category of women, presuming that that guarantee of solidarity is required *in advance,* will necessarily produce factionalization, and that "identity" as a point of department can never hold as the solidifying ground of a feminist political movement. Identity categories are never merely descriptive, but always normative, and as such, exclusionary. This is not to say that the term "women" ought not to be used, or that we ought to announce the death of the category. On the contrary, if feminism presupposes that "women" designates an undesignatable field of differences, one that cannot be totalized or summarized by a descriptive identity category, then the very term becomes a site of permanent openness and resignifiability. I would argue that the rifts between and among women over the content of the term ought to be safeguarded and prized, indeed, that this constant rifting ought to be affirmed as the ungrounded ground of feminist theory. To deconstruct the subject of feminism is not, then, to censure its usage, but, on the contrary, to release the term into a future of multiple significations, to emancipate it from the maternal or racialist ontologies to which it has been restricted, and to give it play as a site where unanticipated meanings might come to bear.

Paradoxically, it may be only through releasing the category of women from a fixed referent that something like 'agency' becomes possible. For if the term permits of a resignification, if its referent is not fixed, then possibilities for new configurations of the term become possible. In a sense, what women signify has been taken for granted for too long, and what has been fixed as the 'referent' of the term has been "fixed," normalized, immobilized, paralyzed in positions of subordination. In effect, the signified has been conflated with the referent, whereby a set of meanings has been taken to inhere in the real nature of women themselves. To recast the referent as the signified, and to authorize or safeguard the category of women as a site of possible resignifications is, on the one hand, to expand the possibilities of what it means to be a woman and in this sense to condition and enable an enhanced sense of agency.

One might well ask: but doesn't there have to be a set of norms that discriminate between those descriptions that ought to adhere to the category of women and those that do not? The only answer to that question is a counter-question: who would set those norms, and what contestations would they produce? To establish a normative foundation for settling the question of what ought properly to be included in the description of women would be only and always to produce a new site of political contest. That foundation would settle nothing, but would of its own necessity founder on its own authoritarian ruse. This is not to say that there is no foundation, but rather, that wherever there is one, there will also be a foundering, a contestation. That such foundations exist only to be put into question is, as it were, the permanent risk of the process of democratization. To refuse that contest is to sacrifice the radical democratic impetus of feminist politics. That the category is unconstrained, even that it comes to serve anti-feminist purposes, will be part of the risk of this procedure. But this is a risk that is produced by the very foundationalism that seeks to safeguard feminism against it. In a sense, this risk is the foundation, and hence is not, of any feminist practice.

In the final part of this paper, I would like to turn to a related question, one that emerges from the concern that a feminist theory cannot proceed without presuming the materiality of women's bodies, the materiality of sex. The chant of anti-postmodernism runs, if everything is discourse, then is there no reality to bodies? How do we understand the material violence that women suffer? In responding to this criticism, I would like to suggest that the very formulation misunderstands the critical point.

It is possible to assert the 'materiality' of bodies, and even the materiality of suffering within poststructuralism, but what constitutes 'materiality' is not immediately clear, and neither is it obvious what constitutes, regulates, and delimits that field of power, violence, sexuality, signification that we call "real" bodies and, in particular, sexed bodies.

I don't know what postmodernism is, but I do have some sense of what it might mean to subject notions of the body and materiality to a deconstructive critique. To deconstruct the concept of matter or that of bodies is not to negate or refuse either term. To deconstruct these terms means, rather, to continue to use them, to repeat them, to repeat them subversively, and to displace them from the contexts in which they have been deployed as instruments of oppressive power. Here it is of course necessary to state quite plainly that the options for theory are not exhausted by *presuming* materiality, on the one hand, and *negating* materiality, on the other. It is my purpose to do precisely neither of these. To call a presupposition into question is not the same as doing away with it; rather, it is to free it up from its metaphysical lodgings in order to occupy and to serve very different political aims. To problematize the matter of bodies entails in the first instance a loss of epistemological certainty, but this loss of certainty does not necessarily entail political nihilism as its result. The body posited as prior to the sign, is always *posited* or *signified* as *prior*. This signification works through producing an *effect* of its own procedure, the body that it nevertheless and simultaneously claims to discover as that which *precedes* signification. If the body signified as prior to signification is an effect of signification, then the mimetic or representational status of language, which claims that signs follow bodies as their necessary mirrors, is not mimetic at all; on the contrary, it is productive, constitutive, one might even argue *performative,* inasmuch as this signifying act produces the body that it then claims to find prior to any and all signification.

If a deconstruction of the materiality of bodies suspends and problematizes the traditional ontological referent of the term, it does not freeze, banish, render useless, or deplete of meaning the usage of the term; on the contrary, it provides the conditions to *mobilize* the signifier in the service of an alternative production.

Consider that most material of concepts, "sex," which Monique Wittig calls a thoroughly political category, and which Michel Foucault calls a regulatory and "fictitious unity." For both theorists, sex does not *describe* a prior materiality, but produces and regulates the *intelligibility* of the *materiality* of bodies. For both, and in different ways, the category of sex imposes a duality and a uniformity on bodies in order to maintain reproductive sexuality as a compulsory order. I've argued elsewhere more precisely how this works, but for our purposes, I would like to suggest that this kind of categorization can be called a violent one, a forceful one, and that this discursive ordering and production of bodies in accord with the category of sex is itself a material violence.

The violence of the letter, the violence of the mark which establishes what will and will not signify, what will and will not be included within the intelligible, takes on a political significance when the letter is the law or the authoritative legislation of what will and will not qualify as the materiality of sex.

Can this kind of poststructural analysis tell us anything about violence and suffering? Is it perhaps that forms of violence are to be understood as more pervasive, more constitutive, and more insidious than prior models have allowed us to see?

Consider the legal restrictions that regulate what does and does not count as rape: here the politics of violence operate through regulating what will and will not be able to appear as an effect of violence. There is, then, already in this foreclosure a violence at work, a marking off in advance of what will or will not qualify under the signs of "rape" or "government violence," or in the case of states in which twelve separate pieces of empirical evidence are required to establish "rape," what then can be called a governmentally facilitated rape.

A similar line of reasoning is at work in discourses on rape when the "sex" of a woman is claimed as that which establishes the responsibility for her own violation. The defense attorney in the New Bedford gang rape case asked the plaintiff, "If you're living with a man, what are you doing running around the streets getting raped?"[9] The "running around" in this sentence collides grammatically with "getting raped," "getting" is procuring, acquiring, having, as if this were a treasure she was running around after, but "getting raped" suggests the passive voice. Literally, of course, it would be difficult to be "running around" and be "getting raped" at the same time, which suggests that there must be an elided passage, here, perhaps a directional that leads from the former to the latter? If the sense of the sentence is, "running around [looking to get] raped," which seems to be the only logical way of bridging the two parts of the sentence, then rape as a passive acquisition is precisely the object of her active search. The first clause suggests that she "belongs" at home, with her man, that the home is a site in which she is the domestic property of that man, and the "streets" establish her as open season. If she is looking to get raped, she is looking to become the property of some other, and this objective is installed in her desire, conceived here as quite frantic in its pursuit. She is "running around," suggesting that she is running around looking under every rock for a rapist to satisfy her. Significantly, the phrase installs as the structuring principle of her desire 'getting raped,' where 'rape' is figured as an act of willful self-expropriation. Since becoming the property of a man is the objective of her "sex," articulated in and through her sexual desire, and rape is the way in which that appropriation occurs "on the

9. Quoted in Catherine Mackinnon, *Toward a Feminist Theory of the State* (Boston: Harvard University Press), 1989, p. 171.

street" [a logic that implies that rape is to marriage as the streets are to the home, that is, that "rape" is street-marriage, a marriage without a home, a marriage for homeless girls, and that marriage is domesticated rape], then "rape" is the logical consequence of the enactment of her sex and sexuality outside domesticity. Never mind that this rape took place in a bar, for the "bar" is within this imaginary but an extension of the "street," or perhaps its exemplary moment, for there is no enclosure, that is, no protection, other than the *home* as domestic marital space. In any case, the single cause of her violation is here figured as her "sex" which, given its natural propensity to seek expropriation, once dislocated from domestic propriety, naturally pursues its rape and is thus responsible for it.

The category of sex here functions as a principle of production and regulation at once, the cause of the violation installed as the formative principle of the body's sexuality. Here sex is a category, but not merely a representation; it is a principle of production, intelligibility, and regulation which enforces a violence and rationalizes it after the fact. The very terms by which the violation is explained *enact* the violation, and concede that the violation was underway before it takes the empirical form of a criminal act. That rhetorical enactment *shows* that "violence" is produced through the foreclosure effected by this analysis, through the erasure and negation that determine the field of appearances and intelligibility of crimes of culpability. As a category that effectively produces the political meaning of what it describes, "sex" here works its silent "violence" in regulating what is and is not designatable.

I place the terms "violence" and "sex" under quotation marks: is this the sign of a certain deconstruction, the end to politics? Or am I underscoring the iterable structure of these terms, the ways in which they yield a repetition, occur ambiguously, and am I doing that precisely to further a political analysis? I place them in quotation marks to show that they are under contest, up for grabs, to initiate the contest, to question their traditional deployment, and call for some other. The quotation marks do not place into question the urgency or credibility of sex or violence as political issues, but, rather, show that the way their very materiality is circumscribed is fully political. The effect of the quotation marks is to denaturalize the terms, to designate these signs as sites of political debate.

If there is a fear that by no longer being able to take for granted the subject, its gender, its sex, or its materiality, that feminism will founder, it might be wise to consider the political consequences of keeping in their place the very premises that have tried to secure our subordination from the start.

9

Subjectivity in social analysis
Renato Rosaldo

According to ethnographies written in the classic mode, the detached observer epitomizes neutrality and impartiality. This detachment is said to produce objectivity because social reality comes into focus only if one stands at a certain distance. When one stands too close, the ethnographic lens supposedly blurs its human subjects. In this view, the researcher must remove observer bias by becoming the emotional, cognitive, and moral equivalent of a blank slate. Translated into ethical terms . . . the myth of detachment gives ethnographers an appearance of innocence, which distances them from complicity with imperialist domination. Prejudice and distortion, however, putatively derive from the vices of subjectivity: passionate concern, prior knowledge, and ethical engagement.

If distance has certain arguable advantages, so too does closeness, and both have their deficits. Yet classic social science has endowed the former with excessive virtue, and the latter with excessive vice. Distance normalizing accounts . . . all too often lead ethnographic writings to translate the compelling events of daily life into the routine performance of conventional acts. The present chapter contests the equation of analytical distance and scientific objectivity by arguing that social analysts should explore their subjects from a number of positions, rather than being locked into any particular one.

In my view, social analysts can rarely, if ever, become detached observers. There is no Archimedean point from which to remove oneself from the mutual conditioning of social relations and human knowledge. Cultures and their "positioned subjects" are laced with power, and power in turn is shaped by cultural forms. Like form and feeling, culture and power are inextricably intertwined. In discussing forms of social knowledge, both of analysts and of human actors, one must consider their social positions. What are the complexities of the speaker's social identity? What life experiences have shaped it? Does the person speak from a position of relative dominance or relative subordination? This chapter uses a series of examples to explore the consequences of thus understanding the factors that condition social analysis.

The heroics of value-free inquiry

Discussions of objectivity in the human sciences ritually invoke Max Weber as their founding ancestor. The Weberian tradition has legitimated research programs that attempt, in the name of value-free inquiry, to clarify the world rather than to change it. Weber's successors have transformed the original demanding ethic of "disinterestedness" into an orthodoxy widespread in the social sciences that equates objectivity with an attitude of emotional disengagement, cognitive distance, and moral indifference.

Weber himself advocated a position that partially overlaps with, but also significantly diverges from, the particular kind of distanced observation so often promoted by his successors. In "Science as a Vocation," for example, he argues that neither the prophet nor the demagogue has any place in the classroom. One should neither preach one's religion nor impose one's politics on a captive audience. Sociological analyses provide no scientific grounds for making judgments about whether the phenomena under study are humanly worthwhile. Questions, for instance, about the ultimate worth of monastic discipline simply cannot be answered within the limits of sociological inquiry. In a historical epoch marked by the "disenchantment of the world," scientific knowledge should not be conflated with ultimate values.

In my view, however, the notion of one's profession as a calling in the pursuit of perfection produces careers that revolve around the twin poles of great effort and tremendous frustration. Arguably, this vocational ethic promotes not only institutional devotion and human unhappiness but also an overly constricted definition of legitimate sources of knowledge. Weberian knowledge emerges more readily from "manly" strength than "womanly" weakness. Yet sources of knowledge other than absolute devotion to a higher standard also provide certain insights for social analysis.

In the present era, feminist thought has made the limitations of the harsh ethic demanded by the warrior priesthood particularly evident. Weber's "manly" ethic should be loosened because its androcentrism has suppressed valuable sources of insight deemed unworthy by bearers of the high standard. This ethic underestimates the analytical possibilities of "womanly weaknesses" and "unmanly states," such as rage, feebleness, frustration, depression, embarrassment, and passion. Victims of oppression, for example, can provide insights into the workings of power that differ from those available to people in high positions. The welfare mother and the chief of police surely differ in their knowledge and feelings about state power. Arguably, human feelings and human failings provide as much insight for social analysis as subjecting oneself to the "manly" ordeals of self-discipline that constitute science as a vocation. Why narrow one's vision to a God's-eye view from on high? Why not use a wider spectrum of less heroic, but equally insightful, analytical positions?

A tent of one's own

Adherence to the vision of anthropology as a vocation has been widespread but not universal. Notable exceptions do exist, particularly among women ethnographers. According to her ethnography *Never in Anger: Portrait of an Eskimo Family,* Jean Briggs worked without Weberian pretensions.[1] In conducting her fieldwork, she did not try to elevate herself to the dignified heights of science as a vocation. Instead, she used her own feelings, particularly depression, frustration, rage, and humiliation, as sources of insight into the emotional life among members of an Eskimo group in the Canadian Northwest Territories.

Briggs struggled to do her research and survive under exceptionally difficult conditions. While conducting fieldwork, she suffered from not altogether unrealistic anxieties about freezing to death, nutritional deprivation, and severe illness. Members of the Eskimo community where she resided were caring, even solicitous of her well-being. According to their norms, however, her desires for domestic privacy were opaque, and her emotional outbursts threatened to rip apart their intricately woven social fabric. In a reversal of usual relations between rational Western Man and the emotional rest, the Eskimos lived with a culturally valued degree of emotional control that the culturally more impulsive ethnographer simply could not attain.

Faced with demanding physical and emotional circumstances, Briggs needed a tent of her own, a place where she could renew body and soul. In time, she closeted herself every evening in her tent, and indulged her cravings for familiar food, books, and work. When summer changed to autumn, her hosts advised her to fold up the tent and move in with them, but she resisted: "Could I tolerate the company of others for twenty-four hours a day? In the past month my tent had become a refuge, into which I withdrew every evening after the rest of the camp was in bed, to repair

1. Jean Briggs, *Never in Anger: Portrait of an Eskimo Family* (Cambridge, Mass.: Harvard University Press, 1970). For more recent reflections on *Never in Anger,* see Jean L. Briggs, "In Search of Emotional Meaning," *Ethos* 15 (1987): 8–15.

the ravages to my spirit with the help of bannock and peanut butter, boiled rice, frozen dates, and Henry James."[2] Briggs often took her penciled notes into her tent and "sat happily typing" for long hours at a time.[3] When mishaps, such as lumps of slush falling into her typewriter, ended her workday, she responded with emotional outbursts that offended her more emotionally disciplined hosts.[4] Like Geertz, she regarded her typewriter as a sacred object, not to be profaned. The typewriter stood for her workspace and her professional identity.

Briggs's ethnography more nearly resembles the captivity narrative, a tale of deprivation and survival, than the romantic quest, a story of adventure and conquest. In commenting on her irrepressible cravings for the "solace of oatmeal, dates, boiled rice, and bannock," the ethnographer accurately depicts her experience as one of isolation, deprivation, and risk: "It is hard for anyone who has not experienced isolation from his familiar world to conceive the vital importance of maintaining symbolic ties with that world and the sense of deprivation that results from their absence. One can be driven to lengths that seem ludicrous once one is safely back on home ground."[5] Although the choice was originally her own, Briggs found herself overwhelmed by an alien world. In response to emotional and physical deprivation, she sought consolation through food, and even went so far as to hoard eight sesame seeds in tin foil. The ethnographer was held prisoner, not by the Eskimos but by her determination to succeed in doing fieldwork under demanding conditions.

Briggs's resolve to survive a demanding test had something of the sentimental heroics of victimization found in certain melodramatic nineteenth-century novels (notably including those of Henry James, and perhaps others she was reading at the time). Yet this resolve did not inspire her to follow the model of masculine heroics in which, as Weber says, the devoted scientist rises "to the height and dignity of the subject he pretends to serve."[6] In everyday fieldwork, she never aspired to perfection. Instead, she made mistakes, felt frustrated, broke into tears, had angry outbursts, grew fatigued, and became depressed. On one occasion, a fishing com-

2. Briggs, *Never in Anger*, pp. 237–38.   3. Ibid., p. 272.
4. Ibid., p. 259. The place of the typewriter in ethnographic discourse clearly merits more extended exploration. The machine appears as often as food and novels. It often symbolizes partially successful, partially frustrated efforts to maintain an academic identity by creating an imaginary "office" while doing fieldwork.
5. Ibid., p. 229.
6. Weber, "Science as a Vocation," in From *Max Weber: Essays in Sociology*, ed. H. H. Gerth and C. Wright Mills (New York: Oxford University Press, 1958), p. 137.

panion warned her to move to a safer spot, but after an initial effort: "Suddenly, something in me gave up. I had no will to struggle further. Dropping to my knees and lowering my head to the ice, I crawled toward home, seething with humiliation and rage but totally unable to stand up. Shielded by the parka and hood that fell over my face, I wept at my ignominy."[7] Even in retrospect, she could not decide whether she fell to her hands and knees because the wind was overwhelming or because she was fatigued from depression. In any case, she survived only by abandoning her dignity and enduring humiliation.[8]

Briggs makes her own depression central to *Never in Anger*. Her final chapter comprises an eighty-two-page case history, depicting the relationship between the ethnographer and her informants as it moved from covert conflicts, through more overt ones, to being shunned. Initially, she was treated as an honored guest, an adopted daughter, a stranger, and a curiosity. Later, she became like a recalcitrant child who oscillated between helpless dependence and mutinous independence. Finally, she suffered the ultimate sanction and was ostracized because, as one Eskimo said in a letter, "she is so annoying, we wish more and more that she would leave."[9]

Briggs explores her fieldwork moods not as an end in itself but as a vehicle for understanding Eskimo family and emotional life. She learned about their conceptions of emotions from their efforts to interpret her unfamiliar ways of acting: "It is possible that in that early period they were watching, weighing, not yet confirming unpleasant judgements but puzzling how to interpret my strange behavior, just as I puzzled how to interpret theirs."[10] Whenever she withdrew from her hosts, they interpreted her behavior by saying she was tired, regardless of whether she felt depressed, cold, or simply in need of solitude. In retrospect, however, Briggs wondered whether the people's caring attention reflected notions about a white woman's feebleness, a perception of emotional fatigue, or both. For

7. Briggs, *Never in Anger*, p. 298.
8. Briggs's account formally resembles works where the anthropologist appears as fall guy, such as in Geertz's typewriter incident, the preface to Evans-Pritchard's classic, *The Nuer*, and Castaneda's *Teachings of Don Juan*. Readers without fieldwork experience often respond to the fall-guy figure with fantasies of "if only I'd been there, I'd have done it right." Such readings both miss the near-parodic conventions that have formed the fall guy and underestimate the powerful effects of deprivation, anxiety, and disorientation often undergone by field-workers. Culture shock consists not only of the confrontation with an alien reality but also of an overwhelming sense of loss, produced by the interruption of one's intimate relations and familiar patterns of love and work.
9. Ibid., p. 286.   10. Ibid., p. 234.

the Eskimos, unpredictable tiredness and emotional upset were closely associated.[11] Their perception of her "tiredness" revealed much about their views of emotions, particularly as experienced in the informal practices of everyday life rather than as articulated in abstract context-free statements.

Briggs delineates transitions in ethnographer-informant relations through a reflexive narrative that highlights cultural conceptions more than the dynamics of power. She displays a grasp of culturally shaped emotional lives, both her own and that of the Eskimos. Yet her analysis of power relations stresses her initial status as honored guest and her later childlike dependence without sufficiently acknowledging her place in a system of domination. During the fieldwork period, as she later realized, the ethnographer failed to recognize the burden her possessions imposed on her host, Inuttiaq: "It was only after I had returned to my own country that I saw, in my photographs of a spring move, the contrast between Inuttiaq's sled load and Ipuituq's, the latter over knee high, the former shoulder high. At the time I was blind."[12] Even in retrospect, however, Briggs was able to perceive the cultural shape of emotions with fine insight, but remained relatively blind to the material differences that divided her from her hosts.

Briggs's relationship with the Eskimos was contradictory, at once vulnerable and dominant. In the local setting, she depended on her hosts for basic survival; in the national setting, she was richer and more powerful than they. Her experience among the Eskimos was colored by feelings of vulnerability, yet her treatment as an honored guest in the beginning and the passive resistance of shunning toward the end were doubtless shaped by the power dynamics between the ethnographer and her informants. Neither her experience nor her relations with the Eskimos were as unified as her narrative persona would make them appear.

Multiplex personal identities and social analysis

Cautionary tales that circulate among field-workers warn against going too far in identifying with the so-called natives. In one such tale, for example, legendary turn-of-the-century North American ethnographer Frank Hamilton Cushing's writings reputedly grew better and better until the day he was initiated into a Zuni secret society. From that time onward, it is said, his ethnography deteriorated. Moral: don't go native. "Going native" is said to mean the end of scientific knowledge. Often

11. Ibid., p. 242.   12. Ibid., p. 247.

traced to Malinowski's legendary fieldwork, this view asserts that the op-
timal field-worker should dance on the edge of a paradox by simultaneously becoming "one of the people" and remaining an academic. The
term *participant-observation* reflects even as it shapes the field-worker's
double persona.

The dilemmas of identification as a source of knowledge have been
forcefully presented in a recent paper by anthropologist Dorinne Kondo.
As a Japanese-American, Kondo was pressured in Japan to conform with
norms more fully than other outsiders. In a vivid anecdote, she describes
herself on a muggy afternoon in Tokyo, pushing a baby in a stroller and
shopping for fish and vegetables: "As I glanced up into the shiny metal
surface of the butcher's display case, I noticed someone who looked ter-
ribly familiar: a typical young housewife, in slip-on sandals and the kind
of cotton shift the Japanese label 'home-wear,' a woman walking with a
characteristically Japanese bend in the knees and sliding of the feet. Suddenly I clutched the handle of the stroller to steady myself as a wave of
dizziness washed over me – for I realized I had caught a glimpse of nothing less than my own reflection."[13] Kondo felt overwhelmed with anxiety.
Had she gone native? Had what Clifford Geertz saw as the tenuous construct shaping field relations become the literal truth? Had she irreversibly
become the dutiful daughter of her Japanese "family"? Would she now become a Japanese housewife rather than a Japanese-American academic?

Kondo thought she had gone too far, and she followed disciplinary
norms by attempting to gain distance on her situation. She returned to
the United States for a month. On returning to Japan, she moved into
an apartment next door to her landlady's family. Rather like Jean Briggs,
she hoped her new situation would allow her to enjoy "the best of
both worlds: the warmth of belonging to a family and the privacy of my
own space."[14]

Yet Kondo could only distance herself to a certain degree. Because of
their cultural expectations about a person who looks so like them, the
Japanese obliged her to act like a "native." Her near-native persona gave
the Japanese-American ethnographer certain advantages, such as rapid
incorporation into a number of social groups. But it also inhibited her in
other areas. Unlike a more foreign researcher, Kondo could neither ask
"indelicate" questions nor speak with people across certain status lines.

The moral Kondo draws from her story is that the process of knowing
involves the whole self. The social analyst is at once cognitive, emotional,
and ethical. She constructs knowledge through contexts of shifting power

13. Dorinne Kondo, "Dissolution and Reconstitution of Self: Implications for
    Anthropological Epistemology," *Cultural Anthropology* 1 (1986): 74–88, at
    p. 74.
14. Ibid., p. 80.

relations that involve varying degrees of distance and intimacy. Rather than uphold detachment as the unified standard of objectivity, Kondo argues for the explicit recognition of multiple sources of knowledge in social analysis.

Kondo's proposal to dissolve the detached observer with his "God's-eye view" of social reality makes most classic ethnographers quake. Are there no standards? Where has objectivity gone? Can this be the advent of unbridled chaos that allows nihilism and relativism to walk hand in hand in a land where "anything goes"? In what follows, I argue, to the contrary, that dismantling objectivism creates a space for ethical concerns in a territory once regarded as value-free. It enables the social analyst to become a social critic.

Social criticism and multiplex communities

In general, social critics attempt to use persuasive eloquence and adept social analysis to make oppression morally unacceptable and human emancipation politically conceivable.[15] In so doing, they invoke local cultural values, such as justice, well-being, or cosmic balance. They engage in arguments about social issues where empirical analyses and ethical judgments are inextricably intertwined. In such cultural arenas, human relations are governed more often by conflict than consensus.

In this recent book entitled *Interpretation and Social Criticism,* political theorist Michael Walzer argues that social criticism involves making complex ethical judgments about existing social arrangements.[16] The moral vision so applied emerges, not from the outside, but from within the society under criticism. In all human societies, everyday life and moral standards overlap, but they also, as Walzer aptly stresses, remain to a certain degree at odds with one another: "The moral world and the social world are more or less coherent," he writes, "but they are never more than more or less coherent. Morality is always potentially subversive of class

15. Because oppressed groups emerge from different social formations, with distinctive cultures and histories, their political visions also differ. Yet a number of otherwise perceptive social thinkers persist in attributing universal goals to such movements. Ernesto Laclau and Chantal Mouffe, for example, posit liberty and equality, driving from the French Revolution, as the only conceivable programs for modern radical democratic movements. Hence they find themselves forced to argue, among other things, that present-day Moslem revolutionary movements are neither radical nor modern. See Ernesto Laclau and Chantal Mouffe, *Hegemony and Socialist Strategy: Towards a Radical Democratic Politics* (London: Verso, 1985).

16. Michael Walzer, *Interpretation and Social Criticism* (Cambridge, Mass.: Harvard University Press, 1987).

and power."[17] Moral visions grow out of specific forms of life that they both unthinkingly reflect and critically call into question. Social critics thus remain grounded in the local cultures to which they direct their exhortations and invectives.

Ideally, according to Walzer, social critics should be meaningfully connected with, rather than utterly detached from, the group under critique. Like my own argument, his assertion contests the conventional wisdom that idealizes the impartial detached observer. Walzer argues that the critic should be socially connected, probably not at the center of things, but neither a complete stranger nor a mere spectator. In his view, the most powerful members of society make better apologists than critics, and those most marginal either perceive their world through distorted lenses or all too readily cave in to efforts to co-opt them.

Unfortunately, Walzer limits the applicability of his analysis by defining the key word *community* too narrowly. It is as if he accepted classic ethnography's notion that each individual can belong to one, and only one, discrete (unambiguous, nonoverlapping) culture. No doubt certain limiting cases exist where a social critic's audience and community are one and the same discrete group. More frequently, however, one finds precisely what Walzer overlooks: a plurality of partially disjunctive, partially overlapping communities that crisscross between the people social critics address and those for whom they speak.

The complexity of a social critic's "community" emerges with a certain clarity in the work of the celebrated social historian E. P. Thompson. The moral vision that informs his committed history is evident, for example, in the conclusion of *The Making of the English Working Class,* where he sketches a "what if" vision of the past in order to critique the present.[18] What if, he asks, the two cultures of nineteenth-century English radicalism – the craftspeople and the romantics – had united in resistance to Utilitarianism and "the exploitive and oppressive relationships intrinsic to industrial capitalism"?:

> After William Blake, no mind was at home in both cultures, nor had the genius to interpret the two traditions to each other. It was a muddled Mr. Owen who offered to disclose the "new moral world," while Wordsworth and Coleridge had withdrawn behind their own ramparts of disenchantment. Hence these years appear at times to display, not a revolutionary challenge, but a resistance movement, in which both the Romantics and the Radical craftsmen opposed the annunciation of Acquis-

17. Ibid., p. 22.
18. E. P. Thompson, *The Making of the English Working Class* (New York: Vintage Books, 1966).

itive Man. In the failure of the two traditions to come to a point of junction, something was lost. How much we cannot be sure, for we are among the losers.[19]

For some fifty years, working-class struggles created and exemplified a "heroic culture" that gave life to the radical tradition. "Their" nineteenth-century failure to unite the two traditions is also "our" twentieth-century failure. As the inheritors of radicalism, "we" have been diminished by the gulf separating romantics and craftspeople. Thompson thus exhorts "us," his readers, to live up to "our" radical heritage by uniting workers, artists, and intellectuals in heroic struggle.

Thompson's shifting use of pronouns indicates the complexity of his identifications. His political communities extend, somewhat ambiguously, to nineteenth-century radicalism; his communities of readers include professional historians and lay radicals. He both distances himself from the nineteenth-century radicals and identifies them as predecessors in "our" tradition of dissent. At the same time, he addresses his social criticism to an international group of present-day historians and radicals, among whom he is an eminent figure.

Let us now juxtapose Thompson's moving conclusion with its rhetorical opposite, the ethnographer Harold of Conklin's classic technical paper, "Shifting Cultivation and Succession to Grassland Climax."[20] This nonobvious comparison underscores the importance of distinguishing the remaking of social analysis from the use of any particular rhetorical form. The attempts of a renewed social analysis to grasp the interplay of culture and power require not only experimentation in writing but also changes in the norms for reading. To maintain older habits of reading is willy-nilly to assimilate new forms of social analysis to the classic period's conventional wisdom. If readers shift their practices, on the other hand, they can recover certain works written in distanced normalizing discourse.

By contrast with Thompson's explicit moral passion, Conklin tacitly claims a "guest membership" in the ethnic Hanunoo community of the Philippines, where he resided for an extended period and whose language he speaks fluently. His paper describes Hanunoo agriculture to an international scientific elite, a community in which he is a prominent member. His communities range as widely in geopolitical terms as his memberships in them vary in their definitions.

19. Ibid., p. 832.
20. Harold C. Conklin, "Shifting Cultivation and Succession to Grassland Climax," *The Proceedings of the Ninth Pacific Science Congress, 1957* 7 (1959): 60–62.

When Conklin meticulously attends to culturally relevant discriminations made by Philippine shifting cultivators, his voice remains scrupulously dispassionate and scientific:

> Where climatic and terrain conditions are ideal for swidden agriculture, a single firing of cut jungle does not – by itself – start a succession to grassland. However, repeated firing of the same site during the following and successive years, for recultivation or by accident, may kill many of the coppicing stumps and young tree seedlings, and discourage the growth of broad leafed shade-providing shrubs, while favoring the spread of erect grasses (especially *Imperata*) whose extensive stoloniferous rhizomes and deep roots are left uninjured.[21]

In other words, under ideal conditions swidden or shifting cultivation (popularly known as "slash and burn") does not start a process that results in the replacement of forest with agriculturally unusable grassland. Ideally, shifting cultivators burn off the forest cover, cultivate the spot for about two years, and then allow the forest to regenerate over an extended fallow period. Such factors as cattle grazing and the dispersal of gardens increase the likelihood of an ideal process. The ecologically destructive succession to grassland climax, in contrast, is associated with such variables as cultivating ridges and hilltops, the simultaneous clearing of adjacent plots, repeatedly burning grass for hunting, and planting grain crops for more than two successive years on a single plot. In its form and content, the analysis appears detached and balanced.

From another angle of vision, however, Conklin's technical article appears as a passionate plea for the ecological soundness of Hanunoo agriculture. In the Philippines, shifting cultivation has long been under assault by public opinion, the media, and governmental policy. The dominant lowland view holds that such agricultural systems, in all times and in all places, destroy the ecological balance by starting a succession to grassland climax. Conklin has chosen a rhetoric designed to persuade an audience of ethnographers, botanists, and agronomists, who conceivably could in turn convince policymakers. Read in this context, the ethnographer emerges as an advocate for the Hanunoo and as a critic of dominant national policy. Like other ethnographers, the author identifies with the underdogs, the people under study. His apparently neutral article has its partisan side. It combines descriptive ethnography, advocacy, and social criticism.

Thus understood, Conklin's technical article becomes an example of committed social analysis. The tacit implications of his article reflect a

21. Ibid., p. 60.

politics grounded in notions of human well-being and ecological concern. To the extent that "Shifting Cultivation" addresses policymakers, it enters an arena of partisan debate where power, knowledge, feeling, and judgment are at play. Those who enter the debate do so from particular positions with complex stakes in the struggle. In this context, Conklin's neutrality and omniscience become a rhetorically strategic means for assuming the authoritative high ground of scientific knowledge divorced from human interests. He appears simply to report the facts, letting the chips fall where they may, but hoping in this manner to convince Filipino politicians to overcome their prejudice and vested interests.

Despite obvious differences of explicitness, politics, and rhetoric, Conklin's "scientific" ethnography compares, in its serious tone and its persuasive moral vision, with the celebrated committed history of E. P. Thompson. Conklin uses self-effacing detachment and scientific authority on behalf of Hanunoo shifting cultivators; Thompson uses flamboyant identification and a compelling moral vision to benefit the working class. Both attempt to give voice to the voiceless. In a dissenting mode, the ethnographer and the social historian aim to articulate the interests and the aspirations of the dispossessed. Where Conklin demands high ethical and scientific standards of his fellow ethnographers and policymakers, Thompson exhorts equally much from his fellow historians and English radicals. As advocates for subordinate groups, they both develop critiques of social domination. As social critics, the "outsider" speaks the universal language of science, and the "insider" uses the orator's impassioned exhortations.

Recapitulation

Using objectivism as a foil, I have contested the masculine heroics of Weber's devotion to "science as a vocation." His passionate detachment brings together thought and feeling in a manner that accomplishes much, but too severely restricts the legitimate sources of knowledge for social analysis. The scientist's twin standards of discipline and dignity exclude insights from "lesser" sources of knowledge, ranging from Geertz's "feebleness" and Briggs's "depression" to Fanon's "rage" and Hurston's "irony."

The analyst's position depends, in part, on the interplay of culture and power. Geertz's "feebleness" resulted from his becoming attuned to the power dynamics at play between himself and his Japanese subjects. The goals of the two parties became more and more painfully incongruous. Briggs's "depression" emerged from her sensitivity to the culturally distinctive emotional lives of her Eskimo hosts. Her impulsiveness came to be increasingly at odds with her informant's self-control. Although one emphasizes power and the other culture, both ethnographers underscore the interaction of their feelings, their observations, and their fieldwork situations.

Kondo's parable of the researcher who looks into a mirror and sees not her analytical self but a Japanese housewife shuffling along the sidewalk argues for using the plural to speak of an observer's identities. More a busy intersection through which multiple identities crisscross than a unified coherent self, the knowing person not only blends a range of cognitive, emotional, and ethical capabilities but her social identities also variously include being a woman, a researcher, and a Japanese-American. That these identities themselves change during fieldwork appears to be the moral of Kondo's deepening awareness of her aversion to becoming a Japanese housewife.

The social analyst's multiple identities at once underscore the potential for uniting an analytical with an ethical project and render obsolete the view of the utterly detached observer who looks down from on high. In this respect, my argument parallels Walzer's discussion of social critic who is connected to a community, not isolated and detached. Rather than work downward from abstract principles, social critics work outward from in-depth knowledge of a specific form of life. Informed by such conceptions as social justice, human dignity, and equality, they use their moral imagination to move from the world as it actually is to a locally persuasive vision of how it ought to be. Because different communities differ in their problems and possibilities, such visions must be more local than universal.

Walzer's discussion of the "connected critic" goes down the wrong path, however, when it assumes that each individual belongs to only one discrete community. The work of Kondo, Thompson, Conklin, and Fanon indicates that individuals often belong to multiple, overlapping communities. Consider how one can be a member of distinct communities of birth, ethnicity, socialization, education, political participation, residence, research, and readership.

In emphasizing the relatively privileged social critic who acts as a broker for the oppressed, Walzer glosses over social criticism made from socially subordinate positions, where one can work more toward mobilizing resistance than persuading the powerful. Such subordinate critical perspectives range from Fanon's uncompromising rage through Flake's modulated anger to Marx's and Hurston's more oblique modes, where wit becomes a tool for apprehending social incongruities and a weapon for use in social conflict.

HUMAN STUDIES AS RHETORIC, NARRATIVE, AND CRITIQUE

- Zygmunt Bauman, *Is there a postmodern sociology?*
- James Clifford, *On ethnographic allegory*
- Richard Harvey Brown, *Rhetoric, textuality, and the postmodern turn in sociological theory*
- Nancy Fraser and Linda Nicholson, *Social criticism without philosophy: An encounter between feminism and postmodernism*

10

Is there a postmodern sociology?
Zygmunt Bauman

Why do we need the concept of 'postmodernity'? On the face of it, this concept is redundant. In so far as it purports to capture and articulate what is novel at the present stage of western history, it legitimizes itself in terms of a job which has been already performed by other, better established concepts – like those of the 'post-capitalist' or 'post-industrial' society. Concepts which have served the purpose well: they sharpened our attention to what is new and discontinuous, and offered a reference point for counter-arguments in favour of continuity.

Is, therefore, the advent of the 'postmodernity' idea an invitation to re-hash or simply replay an old debate? Does it merely signify an all-too-natural fatigue, which a protracted and inconclusive debate must generate? Is it merely an attempt to inject new excitement into an increasingly tedious pastime (as Gordon Allport once said, we social scientists never solve problems; we only get bored with them)? If this is the case, then the idea of 'postmodernity' is hardly worth a second thought, and this is exactly what many a seasoned social scientist suggests.

Appearances are, however, misleading (and the advocates and the detractors of the idea of 'postmodernity' share the blame for confusion). The concept of 'postmodernity' may well capture and articulate a quite different sort of novelty than those the older, apparently similar concepts accommodated and theorized. It can legitimize its right to exist – its cognitive value – only if it does exactly this: if it generates a social-scientific discourse which theorizes different aspects of contemporary experience, or theorizes them in a different way.

I propose that the concept of 'postmodernity' has a value entirely of its own in so far as it purports to capture and articulate the novel experience of just one, but crucial social category of contemporary society: the intellectuals. Their novel experience – that is, their reassessment of their own position within society, their reorientation of the collectively performed function, and their new strategies.

Theory, Culture & Society (SAGE, London, Newbury Park, Beverly Hills and New Delhi). Vol. 5 (1988), 217–37.

Antonio Gramsci called the 'organic intellectuals' of a particular class the part of the educated elite which elaborated the self-identity of the class, the values instrumental to the defence and enhancement of its position within society, an ideology legitimizing its claims to autonomy and domination. One may argue to what extent Gramsci's (1971) 'organic intellectuals' did in fact answer this description; to what extent they were busy painting their own idealized portraits, rather than those of their ostensible sitters; to what extent the likenesses of all other classes represented (unknowingly, to be sure) the painters' cravings for conditions favourable and propitious for the kind of work the intellectuals had been best prepared, and willing, to do. In the discourse of 'postmodernity', however, the usual disguise is discarded. The participants of the discourse appear in the role of 'organic intellectuals' of the intellectuals themselves. The concept of 'postmodernity' makes sense in so far as it stands for this 'coming out' of the intellectuals.

The other way of putting it is to say that the concept of 'postmodernity' connotes the new self-awareness of the 'intellectuals' – this part of the educated elite which has specialized in elaborating principles, setting standards, formulating social tasks and criteria of their success or failure. Like painters, novelists, composers, and to a rapidly growing extent the scientists before them, such intellectuals have now come to focus their attention on their own skills, techniques and raw materials, which turn from tacitly present means into a conscious object of self-perfection and refinement and the true and sufficient subject-matter of intellectual work.

This implosion of intellectual vision, this 'falling upon oneself', may be seen as either a symptom of retreat and surrender, or a sign of maturation. Whatever the evaluation of the fact, it may be interpreted as a response to the growing sense of failure, inadequacy or irrealism of the traditional functions and ambitions, as sedimented in historical memory and institutionalized in the intellectual mode of existence. Yet it was this very sense of failure which rendered the ambitions and the functions visible.

'Postmodernity' proclaims the loss of something we were not aware of possessing until we learned of the loss. This view of past 'modernity' which the 'postmodernity' discourse generates is made entirely out of the present-day anxiety and uneasiness, as a model of a universe in which such anxiety and uneasiness could not arise (much like the view of 'community', of which Raymond Williams (1975) said that it 'always has been'). The concept of 'modernity' has today a quite different content from the one it had before the start of the 'postmodern' discourse; there is little point in asking whether it is true or distorted, or in objecting to the way it is handled inside the 'postmodern' debate. It is situated in that debate, it draws its meaning from it, and it makes sense only jointly with the other side of the opposition, the concept of 'postmodernity', as that negation without which the latter concept would be meaningless. The 'postmodern' discourse generates its own concept of 'modernity', made of the presence of all those things for the lack of which the concept of 'postmodernity' stands.

The anxiety which gave birth to the concept of 'postmodernity' and the related image of past 'modernity' is admittedly diffuse and ill-defined, but nevertheless quite real. It arises from the feeling that the kinds of services the intellectuals have been historically best prepared to offer, and from which they derived their sense of social importance – are nowadays not easy to provide; and that the demand for such services is anyway much smaller than one would expect it to be. It is this feeling which leads to a 'status crisis'; a recognition that the reproduction of the status which the intellectuals got used to seeing as theirs by right, would now need a good deal of rethinking as well as the reorientation of habitual practices.

The services in question amount to the provision of an authoritative solution to the questions of cognitive truth, moral judgment and aesthetic taste. It goes without saying that the importance of such services is a reflection of the size and importance of the demand for them; with the latter receding, their *raison d'être* is eroded. In its turn, the demand in question draws its importance from the presence of social forces which need the authority of cognitive and normative judgments as the legitimation of their actual, or strived-for domination. There must be such forces; they must need such legitimation; and the intellectuals must retain the monopoly on its provision. The 'status crisis', or rather that vague feeling of anxiety for which it can serve as a plausible interpretation, can be made sense of if account is taken of the undermining of the conditions of intellectual status in, at least, three crucial respects.

First of all – the advanced erosion of that global structure of domination, which – at the time the modern intellectuals were born – supplied the 'evidence of reality' of which the self-confidence of the West and its spokesman has been built. Superiority of the West over the rest remained self-evident for almost three centuries. It was not, as it were, a matter of idle comparison. The era of modernity had been marked by an active superiority; part of the world constituted the rest as inferior – either as a crude, still unprocessed 'raw material' in need of cleaning and refinement, or a temporarily extant relic of the past. Whatever could not be brought up to the superior standards, was clearly destined for the existence of subordination. Western practices defined the rest as a pliable or malleable substance still to be given shape. This active superiority meant the right of the superior to proselytize, to design the suitable form of life for the others, to refuse to grant authority to the ways of life which did not fit that design.

Such superiority could remain self-evident as long as the denied authority showed no signs of reasserting itself, and the designs seemed irresistible. A historical denomination could interpret itself as universal and absolute, as long as it could believe that the future would prove it such; the universality of the western mode (the absoluteness of western domination) seemed indeed merely a matter of time. The grounds for certainty and self-confidence could not be stronger. Human reality indeed seemed subject to unshakeable laws and stronger ('progressive') values looked set to supersede or eradicate the weaker ('retrograde', ignorant, superstitious) ones. It was this historically given certainty, grounded in the unchallenged superiority of forces aimed at universal domination, which had been articulated, from the perspective of the intellectual mode, as universality of the standards of truth, judgment and taste. The strategy such articulation legitimated was to supply the forces, bent on universal and active domination, with designs dictated by universal science, ethics and aesthetics.

The certitude of yesteryear is now at best ridiculed as naïvety, at worst castigated as ethnocentric. Nobody but the most rabid of the diehards believes today that the western mode of life, either the actual one or one idealized ('utopianized') in the intellectual mode, has more than a sporting chance of ever becoming universal. No social force is in sight (including those which, arguably, are today aiming at global domination) bent on making it universal. The search for the universal standards has suddenly become gratuitous; there is no credible 'historical agent' to which the findings could be addressed and entrusted. Impracticality erodes interest. The task of establishing universal standards of truth, morality, taste does not seem that much important. Unsupported by will, it appears now misguided and irreal.

Secondly – even the localized powers, devoid of ecumenical ambitions, seem less receptive to the products of intellectual discourse. The time modern intellectuals were born was one of the great 'shake-up': everything solid melted into air, everything sacred was profaned . . . The newborn absolutist state did not face the task of wrenching power from old and jaded hands; it had to create an entirely new kind of social power, capable of carrying the burden of *societal* integration. The task involved the crushing of those mechanisms of social reproduction which had been based in communal traditions. Its performance took the form of a 'cultural crusade'; that is, practical destruction of communal bases of social power, and theoretical delegitimation of their authority. Faced with such tasks, the state badly needed 'legitimation' (this is the name given to intellectual discourse when considered from the vantage point of its power-oriented, political application).

Mais où sont les croisades d'autant? The present-day political domination can reproduce itself using means more efficient and less costly than 'legitimation'. Weber's 'legal–rational legitimation' – the point much too seldom made – is, in its essence, a declaration of the redundancy of legitimation. The modern state is effective without authority; or, rather, its effectivity depends to a large extent on rendering authority irrelevant. It does not matter any more, for the effectivity of state power, and for the reproduction of political domination in general, whether the social area under domination is culturally unified and uniform, and how idiosyncratic are the values, sectors of this area may uphold.

The weapon of legitimation has been replaced with two mutually complementary weapons: this of *seduction* and that of *repression*. Both need intellectually trained experts, and indeed both siphon off, accommodate and domesticate an ever growing section of educated elite. Neither has a need, or a room, for those 'hard-core' intellectuals whose expertise is 'legitimation', i.e. supplying proof that what is being done is universally correct and absolutely true, moral and beautiful.

Seduction is the paramount tool of integration (of the reproduction of domination) in a consumer society. It is made possible once the market succeeds in making the consumers dependent on itself. Market-dependency is achieved through the destruction of such skills (technical, social, psychological, existential) which do not entail the use of marketable commodities; the more complete the destruction, the more necessary become new skills which point organically to market-supplied implements. Market-dependency is guaranteed and self-perpetuating once men and women, now consumers, cannot proceed with the business of life without tuning themselves to the logic of the market. Much debated 'needs creation' by the market means ultimately creation of the need of the market. New technical, social, psychological and existential skills of the consumers are such as to be practicable only in conjunction with marketable commodities; rationality comes to mean the ability to make right purchasing decisions, while the craving for certainty is gratified by conviction that the decisions made have been, indeed, right.

Repression stands for 'panoptical' power, best described by Foucault (1977). It employs surveillance, it is aimed at regimentation of the body, and is diffused (made invisible) in the numerous institutionalizations of knowledge-based expertise. Repression as a tool of domination-reproduction has not been abandoned with the advent of seduction. Its time is not over and the end of its usefulness is not in sight, however overpowering and effective seduction may become. It is the continuous, tangible presence of repression as a viable alternative which makes seduction unchallengeable. In addition, repression is indispensable to reach the areas seduction cannot, and is not meant to, reach: it remains the paramount tool of subordination of the considerable margin of society which cannot be absorbed by market dependency and hence, in market terms, consists of 'non-consumers'. Such 'non-consumers' are people reduced to the satisfaction of their elementary needs; people whose business of life does not transcend the horizon of survival. Goods serving the latter purpose are not, as a rule, attractive as potential merchandise; they serve the needs over which the market has no control and thus undermine, rather than boost, market dependency. Repression reforges the market unattractiveness of non-consumer existence into the unattractiveness of alternatives to market dependency.

Seduction and repression between them, make 'legitimation' redundant. The structure of domination can now be reproduced, ever more effectively, without recourse to legitimation; and thus without recourse to such intellectuals as make the legitimation discourse their speciality. Habermas's (1976) 'legitimation crisis' makes sense, in the final account, as the intellectual perception of 'crisis' caused by the ever more evident irrelevance of legitimation.

The growing irrelevance of legitimation has coincided with the growing freedom of intellectual debate. One suspects more than coincidence. It is indifference on the part of political power which makes freedom of intellectual work possible. Indifference, in its turn, arises from the lack of interest. Intellectual freedom is possible as political power has freed itself from its former dependence on legitimation. This is why freedom, coming as it does in a package-deal with irrelevance, is not received by the intellectuals with unqualified enthusiasm. All the more so as the past political patronage made a considerable part of intellectual work grow in a way which rendered it dependent on the continuation of such a patronage.

What, however, more than anything else prevents the intellectuals from rejoicing is the realization that the withdrawal of the government troops does not necessarily mean that the vacated territory will become now their uncontested domain. What the state has relinquished, is most likely to be taken over by the powers on which the intellectuals have even less hold than they ever enjoyed in their romance with politics.

The territory in question is that of culture. Culture is one area of social life which is defined (cut out) in such a way as to reassert the social function claimed by the intellectuals. One cannot even explain the meaning of the concept without reference to human 'incompleteness', to the need of teachers and, in general, of 'people in the know' to make up for this incompleteness, and to a vision of society as a continuous 'teach-in' session. The idea of culture, in other words, establishes knowledge in the role of power, and simultaneously supplies legitimation of such power. Culture connotes power of the educated elite and knowledge as power; it denotes institutionalized mechanisms of such power – science, education, arts.

Some of these mechanisms, or some areas of their application, remain relevant to the repressive functions of the state, or to the tasks resulting from the state role in the reproduction of consumer society (reproduction of conditions for the integration-through-seduction). As far as this is the case, the state acts as the protector-cum-censor, providing funds but reserving the right to decide on the tasks and the value of their results. The mixed role of the state rebounds in a mixed reaction of the educated elite. The calls for more state resources intermingle with the protests against bureaucratic interference. There is no shortage of the educated willing to serve; neither is there a shortage of criticisms of servility.

Some other mechanisms, or some other areas of their application, do not have such relevance. They are, as a rule, 'underfunded', but otherwise suffer little political interference. They are free. Even the most iconoclastic of their products fail to arouse the intended wrath of the dominant classes and in most cases are received with devastating equanimity. Challenging the capitalist values stirs little commotion in as far as the capitalist domination does not depend on the acceptance of its values. And yet freedom *from* political interference does not result in freedom *for* intellectual creativity. A new protector-cum-censor fills the vacuum left by the withdrawal of the state: the market.

This is the third respect in which the intellectual status is perceived as undermined. Whatever their other ambitions, modern intellectuals always saw culture as their private property; they made it, they lived in it, they even gave it its name. Expropriation of this particular plot hurts most. Or has it been, in fact, an expropriation? Certainly intellectuals never controlled 'popular' consumption of cultural products. Once they felt firmly in the saddle, they saw themselves as members of the circle of 'culture consumers', which, in the sense they would have recognized, was probably significant, if small. It is only now that the circle of people eager to join the culture consumption game has grown to unheard of proportions – has become truly 'massive'. What hurts, therefore, is not so much an expropriation, but the fact that the intellectuals are not invited to stand at the helm of this breath-taking expansion. Instead, it is gallery owners, publishers, TV managers and other 'capitalists' or 'bureaucrats' who are in control. The idea has been wrested out of the intellectual heads and in a truly sorcerer's apprentice's manner, put to action in which the sages have no power.

In another sense, however, what has happened is truly an expropriation, and not just 'stealing the profits.' In the early modern era intellectual forces had been mobilized (or self-mobilized) for the gigantic job of conversion – the culture crusade which involved a thorough revamping or uprooting of the totality of heretofore autonomously reproduced forms of life. The project was geared to the growth of the modern absolutist state and its acute need of legitimation. For reasons mentioned before, this is not the case anymore. Native forms of life have not, however, returned to autonomous reproduction; there are others who manage it – agents of the market, this time, and not the academia. No wonder the old game-keepers view the new ones as poachers. Once bent on the annihilation of 'crude, superstitious, ignorant, bestial' folkways, they now bewail the enforced transformation of the 'true folk culture' into a 'mass' one. Mass culture debate has been the lament of expropriated gamekeepers.

The future does not promise improvement either; the strength of the market forces continues to grow, their appetite seems to grow even faster, and for an increasing sector of the educated élite the strategy 'if you cannot beat them, join them' gains in popularity. Even the areas of intellectual domain still left outside the reach of the market forces are now felt to be under threat. It was the intellectuals who impressed upon the once incredulous population the need for education and the value of information. Here as well their success turns into their downfall. The market is only too eager to satisfy the need and to supply the value. With the new DIY (electronic) technology to offer, the market will reap the rich crop of the popular belief that education is human duty and (any) information is useful. The market will thereby achieve what the intellectual educators struggled to attain in vain: it will turn the consumption of information into a pleasurable, entertaining pastime. Education will become just one of the many variants of self-amusement. It will reach the peak of its popularity and the bottom of its value as measured by original intellectual-made standards.

The three developments discussed above go some way, if not all the way, towards explaining this feeling of anxiety, out-of-placeness, loss of direction which, as I propose, constitutes the true referent of the concept of 'postmodernity'. As a rule, however, intellectuals tend to articulate their own societal situation and the problems it creates as a situation of the society at large, and its, systemic or social, problems. The way in which the passage from 'modernity' to 'postmodernity' has been articulated is not an exception. This time, however, those who articulate it do not hide as thoroughly as in the past behind the role of 'organic intellectuals' of other classes; and the fact that they act as 'organic intellectuals of themselves' is either evident or much easier to discover. Definitions of both 'modernity' and 'postmodernity' refer overtly to such features of respective social situations which have direct and crucial importance for the intellectual status, role and strategy.

The main feature ascribed to 'postmodernity' is thus the permanent and irreducible *pluralism* of cultures, communal traditions, ideologies, 'forms of life' or 'language games' (choice of items which are 'plural' varies with theoretical allegiance); or the awareness and recognition of such pluralism. Things which are plural in the postmodern world cannot be arranged in an evolutionary time-sequence, seen as each other's inferior or superior stages; neither can they be classified as 'right' or 'wrong' solutions to common problems. No knowledge can be assessed outside the context of culture, tradition, language game etc. which makes it possible and endows it with meaning. Hence no criteria of validation are available which could be themselves justified 'out of context'. Without universal standards, the problem of the postmodern world is not how to globalize superior culture, but how to secure communication and mutual understanding between cultures.

Seen from this 'later' perspective, 'modernity' seems in retrospect a time when pluralism was not yet a foregone conclusion; or a time when the ineradicabiliity of pluralism was not duly recognized. Hence the substitution of one, 'supra-communal', standard of truth, judgment and taste for the diversity of local, and therefore inferior, standards, could be contemplated and strived for as a viable prospect. Relativism of knowledge could be perceived as a nuisance, and as a temporary one at that. Means could be sought – in theory and in practice – to exorcize the ghost of relativism once and for all. The end to parochialism of human opinions and ways of life was nigh. This could be a chance – once real, then lost. Or this could be an illusion from the start. In the first case, postmodernity means the failure of modernity. In the second case, it means a step forward. In both cases, it means opening our eyes to the futility of modern dreams of universalism.

The reader will note that I am defining 'modernity' from the perspective of the experience of 'postmodernity', and not vice versa; all attempts to pretend that we proceed in the opposite direction mislead us into believing that what we confront in the current debate is an articulation of the logic of 'historical process', rather than re-evaluation of the past (complete with the imputation of a 'telos' of which the past, in as long as it remained the present, was not aware). If the concept of 'postmodernity' has no other value, it has at least this one: it supplies a new, and external, vantage point, from which some aspects of that world which came into being in the aftermath of Enlightenment and the Capitalist Revolution (aspect not visible, or allotted secondary importance, when observed from inside the unfinished process) acquire saliency and can be turned into a pivotal issue of the discourse.

The reader will note also that I am trying to define both concepts of the opposition in such a way as to make their mutual distinction independent of the 'existential' issue: whether it is the 'actual conditions' which differ, or their perception. It is my view that the pair of concepts under discussion is important first and foremost (perhaps even solely) in the context of the self-awareness of the intellectuals, and in relation to the way the intellectuals perceive their social location, task and strategy. This does not detract from the significance of the concepts. On the contrary, as far as the plight of 'western culture' goes, the way the two concepts are defined here presents them as arguably the most seminal of oppositions articulated in order to capture the tendency of social change in our times.

The change of mood, intellectual climate, self-understanding etc. implied by that vague, but real, anxiety the proposition of the 'advent of postmodernity' attempts to capture, has indeed far-reaching consequences for the strategy of intellectual work in general – and sociology and social philosophy in particular. It does have a powerful impact even on 'traditional' ways of conducting the business of social study. There is no necessity whatsoever for the old procedures to be rescinded or to grind to a halt. One can easily declare the whole idea of 'postmodernity' a sham, obituaries of 'modernity' premature, the need to reorient one's programme non-existent – and stubbornly go where one went before and where one's ancestors wanted to go. One can say that finding the firm and unshakeable standards of true knowledge, true interpretation, defensible morality, genuine art etc. is still a valid, and the major, task. There is nothing to stop one from doing just that. In the vast realm of the academy there is ample room for all sorts of specialized pursuits, and the way such pursuits have been historically institutionalized renders them virtually immune to pressures untranslatable into the variables of their own inner systems; such pursuits have their own momentum; their dynamics subject to internal logic only, they produce what they are capable of producing, rather than what is required or asked of them; showing their own, internally administered measures of success as their legitimation, they may go on reproducing themselves indefinitely. This is particularly true regarding pursuits of a pronouncedly philosophical nature; they require no outside supply of resources except the salaries of their perpetrators, and are therefore less vulnerable to the dire consequences of the withdrawal of social recognition.

Even with their self-reproduction secure, however, traditional forms of philosophizing confront today challenges which must rebound in their concerns. They are pressed now to legitimize their declared purpose – something which used to be taken (at least since Descartes) by and large for granted. For well-nigh three centuries relativism was the *malin génie* of European philosophy, and anybody suspected of not fortifying his doctrine against it tightly enough was brought to book and forced to defend himself against the charges the horrifying nature of which no one put in doubt. Now the tables have been turned – and the seekers of universal standards are asked to prove the criminal nature of relativism; it is they now who are pressed to justify their hatred of relativism, and clear themselves of the charges of dogmatism, ethnocentrism, intellectual imperialism or whatever else their work may seem to imply when gazed upon from the relativist positions.

Less philosophical, more empirically inclined varieties of traditional social studies are even less fortunate. Modern empirical sociology developed in response to the demand of the modern state aiming at the 'total administration' of society. With capital engaging the rest of the society in their roles of labour, and the state responsible for the task of 'recommodifying' both capital and labour, and thus ensuring the continuation of such an engagement – the state needed a huge apparatus of 'social management' and a huge supply of expert social-management knowledge. Methods and skills of empirical sociology were geared to this demand and to the opportunities stemming from it. The social-managerial tasks were large-scale, and so were the funds allotted to their performance. Sociology specialized therefore in developing the skills of use in mass, statistical research; in collecting information about 'massive trends' and administrative measures likely to redirect, intensify or constrain such trends. Once institutionalized, the skills at the disposal of empirical sociologists have defined the kind of research they are capable of designing and conducting. Whatever else this kind of research is, it invariably requires huge funds – and thus a rich bureaucratic institution wishing to provide them. Progressive disengagement of capital from labour, falling significance of the 're-commodification' task, gradual substitution of 'seduction' for 'repression' as the paramount weapon of social integration, shifting of the responsibility for integration from the state bureaucracy to the market – all this spells trouble for traditional empirical research, as state bureaucracies lose interest in financing it.

The widely debated 'crisis of (empirical) sociology' is, therefore, genuine. Empirical sociology faces today the choice between seeking a new social application of its skills or seeking new skills. Interests of state bureaucracy are likely to taper to the management of 'law and order', i.e. a task aimed selectively at the part of the population which cannot be regulated by the mechanism of seduction. And there are private bureaucracies, in charge of the seduction management, who may or may not need the skill of empirical sociology, depending on the extent in which the latter are able, and willing, to reorient and readjust their professional know-how to the new, as yet not fully fathomed, demand.

To sum up: if the radical manifestos proclaiming the end of sociology and social philosophy 'as we know them' seem unfounded – equally unconvincing are the pretentions that nothing of importance has happened and that there is nothing to stop 'business as usual'. The form acquired by sociology and social philosophy in the course of what is now, retrospectively, described as 'modernity' is indeed experiencing at the moment an unprecedented challenge. While in no way doomed, it must adjust itself to new conditions in order to self-reproduce.

I will turn now to those actual, or likely, developments in sociology which do admit (overtly or implicitly) the novelty of the situation and the need for a radical reorientation of the tasks and the strategies of social study.

One development is already much in evidence. Its direction is clearly shown by the consistently expanding assimilation of Heideggerian. Wittgensteinian, Gadamerian and other 'hermeneutical' themes and inspirations. This development points in the direction of sociology as, above all, the skill of interpretation. Whatever articulable experience there is which may become the object of social study – it is embedded in its own 'life-world', 'communal tradition', 'positive ideology', 'form of life', 'language game'. The names for that 'something' in which the experience is embedded are many and different, but what truly counts are not names but the inherent pluralism of that 'something' which all the names emphasize more than anything else. Thus there are *many* 'life-worlds', *many* 'traditions', and *many* 'language-games'. No external point of view is conceivable to reduce this variety. The only reasonable cognitive strategy is therefore one best expressed in Geertz's (1973) idea of 'thick description': recovery of the meaning of the alien experience through fathoming the tradition (form of life, life-world etc.) which constitutes it, and then translating it, with as little damage as possible, into a form assimilable by one's own tradition (form of life, life-world etc). Rather than proselytizing, which would be the task of a cross-cultural encounter in the context of 'orthodox' social science, it is the expected 'enrichment' of one's own tradition, through incorporating other, heretofore inaccessible, experiences, which is the meaning bestowed upon the exercise by the project of 'interpreting sociology'.

As interpreters, sociologists are no more concerned with ascertaining the 'truth' of the experience they interpret – and thus the principle of 'ethnomethodological indifference' may well turn from the shocking heresy it once was into a new orthodoxy. The only concern which distinguishes sociologists-turned-interpreters as professionals is the correctness of interpretation; it is here that their professional credentials as experts (i.e. holders of skills inaccessible to lay and untrained public) are re-established. Assuming that the world is irreducibly pluralist, rendering the messages mutually communicable is its major problem. Expertise in the rules of correct interpretation is what it needs most. It is badly needed even by such powers that are not any more bent on total domination and do not entertain universalistic ambitions; they still need this expertise for their sheer survival. Potential uses are clear; the users, so far, less so – but one may hope they can be found.

As all positions, this one has also its radical extreme. The admission of pluralism does not have to result in the interest in interpretation and translation, or for that matter in any 'social' services sociology may offer. Release from the often burdensome social duty sociology had to carry in the era of modernity may be seen by some with relief – as the advent of true freedom of intellectual pursuits. It is, indeed, an advent of freedom – though freedom coupled with irrelevance: freedom *from* cumbersome and obtrusive interference on the part of powers that be, won at the price of resigning the freedom to influence their actions and their results. If what sociology does does not matter, it can do whatever it likes. This is a tempting possibility: to immerse oneself fully in one's own specialized discourse inside which one feels comfortably at home, to savour the subtleties of distinction and discretion such discourse demands and renders possible, to take the very disinterestedness of one's pursuits for the sign of their supreme value, to take pride in keeping alive, against the odds, a precious endeavour for which the rest, the polluted or corrupted part of the world, has (temporarily – one would add, seeking the comfort of hope) no use. It is one's own community, tradition, form of life etc. which commands first loyalty; however small, it provides the only site wherein the intrinsic value of the discourse can be tended to, cultivated – and enjoyed. After all, the recognition of futility of universal standards, brought along by postmodernity, allows that self-centred concerns treat lightly everything outside criticism. There is nothing to stop one from coming as close as possible to the sociological equivalent of *l'art pour l'art* (the cynic would comment: nothing, but the next round of education cuts).

The two postmodern strategies for sociology and social philosophy, discussed so far, are – each in its own way – internally consistent and viable. Looked at from inside, they both seem invulnerable. Given their institutional entrenchment, they have a sensible chance of survival and of virtually infinite self-reproduction (again, barring the circumstances referred to by the cynic). Whatever critique of these strategies may be contemplated, it may only come from the outside, and thus cut little ice with the insiders.

Such a critique would have to admit its allegiance to ends the insiders are not obliged to share. It would have to cite an understanding of the role of sociology the insiders have every reason to reject, and no reason to embrace. In particular, such a critique would have to declare its own value preference, remarkable above all for the supreme position allotted to the *social relevance* of sociological discourse.

The critique under consideration may be launched in other words only from the intention to preserve the hopes and ambitions of modernity in the age of postmodernity. The hopes and ambitions in question refer to the possibility of a reason-led improvement of the human condition; an improvement measured in the last instance by the degree of human emancipation. For better or worse, modernity was about increasing the volume of human autonomy, but not autonomy which, for the absence of solidarity, results in loneliness; and about increasing the intensity of human solidarity, but not solidarity which, for the absence of autonomy, results in oppression. The alternative strategy for a postmodern sociology would have to take as its assumption that the two-pronged ambition of modernity is still a viable possibility, and one certainly worth promoting.

What makes a strategy which refuses to renounce its modern ('pre-postmodern'?) commitments a 'postmodern' one, is the bluntness with which its premises are recognized as assumptions; in a truly 'postmodern' vein, such a strategy refers to values rather than laws; to assumptions instead of foundations; to purposes, and not to 'groundings'. And it is determined to do without the comfort it once derived from the belief that 'history was on its side', and that the inevitability of its ultimate success had been guaranteed beforehand by inexorable laws of nature (a pleonasm: 'nature' *is* inexorable laws).

Otherwise, there is no sharp break in continuity. There is a significant shift of emphasis, though. The 'meliorative' strategy of social science as formed historically during the era of modernity had two edges. One was pressed against the totalistic ambitions of the modern state; the state, in possession of enough resources and good will to impress a design of a better society upon imperfect reality, was to be supplied with reliable knowledge of the laws directing human conduct and effective skills required to elicit a conduct conforming to the modern ambitions. The other was pressed against the very humans modernity was bent on emancipating. Men and women were to be offered reliable knowledge of the way their society works, so that their life-business may be conducted in a conscious and rational way, and the casual chains making their actions simultaneously effective and constrained become visible – and hence, in principle, amenable to control. To put the same in a different way: the 'meliorative' strategy under discussion was productive of two types of knowledge. One was aimed at rationalization of the state (more generally: societal) power; the other – at rationalization of individual conduct.

Depending on the time and the location, either one or the other of the two types of knowledge was held in the focus of sociological discourse. But both were present at all times and could not but be co-present – due to the ineradicable ambiguity of ways in which any information on social reality can be employed. This ambiguity explains why the relations between social science and the powers that be were at best those of hate-love, and why even during the timespans of wholehearted cooperation there was always more than a trace of mistrust in the state's attitude toward sociological discourse; not without reason, men of politics suspected that such a discourse may well undermine with one hand the self-same hierarchical order it helps to build with the other.

Inside the postmodern version of the old strategy, however, the balance between the two types of knowledge is likely to shift. One circumstance which makes such a shift likely has been already mentioned: the drying up of the state interest in all but the most narrowly circumscribed sociological expertise; no grand designs, no cultural crusades, no demand for legitimizing visions, and no need for models of centrally administered rational society. Yet the effect of this factor, in itself formidable, has been still exacerbated by the gradual erosion of hope that the failure of the rational society to materialize might be due to the weaknesses of the present administrators of the social process, and that an alternative 'historical agent' may still put things right. More bluntly, the faith in a historical agent waiting in the wings to take over and to complete the promise of modernity using the levers of political state – this faith has all but vanished. The first of the two types of knowledge the modern sociological discourse used to turn out is, therefore, without an evident addressee – actual or potential. It may be still used: there are, after all, quite a few powerful bureaucracies which could do with some good advice on how to make the humans behave differently and more to their liking. And they will surely find experts eager to offer such advice. We did discuss such a possibility in the context of strategies which refuse to admit that 'postmodernity' means new situation and calls for rethinking and readjustment of traditional tasks and strategies. For the strategy aimed at the preservation of modern hopes and ambitions under the new conditions of postmodernity, the question *who* uses the administrative knowledge and for what *purpose* is not, however, irrelevant. It would recognize such knowledge as useful only if in the hands of a genuine or putative, yet rationalizing agent. From the vantage point of the political power all this reasoning is redundant anyway. Having lost their interest in its own practical application of sociological knowledge, the state will inevitably tend to identify the totality of sociological discourse with the second of its traditional edges, and thus regard it as an unambiguously subversive force; as a problem, rather than a solution.

The expected state attitude is certain to act as a self-fulfilling prophecy; rolling back the resources and facilities the production of the first type of knowledge cannot do without, it will push the sociological discourse even further toward the second type. It will only, as it were, reinforce a tendency set in motion by other factors. Among the latter, one should count an inevitable consequence of the growing disenchantment with the societal administration as the carrier of emancipation: the shifting of attention to the kind of knowledge which may be used by human individuals in their efforts to enlarge the sphere of autonomy and solidarity. This looks more and more like the last chance of emancipation.

So far, we have discussed the 'push' factors. There is, however, a powerful 'pull' factor behind the shift: a recognition that the task of providing men and women with that 'sociological imagination' for which C.W. Mills (1959) appealed years ago, has never been so important as it is now, under conditions of postmodernity. Emancipation of capital from labour makes possible the emancipation of the state from legitimation; and that may mean in the long run a gradual erosion of democratic institutions and the substance of democratic politics (reproduction of legitimation having been the political democracy major historical function). Unlike the task of reproducing members of society as producers, their reproduction as consumers does not necessarily enlarge the political state and hence does not imply the need to reproduce them as citizens. The 'systemic' need for political democracy is thereby eroded, and the political agency of men and women as citizens cannot count for its reproduction on the centripetal effects of the self-legitimizing concerns of the state. The other factors which could sponsor such reproduction look also increasingly doubtful in view of the tendency to shift political conflicts into the non-political and democratically unaccountable sphere of the market, and the drift toward the substitution of 'needs creation' for 'normative regulation' as the paramount methods of systemic reproduction (except for the part of the society the market is unable or unwilling to assimilate). If those tendencies have been correctly spotted, knowledge which provides the individuals with an accurate understanding of the way society works may not be a weapon powerful enough to outweigh their consequences; but it surely looks like the best bet men and women can still make.

Which leads us into an area not at all unfamiliar; some would say traditional. The third of the conceivable strategies of sociology under the postmodern condition would focus on the very thing on which the sociological discourse did focus throughout its history: on making the opaque transparent, on exposing the ties linking visible biographies to invisible societal processes, on understanding what makes society tick, in order to make it tick, if possible, in a more 'emancipating' way. Only it is a new and different society from the one which triggered off the sociological discourse. Hence 'focusing one the same' means focusing on new problems and new tasks.

I suggest that a sociology bent on the continuation of modern concerns under postmodern conditions would be distinguished not by new procedures and purposes of sociological work, as other postmodern strategies suggest – but by a new *object* of investigation. As far as this strategy is concerned, what matters is that the society (its object) has changed; it does not necessarily admit that its own earlier pursuits were misguided and wasted, and that the crucial novelty in the situation is the dismissal of the old ways of doing sociology and 'discovery' of new ways of doing it. Thus to describe a sociology pursuing the strategy under discussion one would speak, say, of a 'post-full-employment' sociology, or a 'sociology of the consumer society', rather than of a 'post-Wittgensteinian' or 'post-Gadamerian' sociology. In other words, this strategy points toward a sociology of postmodernity, rather than a postmodern sociology.

There is a number of specifically 'postmodern' phenomena which await sociological study. There is a process of an accelerating emancipation of capital from labour; instead of engaging the rest of society in the role of producers, capital tends to engage them in the role of consumers. This means in its turn that the task of reproducing the capital-dominated society does not consist, as before, in the 're-commodification of labour', and that the non-producers of today are not a 'reserve army of labour', to be tended to and groomed for the return to the labour market. This crucial fact of their life is still concealed in their own consciousness, in the consciousness of their political tutors, and of the sociologists who study them, by a historical memory of society which is no more and will not return. The new poor are not socially, culturally or systemically an equivalent of the old poor; the present 'depression', manifested in the massive and stable unemployment, is not a later day edition of the 1930s (one hears about the poor losing their jobs, but one does not hear of the rich jumping out of their windows). 'The two nations' society, mark two, cannot be truly understood by squeezing it into the model of mark one.

'The two nations, mark two' society is constituted by the opposition between 'seduction' and 'repression' as means of social control, integration and the reproduction of domination. The first is grounded in 'market dependency': replacement of old life skills by the new ones which cannot be effectively employed without the mediation of the market; in the shifting of disaffection and conflict from the area of political struggle to the area of commodities and entertainment; in the appropriate redirecting of the needs for rationality and security; and in the growing comprehensiveness of the market-centred world, so that it can accommodate the totality of life business, making the other aspects of systemic context invisible and subjectively irrelevant. The second is grounded in a normative regulation pushed to the extreme, penetration of the 'private' sphere to an ever growing degree, disempowering of the objects of normative regulation as autonomous agents. It is important to know how these two means of social control combine and support each other; and the effects their duality is likely to have on the tendency of political power, democratic institutions and citizenship.

One may guess – pending further research – that while control-through-repression destroys autonomy and solidarity, control-through-seduction generates marketable means serving the pursuit (if not the attainment) of both, and thus effectively displaces the pressures such a pursuit exerts from the political sphere, at the same time redeploying them in the reproduction of capital domination. Thus the opposite alternatives which determine the horizon and the trajectory of life strategies in the postmodern society neutralize the possible threat to systemic reproduction which might emanate from the unsatisfied ambitions of autonomy and solidarity.

Those alternatives, therefore, need to be explored by any sociology wishing seriously to come to grips with the phenomenon of postmodernity. Conscious of the postmodern condition it explores, such a sociology would not pretend that its preoccupations, however skillfully pursued, would offer it the centrality in the 'historical process' to which it once aspired. On the contrary, the problematics sketched above is likely to annoy rather than entice the managers of law and order; it will appear incomprehensible to the seduced, and alluring yet nebulous to the repressed. A sociology determined to tread this path would have to brace itself for the uneasy plight of unpopularity. Yet the alternative is irrelevance. This seems to be the choice sociology is facing in the era of postmodernity

REFERENCES

Foucault, Michel (1977) *Discipline and Punish*. Harmondsworth: Allen Lane.
Geertz, Clifford (1973) *The Interpretation of Culture*. New York: Basic Books.
Gramsci, Antonio (1971) *Selections from the Prison Notebooks*. London: Lawrence & Wishart.
Habermas, Jürgen (1976) *Legitimation Crisis*. London: Heinemann.
Mills, C. Wright (1959) *The Sociological Imagination*. Oxford: Oxford University Press.
Williams, Raymond (1975) *The Country and the City*. St Albans: Paladin.

11

On ethnographic allegory
James Clifford

1. a story in which people, things and happenings have another meaning, as in a fable or parable: allegories are used for teaching or explaining.
2. the presentation of ideas by means of such stories.[1]

In a recent essay on narrative Victor Turner argues that social performances enact powerful stories – mythic and commonsensical – that provide the social process "with a rhetoric, a mode of emplotment, and a meaning" (1980:153). In what follows I treat ethnography itself as a performance emplotted by powerful stories. Embodied in written reports, these stories simultaneously describe real cultural events and

1. *Webster's New Twentieth Century Dictionary,* 2nd ed. In literary studies definitions of allegory have ranged from Angus Fletcher's (1964:2) loose characterization ("In the simplest terms, allegory says one thing and means another") to Todorov's reassertion (1973:63) of a stricter sense: "First of all, allegory implies the existence of at least two meanings for the same words; according to some critics, the first meaning must disappear, while others require that the two be present together. Secondly, this double meaning is indicated in the work in an *explicit* fashion: it does not proceed from the reader's interpretation (whether arbitrary or not)." According to Quintilian, any continuous or extended metaphor develops into allegory; and as Northrop Frye (1971:91) observes, "Within the boundaries of literature we find a kind of sliding scale, ranging from the most explicitly allegorical, consistent with being literature at all, at one extreme, to the most elusive, anti-explicit and anti-allegorical at the other." The various "second meanings" of ethnographic allegory I shall be tracing here are all textually explicit. But ethnographies slide along Frye's scale, exhibiting strong allegorical features, usually without marking themselves *as* allegories.

For helpful criticisms of this paper I would like to thank Richard Handler, Susan Gevirtz, David Schneider, Harry Berger, and the Santa Fe seminar participants, especially Michael Fischer. Reprinted by permission of the University of California Press.

205

make additional, moral, ideological, and even cosmological statements. Ethnographic writing is allegorical at the level both of its content (what it says about cultures and their histories) and of its form (what is implied by its mode of textualization).

An apparently simple example will introduce my approach. Marjorie Shostak begins her book *Nisa: The Life and Words of a !Kung Woman* with a story of childbirth the !Kung way – outside the village, alone. Here are some excerpts:

> I lay there and felt the pains as they came, over and over again. Then I felt something wet, the beginning of the childbirth. I thought, "Eh hey, maybe it is the child." I got up, took a blanket and covered Tashay with it; he was still sleeping. Then I took another blanket and my smaller duiker skin covering and I left. Was I not the only one? The only other woman was Tashay's grandmother, and she was asleep in her hut. So, just as I was, I left. I walked a short distance from the village and sat down beside a tree. . . . After she was born, I sat there; I didn't know what to do. I had no sense. She lay there, moving her arms about, trying to suck her fingers. She started to cry. I just sat there, looking at her. I thought, "Is this my child? Who gave birth to this child?" Then I thought, "A big thing like that? How could it possibly have come out from my genitals?" I sat there and looked at her, looked and looked and looked. (1981:1–3)

The story has great immediacy. Nisa's voice is unmistakable, the experience sharply evoked: "She lay there, moving her arms about, trying to suck her fingers." But as readers we do more than register a unique event. The story's unfolding requires us, first, to imagine a different *cultural* norm (!Kung birth, alone in the bush) and then to recognize a common *human* experience (the quiet heroism of childbirth, feelings of postpartum wonder and doubt). The story of an occurrence somewhere in the Kalahari Desert cannot remain just that. It implies both local cultural meanings and a general story of birth. A difference is posited and transcended. Moreover, Nisa's story tells us (how could it not?) something basic about woman's experience. Shostak's life of a !Kung individual inevitably becomes an allegory of (female) humanity.

I argue below that these kinds of transcendent meanings are not abstractions or interpretations "added" to the original "simple" account. Rather, they are the conditions of its meaningfulness. Ethnographic texts are inescapably allegorical, and a serious acceptance of this fact changes the ways they can be written and read. Using Shostak's experiment as a case study I examine a recent tendency to distinguish allegorical levels as specific "voices" within the text. I argue, finally, that the very activity of ethnographic *writing* – seen as inscription or textualization – enacts a redemptive Western allegory. This pervasive structure needs to be perceived and weighed against other possible emplotments for the performance of ethnography.

> Literary description always opens onto another scene set, so to speak,

> "behind" the this-worldly things it purports to depict.
> MICHEL BEAUJOUR, "Some Paradoxes of Description"

Allegory (Gr. *allos*, "other," and *agoreuein*, "to speak") usually denotes a practice in which a narrative fiction continuously refers to another pattern of ideas or events. It is a representation that "interprets" itself. I am using the term allegory in the expanded sense reclaimed for it by recent critical discussions, notably those of Angus Fletcher (1964) and Paul De Man (1979). Any story has a propensity to generate another story in the mind of its reader (or hearer), to repeat and displace some prior story. To focus on ethnographic allegory in preference, say, to ethnographic "ideology" – although the political dimensions are always present (Jameson 1981) – draws attention to aspects of cultural description that have until recently been minimized. A recognition of allegory emphasizes the fact that realistic portraits, to the extent that they are "convincing" or "rich," are extended metaphors, patterns of associations that point to coherent (theoretical, esthetic, moral) additional meanings. Allegory (more strongly than "interpretation") calls to mind the poetic, traditional, cosmological nature of such writing processes.

Allegory draws special attention to the *narrative* character of cultural representations, to the stories built into the representational process itself. It also breaks down the seamless quality of cultural description by adding a temporal aspect to the process of reading. One level of meaning in a test will always generate other levels. Thus the rhetoric of presence that has prevailed in much post-romantic literature (and in much "symbolic anthropology") is interrupted. De Man's critique of the valorization of symbols over allegory in romantic esthetics also questions the project of realism (De Man 1969). The claim that nonallegorical description was possible – a position underlying both positivist literalism and realist synecdoche (the organic, functional, or "typical" relationship of parts to wholes) – was closely allied to the romantic search for unmediated meaning in the event. Positivism, realism, and romanticism – nineteenth-century ingredients of twentieth-century anthropology – all rejected the "false" artifice of rhetoric along with allegory's supposed abstractness. Allegory violated the canons both of empirical science and of artistic spontaneity. (Ong 1971:6–9). It was too deductive, too much an open imposition of meaning on sensible evidence. The recent "revival" of rhetoric by a diverse group of literary and cultural theorists (Roland Barthes, Kenneth Burke, Gerard Genette, Michel de Certeau, Hayden White, Paul De Man, and Michel Beaujour among others) has thrown serious doubt on the positivist-romantic-realist consensus. In ethnography the current turn to rhetoric coincides with a period of political and epistemological reevaluation in which the constructed, imposed nature of representational authority has become unusually visible and contested. Allegory prompts us to say of any cultural description not "this represents, or symbolizes, that" but rather, "this is a (morally charged) *story* about that."[2]

The specific accounts contained in ethnographies can never be limited to a project of scientific description so long as the guiding task of the work is to make the (often strange) behavior of a different way of life humanly comprehensible. To say that exotic behavior and symbols make sense either in "human" or "cultural" terms is to supply the same sorts of allegorical added meanings that appear in older narratives that saw actions as "spiritually" significant. Culturalist and humanist allegories stand behind the controlled fictions of difference and similitude that we call ethnographic accounts. What is maintained in these texts is a double attention to the descriptive surface and to more abstract, comparative, and explanatory levels of meaning. This twofold structure is set out by Coleridge in a classic definition.

> We may then safely define allegorical writing as the employment of one set of agents and images with actions and accompaniments correspondent, so as to convey, while in disguise, either moral qualities or conceptions of the mind that are not in themselves objects of the senses, or other images, agents, fortunes, and circumstances so that the difference is everywhere presented to the eye or imagination, while the likeness is suggested to the mind; and this connectedly, so that the parts combine to form a consistent whole. (1936:30).

What one *sees* in a coherent ethnographic account, the imaged construct of the other, is connected in a continuous double structure with what one *understands*. At times, the structure is too blatant: "During the ceramic manufacturing process, women converse gently, quietly, always without conflict, about ecosystem dynamics" (Whitten 1978:847). Usually it is less obvious and thus more realistic. Adapting Coleridge's formula, what appears descriptively to the senses (and primarily, as he suggests, to the observing eye) seems to be "other," while what is suggested by the co-

---

2. An "allegorical anthropology" is suggested fairly explicitly in recent works by Boon (1977, 1982), Crapanzano (1980), Taussig (1984), and Tyler (1984a).

herent series of perceptions is an underlying similitude. Strange behavior is portrayed as meaningful within a common network of symbols – a common ground of understandable activity valid for both observer and observed, and by implication for all human groups. Thus ethnography's narrative of specific differences presupposes, and always refers to, an abstract plane of similarity.

It is worth noting, though I cannot pursue the theme here, that before the emergence of secular anthropology as a science of *human* and *cultural* phenomena, ethnographic accounts were connected to different allegorical referents. Father Lafitau's famous comparison (1724) of Native American customs with those of the ancient Hebrews and Egyptians exemplifies an earlier tendency to map descriptions of the other onto conceptions of the " *premiers temps.* " More or less explicit biblical or classical allegories abound in the early descriptions of the New World. For as Johannes Fabian (1983) argues, there has been a pervasive tendency to prefigure others in a temporally distinct, but locatable, space (earlier) within an assumed progress of Western history. Cultural anthropology in the twentieth century has tended to replace (though never completely) these historical allegories with humanist allegories. It has eschewed a search for origins in favor of seeking human similarities and cultural differences. But the representational process itself has not essentially changed. Most descriptions of others continue to assume and refer to elemental or transcendent levels of truth.

This conclusion emerges clearly from the recent Mead-Freeman controversy.[3] Two competing portrayals of Samoan life are cast as scientific projects; but both configure the other as a morally charged alter ego. Mead claimed to be conducting a controlled "experiment" in the field, "testing" the universality of stressful adolescence by examining a counter instance empirically. But despite Boasian rhetoric about the "laboratory" of fieldwork, Mead's experiment produced a message of broad ethical and political significance. Like Ruth Benedict in *Patterns of Culture* (1934), she held a liberal, pluralist vision, responding to the dilemmas of a "complex" American society. The ethnographic stories Mead and Benedict told were manifestly linked to the situation of a culture struggling with diverse values, with an apparent breakdown of established traditions, with utopian visions of human malleability and fears of disaggregation. Their ethnographies were "fables of identity," to adapt Northrop Frye's title (1963). Their openly allegorical purpose was not a kind of

3. Mead (1923), Freeman (1983). I have drawn on my review of Freeman in the *Times Literary Supplement,* May 13, 1983, 475–76, which explores the literary dimensions of the controversy. For another treatment in this vein, see Porter 1984.

moral or expository frame for empirical descriptions, something added on in prefaces and conclusions. The entire project of inventing and representing "cultures" was, for Mead and Benedict, a pedagogical, ethical undertaking.

Mead's "experiment" in controlled cultural variation now looks less like science than allegory – a too sharply focused story of Samoa suggesting a possible America. Derek Freeman's critique ignores any properly literary dimensions in ethnographic work, however, and instead applies its own brand of scientism, inspired by recent developments in sociobiology. As Freeman sees it, Mead was simply wrong about Samoans. They are not the casual, permissive people she made famous, but are beset by all the usual human tensions. They are violent. They get ulcers. The main body of his critique is a massing of counterexamples drawn from the historical record and from his own fieldwork. In 170 pages of empirical overkill, he successfully shows what was already explicit for an alert reader of *Coming of Age in Samoa:* that Mead constructed a foreshortened picture, designed to propose moral, practical lessons for American society. But as Freeman heaps up instances of Samoan anxiety and violence, the allegorical frame for his own undertaking begins to emerge. Clearly something more is getting expressed than simply the "darker side," as Freeman puts it, of Samoan life. In a revealing final page he admits as much, countering Mead's "Apollonian" sense of cultural balance with biology's "Dionysian" human nature (essential, emotional, etc.). But what is the scientific status of a "refutation" that can be subsumed so neatly by a Western mythic opposition? One is left with a stark contrast: Mead's attractive, sexually liberated, calm Pacific world, and now Freeman's Samoa of seething tensions, strict controls, and violent outbursts. Indeed Mead and Freeman form a kind of diptych, whose opposing panels signify a recurrent Western ambivalence about the "primitive." One is reminded of Melville's *Typee,* a sensuous paradise woven through with dread, the threat of violence.

> *Le transfert de l'Empire de la Chine à l'Empire de soi-même est constant.*
> VICTOR SEGALEN

A scientific ethnography normally establishes a privileged allegorical register it identifies as "theory," "interpretation," or "explanation." But once *all* meaningful levels in a text, including theories and interpretations, are recognized as allegorical, it becomes difficult to view one of them as privileged, accounting for the rest. Once this anchor is dislodged, the staging and valuing of multiple allegorical registers, or "voices," becomes an important area of concern for ethnographic writers. Recently this has sometimes meant giving indigenous discourse a semi-independent status in the textual whole, interrupting the privileged monotone of "scientific" representation.[4] Much ethnography, taking its distance from totalizing anthropology, seeks to evoke multiple (but not limitless) allegories.

Marjorie Shostak's *Nisa* exemplifies, and wrestles with, the problem of presenting and mediating multiple stories.[5] I shall dwell on it at some length. Shostak explicitly stages three allegorical registers: (1) the representation of a coherent cultural subject as source of scientific knowledge (Nisa is a "!Kung woman"); (2) the construction of a gendered subject (Shostak asks: what is it to be a woman?); (3) the story of a mode of ethnographic production and relationship (an intimate dialogue). Nisa is the pseudonym of a fifty-year-old woman who has lived most of her life in semi-nomadic conditions. Marjorie Shostak belongs to a Harvard-based research group that has studied the !Kung San hunter-gatherers since the 1950s. The complex truths that emerge from this "life and words" are not limited to an individual or to her surrounding cultural world.

The book's three registers are in crucial respects discrepant. First, the autobiography, cross-checked against other !Kung women's lives, is inserted within an ongoing cultural interpretation (to which it adds "depth"). Second, this shaped experience soon becomes a story of "women's" existence, a story that rhymes closely with many of the experiences and issues highlighted in recent feminist thought. Third, *Nisa* narrates an intercultural encounter in which two individuals collaborate to produce a specific domain of truth. The ethnographic encounter itself becomes, here, the subject of the book, a fable of communication, rapport, and, finally, a kind of fictional, but potent, kinship. *Nisa* is thus manifestly an allegory of scientific comprehension, operating at the levels both of cultural description and of a search for human origins. (Along with other students of gatherer-hunters, the Harvard project – Shostak included – tends to see in this longest stage of human cultural development a baseline for human nature.) *Nisa* is a Western feminist allegory, part of the reinvention of the general category "woman" in the 1970s and 80s. *Nisa* is an allegory of ethnography, of contact and comprehension.

A braided narrative, the book moves constantly, at times awkwardly, between its three meaningful registers. *Nisa* is like many works that portray common human experiences, conflicts, joys, work, and so on. But the text Shostak has made is original in the way it refuses to blend its three registers into a seamless, "full" representation. They remain separate, in dramatic tension. This polyvocality is appropriate to the book's predica-

4. On the origins of this "monotone," see De Certeau 1983:128.
5. The rest of this section is an expanded version of my review of *Nisa* in the *Times Literary Supplement,* September 17, 1982, 994–95.

ment, that of many self-conscious ethnographic writers who find it difficult to speak of well-defined "others" from a stable, distanced position. Difference invades the text; it can no longer be represented; it must be enacted.

Nisa's first register, that of cultural science, holds its subject in firm relation to a social world. It explains Nisa's personality in terms of !Kung ways, and it uses her experience to nuance and correct generalizations about her group. If *Nisa* reveals intersubjective mechanisms in unusual depth, its polyvocal construction shows, too, that the transition to scientific knowledge is not smooth. The personal does not yield to the general without loss. Shostak's research was based on systematic interviews with more than a score of !Kung women. From these conversations she amassed a body of data large enough to reveal typical attitudes, activities, and experiences. But Shostak was dissatisfied by the lack of depth in her interviews, and this led her to seek out an informant able to provide a detailed personal narrative. Nisa was quite unusual in her ability to recall and explain her life; moreover there developed a strong resonance between her stories and Shostak's personal concerns. This posed a problem for the expectations of a generalizing social science.

At the end of her first sojourn in the field, Shostak was troubled by a suspicion that her interlocutor might be too idiosyncratic. Nisa had known severe pain; her life as she recalled it was often violent. Most previous accounts of the !Kung, like Elizabeth Marshall Thomas's *The Harmless People* (1959), had shown them to be peace-loving. "Did I really want to be the one to balance the picture?" (350). On a return trip to the Kalahari, Shostak found reassurance. Though Nisa still exerted a special fascination, she now appeared less unusual. And the ethnographer became "more sure than ever that our work together could and should move forward. The interviews I was conducting with other women were proving to me that Nisa was fundamentally similar to those around her. She was unusually articulate, and she had suffered greater than average loss, but in most other important respects she was a typical !Kung woman" (358).

Roland Barthes (1981) has written poignantly of an impossible science of the individual. An insistent tug toward the general is felt throughout *Nisa,* and it is not without pain that we find Nisa generalized, tied to "an interpretation of !Kung life" (350). The book's scientific discourse, tirelessly contextual, typifying, is braided through the other two voices, introducing each of the fifteen thematic sections of the life with a few pages of background. ("Once a marriage has survived a few years beyond the young wife's first menstruation, the relationship between the spouses becomes more equal" [169]. And so forth.) Indeed, one sometimes feels that the scientific discourse functions in the text as a kind of brake on the book's other voices, whose meanings are excessively personal and inter-subjective. There is a real discrepancy. For at the same time that Nisa's story contributes to better generalizations about the !Kung, its very specificity, and the particular circumstances of its making, create meanings that are resistant to the demands of a typifying science.

The book's second and third registers are sharply distinct from the first. Their structure is dialogical, and at times each seems to exist primarily in response to the other. Nisa's life has its own textual autonomy, as a distinct narrative spoken in characteristic, believable tones. But it is manifestly the product of a collaboration. This is particularly true of its overall shape, a full lifespan – fifteen chapters including "Earliest Memories," "Family Life," "Discovering Sex," "Trial Marriages," "Marriage," "Motherhood and Loss," "Women and Men," "Taking Lovers," "A Healing Ritual," "Growing Older." Although at the start of the interviews Nisa had mapped out her life, sketching the main areas to be covered, the thematic roster appears to be Shostak's. Indeed, by casting Nisa's discourse in the shape of a "life," Shostak addresses two rather different audiences. On one side, this intensely personal collection of memories is made suitable for scientific typification as a "life-history" or "life-cycle." On the other, Nisa's life brings into play a potent and pervasive mechanism for the production of meaning in the West – the exemplary, coherent self (or rather, the self pulling itself together in autobiography). There is nothing universal or natural about the fictional processes of biography and autobiography (Gusdorf 1956; Olney 1972; Lejeune 1975). Living does not easily organize itself into a continuous narrative. When Nisa says, as she often does, "We lived in that place, eating things. Then we left and went somewhere else," or simply, "we lived and lived" (69), the hum of unmarked, impersonal existence can be heard. From this blurred background, a narrative shape emerges in the occasion of speaking, simultaneously to oneself and another. Nisa tells her life, a process textually dramatized in Shostak's book.

As alter ego, provoker, and editor of the discourse, Shostak makes a number of significant interventions. A good deal of cutting and rearranging transforms overlapping stories into "a life" that does not repeat itself unduly and that develops by recognizable steps and passages. Nisa's distinct voice emerges. But Shostak has systematically removed her own interventions (though they can often be sensed in Nisa's response). She has also taken out a variety of narrative markers: her friend's habitual comment at the end of a story, "the wind has taken that away," or at the start, "I will break open the story and tell you what's there"; or in the middle, "What am I trying to do? Here I am sitting, talking about one story, and another runs right into my head and into my thoughts!" (40). Shostak has clearly thought carefully about the framing of her transcripts, and one cannot have everything – the performance with all its divagations, and also an easily understandable story. If Nisa's words were to be widely read, concessions had to be made to the requirements of biographical allegory, to a readership practiced in the ethical interpretation of selves. By these formal means the book's second discourse, Nisa's spoken life, is brought close to its readers, becoming a narration that makes eloquent "human" sense.

The book's third distinct register is Shostak's personal account of fieldwork. "Teach me what it is to be a !Kung woman" was the question she asked of her informants (349). If Nisa responded with peculiar aptness, her words also seemed to answer another question, "What is it to be a woman?" Shostak told her informants "that I wanted to learn what it meant to be a woman in their culture so I could better understand what it meant in my own." With Nisa, the relationship became, in !Kung terms, that of an aunt talking to a young niece, to "a girl-woman, recently married, struggling with the issues of love, marriage, sexuality, work and identity" (4). The younger woman ("niece," sometimes "daughter") is instructed by an experienced elder in the arts and pains of womanhood. The transforming relationship ends with an equality in affection and respect, and with a final word, potent in feminist meaning: "sister" (371). Nisa speaks, throughout, not as a neutral witness but as a person giving specific kinds of advice to someone of a particular age with manifest questions and desires. She is not an "informant" speaking *cultural* truths, as if to everyone and no one, providing information rather than circumstantial responses.

In her account, Shostak describes a search for personal knowledge, for something going beyond the usual ethnographic rapport. She hopes that intimacy with a !Kung woman will, somehow, enlarge or deepen her sense of being a modern Western woman. Without drawing explicit lessons from Nisa's experience, she dramatizes through her own quest the way a narrated life makes sense, allegorically, *for another*. Nisa's story is revealed as a joint production, the outcome of an encounter that cannot be rewritten as a subject-object dichotomy. Something more than explaining or representing the life and words of another is going on – something more open-ended. The book is part of a new interest in revaluing subjective (more accurately, intersubjective) aspects of research. It emerges from a crucial moment of feminist politics and epistemology: consciousness raising and the sharing of experiences by women. A commonality is produced that, by bringing separate lives together, empowers personal action, recognizes a common estate. This moment of recent feminist consciousness is allegorized in *Nisa*'s fable of its own relationality. (In other ethnographies, traditionally masculine stories of initiation and penetration differently stage the productive encounter of self and other.)[6]

6. On ethnography as an allegory of conquest and initiation, see Clifford 1983b.

Shostak's explicit feminist allegory thus reflects a specific moment in which the construction of "woman's" experience is given center stage. It is a moment of continuing importance; but it has been challenged by recent countercurrents within feminist theory. The assertion of common female qualities (and oppressions) across racial, ethnic, and class lines is newly problematic. And in some quarters "woman" is seen, not as a locus of experience, but as a shifting subjective position not reducible to any essence.[7]

Shostak's allegory seems to register these countercurrents in its occasionally complex accounts of the processes of play and transference, which produce the final inscription of commonality. For the book's intimate relationships are based on subtle, reciprocal movements of doubling, imagination, and desire, movements allegorized in one of the stories Shostak tells in counterpoint to Nisa's narrative – an incident turning on the value of a girl-woman's body.

> One day I noticed a twelve-year-old girl, whose breasts had just
> started to develop, looking into the small mirror beside the dri-
> ver's window of our Land Rover. She looked intently at her
> face, then, on tiptoe, examined her breasts and as much of her
> body as she could see, then went to her face again. She stepped
> back to see more, moved in again for a closer look. She was a
> lovely girl, although not outstanding in any way except being in
> the full health and beauty of youth. She saw me watching. I
> teased in the !Kung manner I had by then thoroughly learned,
> "So ugly! How is such a young girl already so ugly?" She
> laughed. I asked, "You don't agree?" She beamed, "No, not at
> all. I'm beautiful!" She continued to look at herself. I said,
> "Beautiful? Perhaps my eyes have become broken with age that
> I can't see where it is?" She said, "Everywhere – my face, my
> body. There is no ugliness at all." These remarks were said eas-
> ily, with a broad smile, but without arrogance. The pleasure
> she felt in her changing body was as evident as the absence of
> conflict about it. (270)

A great deal of the book is here: an old voice, a young voice, a mirror . . . talk of self-possession. Narcissism, a term of deviance applied to women of the West, is transfigured. We notice, too, that it is the ethnographer, assuming a voice of age, who has brought a mirror, just as Nisa provides an allegorical mirror when Shostak takes the role of youth.

7. On racial and class divisions within feminism, see the rethinking of Rich (1979), and the work of Hull, Scott, and Smith (1982), Hooks (1981), and Moraga (1983). Strong feminist critiques of essentialism may be found in Wittig (1981) and Haraway (1985).

Ethnography gains subjective "depth" through the sorts of roles, reflections, and reversals dramatized here. The writer, and her readers, can be both young (learning) and old (knowing). They can simultaneously listen, and "give voice to," the other.[8] *Nisa*'s readers follow – and prolong – the play of a desire. They imagine, in the mirror of the other, a guileless self-possession, an uncomplicated feeling of "attractiveness" that Shostak translates as "I have work," "I am productive," "I have worth" (270).

Anthropological fieldwork has been represented as both a scientific "laboratory" and a personal "rite of passage." The two metaphors capture nicely the discipline's impossible attempt to fuse objective and subjective practices. Until recently, this impossibility was masked by marginalizing the intersubjective foundations of fieldwork, by excluding them from serious ethnographic texts, relegating them to prefaces, memoirs, anecdotes, confessions, and so forth. Lately this set of disciplinary rules is giving way. The new tendency to name and quote informants more fully and to introduce personal elements into the text is altering ethnography's discursive strategy and mode of authority. Much of our knowledge about other cultures must now be seen as contingent, the problematic outcome of intersubjective dialogue, translation, and projection. This poses fundamental problems for any science that moves predominantly from the particular to the general, that can make use of personal truths only as examples of typical phenomena or as exceptions to collective patterns.

Once the ethnographic process is accorded its full complexity of historicized dialogical relations, what formerly seemed to be empirical/interpretive accounts of generalized cultural facts (statements and attributions concerning "the !Kung," "the Samoans," etc.) now appear as just one level of allegory. Such accounts may be complex and truthful; and they are, in principle, susceptible to refutation, assuming access to the same pool of cultural facts. But as written versions based on fieldwork, these accounts are clearly no longer *the* story, but a story among other stories. *Nisa*'s discordant allegorical registers – the book's three, never quite manageable, "voices" – reflect a troubled, inventive moment in the history of cross-cultural representation.

8. Ethnographies often present themselves as fictions of learning, the acquisition of knowledge, and finally of authority to understand and represent another culture. The researcher begins in a child's relationship to adult culture, and ends by speaking with the wisdom of experience. It is interesting to observe how, in the text, an author's enunciative modes may shift back and forth between learning from and speaking for the other. This fictional freedom is crucial to ethnography's allegorical appeal: the simultaneous reconstruction of a culture and a knowing self, a double "coming of age in Samoa."

Welcome of Tears is a beautiful book, combining the stories of
a vanishing people and the growth of an anthropologist.
MARGARET MEAD, blurb for the paperback edition of
Charles Wagley's *Welcome of Tears*

Ethnographic texts are not only, or predominantly, allegories. Indeed, as
we have seen, they struggle to limit the play of their "extra" meanings,
subordinating them to mimetic, referential functions. This struggle
(which often involves disputes over what will count as "scientific" theory
and what as "literary" invention or "ideological" projection) maintains
disciplinary and generic conventions. If ethnography as a tool for positive
science is to be preserved, such conventions must mask, or direct, multiple allegorical processes. For may not every extended description, stylis-
tic turn, story, or metaphor be read to mean something else? (Need we
accept the three explicit levels of allegory in a book like *Nisa?* What about
its photographs, which tell their own story?) Are not readings themselves
undecidable? Critics like De Man (1979) rigorously adopt such a position, arguing that the choice of a dominant rhetoric, figure, or narrative
mode in a text is always an imperfect attempt to impose a reading or range
of readings on an interpretive process that is open-ended, a series of displaced "meanings" with no full stop. But whereas the free play of readings may in theory be infinite, there are, at any historical moment, a
limited range of canonical and emergent allegories available to the com-
petent reader (the reader whose interpretation will be deemed plausible
by a specific community). These structures of meaning are historically
bounded and coercive. There is, in practice, no "free play."

Within this historical predicament, the critique of stories and patterns
that persistently inform cross-cultural accounts remains an important
political as well as scientific task. In the remainder of this essay I explore
a broad, orienting allegory (or more accurately, a pattern of possible
allegories) that has recently emerged as a contested area – a structure
of retrospection that may be called "ethnographic pastoral." Shostak's
book and the Harvard hunter-gatherer studies, to the extent that they
engage in a search for fundamental, desirable human traits, are enmeshed
in this structure.

In a trenchant article, "The Use and Abuse of Anthropology: Reflections on Feminism and Cross-Cultural Understanding," Michelle Rosaldo
has questioned a persistent tendency to appropriate ethnographic data in
the form of a search for origins. Analyses of social "givens" such as gender and sexuality show an almost reflexive need for anthropological just-
so-stories. Beginning with Simone de Beauvoir's founding question,
"What is woman?" scholarly discussions "move . . . to a diagnosis of
contemporary subordination and from then on to the queries 'Were
things always as they are today?' and then 'When did "it" start?' "

(1980:391). Enter examples drawn from ethnography. In a practice not essentially different from that of Herbert Spencer, Henry Maine, Durkheim, Engels, or Freud, it is assumed that evidence from "simple" societies will illuminate the origins and structure of contemporary cultural patterns. Rosaldo notes that most scientific anthropologists have, since the early twentieth century, abandoned the evolutionary search for origins, but her essay suggests that the reflex is pervasive and enduring. Moreover, even scientific ethnographers cannot fully control the meanings – readings – provoked by their accounts. This is especially true of representations that have not historicized their objects, portraying exotic societies in an "ethnographic present" (which is always, in fact, a past). This synchronic suspension effectively textualizes the other, and gives the sense of a reality not in temporal flux, not in the same ambiguous, moving *historical* present that includes and situates the other, the ethnographer, and the reader. "Allochronic" representations, to use Johannes Fabian's term, have been pervasive in twentieth-century scientific ethnography. They invite allegorical appropriations in the mythologizing mode Rosaldo repudiates.

Even the most cooly analytic accounts may be built on this retrospective appropriation. E. E. Evans-Pritchard's *The Nuer* (1940) is a case in point, for it portrays an appealingly harmonious anarchy, a society uncorrupted by a Fall. Henrika Kuklick (1984) has analyzed *The Nuer* (in the context of a broad trend in British political anthropology concerned with acephalous "tribal" societies) as a political allegory reinscribing a recurrent "folk model" of Anglo-Saxon democracy. When Evans-Pritchard writes, "There is no master and no servant in their society, but only equals who regard themselves as God's noblest creation," it is not difficult to hear echoes of a long political tradition of nostalgia for "an egalitarian, contractual union" of free individuals. Edenic overtones are occasionally underscored, as always with Evans-Pritchard, drily.

> Though I have spoken of time and units of time the Nuer have no expression equivalent to "time" in our language, and they cannot, therefore, as we can, speak of time as though it were something actual, which passes, can be wasted, can be saved, and so forth. I do not think that they ever experience the same feeling of fighting against time or of having to coordinate activities with an abstract passage of time, because their points of reference are mainly the activities themselves, which are generally of a leisurely character. Events follow a logical order, but they are not controlled by an abstract system, there being no autonomous points of reference to which activities have to conform with precision. Nuer are fortunate. (103)

For a readership caught up in the post-Darwinian bourgeois experience of time – a linear, relentless progress leading nowhere certain and permitting no pause or cyclic return, the cultural islands out of time (or "without history") described by many ethnographers have a persistent prelapsarian appeal. We note, however, the ironic structure (which need not imply an ironic tone) of such allegories. For they are presented through the detour of an ethnographic subjectivity whose attitude toward the other is one of participant-observation, or better perhaps, belief-skepticism (See Webster 1982:93). Nuer are fortunate. (We are unfortunate.) The appeal is fictional, the temporal ease and attractive anarchy of Nuer society are distant, irretrievable. They are lost qualities, textually recovered.

This ironic appeal belongs to a broad ideological pattern that has oriented much, perhaps most, twentieth century cross-cultural representation. "For us, primitive societies [*Naturvölker*] are ephemeral. . . . At the very instant they become known to us they are doomed." Thus, Adolph Bastian in 1881 (quoted in Fabian 1983:122). In 1921, Bronislaw Malinowski: "Ethnology is in the sadly ludicrous, not to say tragic position, that at the very moment when it begins to put its workshop in order, to forge its proper tools, to start ready for work on its appointed task, the material of its study melts away with hopeless rapidity" (1961:xv). Authentic Trobriand society, he implied, was not long for this world. Writing in the 1950s, Claude Lévi-Strauss saw a global process of entropy. *Tristes Tropiques* sadly portrays differentiated social structures disintegrating into global homogeneity under the shock of contact with a potent monoculture. A Rousseauian quest for "elementary" forms of human collectivity leads Lévi-Strauss to the Nambikwara. But their world is falling apart. "I had been looking for a society reduced to its simplest expression. That of the Nambikwara was so truly simple that all I could find in it was individual human beings" (1975:317).

The theme of the vanishing primitive, of the end of traditional society (the very act of naming it "traditional" implies a rupture), is pervasive in ethnographic writing. It is, in Raymond Williams's phrase, a "structure of feeling" (1973:12). Undeniably, ways of life can, in a meaningful sense, "die"; populations are regularly violently disrupted, sometimes exterminated. Traditions are constantly being lost. But the persistent and repetitious "disappearance" of social forms at the moment of their ethnographic representation demands analysis as a narrative structure. A few years ago the *American Ethnologist* printed an article based on recent fieldwork among the Nambikwara – who are still something more than "individual human beings." And living Trobriand culture has been the object of recent field study (Weiner 1976). The now-familiar film *Tro-*

briand Cricket shows a very distinct way of life, reinventing itself under the conditions of colonialism and early nationhood.

Ethnography's disappearing object is, then, in significant degree, a rhetorical construct legitimating a representational practice: "salvage" ethnography in its widest sense. The other is lost, in disintegrating time and space, but saved in the text. The rationale for focusing one's attention on vanishing lore, for rescuing in writing the knowledge of old people, may be strong (though it depends on local circumstances and cannot any longer be generalized). I do not wish to deny specific cases of disappearing customs and languages, or to challenge the value of recording such phenomena. I do, however, question the assumption that with rapid change something essential ("culture"), a coherent differential identity, vanishes. And I question, too, the mode of scientific and moral authority associated with salvage, or redemptive, ethnography. It is assumed that the other society is weak and "needs" to be represented by an outsider (and that what matters in its life is its past, not present or future). The recorder and interpreter of fragile custom is custodian of an essence, unimpeachable witness to an authenticity. (Moreover, since the "true" culture has always vanished, the salvaged version cannot be easily refuted.)

Such attitudes, though they persist, are diminishing. Few anthropologists today would embrace the logic of ethnography in the terms in which it was enunciated in Franz Boas's time, as a last-chance rescue operation. But the allegory of salvage is deeply ingrained. Indeed, I shall argue in a moment that it is built into the conception and practice of ethnography as a process of writing, specifically of textualization. Every description or interpretation that conceives itself as "bringing a culture into writing," moving from oral-discursive experience (the "native's," the fieldworker's) to a written version of that experience (the ethnographic text) is enacting the structure of "salvage." To the extent that the ethnographic process is seen as inscription (rather than, for example, as transcription, or dialogue) the representation will continue to enact a potent, and questionable, allegorical structure.

This structure is appropriately located within a long Western tradition of pastoral. Raymond Williams's *The Country and the City* (1973), while drawing on an established tradition of scholarship on pastoral (Empson 1950, Kermode 1952, Frye 1971, Poggioli 1975, among others) strains toward a global scope wide enough to accommodate ethnographic writing. He shows how a fundamental contrast between city and country aligns itself with other pervasive oppositions: civilized and primitive, West and "non-West," future and past. He analyzes a complex, inventive, strongly patterned set of responses to social dislocation and change, stretching from classical antiquity to the present. Williams traces the constant reemergence of a conventionalized pattern of retrospection that laments the loss of a "good" country, a place where authentic social and natural contacts were once possible. He soon, however, notes an unsettling regression. For each time one finds a writer looking back to a happier place, to a lost, "organic" moment, one finds another writer of that earlier period lamenting a similar, previous disappearance. The ultimate referent is, of course, Eden (9–12).

Williams does not dismiss this structure as simply nostalgic, which it manifestly is; but rather follows out a very complex set of temporal, spatial, and moral positions. He notes that pastoral frequently involves a *critical nostalgia,* a way (as Diamond [1974] argues for a concept of the primitive) to break with the hegemonic, corrupt present by asserting the reality of a radical alternative. Edward Sapir's "Culture, Genuine and Spurious" (1966) recapitulates these critical pastoral values. And indeed every imagined authenticity presupposes, and is produced by, a present circumstance of felt inauthenticity. But Williams's treatment suggests that such projections need not be consistently located in the past; or, what amounts to the same thing, that the "genuine" elements of cultural life need not be repetitiously encoded as fragile, threatened, and transient. This sense of pervasive social fragmentation, of a constant disruption of "natural" relations, is characteristic of a subjectivity Williams loosely connects with city life and with romanticism. The self, cut loose from viable collective ties, is an identity in search of wholeness, having internalized loss and embarked on an endless search for authenticity. Wholeness by definition becomes a thing of the past (rural, primitive, childlike) accessible only as a fiction, grasped from a stance of incomplete involvement. George Eliot's novels epitomize this situation of participant-observation in a "common condition . . . a knowable community, belong[ing] ideally in the past." *Middlemarch,* for example, is projected a generation back from the time of its writing to 1830. And this is approximately the temporal distance that many conventional ethnographies assume when they describe a passing reality, "traditional" life, in the present tense. The fiction of a knowable community "can be recreated there for a widely ranging moral action. But the real step that has been taken is withdrawal from any full response to an existing society. Value is in the past, as a general retrospective condition, and is in the present only as a particular and private sensibility, the individual moral action" (180).

In George Eliot we can see the development of a style of sociological writing that will describe whole cultures (knowable worlds) from a specific temporal distance and with a presumption of their transience. This will be accomplished from a loving, detailed, but ultimately disengaged, standpoint. Historical worlds will be salvaged as textual fabrications disconnected from ongoing lived milieux and suitable for moral, allegorical appropriation by individual readers. In properly *ethnographic* pastoral this textualizing structure is generalized beyond the dissociations of nineteenth-century England to a wider capitalist topography of Western/non-Western, city/country oppositions. "Primitive," nonliterate, underdeveloped, tribal societies are constantly yielding to progress, "losing" their traditions. "In the name of science, we anthropologists compose requiems," writes Robert Murphy (1984). But the most problematic, and politically charged, aspect of this "pastoral" encodation is its relentless placement of others in a present-becoming-past. What would it require, for example, consistently to associate the inventive, resilient, enormously varied societies of Melanesia with the cultural *future* of the planet? How might ethnographies be differently conceived if this standpoint could be seriously adopted? Pastoral allegories of cultural loss and textual rescue would, in any event, have to be transformed.[9]

Pervasive assumptions about ethnography as writing would also have to be altered. For allegories of salvage are implied by the very practice of textualization that is generally assumed to be at the core of cultural description. Whatever else an ethnography does, it translates experience into text. There are various ways of effecting this translation, ways that have significant ethical and political consequences. One can "write up" the results of an individual experience of research. This may generate a realistic account of the unwritten experience of another group or person. One can present this textualization as the outcome of observation, of interpretation, of dialogue. One can construct an ethnography composed of dialogues. One can feature multiple voices, or a single voice. One can portray the other as a stable, essential whole, or one can show it to be the product of a narrative of discovery, in specific historical circumstances. I have discussed some of these choices elsewhere (1983a). What is irreducible, in all of them, is the assumption that ethnography brings experience and discourse into writing.

Though this is manifestly the case, and indeed reflects a kind of common sense, it is not an innocent common sense. Since antiquity the story

9. In my reading, the most powerful attempt to unthink this temporal setup, by means of an ethnographic invention of Melanesia, is the work of Roy Wagner (1979, 1980). He opposes, perhaps too sharply, Western "anticipations of the past" with Melanesian "anticipations of the future." The former are associated with the idea of culture as a structuring tradition (1979:162). Hugh Brody's *Maps and Dreams* (1982) offers a subtle and precise attempt to portray the hunting life of Beaver Indians in northwest Canada as they confront world-system forces, an oil pipeline, hunting for sport, etc. He presents his work as a political collaboration. And he is careful to keep the future open, uncertain, walking a fine line between narratives of "survival," "acculturation," and "impact."

of a passage from the oral/aural into writing has been a complex and charged one. Every ethnography enacts such a movement, and this is one source of the peculiar authority that finds both rescue and irretrievable loss – a kind of death in life – in the making of texts from events and dialogues. Words and deeds are transient (and authentic), writing endures (as supplementarity and artifice). The text embalms the event as it extends its "meaning." Since Socrates' refusal to write, itself powerfully written by Plato, a profound ambivalence toward the passage from oral to literate has characterized Western thinking. And much of the power and pathos of ethnography derives from the fact that it has situated its practice within this crucial transition. The fieldworker presides over, and controls in some degree, the making of a text out of life. His or her descriptions and interpretations become part of the "consultable record of what man has said" (Geertz 1973:30). The text is a record of something enunciated, in a *past*. The structure, if not the thematic content, of pastoral is repeated.

A small parable may give a sense of why this allegory of ethnographic rescue and loss has recently become less self-evident. It is a true parable.[10] A student of African ethno-history is conducting field research in Gabon. He is concerned with the Mpongwé, a coastal group who, in the nineteenth century, were active in contacts with European traders and colonists. The "tribe" still exists, in the region of Libreville, and the ethno-historian has arranged to interview the current Mpongwé chief about traditional life, religious ritual, and so on. In preparation for his interview the researcher consults a compendium of local custom compiled in the early twentieth century by a Gabonese Christian and pioneering ethnographer, the Abbé Raponda-Walker. Before meeting with the Mpongwé chief the ethnographer copies out a list of religious terms, institutions and concepts, recorded and defined by Raponda-Walker. The interview will follow this list, checking whether the customs persist, and if so, with what innovations. At first things go smoothly, with the Mpongwé authority providing descriptions and interpretations of the terms suggested, or else noting that a practice has been abandoned. After a time, however, when the researcher asks about a particular word, the chief seems uncertain, knits his brows. "Just a moment," he says cheerfully, and disappears into his house to return with a copy of Raponda-Walker's compendium. For the rest of the interview the book lies open on his lap.

Versions of this story, in increasing numbers, are to be heard in the folklore of ethnography. Suddenly cultural data cease to move smoothly from

10. My thanks to Henry Bucher for this true story. I have told it as a parable, both because it is one, and because I suspect he would tell it somewhat differently, having been there.

oral performance into descriptive writing. Now data also move from text to text, inscription becomes transcription. Both informant and researcher are readers and re-*writers* of a cultural invention. This is not to say, as some might, that the interview has ended in a sterile short circuit. Nor need one, like Socrates in the *Phaedrus,* lament the erosion of memory by literacy. The interview has not, suddenly, become "inauthentic," the data merely imposed. Rather, what one must reckon with are new conditions of ethnographic production. First, it is no longer possible to act as if the outside researcher is the sole, or primary, bringer of the culture into writing. This has, in fact, seldom been the case. However, there has been a consistent tendency among fieldworkers to hide, discredit, or marginalize prior written accounts (by missionaries, travelers, administrators, local authorities, even other ethnographers). The fieldworker, typically, starts from scratch, from a research *experience,* rather than from reading or transcribing. The field is not conceived of as already filled with texts. Yet this intertextual predicament is more and more the case (Larcom 1983). Second, "informants" increasingly read and write. They interpret prior versions of their culture, as well as those being written by ethnographic scholars. Work with texts – the process of inscription, rewriting, and so forth – is no longer (if it ever was) the exclusive domain of outside authorities. "Nonliterate" cultures are already textualized; there are few, if any, "virgin" lifeways to be violated and preserved by writing. Third, a very widespread, empowering distinction has been eroded: the division of the globe into literate and nonliterate peoples. This distinction is no longer widely accurate, as non-Western, "tribal" peoples become increasingly literate. But furthermore, once one begins to doubt the ethnographer's monopoly on the power to inscribe, one begins to see the "writing" activities that have always been pursued by native collaborators – from an Ambrym islander's sketch (in a famous gesture) of an intricate kinship system in the sand for A. B. Deacon to the Sioux George Sword's book-length cultural description found in the papers of James Walker.

But the most subversive challenge to the allegory of textualization I have been discussing here is found in the work of Derrida (1974). Perhaps the most enduring effect of his revival of "grammatology" has been to expand what was conventionally thought of as writing. *Alphabetic* writing, he argues, is a restrictive definition that ties the broad range of marks, spatial articulations, gestures, and other inscriptions at work in human cultures too closely to the representation of speech, the oral/aural word. In opposing logocentric representation to *écriture,* he radically extends the definition of the "written," in effect smudging its clear distinction from the "spoken." There is no need here to pursue in detail a disorienting project that is by now well known. What matters for ethnography is the claim that *all* human groups write – if they articulate, classify, possess an "oral-literature," or inscribe their world in ritual acts. They repeatedly "textualize" meanings. Thus, in Derrida's epistemology, the writing of ethnography cannot be seen as a drastically new form of cultural inscription, as an exterior imposition on a "pure," unwritten oral/aural universe. The logos is not primary and the *gramme* its mere secondary representation.

Seen in this light, the processes of ethnographic writing appear more complex. If, as Derrida would say, the cultures studied by anthropologists are always already writing themselves, the special status of the fieldworker-scholar who "brings the culture into writing" is undercut. Who, in fact, writes a myth that is recited into a tape recorder, or copied down to become part of field notes? Who writes (in a sense going beyond transcription) an interpretation of custom produced through intense conversations with knowledgeable native collaborators? I have argued that such questions can, and should, generate a rethinking of ethnographic authority (Clifford 1983a). In the present context I want merely to underline the pervasive challenge, both historical and theoretical in origin, that presently confronts the allegory of ethnographic practice as textualization.

It is important to keep the allegorical dimensions in mind. For in the West the passage from oral to literate is a potent recurring *story* – of power, corruption, and loss. It replicates (and to an extent produces) the structure of pastoral that has been pervasive in twentieth-century ethnography. Logocentric writing is conventionally conceived to be a *representation* of authentic speech. Pre-literate (the phrase contains a story) societies are oral societies; writing comes to them from "outside," an intrusion from a wider world. Whether brought by missionary, trader, or ethnographer, writing is both empowering (a necessary, effective way of storing and manipulating knowledge) and corrupting (a loss of immediacy, of the face-to-face communication Socrates cherished, of the presence and intimacy of speech). A complex and fertile recent debate has circled around the valorization, historical significance, and epistemological status of writing.[11] Whatever may or may not have been settled in the debate, there is no doubt of what has become unsettled: the sharp distinction of the world's cultures into literate and pre-literate; the notion that ethnographic textualization is a process that enacts a fundamental transition from oral experience to written representation; the assumption that something essential is lost when a culture becomes "ethnographic"; the

11. The "debate" centers on the confrontation of Ong (1967, 1977, 1982) and Derrida (1973, 1974). Tyler (1978, 1984b) tried to work past the opposition. Goody (1977) and Eisenstein (1979) have made important recent contributions.

strangely ambivalent authority of a practice that salvages as text a cultural life becoming past.

These components of what I have called ethnographic pastoral no longer appear as common sense. Reading and writing are generalized. If the ethnographer reads culture over the native's shoulder, the native also reads over the ethnographer's shoulder as he or she writes each cultural description. Fieldworkers are increasingly constrained in what they publish by the reactions of those previously classified as nonliterate. Novels by a Samoan (Alfred Wendt) can challenge the portrait of his people by a distinguished anthropologist. The notion that writing is a corruption, that something irretrievably pure is lost when a cultural world is textualized is, after Derrida, seen to be a pervasive, contestable, Western allegory. Walter Ong and others have shown that something is, indeed, lost with the generalization of writing. But authentic culture is not that something – to be gathered up in its fragile, final truth by an ethnographer or by anyone else.

Modern allegory, Walter Benjamin (1977) tells us, is based on a sense of the world as transient and fragmentary. "History" is grasped as a process, not of inventive life, but of "irresistible decay." The material analogue of allegory is thus the "ruin" (178), an always-disappearing structure that invites imaginative reconstruction. Benjamin observes that "appreciation of the transience of things, and the concern to redeem them for eternity, is one of the strongest impulses in allegory" (quoted by Wolin 1982:71). My account of ethnographic pastoral suggests that this "impulse" is to be resisted, not by abandoning allegory – an impossible aim – but by opening ourselves to different histories.

> Allegories are secured . . . by teaching people to read in certain ways.
> TALAL ASAD (comment on this essay at the Santa Fe seminar)

I have explored some important allegorical forms that express "cosmological" patterns of order and disorder, fables of personal (gendered) identity, and politicized models of temporality. The future of these forms in uncertain; they are being rewritten and criticized in current practice. A few conclusions, or at least assertions, may be drawn from this exploration.

- There is no way definitely, surgically, to separate the factual from the allegorical in cultural accounts. The data of ethnography make sense only within patterned arrangements and narratives, and these are conventional, political, and meaningful in a more than referential sense. Cultural facts are not true and cultural allegories false. In the human sciences the relation of fact to allegory is a domain of struggle and institutional discipline.

The meanings of an ethnographic account are uncontrollable. Neither an author's intention, nor disciplinary training, nor the rules of genre can limit the readings of a text that will emerge with new historical, scientific, or political projects. But if ethnographies are susceptible to multiple interpretations, these are not at any given moment infinite, or merely "subjective" (in the pejorative sense). Reading is indeterminate only to the extent that history itself is open-ended. If there is a common resistance to the recognition of allegory, a fear that it leads to a nihilism of reading, this is not a realistic fear. It confuses contests for meaning with disorder. And often it reflects a wish to preserve an "objective" rhetoric, refusing to locate its own mode of production within inventive culture and historical change.

A recognition of allegory inescapably poses the political and ethical dimensions of ethnographic writing. It suggests that these be manifested, not hidden. In this light, the open allegorizing of a Mead or a Benedict enacts a certain probity – properly exposing itself to the accusation of having *used* tribal societies for pedagogical purposes. (Let those free of such purposes cast the first stone!) One need not, of course, purvey heavy-handed "messages," or twist cultural facts (as presently known) to a political purpose. I would suggest as a model of allegorical tact Marcel Mauss's *The Gift*. No one would deny its scientific importance or scholarly commitment. Yet from the outset, and especially in its concluding chapter, the work's aim is patent: "to draw conclusions of a moral nature about some of the problems confronting us in our present economic crisis" (1967:2). The book was written in response to the breakdown of European reciprocity in World War I. The troubling proximity it shows between exchange and warfare, the image of the round table evoked at the end, these and other urgent resonances mark the work as a socialist-humanist allegory addressed to the political world of the twenties. This is not the work's only "content." The many rereadings *The Gift* has generated testify to its productivity as a text. It can even be read – in certain graduate seminars – as a classic comparative study of exchange, with admonitions to skim over the final chapter. This is a sad mistake. For it misses the opportunity to learn from an admirable example of science deploying itself *in* history.

A recognition of allegory complicates the writing and reading of ethnographies in potentially fruitful ways. A tendency emerges to specify and separate different allegorical registers within the test. The marking off of extended indigenous discourses shows the ethnography to be a hierarchical structure of powerful stories that translate, encounter, and recontextualize other powerful stories. It is a palimpset (Owens 1980). Moreover, an awareness of allegory heightens awareness of the narratives, and other temporal setups, implicitly or explicitly at work. Is the redemptive structure of salvage-textualization being replaced? By what new allegories? Of conflict? Of emergence? Of syncretism?[12]

Finally, a recognition of allegory requires that as readers and writers of ethnographies, we struggle to confront and take responsibility for our systematic constructions of others and of ourselves through others. This recognition need not ultimately lead to an ironic position – though it must content with profound ironies. If we are condemned to tell stories we cannot control, may we not, at least, tell stories we believe to be true.

12. For recent changes in these underlying stories, see note 9, above, and Bruner 1985. See also James Boon's 1983 exploration of anthropology's satiric dimensions. A partial way out can perhaps be envisioned in the pre-modern current that Harry Berger has called "strong" or "metapastoral" – a tradition he finds in the writing of Sidney, Spenser, Shakespeare, Cervantes, Milton, Marvell, and Pope. "Such pastoral constructs within itself an image of its generic traditions in order to criticize them and, in the process, performs a critique on the limits of its own enterprise even as it ironically displays its delight in the activity it criticizes" (1984:2). Modern ethnographic examples are rare, although much of Lévi-Strauss's *Tristes Tropiques* certainly qualifies.

12

Rhetoric, textuality, and the postmodern turn in sociological theory

Richard Harvey Brown

During the past decade the "rhetorical turn" has become an important intellectual movement in the human sciences. It has become a commonplace that social and cultural reality, and the social sciences themselves, are linguistic constructions. Not only is society viewed increasingly as a text, but scientific texts themselves are seen as rhetorical constructions. In this rhetorical view, reality and truth are formed through practices of representation and interpretation by rhetors and their publics. This view can be located in the contexts of poststructuralism, critical rhetoric of inquiry, and the social construction (and reconstruction) of science. All these tendencies of thought reject the simple of bifurcation of reason and persuasion, or of thought and its expression. Instead, knowledge is viewed as poetically and politically constituted, "made" by human communicative action that develops historically and is institutionalized politically.

In this view, realistic representations become true descriptions not by correspondence to noumenal objects, but by conformity to orthodox practices of writing and reading. Thus theories can be seen as the practices through which things take on meaning and value, and not merely as representations of a reality that is wholly exterior to them. Indeed, insofar as a theoretical representation is regarded as objectively true, it is viewed in that way because its methods of construction have become so familiar that they operate transparently (Shapiro 1988, p. XI). For example if we show a chart and call it "Income Distribution in the United States," we assume that the chart has a certain equivalence with things

This essay is a collaborative effort, especially with Scott Baker, whose thought and prose infuse the opening sections, and with Robert Brulle, who co-authored the section on the rhetorical construction of social reality. I also have drawn heavily on the works of Kenneth Gergen, Alan Gross, Julie Klein, and Herbert Simons, as well as on conversations with James Klumpp, Jerald Hage, Remi Clignet, and other members of our seminar on postmodern social theory. The limitations of this essay are of course entirely my own. Reprinted with permission of the American Sociological Association.

229

that people have or do. That is, we see the realism of the chart as independent of our conceptions of statistics, demographic research, and social theory that guide our way of seeing and reading that image. Yet every representation is always a representation from some point of view, within some frame of vision. Absolutist conceptions of sociological truth are merely those modes of representation which have "made it" socially and thence deny their necessary partiality. The distinctions between fact and fiction are thereby softened because both are seen as the products of, and sources for, communicative action; both are viewed as representations of reality that also represent various groups, interests, ideologies, and historical impositions. By untangling the relationship between textual and political practices, we gain insight into the ways in which the true has been fashioned, and could be refashioned anew.

In the presence of such a relativization of formerly privileged discourses of truth, many people feel nostalgia for a lost foundation for lawlike knowledge, whereas others hope for the creation of a new ethical ontology and normative epistemology. That is, even after deconstructive criticism has done its work, we still are faced with the challenge of establishing cognitive authority and inventing positive values as central elements of any rational moral polity. What is needed, then, is a critical assessment of the deconstructivist, rhetorical effort to date, a clearer understanding of its dialectical relationship to intelligibility within historical communities of discourse, and an analysis of how such academic discourses both reflect and influence their larger political contexts of production. In other words, we need to extend sociological analysis to uncover the methods by which, as sociologists and as citizens, we encode what is taken as real, normal, and to be accepted without question and even without awareness.

Thus the postmodernist project has the potential to radicalize the methods, the objects, and the very conceptions of our sociological enterprise. In particular, the postmodern transvaluation of epistemology wrenches us away from our most treasured beliefs about the constitution of science, knowledge, and even reason itself. It does so by leading us to question the traditional foundations of knowledge and scientific inquiry; then it asks us to adopt a *rhetorical* posture as we are subsequently faced with redefining, metatheoretically, what theory and research are. Then the task will be to define a more intellectually reflective and politically responsible sociological practice.

In the modernist past, postmodernists argue, our understanding of how science and knowledge were constituted relied upon an assumed polarity and hierarchy between truth and its medium of expression. Foundationalist epistemology and modern scientific method insisted that objective truth existed independently of any symbols that might be used to convey it. In this bifurcation, reason was authoritatively superior to its own external systems of expression. Since the Enlightenment, science has thrived on the self-endorsing assumption that the "rhetorical" is by definition separate from the true, ontologically and epistemologically. By contrast, postmoderns subvert the authority of modernist metatheory with a rhetorical conception of science. They relativize reason radically by conflating the traditionally bifurcated hierarchies of truth and expression, *doxa* and *episteme*, rationality and language, appearance and reality, and meaning and metaphor. They do so by focusing on the *how* rather than the *what* of knowledge, its poetic and political enablements rather than its logical and empirical entailments.

Through such shifts of focus, knowledge is relocated in the act of symbolic construction, and no longer is regarded as that which symbols subserviently convey. Knowledge about social reality is not viewed merely as objective product, but also as symbolic process that is inherently persuasive. Humans *enact* truth not by legislating it scientifically, but by performing it rhetorically. Our knowledge of truth is not based on some extralinguistic rationality, because rationality itself is demystified and reconstituted as a historical construction and deployment by human rhetors. Logic and reason are brought down from their absolute, preexistent heights into the creative, contextual web of history and action (Brown 1987, 64–79). The arena of conversation and contention that logic is closed to all but experts is thus prised open by rhetoric, with its emphasis upon audience, narrative, and prudent judgment in the face of historical contingency.

Accordingly, postmodernism shifts the agenda of social theory and research from explanation and verification to a conversation of scholars/rhetors who seek to guide and persuade themselves and each other. Theoretical truth is not a fixed entity discovered according to a metatheoretical blueprint of linearity or hierarchy, but is invented within an ongoing self-reflective community in which "theorist," "social scientist," "agent," and "critic" become relatively interchangeable (Burke 1964; Rorty 1979). This picture of the sociological enterprise suggests that critique of theory and method must be permanently imminent precisely because theories and methods themselves cannot be universalized. This view requires us to acknowledge our own rhetorical constitution – our selves as subjects and our fields as disciplinary objects – and then to maintain and apply the consciousness and the practice of rhetorical awareness.

A postmodern rhetoric for sociological theory

The status of the postmodernist critique of sociological theory can be framed in terms of the old question of the scope of rhetoric. If we accept the Aristotelian view that science is a specialized, somewhat exclusive practice of theoretical inquiry into certainty, whereas rhetoric treats the contingencies of public life, then the scope of rhetoric, and of any textualist deconstruction, must stop at the gates of science.

Conversely, critical rhetoric of inquiry has sought to subsume philosophical-scientific inquiry. A fuller intellectual justification for such a subsumption would require us to reexamine Plato's dispute with the rhetorical epistemology of the Sophists, and to reappraise the eventual emergence and maintenance of a strict disciplinary division between philosophy-science and rhetoric from Aristotle, through Cicero, through the medieval Church, and into the Enlightenment, with philosophy almost always on top.

We also would need to inspect the humanist rhetoricians of the Renaissance, and their responses to the mechanistic science of Descartes and Bacon. Vico's contribution, elaborated later by Kenneth Burke, is most important here if we conceived of rhetoric as the poetic-metaphoric view that reality and truth are projected through language. Vico's main thesis is that knowledge is not possible without language because through language we project an experienceable world. We create a human reality through metaphor (what Vico called *ingenium*), and in this rhetorical process every perception becomes an argument for seeing and acting toward reality in a certain way.

An intellectual justification for the postmodern, rhetorical deconstruction of social theory also would have to reframe Thomas Kuhn's suggestion that science itself is not a sacrosanct process of pure, incremental accumulation of knowledge, but a *community* of persons and schools guided by conceptual systems that he called paradigms. Kuhn advanced two claims that gave theorists the license to reveal the rhetorical character of science: first, that paradigms are sets of presuppositions which constrain what counts as evidence and what evidence counts; and second, that scientific discovery is guided by a given paradigm until another emerges to challenge and convert its practitioners.

Rhetorical theorists used this license to advance several arguments. First, some thinkers extended Kuhn's ideas by showing that paradigm enforcement is a practice of social and political control. Others conceptualized scientific inquiry as rhetorical because the theories themselves had to be linguistic constructs which, if adopted in periods of crisis ("paradigm shifts"), would be made attractive only through rhetorical persuasion. Others argued that knowing is itself poetic and political – that is, rhetorical (Weimer 1977). Still others asserted that if even the most rigorous processes of theory, such as mathematical demonstration and logical argument, were governed by consensus, then all theory would be capable of being metatheorized rhetorically (see Brown 1989b, pp. 123–42; Cherwitz 1977; Immershiem and Kaplan 1974; Perelman and Olbrechts-Tyteca 1969; Weimer 1977; Wolin 1960).

In the field of sociology, the emergence of labeling theory, ethnomethodology, and the sociology of knowledge have played out the same theme. From their respective standpoints, what we take to be the facts of any matter are not the results of events in themselves. Instead, a forestructure of labels or methods is deployed socially to negotiate what is to be marked as deviance, suicide, and the like. For sociologists of knowledge such as Collins (1985), Knorr-Cetina and Mulkay (1983), or Latour and Woolgar (1979), this means that the scientific laboratory becomes another site for ethnographic research – a place to note the social processes that produce the normalcies and deviance, the true and false, of science (see Gergen 1987).

All of these developments illustrate those shifts of discourse that have revived the ancient field of rhetoric. Language, and communicative action more generally, are now seen as the very condition of thought. Similarly, the idea of "text" is no longer restricted to a written representation. Any statement of experience or (more strongly) any lived or imagined experience is a discursive practice that is both culturally embedded and historically situated. A text might be a mathematical model or an archival record, a novel or a myth, a ritual or a public program. Indeed, culture itself is seen as an "ensemble of texts" (Geertz 1973, p. 452; Klein forthcoming). Correspondingly, meaning does not reside autonomously within a text but is created in the process of transforming experience into text in a dialogical relation with other texts and contexts (Todorov 1984, p. 48). Thus a text becomes an intertextual network, "a kind of juncture, where other texts, norms and values meet and work upon each other" (Iser 1987, p. 219). As a result, there is not one privileged meaning but many meanings and many voices. Necessarily, then, we are all engaged in textual problems and production. "Texts are no longer the sole province of English Departments, narrative the stuff of fiction, point of view the business of literary critics" (Klein forthcoming). Instead, society becomes a text, and sociological theory becomes an authorial voice of significant power.

In this view, what a social theoretical text says may be less the product of its own "inherent" properties than of the predispositions brought to the text by the reader (Klein forthcoming; Suleiman and Crossman 1980). Theoretically, then, a given text is open to as many different interpretations as there are articulate readers. Writers in the destructionist mode push this line of thinking to its limits. As Derrida (1974), de Man (1973), and others propose, writing, and by extension sociological theory, are not mimetic. Writing does not describe a world independent of itself. Rather, critical or expository writing is self-referential, governed by rules for its own construction (Gergen 1987). Thus "discovery" in science is more an honorific than a descriptive appellation; and it is ideological too because it disguises the very practices of reality projection that postmodernists deconstruct.

The rhetorical construction of social reality

The textualist approach also illuminates how selves and societies are constructed and deconstructed through rhetorical practices. In this view, the creation of meaningful personal or collective reality involves the intersubjective deployment of symbol structures through which happenings are organized into events and experience. Peoples establish repertoires of categories by which certain aspects of what is to be the case are fixed, focused, or forbidden. These aspects are put in the foreground of awareness and become articulated or conscious experience against a background of unspoken existence. The knowledge that emerges from this process takes a narrative form (Brown 1990; Greimas 1987, Chapter 6). Reciprocally, the sequential ordering of a past, a present, and a future enables the structuring of perceptual experience, the organization of memory, and the constructions of the events, identities, and lives that they express (Bruner 1987, p. 15). This rhetorically constructed narrative unity provides models of identity for people in particular symbolic settings or lifeworlds. It also guides individuals and groups in knowing what is real and what is illusion, what is permissible and what is proscribed, what goes without saying and what must not be said. "The construction of a worldview is thus a rhetorical act of creative human agency; it is a practical accomplishment of a human community over time" (Brulle 1988, p. 4).

In so constructing a world, other worlds are foreclosed. There is always a "surplus reality" because existence (potential experience) is always larger than actual experience. Moreover, as shown in Laurence Sterne's *Tristram Shandy*, there also is always a "surplus of the signified" because we experience more than we know, and we know more tacitly than we can state. Hence the unreflected, signified world is always larger than whatever version of it becomes canonized into formal knowledge. The land is always larger than the maps, and in mapping it in one official way we narrow awareness of alternative ways of experiencing the terrain. Likewise with human conduct: what is mapped as catatonic seizure in one culture may be seen as a divine trance in another; each is equally real for those who name their world in that way (Foucault 1973).

In articulating experience through categories, discursive practices realize differences and distinctions; they define what is normal and deviant, and hence express and enact forms of domination. Thus the processes of definition and exclusion are not only logical properties of discourse; they also are preconditions of intelligibility, sociation, social order, and social control. To make reality mutually comprehensible in an intersubjective group and to regularize symbolically guided social behavior, some versions of reality must be legitimized at the expense of their competitors. As Robert Brulle (1988) has discussed, such legitimation is an operation of closure. That is, it discounts the value of pursuing further implications and protects established interpretations by means of social sanctions that marginalize or silence dissident voices. Thus legitimation is a rhetorical achievement (Brinton 1985, p. 281; Brulle 1988, p. 4; Stanley 1978, p. 131). In Foucault's phrase (1970, 1972), it establishes a "regime of truth," a metanarrative by which the society lives.

Orthodox political theories hold that human nature generates social order; for example, for Hobbes brutish human nature necessitated a Leviathan state. Yet it is much more useful to understand both states and persons as cogenerated through discursive practices. Different dominant discursive practices reflect different collective habits of mind and action. In Pierre Bourdieu's (1977, p. 73) usage, the habitus is a system of durable, transposable dispositions that help generate and structure practices and representations. The habitus guides people's improvisations as they respond to changing situations. By helping to routinize actions and accounts, the habitus secures a commonsense world endowed with objectivity based on a consensus of the meanings of practice and reality (Brulle 1988, p. 4). These shared onto-operational assumptions make intelligibility and predictability possible, and therefore require and permit the coordination of the actions of members of a given group.

Reciprocally, from such routinized coordinated actions emerge institutions, social structures, and ontological assumptions. Temporally stable patterned and coordinated actions – that is, institutions – may realize "emergent properties" in the sense that their operations cannot be understood fully in terms of the intentions of their members. Moreover, for members such institutions may become icons, human artifacts thought to have a life of their own, independent of the volition of actors within them. Yet such institutions, cognitive structures, and other collective phenomena cannot be realized except in and through the system of rhetorical postures and discursive practices of the agents who constitute them (Brubaker 1985).

As noted, closure and legitimation also involve the repression of alternative realities. The establishment of an orthodoxy thus creates heterodoxies – subjugated discourses that stand outside the regime of truth. Foucault characterizes these discourses as "a whole set of knowledge that has been disqualified as inadequate to their task or insufficiently elaborated; naive knowledge, located low down on the hierarchy, beneath the required level of cognition or scientificity" (Foucault 1980, p. 82; see Kristeva 1973). In modern Western societies, such alternative realities are different and deviant from the dominant scientific habitus. They include dream time, carnal wisdom, mystic experience, feminine intuition, primal thought, aesthetic perception, hand intelligence, street smarts, lower-class lore, folkways, dopeways, old wives' tales, grace, and other forms of knowing.

These alternative realities are delegitimated by marginalizing the discursive practices through which they are constructed. Such practices become unofficial, extrainstitutional, and "backstage," expressed in the "restricted" rather than the "elaborated" code (see Bernstein 1971; Brown 1987; Goffman 1959, Chapter 1). From the view point of the dominant habitus, these discourses are linguistically deprived. Their delegitimation also delegitimates the lifeworlds of their users. The official discourse becomes the only one that provides symbolic capital that could be fruitfully invested in institutional relations. This limits the power and autonomy of speakers of marginalized discourses and forces them to adopt the dominant definition of reality and its regime of truth if they are to participate as full members in the collective institutional life. Indeed, compliance and full membership are expressed practically through adequate performance of the dominant mode of speech.

Thus relations of domination are produced through practice and are reified for members as things given by God, Nature, Tradition, History, or Reason. This movement from creative agency to reified structure is enacted through various persuasive strategies that conceal from social members their own rhetorical construction of the social text. Society comes to be seen as a natural fact rather than a cultural artifact. Reification thus allows relations of domination and authority to be seen as natural instead of created; it thereby facilitates conformity and continued reproduction of the social order. This ascription of naturalness inclines agents to accept the social order as it is. It becomes a "realized morality" to its members (Bourdieu 1977, pp. 163–64).

The appearance of society as a moral entity leads individuals to actions designed to maintain their self-image by avoiding shame and exclusion. Everyday interactions therefore are polite exchanges, aimed at avoiding embarrassment. Should the social fabric and persons' moral esteem be torn temporarily, this damage is repaired with excuses and justifications (Gamson 1985; Goffman 1959; Lyman and Scott 1970; Schudson and Crellanin 1984). In everyday life, Goffman tells us, we are occupied with "maintaining the definition of the situation" in order to "cope with the bizarre potentials of social life" (1974, p. 14). "Definitional disruptions . . . would occur much more frequently were not constant precaution taken" (Goffman 1959, pp. 2, 13). The social order, in other words, requires that "others" be "forced to accept some events as conventional or natural signs of something not directly available to the senses" (Goffman 1959, p. 2). Thus the realized morality of everyday interactions makes successful challenges to authority a risky, difficult, and sometimes unimaginable task. In these ways both social structure and personal identity are achieved rhetorically.

Postmodernism, sociological theory, and the political community

What is the relationship between the rhetorical, textualist perspective of postmodernism and the *telos* of nonideological, emancipatory discourse? Can the postmodernist project also contribute to a more reflexive, more enlightened polity? An adequate paradigm for democratic civic communication must join efficiency in managing complex systems with self-understanding and significance in the lifeworld. That is, it must enable us to govern our polities in a rational manner to ensure collective survival while providing us with meaning and dignity in our existential experience of ourselves. Hence such a discourse must be adequate not only on the level of science and technique, but also on the level of ethics and politics. After we have deconstructed traditional humanism and traditional science, we still confront these challenges. But with what intellectual resources, and with what disciplinary strategies? What additional problems are we likely to confront? How might they be usefully framed and addressed? How are analytic and existential truths to be conjoined within one discourse? How can we put ourselves within our scholarly texts?

The metaphor of scientific and social realities as rhetorical construction helps us to address such questions. First, it allows us to abandon the views both of social structures as objective entities acting on individuals and of subjective agents inventing their worlds out of conscious intentions. Instead both structure and consciousness are seen as practical, historical accomplishments, brought about through everyday communicative action, the result of rhetorical (poetic and political) struggles over the nature and meaning of reality.

In this discursive view, language is not a natural fact of daily life or a mere epiphenomenon of forces and relations of production. Instead it expresses and enables a social "covenant." As de Saussure put it, this covenant is

> the social side of language, outside the individual who can
> never create or modify it by himself; it exists only by virtue of a
> sort of contract signed by the members of the community. The
> community is necessary . . . ; by himself the individual cannot

fix a single value (1965, pp. 14, 113, 109). Each time I say [a] word I renew its substance (1965, p. 109).

What is true of discourse is, conversely, also true of persons. Because individuals are the *loci* from which discursive practices take their empowerment, the ontological status of human agents is a central condition for rhetorical awareness and practice. Thus a critical rhetoric for sociological theory appears to project two dialectically interrelated conditions: First, language and rhetoric are the constitutive conditions for selves, society, and knowledge; second, human agents are the condition for language and thus for human knowledge (Gergen 1987).

In such a manner, absolutist dichotomies of structure and agency or of base and superstructure may be dissolved in the metaphor of society as textual enactment. The structure (language) is both a constraint and a resource for performance (speech). The semiotic moment of the rhetorical approach deals effectively with structure; its hermeneutic moment treats of meaning and action. Both these dimensions – syntactics and grammatics, on the one hand, and semantics and pragmatics, on the other – are contained and logically consisted within the rhetorical or textualist metaphor. This metaphor combines in linguistic terms Durkheim's conception of constraining structures with Marx's idea that the system of exchanges is the source of values (Lemert 1990). Yet it also incorporates Mead's and Garfinkel's conceptions of social reality as constructed through communicative interaction.

In addition, unlike either positivism or subjective hermeneutics, this discursive approach is critical and reflexive. It sees cultural representations, and especially sociological theory, as providing *logoi* by which members can generate their own social texts. Thus social theory on the model of rhetoric recognizes explicity its moral and political functions. That is, it acknowledges that its discourse *about* society embodies members' representations *of* society and engenders further discourse *within* society. It thus sees sociological theory as value-soaked civic talk about our common life.

After we have perfected a hermeneutics of suspicion, there still is work to be done. Rhetoric, Richard McKeon reminds us, "provides the devices by which to determine the characteristics and problems of our times and to form the art by which to guide actions for the . . . improvement of our circumstances." Rhetoric enables us to "constitute new fields more relevant to the problems we encounter, and more viable to processes of inquiry and action" (McKeon 1971, pp. 52, 57).

The discursive approach also abandons the distorting notion of disciplines as well as of positivist and hermeneutic dichotomies within these disciplines. Instead it enables us to slice modes of argumentation differently and to understand "theory construction" as itself the deployment of various rhetorical strategies. Such an approach highlights the presuppositions and metalogics of all forms of sociological theory and thus brings values back to the fore. The devices of discovery and judgment, or of invention and legitimation, of course are rhetorical terms; within the rhetorical metaphor of society they now can be used to develop general social theories that are discourses for reasoned civic judgment.

In abandoning the antirhetorical rhetoric of positivism, the discursive approach recovers the ancient function of social thought as a moral and political practice. In this new critical rhetorical view, in constructing social theory we should attend not only to logical propositions and empirical contents, but also to linguistic methods and existential functions. We then see the linguistic dimension of social theory as an integral part of its truth or falsity to social life. This is the case for two reasons. First, truth and validity are themselves rhetorically constructed and hence are a part of our civic life. Second, as rhetorical interventions, social scientific theories convey an existential as well as a propositional truth. Sociological theories provide a truth of facts or meanings, an appeal to the *telos* of elegance and precision, predictability or comprehension. Yet when seen rhetorically, such truth is also an implicit call to action. Its existential *telos* is self-understanding, critique, and emancipation. Reductionists have sought to silence this existential dimension of sociological theory by treating it as an object external to society that makes no personal moral claim upon us. But social theories do convey an existential truth. And, unlike propositional truth, existential truth is not merely to be cross-examined. Instead, when it speaks we ourselves become the "object," for it is we who are addressed.

REFERENCES

Bernstein, Basil. 1971. *Class, Codes, and Control*. London: Routledge and Kegan Paul.

Bourdieu, Pierre. 1977. *Outline of a Theory of Practice*. Cambridge: Cambridge University Press.

Brinton, Alan. 1985. "On Viewing Knowledge as Rhetorical." *Central States Speech Journal* 36 (4): 270–81.

Brown, Richard Harvey. 1987. *Society as Text, Essays on Rhetoric, Reason, and Reality*. Chicago: University of Chicago Press.

1989a(1977). *A Poetic for Sociology, Toward a Logic of Discovery for the Human Sciences*. Chicago: University of Chicago Press.

1989b. *Social Science as Civic Discourse. Essays on the Invention, Legitimation, and Uses of Social Theory*. Chicago: University of Chicago Press.

1990. "Narrative in Scientific Knowledge and Civic Discourse." *Current Perspectives in Social Theory*. 11: In press.

Brubaker, Roger. 1985. "Rethinking Classical Theory: The Sociological Vision of Pierre Bourdieu." *Theory and Society* 14 (6): 745–75.

Brulle, Robert J. 1988. "Power, Discourse, and Social Movements." Unpublished paper: Washington, DC. Department of Sociology, George Washington University.

Bruner, Jerome. 1987. "Life as Narrative." *Social Research* 54 (1): 11–32.

Burke, Kenneth. 1964. *Perspectives by Incongruity*. Bloomington: Indiana University Press.

Cherwitz, Richard. 1977. "Rhetoric as a 'Way of Knowing' ": An Attenuation of the Epistemological Claims of the 'New Rhetoric'." *Southern Speech Communication Journal* 42: 207–19.

Collins, Harry M. 1985. *Changing Order*. Los Angeles: Sage.

de Man, Paul. 1973. "Semiology and Rhetoric." *Diacritics* 3 (3): 27–33.

Derrida, Jacques, 1974. *Of Grammatology*. Baltimore: Johns Hopkins University Press.

de Saussure, Ferdinand. 1965. *Cours de Linguistique Generale*. Paris: Presses Universitaires de France.

Foucault, Michel. 1970. *The Order of Things: An Archaeology of the Human Sciences*. New York: Pantheon.

1972. *The Archaeology of Knowledge*, translated by A.M. Sheridan. New York: Harper.

1973. *Madness and Civilization: A History of Insanity in the Age of Reason*, translated by R. Howard. New York: Vintage.

Gamson, William A. 1985. "Goffman's Legacy to Political Sociology." *Theory and Society* 14 (5): 605–22.

Geertz, Clifford. 1973. *The Interpretation of Cultures*. New York: Basic Books.

Gergen, Kenneth J. 1982. *Toward a Transformation of Social Knowledge*. New York: Springer-Verlag.

1987. "The Checkmate of Rhetoric (But Can Our Reasons Become Causes?)" Presented to the Conference on Case Studies in Rhetoric, Temple University, Philadelphia.

Goffman, Erving. 1959. *The Presentation of the Self in Everyday Life*. Garden City, NY: Doubleday.

1974. *Frame Analysis: An Essay on the Organization of Experience*. New York: Harper.

Greimas, Algirdas Julien. 1987. *On Meaning: Selected Writings in Semiotic Theory*. Minneapolis: University of Minnesota Press.

Immersheim, Allen W. and Howard M. Kaplan. 1974. "Organizational Change as a Paradigm Shift: The Case of Health Care Delivery." Presented to the American Sociological Association, Montreal.

Iser, Wolfgang. 1987. "Representation: A Performative Act." Pp. 217–32 in *The Aims of Representation: Subject/Text/History*, edited by Murray-Kreiger. New York: Columbia University Press.

Klein, Julie. Forthcoming. "Text/Context: A Rhetoric of Integration in the Human Sciences." In *Writing the Social Text: Poetics and Politics in Social-Science Discourse*, edited by Richard Harvey Brown.

Knorr-Cetina, Karin D. and Michael Mulkay. 1983. *Science Observed: Perspectives on the Social Study of Science*. London: Sage.

Kristeva, Julia. 1973. "The System and the Speaking Subject." *The Times Literary Supplement*, October 12 (3, 736): 1249–50.

Kuhn, Thomas. 1972. *The Structure of Scientific Revolutions*. Chicago: University of Chicago Press.

Latour, Bruno and Steve Woolgar. 1979. *Laboratory Life*. Princeton: Princeton University Press.

Lemert, Charles. 1990. "Social Theory? Theoretical Play after Difference." In *Postmodernism and Social Theory*, edited by Steven Seidman and David Wagner. Oxford: Basil Blackwell.

Lyman, Stanford M. and Marvin B. Scott. 1970. "Accounts." In *A Sociology of the Absurd*, New York: Appleton-Century-Crofts.

McKeon, Richard. 1971. "The Uses of Rhetoric in a Technological Age: Architectonic Productive Arts." Pp. 44–63 in *The Prospect of Rhetoric*, edited by Lloyd F. Bitzer and Edwin Black. Englewood Cliffs, NJ: Prentice-Hall.

Perelman, Chaim and Lucie Olbrechts-Tyteca. 1969. *The New Rhetoric. A Treatise on Argumentation*. Notre Dame: University of Notre Dame Press.

Rorty, Richard. 1979. *Philosophy and the Mirror of Nature*. Princeton: Princeton University Press.

Schudson, Michael. 1984. "Embarrassment and Erving Goffman's Idea of Human Nature." *Theory and Society* 13 (5):633–48.

Shapiro, Michael J. 1988. *The Politics of Representation: Writing Practices in Biography, Photography, and Policy Analysis*. Madison: University of Wisconsin Press.

Stanley, Manfred. 1978. *The Technological Conscience. Survival and Dignity in an Age of Expertise*. Chicago: University of Chicago Press.

Sterne, Laurence. 1940. *The Life and Opinions of Tristram Shandy*. New York: Odyssey.

Suleiman, Susan R. and Inge Crossman, eds. 1980. *The Reader in the Text: Essays on Audience and Interpretation*. Princeton: Princeton University Press.

Todorov, Tzvetan. 1984. *Mikhail Bakhtin: The Dialogal Principle*, translated by Wead Godzich. Minneapolis: University of Minnesota Press.

Vico, Giambattista. 1972.(1744). *The New Science of Giambattista Vico*, translated by Thomas Goddard and Max Harold Frish. Ithaca: Cornell University Press.

Weimer, Walter B. 1977. "Sciences as a Rhetorical Transaction: Toward a Nonjustificational Conception of Rhetoric." *Philosophy and Rhetoric* 10: 1–29.

Wolin, Sheldon. 1960. *Politics and Vision: Continuity and Innovation in Western Political Thought*. Boston: Little, Brown.

13

Social criticism without philosophy:
An encounter between feminism
and postmodernism

Nancy Fraser and Linda Nicholson

Feminism and postmodernism have emerged as two of the most important political-cultural currents of the last decade. So far, however, they have kept an uneasy distance from one another. Indeed, so great has been their mutual wariness that there have been remarkably few extended discussions of the relations between them (exceptions are: Flax, 1986; Harding, 1986a, 1986b; Haraway, 1983; Jardine, 1985; Lyotard, 1978; Owens, 1983).

Initial reticences aside, there are good reasons for exploring the relations between feminism and postmodernism. Both have offered deep and far-reaching criticisms of the 'institution of philosophy'. Both have elaborated critical perspectives on the relation of philosophy to the larger culture. And, most central to the concerns of this essay, both have sought to develop new paradigms of social criticism which do not rely on traditional philosophical underpinnings. Other differences notwithstanding, one could say that, during the last decade, feminists and postmodernists have worked independently on a common nexus of problems: they have tried to rethink the relation between philosophy and social criticism so as to develop paradigms of 'criticism without philosophy'.

On the other hand, the two tendencies have proceeded, so to speak, from opposite directions. Postmodernists have focused primarily on the philosophy side of the problem. They have begun by elaborating antifoundational metaphilosophical perspectives and from there have gone on to draw conclusions about the shape and character of social criticism.

Theory, Culture & Society (SAGE, London, Newbury Park, Beverly Hills and New Delhi), Vol. 5 (1988), 373–94 We are grateful for the helpful suggestions of many people, especially Jonathan Arac, Ann Ferguson, Marilyn Frye, Nancy Hartsock, Alison Jaggar, Berel Lang, Thomas McCarthy, Karsten Struhl, Iris Young, Thomas Wartenburg and the members of SOFPHIA. We are also grateful for word-processing help from Marina Rosiene.

For feminists, on the other hand, the question of philosophy has always been subordinate to an interest in social criticism. So they have begun by developing critical political perspectives and from there have gone on to draw conclusions about the status of philosophy. As a result of this difference in emphasis and direction, the two tendencies have ended up with complementary strengths and weaknesses. Postmodernists offer sophisticated and persuasive criticisms of foundationalism and essentialism, but their conceptions of social criticism tend to be anaemic. Feminists offer robust conceptions of social criticism, but they tend, at times, to lapse into foundationalism and essentialism.

Thus, each of the two perspectives suggest some important criticisms of the other. A postmodernist reflection on feminist theory reveals disabling vestiges of essentialism while a feminist reflection on postmodernism reveals androcentrism and political naivete.

It follows that an encounter between feminism and postmodernism will initially be a trading of criticisms. But there is no reason to suppose that this is where matters must end. In fact, each of these tendencies has much to learn from the other; each is in possession of valuable resources which can help remedy the deficiencies of the other. Thus, the ultimate stake of an encounter between feminism and postmodernism is the prospect of a perspective which integrates their respective strengths while eliminating their respective weaknesses. It is the prospect of a postmodernist feminism.

In what follows, we aim to contribute to the development of such a perspective by staging the initial, critical phase of the encounter. In section I, we examine the ways in which one exemplary postmodernist, Jean-François Lyotard, has sought to derive new paradigms of social criticism from a critique of the institution of philosophy. We argue that the conception of social criticism so derived is too restricted to permit an adequate critical grasp of gender dominance and subordination. We identify some internal tensions in Lyotard's arguments; and we suggest some alternative formulations which could allow for more robust forms of criticism without sacrificing the commitment to anti-foundationalism. In section II, we examine some representative genres of feminist social criticism. We argue that, in many cases, feminist critics continue tacitly to rely on the sorts of philosophical underpinnings which their own commitments, like those of postmodernists, ought, in principle, to rule out. And we identify some points at which such underpinnings could be abandoned without any sacrifice of social-critical force. Finally, in a brief conclusion, we consider the prospects for a postmodernist feminism. We discuss some requirements which constrain the development of such a perspective and we identify some pertinent conceptual resources and critical strategies.

I. Postmodernism

Postmodernists seek, inter alia, to develop conceptions of social criticism which do not rely on traditional philosophical underpinnings. The typical starting point for their efforts is a reflection on the condition of philosophy today. Writers like Richard Rorty and Jean-François Lyotard begin by arguing that Philosophy with a capital 'P' is no longer a viable or credible enterprise. From here, they go on to claim that philosophy, and, by extension, theory more generally, can no longer function to *ground* politics and social criticism. With the demise of foundationalism comes the demise of the view that casts philosophy in the role of *founding* discourse vis-à-vis social criticism. That 'modern' conception must give way to a new 'postmodern' one in which criticism floats free of any universalist theoretical ground. No longer anchored philosophically, the very shape or character of social criticism changes; it becomes more pragmatic, ad hoc, contextual and local. And with this change comes a corresponding change in the social role and political function of intellectuals.

Thus, in the postmodern reflection on the relationship between philosophy and social criticism, the term 'philosophy' undergoes an explicit devaluation; it is cut down to size, if not eliminated altogether. Yet, even as this devaluation is argued explicitly, the term 'philosophy' retains an implicit structural privilege. It is the changed condition of philosophy which determines the changed characters of social criticism and of engaged intellectual practice. In the new postmodern equation, then, philosophy is the independent variable while social criticism and political practice are dependent variables. The view of theory which emerges is not determined by considering the needs of contemporary criticism and engagement. It is determined, rather, by considering the contemporary status of philosophy. As we hope to show, this way of proceeding has important consequences, not all of which are positive. Among the results is a certain underdescription and premature foreclosing of possibilities for social criticism and engaged intellectual practice. This limitation of postmodern thought will be apparent when we consider its results in the light of the needs of contemporary feminist theory and practice.

Let us consider as an example the postmodernism of Jean-François Lyotard, since it is genuinely exemplary of the larger tendency. Lyotard is one of the few social thinkers widely considered postmodern who actually uses the term; indeed, it was he himself who introduced it into current discussions of philosophy, politics, society and social theory. His book, *The Postmodern Condition,* has become the *locus classicus* for contemporary debates, and it reflects in an especially acute form the characteristic concerns and tensions of the movement (Lyotard, 1984a).

For Lyotard, postmodernism designates a general condition of contemporary western civilization. The postmodern condition is one in which 'grand narratives of legitimation' are no longer credible. By 'grand narratives' he means, in the first instance, overarching philosophies of history like the Enlightenment story of the gradual but steady progress of reason and freedom, Hegel's dialectic of Spirit coming to know itself, and, most important, Marx's drama of the forward march of human productive capacities via class conflict culminating in proletarian revolution. For Lyotard, these 'metanarratives' instantiate a specifically modern approach to the problem of legitimation. Each situates first-order discursive practices of inquiry and politics within a broader totalizing metadiscourse which legitimates them. The metadiscourse narrates a story about the whole of human history which purports to guarantee that the 'pragmatics' of the modern sciences and of modern political processes, that is, the norms and rules which govern these practices, determining what counts as a warranted move within them, are themselves legitimate. The story guarantees that some sciences and some politics have the *right* pragmatics and, so, are the *right* practices.

We should not be misled by Lyotard's focus on narrative philosophies of history. In his conception of legitimating metanarrative, the stress properly belongs on the 'meta' and not the 'narrative'. For what most interests him about the Enlightenment, Hegelian and Marxist stories is what they share with other, non-narrative forms of philosophy. Like ahistorical epistemologies and moral theories, they aim to show that specific first-order discursive practices are well-formed and capable of yielding true and just results. 'True' and 'just' here mean something more than results reached by adhering scrupulously to the constitutive rules of some given scientific and political games. They mean, rather, results which correspond to Truth and Justice as they really are in themselves independent of contingent, historical, social practices. Thus, in Lyotard's view, a metanarrative is meta in a very strong sense. It purports to be a privileged discourse capable of situating, characterizing and evaluating all other discourses, but not itself infected by the historicity and contingency which render first-order discourses potentially distorted and in need of legitimation.

In *The Postmodern Condition,* Lyotard argues that metanarratives, whether philosophies of history or non-narrative foundational philosophies, are merely modern and dépassé. We can no longer believe, he claims, in the availability of a privileged metadiscourse capable of capturing once and for all the truth of every first-order discourse. The claim to meta status does not stand up. A so-called metadiscourse is in fact simply one more discourse among others. It follows for Lyotard that legitimation, both epistemic and political, can no longer reside in philosophical metanarratives. Where, then, he asks, does legitimation reside in the postmodern era?

Much of *The Postmodern Condition* is devoted to sketching an answer to this question. The answer, in brief, is that in the postmodern era legitimation becomes plural, local and immanent. In this era, there will necessarily be many discourses of legitimation dispersed among the plurality of first-order discursive practices. For example, scientists no longer look to prescriptive philosophies of science to warrant their procedures of inquiry. Rather, they themselves problematize, modify and warrant the constitutive norms of their own practice even as they engage in it. Instead of hovering above, legitimation descends to the level of practice and becomes immanent in it. There are no special tribunals set apart from the sites where inquiry is practiced. Rather, practitioners assume responsibility for legitimizing their own practice.

Lyotard intimates that something similar is or should be happening with respect to political legitimation. We cannot have and do not need a single, overarching theory of justice. What is required, rather, is a 'justice of multiplicities' (Lyotard, 1984a; see also: Lyotard and Thébaud, 1987; Lyotard, 1984b). What Lyotard means by this is not wholly clear. On one level, he can be read as offering a normative vision in which the good society consists in a decentralized plurality of democratic, self-managing groups and institutions whose members problematize the norms of their practice and take responsibility for modifying them as situations require. But paradoxically, on another level, he can be read as ruling out the sort of larger scale, normative political theorizing which, from a 'modern' perspective at least, would be required to legitimate such a vision. In any case, his justice of multiplicities conception precludes one familiar, and arguably essential, genre of political theory: identification and critique of macrostructures of inequality and injustice which cut across the boundaries separating relatively discrete practices and institutions. There is no place in Lyotard's universe for critique of pervasive axes of stratification, for critique of broad-based relations of dominance and subordination along lines like gender, race and class.

Lyotard's suspicion of the large extends to historical narrative and social theory as well. Here, his chief target is Marxism, the one metanarrative in France with enough lingering credibility to be worth arguing against. The problem with Marxism, in his view, is twofold. On the one hand, the Marxian story is too big, since it spans virtually the whole of human history. On the other hand, the Marxian story is too theoretical, since it relies on a *theory* of social practice and social relations which claims to *explain* historical change. At one level, Lyotard simply rejects the specifics of this theory. He claims that the Marxian conception of practice as production occludes the diversity and plurality of human prac-tices. And the Marxian conception of capitalist society as a totality tra-versed by one major division and contradiction occludes the diversity and plurality of contemporary societal differences and oppositions. But Ly-otard does not occlude that such deficiencies can and should be remedied by a better social theory. Rather, he rejects the project of social theory *tout court.*

Once again, Lyotard's position is ambiguous, since his rejection of social theory depends on a theoretical perspective of sorts of its own. He offers a 'postmodern' conception of sociality and social identity, a con-ception of what he calls 'the social bond'. What holds a society together, he claims, is not a common consciousness or institutional substructure. Rather, the social bond is a weave of criss-crossing threads of discursive practices, no single one of which runs continuously throughout the whole. Individuals are the nodes or 'posts' where such practices intersect and, so, they participate in many simultaneously. It follows that social identities are complex and heterogeneous. They cannot be mapped onto one an-other nor onto the social totality. Indeed, strictly speaking, there is no so-cial totality and a fortiori no possibility of a totalizing social theory.

Thus, Lyotard insists that the field of the social is heterogeneous and nontotalizable. As a result, he rules out the sort of critical social theory which employs general categories like gender, race and class. From his perspective, such categories are too reductive of the complexity of social identities to be useful. And there is apparently nothing to be gained, in his view, by situating an account of the fluidity and diversity of discursive practices in the context of a critical analysis of large-scale institutions and social structures.

Thus, Lyotard's postmodern conception of criticism without philoso-phy rules out several recognizable genres of social criticism. From the premise that criticism cannot be grounded by a foundationalist philo-sophical metanarrative, he infers the illegitimacy of large historical sto-ries, normative theories of justice and social-theoretical accounts of macrostructures which institutionalize inequality. What, then, *does* post-modern social criticism look like?

Lyotard tries to fashion some new genres of social criticism from the discursive resources that remain. Chief among these is smallish, localized narrative. He seeks to vindicate such narrative against both modern to-talizing metanarrative and the scientism that is hostile to all narrative. One genre of postmodern social criticism, then, consists in relatively dis-crete, local stories about the emergence, transformation and disappear-ance of various discursive practices treated in isolation from one another. Such stories might resemble those told by Michel Foucault, though with-out the attempts to discern larger synchronic patterns and connections that Foucault (1979) sometimes made. And like Michael Walzer (1983), Lyotard seems to assume that practitioners would narrate such stories when seeking to persuade one another to modify the pragmatics or constitutive norms of their practice.

This genre of social criticism is not the whole postmodern story, however. For it casts critique as strictly local, ad hoc and ameliorative, thus supposing a political diagnosis according to which there are no large scale, systemic problems which resist local, ad hoc, ameliorative initiatives. Yet Lyotard recognizes that postmodern society does contain at least one unfavourable structural tendency which requires a more coordinated response. This is the tendency to universalize instrumental reason, to subject *all* discursive practices indiscriminately to the single criterion of efficiency or 'performativity'. In Lyotard's view, this threatens the autonomy and integrity of science and politics, since these practices are not properly subordinated to performative standards. It would pervert and distort them, thereby destroying the diversity of discursive forms.

Thus, even as he argues explicitly against it, Lyotard posits the need for a genre of social criticism which transcends local mininarrative. And despite his strictures against large, totalizing stories, he narrates a fairly tall tale about a large-scale social trend. Moreover, the logic of this story, and of the genre of criticism to which it belongs, calls for judgments which are not strictly practice-immanent. Lyotard's story presupposes the legitimacy and integrity of the scientific and political practices allegedly threatened by 'performativity'. It supposes that one can distinguish changes or developments which are *internal* to these practices from externally induced distortions. But this drives Lyotard to make normative judgments about the value and character of the threatened practices. These judgments are not strictly immanent in the practices judged. Rather, they are 'metapractical'.

Thus, Lyotard's view of postmodern social criticism is neither entirely self-consistent nor entirely persuasive. He goes too quickly from the premise that Philosophy cannot ground social criticism to the conclusion that criticism itself must be local, ad hoc and non-theoretical. As a result, he throws out the baby of large historical narrative with the bathwater of philosophical metanarrative and the baby of social-theoretical analysis of large scale inequalities with the bathwater of reductive Marxian class theory. Moreover, these allegedly illegitimate babies do not in fact remain excluded. They return like the repressed within the very genres of postmodern social criticism with which Lyotard intends to replace them.

We began this discussion by noting that postmodernists orient their reflections on the character of postmodern social criticism by the falling star of foundationalist philosophy. They posit that, with philosophy no longer able credibly to ground social criticism, criticism itself must be local, ad hoc and untheoretical. Thus, from the critique of foundationalism, they infer the illegitimacy of several genres of social criticism. For Lyotard, the illegitimate genres include large-scale historical narrative and social-theoretical analyses of pervasive relations of dominance and subordination.[1]

Suppose, however, one were to choose another starting point for reflecting on postfoundational social criticism. Suppose one began, not with the condition of Philosophy, but with the nature of the social object one wished to criticize. Suppose, further, that one defined that object as the subordination of women to and by men. Then, we submit, it would be apparent that many of the genres rejected by postmodernists are necessary for social criticism. For a phenomenon as pervasive and multi-faceted as male dominance simply cannot be adequately grasped with the meagre critical resources to which they would limit us. On the contrary, effective criticism of this phenomenon requires an array of different methods and genres. It requires at minimum large narratives about changes in social organization and ideology, empirical and social-theoretical analyses of macrostructures and institutions, interactionist analyses of the micropolitics of everyday life, critical-hermeneutical and institutional analyses of cultural production, historically and culturally specific sociologies of gender. . . . The list could go on.

Clearly, not all of these approaches are local and 'untheoretical'. But all are nonetheless essential to feminist social criticism. Moreover, all can, in principle, be conceived in ways that do not take us back to foundationalism even though, as we argue in the next section, many feminists have so far not wholly succeeded in avoiding that trap.

II. Feminism

Feminists, like postmodernists, have sought to develop new paradigms of social criticism which do not rely on traditional philosophical underpinnings. They have criticized modern foundationalist epistemologies and moral and political theories, exposing the contingent, partial and historically situated character of what have passed in the mainstream for nec-

1. It should be noted that, for Lyotard, the choice of Philosophy as a starting point is itself determined by a metapolitical commitment, namely, to anti-totalitarianism. He assumes, erroneously, in our view, that totalizing social and political theory necessarily eventuates in totalitarian societies. Thus, the 'practical intent' which subtends Lyotard's privileging of philosophy (and which is in turn attenuated by the latter) is anti-Marxism. Whether it should also be characterized as 'neo-liberalism' is a question too complicated to be explored here.

essary, universal and ahistorical truths. And they have called into question the dominant philosophical project of seeking objectivity in the guise of a 'God's eye view' which transcends any situation of perspective (see for example Harding and Hintikka, 1983).

However, if postmodernists have been drawn to such views by a concern with the status of philosophy, feminists have been led to them by the demands of political practice. This practical interest has saved feminist theory from many of the mistakes of postmodernism: women whose theorizing was to serve the struggle against sexism were not about to abandon powerful political tools merely as a result of intramural debates in professional philosophy.

Yet even as the imperatives of political practice have saved feminist theory from one set of difficulties, they have tended at times to incline it toward another. Practical imperatives have led some feminists to adopt modes of theorizing which resemble the sorts of philosophical metanarrative rightly criticized by postmodernists. To be sure, the feminist theories we have in mind here are not 'pure' metanarratives; they are not ahistorical normative theories about the transcultural nature of rationality or justice. Rather, they are very large social theories, theories of history, society, culture and psychology which claim, for example, to identify causes and/or constitutive features of sexism that operate cross-culturally. Thus, these social theories purport to be empirical rather than philosophical. But, as we hope to show, they are actually 'quasi-metanarratives'. They tacitly presuppose some commonly held but unwarranted and essentialist assumptions about the nature of human beings and the conditions for social life. In addition, they assume methods and/or concepts which are uninflected by temporality or historicity and which therefore function de facto as permanent, neutral matrices for inquiry. Such theories, then, share some of the essentialist and ahistorical features of metanarratives: they are insufficiently attentive to historical and cultural diversity; and they falsely universalize features of the theorist's own era, society, culture, class, sexual orientation, and/or ethnic or racial group.

On the other hand, the practical exigencies inclining feminists to produce quasi-metanarratives have by no means held undisputed sway. Rather, they have had to co-exist, often uneasily, with counterexigencies which have worked to opposite effect, for example, political pressures to acknowledge differences among women. In general, then, the recent history of feminist social theory reflects a tug of war between forces which have encouraged and forces which have discouraged metanarrative-like modes of theorizing. We can illustrate this dynamic by looking at a few important turning points in this history.

When, in the 1960s, women in the new left began to extend prior talk about 'women's rights' into the more encompassing discussion of 'wom-

en's liberation', they encountered the fear and hostility of their male comrades and the use of Marxist political theory as a support for these reactions. Many men of the new left argued that gender issues were secondary
because subsumable under more basic modes of oppression, namely, class
and race.

In response to this practical-political problem, radical feminists such as
Shulamith Firestone (1970) resorted to an ingenious tactical manoeuvre:
Firestone invoked biological differences between women and men to explain sexism. This enabled her to turn the tables on her Marxist comrades
by claiming that gender conflict was the most basic form of human conflict and the source of all other forms, including class conflict. Here, Firestone drew on the pervasive tendency within modern culture to locate the
roots of gender differences in biology. Her coup was to use biologism to
establish the primacy of the struggle against male domination rather than
to justify acquiescence to it.

The trick, of course, is problematic from a postmodernist perspective
in that appeals to biology to explain social phenomena are essentialist and
monocausal. They are essentialist insofar as they project onto all women
and men qualities which develop under historically specific social conditions. They are monocausal insofar as they look to one set of characteristics, such as women's physiology or men's hormones, to explain
women's oppression in all cultures. These problems are only compounded
when appeals to biology are used in conjunction with the dubious claim
that women's oppression is the cause of all other forms of oppression.

Moreover, as Marxists and feminist anthropologists began insisting in
the early 1970s, appeals to biology do not allow us to understand the
enormous diversity of forms which both gender and sexism assume in different cultures. And in fact, it was not long before most feminist social
theorists came to appreciate that accounting for the diversity of the forms
of sexism was as important as accounting for its depth and autonomy.
Gayle Rubin (1975: 160) aptly described this dual requirement as the
need to formulate theory which could account for the oppression of
women in its 'endless variety and monotonous similarity'. How were feminists to develop a social theory adequate to both demands?

One approach which seemed promising was suggested by Michelle
Zimbalist Rosaldo and other contributors to the influential 1974 anthropology collection, *Woman, Culture and Society*. They argued that common to all know societies was some type of separation between a
'domestic sphere' and a 'public sphere', the former associated with
women and the latter with men. Because in most societies to date women
have spent a good part of their lives bearing and raising children, their
lives have been more bound to 'the domestic sphere'. Men, on the other
hand, have had both the time and mobility to engage in those out of the

home activities which generate political structures. Thus, as Rosaldo (1974) argued, while in many societies women possess some or even a great deal of power, women's power is always viewed as illegitimate, disruptive and without authority.

This approach seemed to allow for both diversity and ubiquity in the manifestations of sexism. A very general identification of women with the domestic and of men with the extra-domestic could accommodate a great deal of cultural variation both in social structures and in gender roles. At the same time, it could make comprehensible the apparent ubiquity of the assumption of women's inferiority above and beyond such variation. This hypothesis was also compatible with the idea that the extent of women's oppression differed in different societies. It could explain such differences by correlating the extent of gender inequality in a society with the extent and rigidity of the separation between its domestic and public spheres. In short, the domestic/public theorists seemed to have generated an explanation capable of satisfying a variety of conflicting demands.

However, this explanation turned out to be problematic in ways reminiscent of Firestone's account. Although the theory focused on differences between men's and women's spheres of activity rather than on differences between men's and women's biology, it was essentialist and monocausal nonetheless. It posited the existence of a 'domestic sphere' in all societies and thereby assumed that women's activities were basically similar in content and significance across cultures. (An analogous assumption about men's activities lay behind the postulation of a universal 'public sphere'.) In effect, the theory falsely generalized to all societies an historically specific conjunction of properties: women's responsibility for early child-rearing, women's tendency to spend more time in the geographical space of the home, women's lesser participation in the affairs of the community, a cultural ascription of triviality to domestic work, and a cultural ascription of inferiority to women. The theory thus failed to appreciate that, while each individual property may be true of many societies, the conjunction is not true of most.[2]

One source of difficulty in these early feminist social theories was the presumption of an overly grandiose and totalizing conception of theory. Theory was understood as the search for the one key factor which would explain sexism cross-culturally and illuminate all of social life. In this sense, to theorize was by definition to produce a quasi-metanarrative.

Since the late 1970s, feminist social theorists have largely ceased speaking of biological determinants or a cross-cultural domestic/public separa-

2. These and related problems were soon apparent to many of the domestic/public theorists themselves. See Rosaldo's (1980) self criticism. A more recent discussion, which points out the circularity of the theory, appears in Sylvia J. Yanagisako and Jane F. Collier (1988).

tion. Many, moreover, have given up the assumption of monocausality. Nevertheless, some feminist social theorists have continued implicitly to suppose a quasi-metanarrative conception of theory. They have continued to theorize in terms of a putatively unitary, primary, culturally universal type of activity associated with women, generally an activity conceived as 'domestic' and located in 'the family'.

One influential example is the analysis of 'mothering' developed by Nancy Chodorow (1978). Setting herself to explain the internal, psychological, dynamics which have led many women willingly to reproduce social divisions associated with female inferiority, Chodorow posited a cross-cultural activity, mothering, as the relevant object of investigation. Her question thus became: how is mothering as a female-associated activity reproduced over time? How does mothering produce a new generation of women with the psychological inclination to mother and a new generation of men not so inclined? The answer she offered was in terms of 'gender identity': female mothering produces women whose deep sense of self is 'relational' and men whose deep sense of self is not.

Chodorow's theory has struck many feminists as a persuasive account of some apparently observable psychic differences between men and women. Yet the theory has clear metanarrative overtones. It posits the existence of a single activity, 'mothering', which, while differing in specifics in different societies, nevertheless constitutes enough of a natural kind to warrant one label. It stipulates that this basically unitary activity gives rise to two distinct sorts of deep selves, one relatively common across cultures to women, the other relatively common across cultures to men. And it claims that the difference thus generated between 'feminine and masculine gender identity' causes a variety of supposedly cross-cultural social phenomena, including the continuation of female mothering, male contempt for women and problems in heterosexual relationships.

From a postmodern perspective, all of these assumptions are problematic because essentialist. But the second one, concerning 'gender identity', warrants special scrutiny, given its political implications. Consider that Chodorow's use of the notion of gender identity presupposes three major premises. One is the psychoanalytic premise that everyone has a deep sense of self which is constituted in early childhood through one's interactions with one's primary parent and which remains relatively constant thereafter. Another is the premise that this 'deep self' differs significantly for men and for women but is roughly similar among women, on the one hand, and among men, on the other hand, both across cultures and within cultures across lines of class, race and ethnicity. The third premise is that this deep self colours everything one does; there are no actions, however trivial, which do not bear traces of one's masculine or feminine gender identity.

One can appreciate the political exigencies which made this conjunction of premises attractive. It gave scholarly substance to the idea of the pervasiveness of sexism. If masculinity and femininity constitute our basic and ever-present sense of self, then it is not surprising that the manifestations of sexism are systemic. Moreover, many feminists had already sensed that the concept of 'sex-role socialization', an idea Chodorow explicitly criticized, ignored the depth and intractability of male dominance. By implying that measures such as changing images in school textbooks or allowing boys to play with dolls would be sufficient to bring about equality between the sexes, this concept seemed to trivialize and coopt the message of feminism. Finally, Chodorow's depth-psychological approach gave a scholarly sanction to the idea of sisterhood. It seemed to legitimate the claim that the ties which bind women are deep and substantively based.

Needless to say, we have no wish to quarrel with the claim of the depth and pervasiveness of sexism, nor with the idea of sisterhood. But we do wish to challenge Chodorow's way of legitimating them. The idea of a cross-cultural, deep sense of self, specified differently for women and men, becomes problematic when given any specific content. Chodorow states that women everywhere differ from men in their greater concern with 'relational interaction'. But what does she mean by this term? Certainly not any and every kind of human interaction, since men have often been more concerned than women with some kinds of interactions, for example, those which have to do with the aggrandizement of power and wealth. Of course, it is true that many women in modern western societies have been expected to exhibit strong concern with those types of interactions associated with intimacy, friendship and love, interactions which dominate one meaning of the late twentieth-century concept of 'relationship'. But surely this meaning presupposes a notion of private life specific to modern western societies of the last two centuries. Is it possible that Chodorow's theory rests on an equivocation on the term 'relationship'?[3]

Equally troubling are the aporias this theory generates for political practice. While 'gender identity' gives substance to the idea of sisterhood, it does so at the cost of repressing differences among sisters. Although the

3. A similar ambiguity attends Chodorow's discussion of 'the family'. In response to critics who object that her psychoanalytic emphasis ignores social structures, Chodorow has rightly insisted that the family is itself a social structure, one frequently sighted in social explanations. Yet she generally does not discuss families as historically specific institutions whose specific relations with other institutions can be analysed. Rather, she tends to invoke 'the family' in a very abstract and general sense defined only as the locus of female mothering.

theory allows for some differences among women of different classes, races, sexual orientations and ethnic groups, it construes these as subsidiary to more basic similarities. But it is precisely as a consequence of the request to understand such differences as secondary that many women have denied an allegiance to feminism.

We have dwelt at length on Chodorow because of the great influence her work has enjoyed. But she is not the only recent feminist social theorist who has constructed a quasi-metanarrative around a putatively cross-cultural female-associated activity. On the contrary, theorists like Ann Ferguson and Nancy Folbre (1981), Nancy Hartsock (1983) and Catharine MacKinnon (1982) have done something analogous with 'sex-affective production', 'reproduction' and 'sexuality' respectively. Each claims to have identified a basic kind of human practice found in all societies which has cross-cultural explanatory power. In each case, the practice in question is associated with a biological or quasi-biological need and is construed as functionally necessary to the reproduction of society. It is not the sort of thing, then, whose historical origins need be investigated.

The difficulty here is that categories like sexuality, mothering, reproduction and sex-affective production group together phenomena which are not necessarily conjoined in all societies, while separating off from one another phenomena which are not necessarily separated. As a matter of fact, it is doubtful whether these categories have any determinate cross-cultural content. Thus, for a theorist to use such categories to construct a universalistic social theory is to risk projecting the socially dominant conjunctions and dispersions of her own society onto others, thereby distorting important features of both. Social theorists would do better first to construct genealogies of the *categories* of sexuality, reproduction and mothering before assuming their universal significance.

Since around 1980, many feminist scholars have come to abandon the project of grand social theory. They have stopped looking for *the* causes of sexism and have turned to more concrete inquiry with more limited aims. One reason for this shift is the growing legitimacy of feminist scholarship. The institutionalization of Women's Studies in the US has meant a dramatic increase in the size of the community of feminist inquirers, a much greater division of scholarly labour and a large growing fund of concrete information. As a result, feminist scholars have come to regard their enterprise more collectively, more like a puzzle whose various pieces are being filled in by many different people than a construction to the be completed by a single grand theoretical stroke. In short, feminist scholarship has attained its maturity.

Even in this phase, however, traces of youthful quasi-metanarratives remain. Some theorists who have ceased looking for *the* causes of sexism still rely on essentialist categories like 'gender identity'. This is especially true of those scholars who have sought to develop 'gynocentric' alternatives to mainstream androcentric perspectives, but who have not fully abandoned the universalist pretensions of the latter.

Consider, as an example, the work of Carol Gilligan (1982). Unlike most of the theorists we have considered so far, Gilligan has not sought to explain the origins or nature of cross-cultural sexism. Rather, she set herself the more limited task of exposing and redressing androcentric bias in the model of moral development of psychologist Lawrence Kohlberg. Thus, she argued that it is illegitimate to evaluate the moral development of women and girls by reference to a standard drawn exclusively from the experience of men and boys. And she proposed to examine women's moral discourse on its own terms in order to uncover its immanent standards of adequacy.

Gilligan's work has been rightly regarded as important and innovative. It challenged mainstream psychology's persistent occlusion of women's lives and experiences and its insistent but false claims to universality. Yet insofar as Gilligan's challenge involved the construction of an alternative 'feminine' model of moral development, her position was ambiguous. On the one hand, by providing a counter-example to Kohlberg's model, she cast doubt on the possibility of any single universalist developmental schema. On the other hand, by constructing a female countermodel, she invited the same charge of false generalization she had herself raised against Kohlberg, though now from other perspectives such as class, sexual orientation, race and ethnicity. Gilligan's (1982: 2) disclaimers notwithstanding, to the extent that she described women's moral development in terms of *a* different voice; to the extent that she did not specify which women, under which specific historical circumstances have spoken with the voice in question; and to the extent that she grounded her analysis in the explicitly cross-cultural framework of Nancy Chodorow, her model remained essentialist. It perpetuated in a newer, more localized fashion traces of previous, more grandiose quasi-metanarratives.

Thus, vestiges of essentialism have continued to plague feminist scholarship even despite the decline of grand theorizing. In many cases, including Gilligan's, this represents the continuing subterranean influence of those very mainstream modes of thought and inquiry with which feminists have wished to break.

On the other hand, the practice of feminist politics in the 1980s has generated a new set of pressures which have worked against metanarratives. In recent years, poor and working class women, women of colour and lesbians have finally won a wider hearing for their objections to feminist theories which fail to illuminate their lives and address their problems. They have exposed the earlier quasi-metanarratives, with their assumptions of universal female dependence and confinement to 'the domestic sphere', as false extrapolations from the experience of the white, middle-class, heterosexual women who dominated the beginnings of the second wave. For example, writers like Bell Hooks (1984), Gloria Joseph (1981), Audre Lord (1981), Maria Lugones and Elizabeth Spelman (1983; 1980–1) have unmasked the implicit reference to white Anglo women in many classic feminist texts; likewise, Adrienne Rich (1980) and Marilyn Frye (1983) have exposed the heterosexist bias of much mainstream feminist theory. Thus, as the class, sexual, racial and ethnic awareness of the movement has altered, so has the preferred conception of theory. It has become clear that quasi-metanarratives hamper rather than promote sisterhood, since they elide differences among women and among the forms of sexism to which different women are differentially subject. Likewise, it is increasingly apparent that such theories hinder alliances with other progressive movements, since they tend to occlude axes of domination other than gender. In sum, there is growing interest among feminists in modes of theorizing which are attentive to differences and to cultural and historical specificity.

In general, then, feminist scholarship of the 1980s evinces some conflicting tendencies. On the one hand, there is decreasing interest in grand social theories as scholarship has become more localized, issue-oriented and explicitly fallibilistic. On the other hand, essentialist vestiges persist in the continued use of ahistorical categories like 'gender identity' without reflection as to how, when and why such categories originated and were modified over time. This tension is symptomatically expressed in the current fascination, on the part of US feminists, with French psychoanalytic feminisms: the latter propositionally decry essentialism even as they performatively enact it (Cixous, 1980; Cixous and Clément, 1986; Irigaray, 1985a, 1985b; Kristeva, 1980, 1981; see also critical discussions by Jones, 1985; Moi, 1985). More generally, feminist scholarship has remained insufficiently attentive to the *theoretical* prerequisites of dealing with diversity, despite widespread commitment to accepting it politically.

By criticizing lingering essentialism in contemporary feminist theory, we hope to encourage such theory to become more consistently postmodern. This is not, however, to recommend merely *any* form of postmodernism. On the contrary, as we have shown, the version developed by Jean-François Lyotard offers a weak and inadequate conception of social criticism without philosophy. It rules out genres of criticism, such as large historical narrative and historically situated social theory, which feminists rightly regard as indispensable. But it does not follow from Lyotard's shortcomings that criticism without philosophy is in principle incompatible with criticism with social force. Rather, as we argue next, a robust, postmodern-feminist paradigm of social criticism without philosophy is possible.

III. Towards a Postmodern Feminism

How can we combine a postmodernist incredulity toward metanarratives with the social-critical power of feminism? How can we conceive a version of criticism without philosophy which is robust enough to handle the tough job of analyzing sexism in all its 'endless variety and monotonous similarity'?

A first step is to recognize, *contra* Lyotard, that postmodern critique need foreswear neither large historical narratives nor analyses of societal macrostructures. This point is important for feminists, since sexism has a long history and is deeply and pervasively embedded in contemporary societies. Thus, postmodern feminists need not abandon the large theoretical tools needed to address large political problems. There is nothing inconsistent in the idea of postmodern theory.

However, if postmodern-feminist critique must remain 'theoretical', not just any kind of theory will do. Rather, theory here would be explicitly historical, attuned to the cultural specificity of different societies and periods, and to that of different groups within societies and periods. Thus, the categories of postmodern-feminist theory would be inflected by temporality, with historically specific institutional categories like 'the modern, restricted, male-headed, nuclear family' taking precedence over ahistorical, functionalist categories like 'reproduction' and 'mothering'. Where categories of the latter sort were not eschewed altogether, they would be genealogized, that is, framed by a historical narrative and rendered temporally and culturally specific.

Moreover, postmodern-feminist theory would be non-universalist. When its focus became cross-cultural or transepochal, its mode of attention would be comparativist rather than universalizing, attuned to changes and contrasts instead of to 'covering laws'. Finally, postmodern-feminist theory would dispense with the idea of a subject of history. It would replace unitary notions of 'woman' and 'feminine gender identity' with plural and complexly constructed conceptions of social identity, treating gender as one relevant strand among others, attending also to class, race, ethnicity, age and sexual orientation.

In general, postmodern-feminist theory would be pragmatic and fallibilistic. It would tailor its methods and categories to the specific task at hand, using multiple categories when appropriate and foreswearing the metaphysical comfort of a single 'feminist method' or 'feminist epistemology'. In short, this theory would look more like a tapestry composed of threads of many different hues than one woven in a single colour.

The most important advantage of this sort of theory would be its usefulness for contemporary feminist political practice. Such practice is increasingly a matter of alliances rather than one of unity around a universally shared interest or identity. It recognizes that the diversity of women's needs and experiences means that no single solution, on issues like child care, social security and housing, can be adequate for all. Thus, the underlying premise of this practice is that, while some women share some common interests and face some common enemies, such commonalities are by no means universal; rather, they are interlaced with differences, even with conflicts. This, then, is a practice made up of a patchwork of overlapping alliances, not one circumscribable by an essential definition. One might best speak of it in the plural as the practice of 'feminisms'. In a sense, this practice is in advance of much contemporary feminist theory. It is already implicitly postmodern. It would find its most appropriate and useful theoretical expression in a postmodern-feminist form of critical inquiry. Such inquiry would be the theoretical counterpart of a broader, richer, more complex and multi-layered feminist solidarity, the sort of solidarity which is essential for overcoming the oppression of women in its 'endless variety and monotonous similarity'.

REFERENCES

Chodorow, Nancy (1978) *The Reproduction of Mothering: Psychoanalysis and the Sociology of Gender*. Berkeley: University of California Press.

Cixous, Hélène (1981) 'The Laugh of the Medusa'. Translated by K. Cohen and P. Cohen in E. Marks and I. de Courtivron (eds) *New French Feminisms*. New York: Schocken Books.

Cixous, Hélène and Clément, Catherine (1986) *The Newly Born Woman*. Minneapolis: University of Minnesota PRess.

Ferguson, Ann and Folbre, Nancy (1981) 'The Unhappy Marriage of Patriarchy and Capitalism', in L. Sargent (ed.) *Women and Revolution*. Boston: South End Press.

Firestone, Shulamith (1970) *The Dialectic of Sex*. New York: Bantam.

Flax, Jane (1986) 'Gender as a Social Problem: In and For Feminist Theory', *American Studies/Amerika Studien* June.

Foucault, Michel (1979) *Discipline and Punish: The Birth of the Prison*. Translated by Alan Sheridan. New York: Vintage Books.

Frye, Marilyn (1983) *The Politics of Reality: Essays in Feminist Theory*. Trumansburg, NY: The Crossing Press.

Gilligan, Carol (1982) *In a Different Voice: Psychological Theory and Women's Development*. Cambridge, Mass.: Harvard University Press.

Haraway, Donna (1983) 'A Manifesto for Cyborgs: Science, Technology and Socialist Feminism in the 1980s', *Socialist Review* 80: 65–107.

Harding, Sandra (1986a) *The Science Question in Feminism*. Ithaca, NY: Cornell University Press.

(1986b) 'The Instability of the Analytical Categories of Feminist Theory', *Signs: Journal of Women in Culture and Society* 11(4): 645–64.

Harding, Sandra and Hintikka, Merrill B. (eds) (1983) *Discovering Reality: Feminist Perspectives on Epistemology, Metaphysics, Methodology and Philosophy of Science.* Dordrecht: D. Reidel.

Hartsock, Nancy (1983) *Money, Sex and Power: Toward a Feminist Historical Materialism.* New York: Longman.

Hooks, Bell (1984) *Feminist Theory: From Margin to Center.* Boston: South End Press.

Irigaray, Luce (1985a) *Speculum of the Other Woman,* Ithaca, NY: Cornell University Press.

(1985b) *This Sex Which is Not One.* Ithaca, NY: Cornell University Press.

Jardine, Alice A. (1985) *Gynesis: Configurations of Women and Modernity.* Ithaca, NY: Cornell University Press.

Jones, Ann Rosalind (1985) 'Writing the Body: Toward an Understanding of l'Ecriture féminine', in E. Showalter (ed.) *The New Feminist Criticism: Essays on Women, Literature and Theory.* New York: Pantheon Books.

Joseph, Gloria (1981) 'The Incompatible Menage à Trois: Marxism, Feminism and Racism', in L. Sargent (ed.) *Women and Revolution.* Boston: South End Press.

Kristeva, Julia (1980) *Desire in Language: A Semiotic Approach to Literature and Art,* in L. S. Roudiez (ed.). New York: Columbia University Press.

Lorde, Audre (1981) 'An Open Letter to Mary Daly', in C. Moraga and G. Anzaldua (eds) *This Bridge Called My Back: Writings by Radical Women of Color,* Watertown, MA: Persephone Press.

Lugones, Maria C. and Spelman, Elizabeth V. (1983) 'Have We Got a Theory for You! Feminist Theory, Cultural Imperialism and the Demand for the Women's Voice', *Hypatia, Women's Studies International Forum* 6(6): 578–81.

Lyotard, Jean-François (1978) 'Some of the Things at Stake in Women's Struggles'. Translated by D. J. Clarke, W. Woodhull and J. Mowitt, *Sub-Stance* 20.

(1984a) *The Postmodern Condition: A Report on Knowledge.* Translated by G. Bennington and B. Massumi. Minneapolis: Minnesota University Press.

(1984b) 'The Differend'. Translated by G. Van Den Abbeele, *Diacritics* Fall: 4–14.

Lyotard, Jean-François and Thebaud, Jean-Loup (1987) *Just Gaming.* Minneapolis: Minnesota University Press.

MacKinnon, Catharine A. (1982) 'Feminism, Marxism, Method, and the State: An Agenda for Theory', *Signs: Journal of Women in Culture and Society* 7(3): 515–44.

Moi, Toril (1985) *Sexual/Textual Politics: Feminist Literary Theory.* London: Methuen.

Owens, Craig (1983) 'The Discourse of Others: Feminists and Postmodernism', in H. Foster (ed.) *The Anti-Aesthetic: Essays on Postmodern Culture.* Port Townsend, WA: Bay Press.

Rich, Adrienne (1980) 'Compulsory Heterosexuality and Lesbian Existence', *Signs: Journal of Women in Culture and Society* 5(4): 631–60.

Rosaldo, Michelle Zimbalist (1974) 'Women, Culture and Society: A Theoretical Overview', in M. Z. Rosaldo and L. Lamphere (eds) *Woman, Culture and Society*. Stanford: Stanford University Press.

Rosaldo, Michelle Zimbalist (1980) 'The Use and Abuse of Anthropology: Reflections on Feminism and Cross-cultural Understanding', *Signs: Journal of Women in Culture and Society* 5(3): 389–417.

Rubin, Gayle (1975) 'The Traffic in Women', in R. R. Reiter (ed.) *Toward an Anthropology of Women*. New York: Monthly Review Press.

Spelman, Elizabeth (1980–1) 'Theories of Race and Gender: The Erasure of Black Women', *Quest* 5(4): 36–62.

Walzer, Michael (1983) *Spheres of Justice: A Defense of Pluralism and Equality*. NY: Basic Books.

Yanagisako, Sylvia J. and Collier, Jane F. (1988) 'Toward a Unified Analysis of Gender and Kinship', in J. F. Collier and S. J. Yanagisako (eds) *Gender and Kinship: Toward a Unified Analysis*. Stanford: Stanford University Press.

POSTMODERN SOCIAL ANALYSIS: EMPIRICAL ILLUSTRATIONS

- Charles C. Lemert, *Post-structuralism and sociology*
- Joan W. Scott, *Deconstructing equality-versus-difference: Or, the uses of poststructuralist theory for feminism*
- Lee Edelman, *The plague of discourse: Politics, literary theory, and AIDS*

14

Post-Structuralism and Sociology
Charles C. Lemert

Against philosophies of the Center, modernism in particular, poststructuralism introduced an intellectual politics based on the now famous concept of decentering. It is not always understood that decentering is less a philosophy, or a rival concept to those of modernism, than a practice. This is, in part, the point of post-structuralism's unsettling approach to writing.

From one point of view, decentering is a reasonably precise philosophical concept conveying Deridda's and Foucault's (1972) original attacks on centered philosophies, most especially phenomenology's extreme subjectivist philosophy of consciousness. This is the sense most accurately associated with the postmodernist rejection of Enlightenment theories of knowledge. From another point of view, decentering suggests a broad political opposition to all traditional and modern social forms, philosophy included, in which structures serve to inhibit social freedom. It is advisable, therefore, to think of post-structuralism and postmodernism as first and foremost a form of knowledge derived from a political practice. This attitude conveys not only post-structuralism's attempt to overcome philosophy for political purposes but also its claim that discourse and writing must be taken as the subject matter and means of intellectual work.

Such an interpretation of decentering makes a heavy demand on sociologists accustomed to viewing politics as something totally other than science, or, at most, that to which sociologists contribute expertise. Post-structuralism claims that intellectual work is political, and it does so with reference to concepts most sociologists would consider anything but political – text and discourse.

Roland Barthes defines the Text as "that *social* space that leaves no language safe or untouched, that allows no enunciative subject to hold the position of judge, teacher, analyst, confessor, or decoder. The theory of the Text can only coincide with the activity of writing" (Barthes 1979, 81, emphasis original). This statement is linked to the claim that decentering

Frontiers of Social Theory, George Ritzer, ed., 1990 © Columbia University Press, New York. Reprinted with the permission of the publisher.

is an ongoing intellectual practice deriving from the theoretical decision to interpret the Text in relation to other texts, rather than in relation to its author. For Barthes this involves the distinction between the work and the Texts

> The work is concrete, occupying a portion of book-space (in a library, for example), the Text, on the other hand, is a methodological field. . . . This opposition recalls the distinction proposed by Lacan between "reality" and the "real"; the one is displayed, the other demonstrated. In the same way, the work can be seen in bookstores, in card catalogues, and on course lists, while the Text reveals itself, articulates itself according to and against certain rules. While the work is held in the hand, the text is held in language. (Barthes 1979, 74–75)

The work, therefore, is seen as the unit of modernist writing in which writing is a transitive activity – the production of literary objects by subjects, authors. Thus, the privileging of the Text over the work is another instance of the philosophical side of decentering, here the rejection of the purportedly modernist belief that the social world is inhabited by self-conscious subjects who project meaning into their works. It is a rejection of subjectivism as a cryptometaphysics.

This move replaces the original modernist couplet – *subject* (author)/ *object* (work) – with something else which itself has the appearance of a couplet – *practices* (writing)/(intertextual) *field*. But the relationship of text to its intertextual field is active, creative, and practical. Practices/ field has the form but not the substance of a conceptual dichotomy. It looks the same but different – postdichotomous. Texts are products of intransitive writing, they are outside the subject-object dichotomy. "The Text cannot be thought of as a defined object" (Barthes 1979, 74.) It is, as noted, a methodological field, while the work is a concrete object. Texts are, therefore, play in a forever open and open-ended field which they produce and by which they are produced, and in which they must be interpreted.

The important thing to keep in mind is that post-structuralists view this reorientation as a general social theoretical move. Though they remain close to the language of text and discourse, post-structuralists situate their views with respect to a theory of society. The critique of the subject-author is an instance of opposition to all forms of social domination. Much of Foucault's writing on various topics, from *The Order of Things* to *The History of Sexuality,* is in opposition to dominations represented by the engendered, Europeanized humanism which, in another context, is characterized by the term patriarchy.[1] The link between a general social

1. Foucault's attacks on the logocentric and anthropocentric basis of modernism are explicit, though sometimes overlooked, in this regard. See Lemert 1979b.

theory and the problem of the author is apparent in Foucault's "What Is an Author?" (Foucault 1979, 158–159).

> We are accustomed . . . to saying that the author is a general creator of a work in which he deposits with infinite wealth and generosity, an inexhaustible world of significations. We are used to thinking that the author is so different from other men, and so transcendent with regard to all languages, that as soon as he speaks meanings begin to proliferate. . . . The truth is quite contrary . . . the author does not precede the works, he is a certain fundamental principle by which, in our culture, one limits, excludes, and chooses. . . . The author is the ideological figure by which one marks the manner in which we fear the proliferation of meanings.

In this respect, post-structuralism is a social theory articulated within concrete studies of literary, historical, and philosophical questions.

Post-structuralism is very much a product of the political and social events leading to and ensuing from May 1968 in Paris. Foucault's (1978) sexual politics, Lacan's (1977) engendering of psychoanalysis, Kristeva and Irigaray's (*see* Moi 1987) feminist theories, Derrida's (1985) politics of difference, Deleuze and Guattari's (1977) schizoanalytic politics all are rooted, one way or another, in the late sixties revolutionary politics that challenged the world-centered ambitions of post-war Gaullism. If, at that same moment, left intellectuals in the United States sought a coherent New Left alternative to both Old Left Marxism and Johnson-Humphrey liberalism, French intellectuals searched for an alternative that rejected traditional communist and socialist party politics and was post-Marxist without being anti-Marxist. In the one joint programmatic statement of the post-structuralist movement, when Foucault, Barthes, Derrida, Sollers, and Kristeva allowed and caused their separate projects to be joined in an edition of *Tel Quel* titled "Théorie d'ensemble" (published not incidentally in the early autumn of 1968), these politics were quite explicit. The introduction stated that their joint project was, in part, "to articulate a politics logically bound to a dynamically non-representative writing, that is to say: analysis of the confusion created by this position, explicition of their social and economic character, construction of the relations of this writing with historical materialism and dialectical materialism" (*Tel Quel* 1968, 10). It would be an uncomfortable stretch to consider this a social theory in the usual sense, but that theory is there, however faintly. It is the basis for a positive connection with social theoretical work in sociology.

In more sociological terms, the implication of this attitude toward writing as an intellectual practice is that action is oriented to an open field of play that lacks inherent, limiting rules. Rules become resources in Giddens' sense, limits are social arbitraries serving only to define the possibilities of transgression in Foucault's sense, the field defines the conditions and terms of practices in Bourdieu's sense. The structured field is viewed as open, that is, characterized by differences, absence, play. Hence the various descriptive terms one associates with post-structuralist thinkers; discursive formation (Foucault), intertextuality (Barthes), *la langue* (Saussure), *champ* (Bourdieu). To these sometimes implicit visions of a field of play are juxtaposed the correlative notions that describe intransitive actions: practices, writing, speaking, habitus.[2]

On first examination, this would appear to be an interesting theoretical model in the form: *Think of social action as intransitive practices in a dynamically open field of play.* But this would not be a sufficient interpretation of post-structuralist thinking. Models, in its view, are modernist attempts to mirror the social world. Models depend on the assumption that the social (or natural) world can be represented, that is, "presented again" in the language of knowledge. Post-structuralism, implicitly, and postmodernism, explicitly, reject the Enlightenment ideas that knowledge is an autonomous and constituting feature of social life.

> The notion that our chief task is to mirror accurately, in our Glassy Essence, the universe around us is the complement to the notion, common to Democritus and Descartes, that the universe is made up of very simple, clearly and distinctly knowable things, knowledge of whose essences provides the master vocabulary which permits commensuration of discourses. (Rorty 1979, 357)

There are no post-structuralist models. "Let us wage a war on totality; let us be witnesses to the unpresentable; let us activate the differences and save the honor of the name" (Lyotard 1979, 82). Postmodernist knowledge, such as it is, is the consequence, not a representation, of action in a field of play.

Therefore, what is at stake in a possible post-structuralist sociology is a willingness to move sociology away from its historic role as a discipline, a social science, a type of knowledge, and toward a more politically self-conscious practice that is neither traditionally Marxist nor liberal. Postmodern knowledge entails a postmodern politics. Like the strange space Derrida sought to open and use in the first words of "Structure, Sign, and Play in the Human Sciences," a post-structuralist sociology would have to be willing to tolerate the idea of working in a confusing, different social space that is neither epistemological nor political, but both yet neither.

2. In reference to the concepts presented in this paragraph see Giddens (1984), Foucault (1972), Bourdieu (1977), and Barthes (1970, 1979).

In a certain sense this is not an alien idea to sociology. We have been, from the beginning, the most artificial of disciplines and the clumsiest of sciences because sociology is, by its nature, a situated practice. It is only in recent years that sociologists have reincorporated ideas from ethnomethodology and other parasociological sources (including some of the post-structuralist literature) to recover the centrality of what Giddens (1984, xxxv) describes as the double hermeneutic, the fact that theories of society interpret that which they also help constitute, even while interpreting. Though post-structuralism makes a more radical claim than such indigenous sociological practices as ethnomethodology and Giddens' structuration theory, it bears this point of positive comparison with those aspects of sociology that forthrightly work within a recognition of the unique double nature of sociological knowledge. Ideas like the "double hermeneutic" and "writing as intransitive practice" are similarly comfortable with the uncomfortable social space in which knowledge is no longer the foundation of that which is, where instead language both is the universal problematic and, insofar as "knowledge" is concerned, is all that is.

Within post-structuralist perspectives, the generic name for this knowledge which is (nothing but) language is discourse. Discourse expresses, and is, the inherently transgressive quality of post-structuralist intellectual politics, as one can see in Hayden White's (1978, 4) definition:

> A discourse moves "to and fro" between received encodations of experience and the clutter of phenomena which refuses incorporation into conventionalized notions of "reality," "truth," or "possibility." . . . Discourse, in a word, is quintessentially a *mediative* enterprise. As such it is both interpretive and preinterpretive; it is always *about* the nature of interpretation itself as it is *about* the subject matter which is the manifest occasion of its own elaboration.

Post-structuralist social theory, whether avowedly sociological or not, is discursive in this sense of transgressing the subject matter it interprets by constantly reflecting on the necessity and nature of interpretation itself.[3]

Of course, there are problems with a proposal to make discourse both the subject matter and the medium of sociological analysis. A discursive sociology, as we have already seen, would require an uprooting of deeply ingrained convictions – belief in the subject-object dichotomy and other classical dualities; loyalty to the ideal of sociology as a well-founded, scientific source of knowledge, expectations that good work will produce identifiably worthwhile political and intellectual outcomes.

The far more serious problem with a discursive sociology in the post-structuralist tradition is that posed by taking discourse as an object of

3. Compare Gidens' idea of discursive consciousness (Giddens 1984, 41–45).

study. It is one thing to accept a discursive, transgressive method as the condition of sociological practice, another to deal with evident dilemmas in the discursive analysis of discourse. Sociologists and other intellectual practitioners can be discursive in the sense of appropriating the attitude of constant, as White puts it, to-ing and fro-ing with the real world. Social theory as reflective, intransitive action is thinkable even if objectionable to some. But what are the limits of discourse as an "object" of study? This question demonstrates the severity of the challenges posed by post-structuralism. One must bracket even the term "object." But what do the brackets mean? Does a discursive social theory mean there are no "objects," that is to say, no contents to intellectual practices? Is such a practice forever doomed to a world of talk about talk itself, of the interpretation of interpretation, of a program without performances? The problem is acute when one considers the question, Is there in the "real" world nondiscursive social action? It is one thing for a discursive intellectual work to treat other discursive materials of the same sort. This is what the post-structuralists mean by intertextuality in the strictest sense of the concept.

The success of post-structuralism in literary studies may rely considerably on the fact that, in this area, other texts are the proper subject matter. The most compelling successes, in my opinion, of applied post-structuralism have been among feminist, third world, and Afro-American critics who uncover the discursive power of hitherto silent, oppressed women, black, or third-world writers (Gates 1985, 1988; Carby 1987). In a case like Henry Louis Gates' (1988) discussion of the confluence between the African Esu-Elegbara and the Afro-American signifying monkey figures in two separated but historically bound cultural systems, the analyst is applying a discursive method to texts that are found to be surprisingly discursive themselves. Both figures served to contain and express the doubled cultural experience of those who are simultaneously African and in some fractured way American. The figures were discursive in that they mediate the divided social reality of people for whom colonial oppression and slavery were the decisive social attribute. This discovery of the discursive, and political consciousness of so-called nonliterate or otherwise excluded people is parallel to similar discoveries of the study of oppressed women, the working class, and other victims of colonial domination, and this literature – of which E.P. Thompson's *The Making of the English Working Class* is a locus classicus[4] – is familiar and assimilable to even normal sociological thought.

The greater difficulty concerns the hint strong within post-structuralist thought that everything social is discourse. Are there no events in the

4. Cultural studies, a movement with strong ties to sociology and to post-structuralism, expressly takes Thompson's work as among its classical references (*see* Hall et al. 1980).

"real" world that lack this transgressive, mediative quality? This, of course, is a very familiar question, arrived at by a different route. What are we to make of the silence of oppressed people? Is there silence merely a latent discursivity, covered by false consciousness? It is one thing to say that certain slave narratives are discursive, and another to suggest that all which is said by or inscribed on behalf of slaves is discursive, and still another, by extension, to suggest that slavery is nothing but discourse. This is the question that separates a prospective sociological post-structuralism from the actual post-structuralist literary criticism. Sociologists should have little difficulty accepting the idea that there are hidden or underlying variables behind surface appearances. But they will have trouble with the suggestion that those variables are exclusively discursive. Is there nothing in the "real" world but texts and discursive talk? Literary theorists and others; including social historians, can plausibly study nothing but texts. Can sociologists? Or, better put, what does it mean to propose that sociology be the discursive study of nothing but discursive texts?

In a different guise this is the familiar problem of the presumption of a necessary difference between theory and concrete empirical data. Most sociologists could, if pressed, consider the proposition that theory is the discursive property of any sociological work. This would amount to little more than granting that in theory, whatever else we do, we state and describe both a statement about the "real" world and the rules by which we arrive at that interpretation. Usually, however, even in a radical version of this conviction, sociologists hold to the existence of a "real" world outside of the discursive sway of theory. The world's "reality" is taken, normally, as the source of concrete empirical data. This conviction, we can now see, would be treated with great skepticism by poststructuralism and postmodernism. The idea of a free-standing reality as the source of empirical data partakes of the modernist distinction between the knowing subject and the world of objects, and relies on a belief in attainable knowledge as the arbiter of that distinction. We might grant, therefore, that post-structuralism would have this particular philosophical attitude toward the division of theory and data. But, can we grant that sociology can get along without free-standing data, that is, without data from the world as the resource of theory? Viewed through the lens of a post-structuralist critique, we can see that the question need not be posed so narrowly. We can agree that data are necessary to even a poststructuralist sociology and *still* accept the proposition that those data are neither necessarily of an order different from theory nor nondiscursive.

This line of questioning requires a reconsideration of the status of our concept of reality; clearly postmodernism would abandon the notion altogether. But it seems possible, even if only for tactical purposes, that one can avoid the threats of such a course. Here is where the post-structuralist ideas of discourse and textuality offer considerable leverage even with their terrible philosophical troubles.

Texts, discursive sociology and vietnam: An illustration

A post-structuralist or postmodernist approach to the concept of "reality" would be pragmatic. What do we intend by it? And can we get around it in order to enhance our ability to know and discuss? Can, therefore, the theory of Texts, including discursive texts, get us around the problems sociology, and other sciences, usually solve with reference to ideas like "empirical reality"?

The prospect of such an alternative depends on the plausibility of four assumptions already presented, explicitly or implicitly:

1. that theory is an inherently discursive activity;
2. that the empirical reality in relation to which theoretical texts are discursive is without exception textual;
3. that empirical texts depend on this relationship to theoretical texts for their intellectual or scientific value; and
4. that in certain, if not all, cases a discursive interpretation yields more, not less, adequate understanding.

Assumption #1 was stipulated in the above discussion. Assumptions #2 and #3 require further discussion. Assumption #4 is best considered with reference to a case study.

Theoretical statements mediate the "reality" contained in empirical texts – answers to questionnaires, performed rituals and observed behaviors (usually inscribed on film or tape or in notebooks), letters, corporate reports, transcripts, interviews, archives, census tracts. It is far from clear that there are any data "purer," that is, "more real," than these. And none of these is anything but textual in the two senses poststructuralism employs. First, they are literally inscribed on one medium or another and are never used for analysis without being thus written. Secondly, they are useful for knowledge only to the extent that they exist in an intertextual field – with other empirical texts of the same sort, without other empirical texts of a different kind, and, most of all, with the theoretical texts out of which sense is made of them. It hardly need be said that raw data, in whatever form, are useless until they are situated with respect to theoretical statements. Theoretical statements, regardless of the "school" or methodological style in which they are expressed (scientific, humanistic, qualitative, ethnographic, etc.), are never made without a relationship to empirical data or an empirical reference, however abstract. Parsons' most abstract theory of the AGIL paradigm requires a great number of assumptions about the reality of the social world, such as a willingness to believe that societies are patterned, that culture is an effective control over society, that societies need integrative mechanisms like laws. None of these beliefs, however arguable, is held without reference to a wealth of empirical references. These references when held by a reader are necessary to the sense of Parsons' theory. They arise from the many empirical texts ranging from survey results to everyday life conversations and everything in between – that inform a reader's ability to read. Similarly, such texts are also written, whether consciously or not, as an intervention in the field of existing texts sociologists variously consider germane to their work. It is not at all clear why one needs the idea of an empirical reality existing beyond such an intertextual field.

Of the four assumptions, #4 is the sternest test of the prospects of a post-structuralist sociology. In the end, it is hardly worth the while to try something with so many inherent difficulties if there are no anticipated advantages over what we have now.

As I have indicated, some theoretical advantages are clear, and they have been reasonably well developed in other areas. The most significant of these is the articulation of the principle of difference as the substance of a decentering social theory. There is now an important body of work indebted to the post-structuralist idea that when the world is decentered the primacy of social differences becomes apparent (Abel 1980; Gates 1985; Marcus and Fischer 1986; Harding 1986). One of the most interesting is Sandra Harding's argument against all theories, including feminist standpoint theories, that would reduce social analysis to a totalizing principle. She proposes the concept of "fractured identities," explaining that one cannot account for and resolve the problems of sexism by reversing the gender principle because there is no such thing as an essential woman any more than there is an essential man. Rather, women must think of themselves (and they must act) in reference to identities fractured not only by gender but race, class, and world position as well. There is no abstract total woman, only black-African, or white-working class, wealthy American, . . . women.

> Once "woman" is deconstructed into "women," and "gender" is recognized to have no fixed referents, feminism itself dissolves as a theory that can reflect the voice of a naturalized or essentialized speaker. It does not dissolve as a fundamental part of our political identities, as a motivation for developing political solidarities – how could it in a world where we can now name the plethora of moral outrages designed exactly to con-

tain us, to coerce us, within each of our culturally specific
womanly activities? But because of the historical specificity of
sexism's structures, this strain of feminist thought encourages
us to cherish and defend our "hyphens" – those theoretical expressions of our multiple struggles. (Harding 1986, 246)

The value of the concept fractured identities is apparent. It is no coincidence that it arises at the very time when social theorists are reevaluating
hitherto segregated categories such as race, class, and gender. This is one
instance of a theoretical shift caused by the post-structuralist movement.
Yet, as powerful as the idea of difference is, it is still not enough to suggest the advantages of a post-structuralist sociology.

I will conclude by proposing a case illustration that lends itself to post-
structuralist analysis. Important as it is to recent American, and global,
history the reality of Vietnam is far from certain. For the majority of persons who make any attempt to interpret it their most vivid impressions
come not from direct experience but from a strange conglomeration of
texts – the memorial on the Mall in Washington, films, firsthand accounts
of speakers, friends, or relatives, novels, Neil Sheehan's *New Yorker* articles and prize-winning book, college and high school courses, rhetorical
allusions by politicians, archives, microfilm and microfiche, and so on. Is
it an accident that the most searing film account, if not the roulette scene
in *The Deer Hunter,* is *Apocalypse Now,* a montage of craziness and
dream-like irreality in which the viewer is made to feel that nothing real
was there? Was Vietnam after all nothing more than a repetition of a classic Conradian narrative – a crazed voyage through an exotic jungle in
search of an unattainable kingdom? One wants to argue that this is a fiction and that the reality is still there. Reviews of each serious Vietnam film
center on the question, did this one, *Platoon* perhaps, finally capture the
reality of the war?

It is possible that the search for the reality of social things is the true
Conradian search. Where would one look for the reality of Vietnam? Are
recollections of veterans or POWs more real than *Apocalypse Now?* Are
the *Pentagon Papers?* Are Neil Sheehan's articles? Are Stanley Karnow's
history and PBS documentary? Is that finer reality still buried in an
archive somewhere? And cannot these questions be asked of most complex social historical events?

In pursuit of a post-structuralist sociology, what can then be said about
the empirical reality of a series of events like the war in Vietnam? I propose that we ignore, for the moment, our sociological thirst for reality,
and consider it simply and straightforwardly as though it were, for all in-
tents and purposes, a huge, ugly but plausibly discursive text. In this respect we should have to entertain the proposition that the war itself was

discursive, a global inscription in which the United States sought to mediate its own sense of the irreality of world history.[5]

In the years following the Second World War, the United States quickly encountered an intolerable set of contradictions. On the one hand, the United States emerged from the world war as the greatest military and industrial power in history. On the other hand, as early as 1947, the year of George Kennan's famous long telegram enunciating the policy of containment, the Soviet Union was taken seriously, as well it should have been, as a rival power. The United States suffered the contradiction of being the supreme world power, but one of two supreme powers, hence not supreme. The McCarthy blight, in the early fifties, was a flawed attempt to mediate this contradiction by turning inward with the unreal insistence that anyone and everyone could be communist, the cause of America's loss of world potency. In 1954 Joseph McCarthy was censured by the United States Senate. In the same year Dienbienphu fell. In 1955 Eisenhower approved direct military aid to the Saigon government, thus beginning the U.S. presence in Southeast Asia.

Was that presence, and the war which ensued, an attempt to resolve, discursively, the contradiction that McCarthyism failed to resolve? The answer lies in an analysis of the specific texts which articulate the theory that governed American war policy.

The decisive event which led to war was President Lyndon Johnson's decision in the first few days of February 1965 to escalate the bombing in the north. The previous summer, Johnson and his advisers invented an incident in the Gulf of Tonkin as cause to push through Congress the resolution that gave him virtually unchecked authority to engage in war. His defeat of Barry Goldwater in the November 1964 election added substantially to his mandate both for foreign policy leadership and the pursuit of his plans of a Great Society at home. In 1965 Johnson submitted sixty-three pieces of social legislation, a domestic program that exceeded even Roosevelt's for its ambition and commitment to America's disadvantaged. Few, if any, American presidents possessed so extensive a social vision. Yet that vision is easily forgotten because it was held along with a view of America's world position that led to Vietnam.

On February 5, 1965, the Vietcong attacked an American installation at Pleiku, killing nine, and wounding a hundred American advisers. Johnson responded immediately by authorizing "Operation Flaming Dart," air raids against the north carefully selected because Soviet Prime

5. Sources for following section are: the Pentagon Papers (Gravel 1971), Kearns (1976), Gibson (1986), Hodgson (1976), Karnow (1983). One should also not forget that though this is stated with reference to the American discursive dilemma the same analysis can, and should, be applied to the people of Southeast Asia.

Minister Aleksi Kosygin was then visiting Hanoi. The question before Johnson was, shall the air strikes be expanded and the American engagement enlarged?

At the same time, on February 6 and 7, Johnson's adviser McGeorge Bundy, en route home from Vietnam, completed the draft of a memorandum that confirmed an earlier (January 27) report that the situation in Vietnam was deteriorating. Bundy's February 7 memorandum coined the ironic, and highly discursive phrase, "sustained reprisal." This evidently duplicitous phrase came to justify and be the name for Johnson's evolving war policy. The memorandum argued that a policy of reprisals against the north would eventually "improve the situation in the South" by demonstrating to Hanoi the military resolve of the United States. The policy decision came quickly. On February 24, 1965, Johnson ordered Operation Rolling Thunder, sustained air raid on the north which by year's end totaled 55,000 sorties.

Like George Kennan's famous long telegram twenty years earlier which invented the equally discursive concept of containment, Bundy's sustained reprisal memorandum defined Johnson's fatal policy. By December 1965, 200,000 troops had replaced the 20,000 or so advisers in Vietnam at the beginning of the year. And by 1968 Johnson's presidency and his Great Society program would be in ruins, and the direction of American foreign and domestic policies would be, it now seems, irreversibly altered.

Bundy's February 7 memorandum did not cause the war. Texts don't cause anything in the traditional sense. They are practices in an intertextual field. Their significance relies on their relationship to that field. It is easy to see both the discursive nature of the Bundy text and its crucial place in an intertextual field that included Johnson's own statements, the preceding generation's dilemma over America's contradictory world position, and subsequent interpretations of the war itself.

As Godfrey Hodgson (1976, 229) points out, Bundy's phrase, sustained reprisal, is a subtly double-sided notion that suits a former dean of Harvard College. Operation Rolling Thunder and all that went with it was surely "sustained" but in the dramatic escalation that followed the very meaning of "reprisal" was subverted. The supposed reprisal for Pleiku (and more remotely the nonexistent Tonkin incident) became initiative. The restraint suggested by the term reprisal was confounded by the reality of devastation that came to pass. Though the Pentagon wanted even more, the reality of over 500,000 troops and countless air sorties in the north and south altered, as we now know, the map of Southeast Asia, just as it altered the terrain of American political and moral conscience. In some very specific sense, "sustained reprisal" literally rewrote the reality of American life as it rewrote the geopolitical boundaries of Asia.

Again, one must resist the temptation to say that Bundy's memo caused all this. It was, rather, a crucial discursive text that provided the theory which encouraged American desires to have it all – to be supreme abroad, while being a Great Society at home. The text's meaning is lodged in this more complex field, and its discursive value was that it both revealed and masked (to-ed and fro-ed so to speak) the reality of the policy's appeal to the best and brightest who advised Johnson and to Johnson himself. Johnson's famous complex about his Harvardian advisers did not prevent him from sharing their theory. He could not use the language of a Harvard dean, but he could understand it. His own public statement announcing Flaming Dart used quite a different, and richer, metaphor: "We have kept our guns over the mantel and our shells in the cupboard for a long time. . . . I can't ask our American soldiers out there to fight with one hand tied behind their backs" (Kearns 1976, 261). This Alamo metaphor from Johnson's Texas frontier background conveyed the same meaning as did "sustained reprisal." It lacked only the (to him) noxious qualities of a more Harvardian abstraction. He saw himself, as Doris Kearns' (1976) biography shows, as a tough, virile man of peace, defending America against an aggressor. "Rolling Thunder," to Johnson, was an act of peace, an instance of what William Gibson (1986) rightly calls doublethink. But as discourse it has the same attributes as "sustained reprisal" – a play with words that plays with reality, simultaneously constituting and deconstituting the reality of the words and the world. And both figures of speech take their place alongside the war's most famous expression of doublethink, "We had to destroy the village in order to save it."

Doublethink is the discursive form required when there is no plausible reality on the ground to support the actions taken in the air of a contradictory theory of the world. This is not to say that nothing happened on the ground of Vietnam, that no one died. It does say, however, that we have no interpretive access to that reality, in large part because those who lived and died in the jungles did so because of the real irreality of a series of highly theoretical texts. The war was whatever reality it was because of a theoretical field in which sustained reprisal and Johnson's Alamo figure stood side by side, without prejudice to all the contradictions they contained.

This intertextual field in which the war in Vietnam was constituted stretches along several axes – horizontally across the differences of language between Johnson and Bundy, and vertically from their gross theory of the world to the irreality experienced by men and women on the ground. Bundy's abstract theory was not of a different order from the accounts of combatants. Hundreds of firsthand accounts by veterans describe the bizarre incongruence between hours spent when nothing happened, a fleeting and often unseen enemy, and eerie nothingness punctuated by deat – of buddies, of the enemy, of people who looked like but were not enemy, of old women and children, and eventually of fragged soldiers. Foot soldiers lost all sense of the reality of normal distinctions – between war and just walking around, between enemy and ally, between combatant and civilian. "We knew," said Specialist Fourth Class Charles Strong, "where the North Vietnamese were, but we knew that if we got into it, they would probably have wiped a big portion of the company out. We were really dropped there to find the North Vietnamese, and here we was hiding from them. Running because we was hungry. We were so far up in the hills that the place was so thick you didn't have to pull guard at night" (Terry 1984, 55). This collapse of reality on the ground is perfectly well explained by the irreality of the theoretical policy that invoked the war. Some might think this destroys the material reality of jungles, death, and Vietnam. But does it? Is it not certain that our men would never find the enemy, or recognize them when they found them, when the war itself had little to do with anything real? After all, Bundy and Johnson could have learned from Dienbienphu that this was to be a war with enemies that could not be found. They ignored this lesson because they were creating another, textual reality having more to do with the Alamo and postwar fear of communism than anything actually on the ground in Vietnam.

From Hamburger Hill to Johnson's situation room the reality of Vietnam was created, then breached, then recreated in countless texts. What after all truly went on there? Where was there? And what is the meaningful distinction among the realities written in journals of American and Vietcong combatants, Johnson's memoirs, Bundy's memorandum, the Pentagon Papers, *Apocalypse Now,* the heartwrenching V-shaped memorial on the Mall, deaths which rewrote family histories, defoliation which rewrote the ecology of Southeast Asia, a military failure that rewrote the boundaries of Vietnam? How could there be a study, including a sociological study, of Vietnam based on anything but these texts? Nothing else is out there, not now, and in an eerie sense not then.

It is certainly not by chance that the single most successful piece of poststructuralist sociology is about Vietnam. William Gibson's *The Perfect War* argues in the terms of a Foucauldian semiotics that Vietnam was an extensive elaboration of the codes contained in late liberal technocracy of which the Johnson administration was the epiphany. He demonstrates, to take one example, that the bombing around which the war was built was nothing more than an elaborate code for communications with Hanoi. The message was: "We want peace. We are resolved. You stop and we will too." Yet the message had no receiver to whom it made sense. In fact, the air raids on Hanoi's oil storage facilities were based on a certifiable denial of reality. The manifest purpose of these bombings was, Gibson shows, to communicate American resolve by destroying the bulk of Hanoi's oil reserves supporting infiltration of the south. By July 1965, when sorties reached more than 10,000 a month, almost seventy percent of the north's oil reserves had, in fact, been destroyed. Yet the actual daily need for petroleum fuel in the south was an amount that could be carried in fifteen pickup trucks. The thirty percent reserve not destroyed was more than enough. This reality was knowable by the simplest of intelligence reports. But the bombing continued, directed in part by Secretary of Defense Robert McNamara who, as a younger man, had directed a study demonstrating that allied bombing missions in World War Two had similarly little effect on the course of that war. What did the bombings mean? Their sense had nothing at all to do with an external reality. They were the necessary utterance dictated by a theoretical war policy code.

Gibson ends his book with a statement in which he means every word in a strict post-structuralist sense. He says, referring to the irrelevance of a distinction between his sociological text on the war and the fated experiences of men and women who lived the war's irreality: "In this *corpus* men and women live and die; the stories of their lives and their deaths have truths beyond in*corp*oration in any theoretical arguments" (Gibson 1986, 476). In a world where reality is constituted in and by means of texts, everything is theoretical in some sense, because everything is discursive and, in situations where this is the case, what other reality is there?

What then are the prospects for a post-structuralist sociology? One answer might be found in the fact, reported by Russell Jacoby (1987), that between 1959 and 1969, the crucial years of the war, the three leading political science journals published 924 pieces of which exactly one concerned Vietnam. Sociology did not do much better. In the forty-six years between 1936 and 1982, the *American Sociological Review* published 2,559 articles, of which a scant five percent concerned political and social issues of any kind. This does not speak well for social science's grasp of reality.

Quite possibly a post-structuralist sociology would do better, however high the stakes. It would not be difficult to do as well.

REFERENCES

Abel, Elizabeth, ed. 1980. *Writing and Sexual Difference*. Chicago: University of Chicago Press.
Althusser, Louis. 1970. *For Marx*. New York: Vintage.
Barthes, Roland. 1970. *Writing Degree Zero and Elements of Semiology*. Boston: Beacon Press.
    1979. "From Work to Text." In Josue Hariri, ed., *Textual Strategies: Perspectives in Poststructuralist Criticism*. Ithaca: Cornell University Press.
Bernstein, Richard, ed. 1985. *Habermas and Modernity*. Cambridge: MIT Press.

Boudon, Raymond. 1971. *The Uses of Structuralism.* London: Heinemann.

Bourdieu, Pierre. 1977. *Outline of a Theory of Practice.* Cambridge: Cambridge University Press.

Brown, Richard Harvey. 1987. *Society as Text.* Chicago: University of Chicago Press.

Carby, Hazel. 1987. *Reconstructing Womanhood: The Emergence of the Afro-American Woman Novelist.* New York: Oxford University Press.

Deleuze, Gilles, and Felix Guattari. 1977. *Anti-Oedipus: Capitalism and Schizophrenia.* New York: Viking Press.

Derrida, Jacques. 1978. "Structure, Sign and Play in the Discourse of the Human Science." In Jacques Derrida, *Writing and Difference.* Chicago: University of Chicago Press.

   1985. "Racism's Last Word." In Gates, ed., *"Race," Writing and Difference.*

Foucault, Michel. 1972. *The Archaeology of Knowledge.* New York: Pantheon.

   1978. *History of Sexuality.* Vol. I. New York: Pantheon.

   1979. "What Is an Author?" In Josue V. Hariri, ed., *Textual Strategies: Perspectives in Post-Structuralist Criticism.* Ithaca: Cornell University Press.

Gates, Henry Louis, 1985. *"Race," Writing and Difference.* Chicago: University of Chicago Press.

   1988. *The Signifying Monkey: A Theory of Afro-American Literary Criticism.* New York: Oxford University Press.

Gibson, William. 1986. *The Perfect War.* Boston: Atlantic Monthly Press.

Giddens, Anthony. 1984. *The Constitution of Society.* Berkeley: University of California Press.

Gitlin, Todd. 1988. "Hip-Deep in Post-Modernism." *New York Times Book Review,* November 7.

Gravel, Mike, ed. 1971. *The Pentagon Papers.* Vols. I–IV. Boston: Beacon Press.

Hall, Stuart, et al. 1980. *Culture, Media, and Language: Working Papers in Cultural Studies, 1972–79.* London: Hutchinson.

Harding, Sandra. 1986. *The Science Question in Feminism.* Ithaca: Cornell University Press.

Hodgson, Godfrey. 1976. *America in Our Time.* New York: Vintage.

Jacoby, Russell. 1987. *The Last Intellectuals.* New York: Basic Books.

Jameson, Fredric. 1984. "Foreword." In Lyotard, *The Postmodern Condition.*

Jencks, Charles. 1977. *The Language of Post-Modern Architecture.* New York: Rizzoli.

Karnow, Stanley. 1983. *Vietnam: A History.* New York: Penguin.

Kearns, Doris. 1976. *Lyndon Johnson and the American Dream.* New York: Harper and Row.

Kristeva, Julia. 1974. *La révolution du language poétique.* Paris: Editions du Seuil.

Lacan, Jacques. 1968. *The Language of the Self.* New York: Delta.

   1977. *Ecrits: A Selection.* New York: Norton.

Lemert, Charles, 1979a. "Language, Structure, and Measurement: Structuralist Semiotics and Sociology." *American Journal of Sociology* 84:929–957.

   1979b. *Sociology and the Twilight of Man: Homocentrism and Discourse in Sociological Theory.* Carbondale: Southern Illinois University Press.

1982. *Michel Foucault: Social Theory and Transgression*. New York: Columbia University Press.

Lévi-Strauss, Claude. 1967. "The Structural Study of Myth." In Claude Lévi-Strauss, *Structural Anthropology*. New York: Anchor.

1970. "Overture to *le Cru et le cuit*." In Jacques Ehrmann, ed., *Structuralism*. New York: Anchor.

Lyotard, Jean-François. 1984. *The Postmodern Condition: A Report on Knowledge*. Minneapolis: University of Minnesota Press.

Marcus, George, and Michael M. J. Fischer. 1986. *Anthropology as Cultural Critique*. Chicago: University of Chicago Press.

Moi, Toril, ed. 1987. *French Feminist Thought: Politics, Patriarchy, and Sexual Difference*. New York: Basil Blackwell.

Portoghesi, Paolo. 1980. *After Modern Architecture*. New York: Rizzoli.

Rorty, Richard. 1979. *Philosophy and the Mirror of Nature*. Princeton: Princeton University Press.

1985. "Habermas and Lyotard on Postmodernity." In Bernstein, ed., *Habermas and Modernity*.

Rossi, Ino. 1983. *From the Sociology of Symbols to the Sociology of Signs*. New York: Columbia University Press.

Tel Quel. 1968. "Théorie d'ensemble." Paris: Editions du Seuil.

Terry, Wallace. 1984. *Bloods*. New York: Ballantine Books.

White, Hayden. 1978. *Tropics of Discourse*. Baltimore: Johns Hopkins University Press.

15

Deconstructing equality-versus-difference: Or, the uses of poststructuralist theory for feminism

Joan W. Scott

That feminism needs theory goes without saying (perhaps because it has been said so often). What is not always clear is what that theory will do, although there are certain common assumptions I think we can find in a wide range of feminist writings. We need theory that can analyze the workings of patriarchy in all its manifestations – ideological, institutional, organizational, subjective – accounting not only for continuities but also for change over time. We need theory that will let us think in terms of pluralities and diversities rather than of unities and universals. We need theory that will break the conceptual hold, at least, of those long traditions of (Western) philosophy that have systematically and repeatedly construed the world hierarchically in terms of masculine universals and feminine specificities. We need theory that will enable us to articulate alternative ways of thinking about (and thus acting upon) gender without either simply reversing the old hierarchies or confirming them. And we need theory that will be useful and relevant for political practice.

It seems to me that the body of theory referred to as poststructuralism best meets all these requirements. It is not by any means the only theory nor are its positions and formulations unique. In my own case, however, it was reading poststructuralist theory and arguing with literary scholars that provided the elements of clarification for which I was looking. I found a new way of analyzing constructions of meaning and relationships of power that called unitary, universal categories into question and historicized concepts otherwise treated as natural (such as man/woman) or

I am extremely grateful to William Connolly, Sanford Levinson, Andrew Pickering, Barbara Herrnstein Smith, and Elizabeth Weed for their thoughtful suggestions, which sharpened and improved my argument.
This article is reprinted from FEMINIST STUDIES, volume 14, number 1 (1988):33–50, by permission of the publisher, FEMINIST STUDIES, Inc., c/o Women's Studies Program, University of Maryland, College Park, MD 20742.

absolute (such as equality or justice). In addition, what attracted me was the historical connection between the two movements. Poststructuralism and contemporary feminism are late-twentieth-century movements that share a certain self-conscious critical relationship to established philosophical and political traditions. It thus seemed worthwhile for feminist scholars to exploit that relationship for their own ends.[1]

This article will not discuss the history of these various "exploitations" or elaborate on all the reasons a historian might look to this theory to organize her inquiry.[2] What seems most useful here is to give a short list of some major theoretical points and then devote most of my effort to a specific illustration. The first part of this article is a brief discussion of concepts used by poststructuralists that are also useful for feminists. The second part applies some of these concepts to one of the hotly contested issues among contemporary (U.S.) feminists – the "equality-versus-difference" debate.

Among the useful terms feminists have appropriated from poststructuralism are language, discourse, difference, and deconstruction.

Language. Following the work of structuralist linguistics and anthropology, the term is used to mean not simply words or even a vocabulary and set of grammatical rules but, rather, a meaning-constituting system: that is, any system – strictly verbal or other – through which meaning is constructed and cultural practices organized and by which, accordingly, people represent and understand their world, including who they are and how they relate to others. "Language," so conceived, is a central focus of poststructuralist analysis.

Language is not assumed to be a representation of ideas that either cause material relations or from which such relations follow; indeed, the idealist/materialist opposition is a false one to impose on this approach. Rather, the analysis of language provides a crucial point of entry, a starting point for understanding how social relations are conceived, and therefore – because understanding how they are conceived means understanding how they work – how institutions are organized, how relations of production are experienced, and how collective identity is established. Without attention to language and the processes by which meanings and categories are constituted, one only imposes oversimplified models on the

1. On the problem of appropriating poststructuralism for feminism, see Biddy Martin, "Feminism, Criticism, Foucault," *New German Critique* 27 (Fall 1982): 3–30.
2. Joan W. Scott, "Gender: A Useful Category of Historical Analysis," *American Historical Review* 91 (December 1986): 1053–75; Donna Haraway. "A Manifesto for Cyborgs: Science, Technology, and Socialist Feminism in the 1980s." *Socialist Review* 15 (March-April 1985): 65–107

world, models that perpetuate conventional understandings rather than open up new interpretive possibilities.

The point is to find ways to analyze specific "texts" – not only books and documents but also utterances of any kind and in any medium, including cultural practices – in terms of specific historical and contextual meanings. Poststructuralists insist that words and texts have no fixed or intrinsic meanings, that there is no transparent or self-evident relationship between them and either ideas or things, no basic or ultimate correspondence between language and the world. The questions that must be answered in such an analysis, then, are how, in what specific contexts, among which specific communities of people, and by what textual and social processes has meaning been acquired? More generally, the questions are: How do meanings change? How have some meanings emerged as normative and others have been eclipsed or disappeared? What do these processes reveal about how power is constituted and operates?

Discourse. Some of the answers to these questions are offered in the concept of discourse, especially as it has been developed in the work of Michel Foucault. A discourse is not a language or a text but a historically, socially, and institutionally specific structure of statements, terms, categories, and beliefs. Foucault suggests that the elaboration of meaning involves conflict and power, that meanings are locally contested within discursive "fields of force," that (at least since the Enlightenment) the power to control a particular field resides in claims to (scientific) knowledge embodied not only in writing but also in disciplinary and professional organizations, in institutions (hospitals, prisons, schools, factories), and in social relationships (doctor/patient, teacher/student, employer/worker, parent/child, husband/wife). Discourse is thus contained or expressed in organizations and institutions as well as in words; all of these constitute texts or documents to be read.[3]

Discursive fields overlap, influence, and compete with one another; they appeal to one another's "truths" for authority and legitimation. These truths are assumed to be outside human invention, either already known and self-evident or discoverable through scientific inquiry. Precisely because they are assigned the status of objective knowledge, they seem to be beyond dispute and thus serve a powerful legitimating function. Darwinian theories of natural selection are one example of such legitimating truths; biological theories about sexual difference are another.

3. Examples of Michel Foucault's work include *The Archaeology of Knowledge* (New York: Harper & Row, 1976), *The History of Sexuality,* vol. 1, *An Introduction* (New York: Vintage, 1980), and *Power/Knowledge: Selected Interviews and Other Writings, 1972–1977* (New York: Pantheon, 1980). See also Hubert L. Dreyfus and Paul Rabinow, *Michel Foucault: Beyond Structuralism and Hermeneutics* (Chicago: University of Chicago Press, 1983).

The power of these "truths" comes from the way they function as givens or first premises for both sides in an argument, so that conflicts within discursive fields are framed to follow from rather than question them. The brilliance of so much of Foucault's work has been to illuminate the shared assumptions of what seemed to be sharply different arguments, thus exposing the limits of radical criticism and the extent of the power of dominant ideologies or epistemologies.

In addition, Foucault has shown how badly even challenges to fundamental assumptions often fared. They have been marginalized or silenced, forced to underplay their most radical claims in order to win a short-term goal, or completely absorbed into an existing framework. Yet the fact of change is crucial to Foucault's notion of "archaeology," to the way in which he uses contrasts from different historical periods to present his arguments. Exactly how the process happens is not spelled out to the satisfaction of many historians, some of whom want a more explicit causal model. But when causal theories are highly general, we are often drawn into the assumptions of the very discourse we ought to question. (If we are to question those assumptions, it may be necessary to forgo existing standards of historical inquiry.) Although some have read Foucault as an argument about the futility of human agency in the struggle for social change, I think that he is more appropriately taken as warning against simple solutions to difficult problems, as advising human actors to think strategically and more self-consciously about the philosophical and political implications and meanings of the programs they endorse. From this perspective, Foucault's work provides an important way of thinking differently (and perhaps more creatively) about the politics of the contextual construction of social meanings, about such organizing principles for political action as "equality" and "difference."

Difference. An important dimension of poststructuralist analyses of language has to do with the concept of difference, the notion (following Ferdinand de Saussure's structuralist linguistics) that meaning is made through implicit or explicit contrast, that a positive definition rests on the negation or repression of something represented as antithetical to it. Thus, any unitary concept in fact contains repressed or negated material; it is established in explicit opposition to another term. Any analysis of meaning involves teasing out these negations and oppositions, figuring out how (and whether) they are operating in specific contexts. Oppositions rest on metaphors and cross-references, and often in patriarchal discourse, sexual difference (the contrast masculine/feminine) serves to encode or establish meanings that are literally unrelated to gender or the body. In that way, the meanings of gender become tied to many kinds of cultural representations, and these in turn establish terms by which relations between women and men are organized and understood. The possibilities of this kind of analysis have, for obvious reasons, drawn the interest and attention of feminist scholars.

Fixed oppositions conceal the extent to which things presented as oppositional are, in fact, interdependent – that is, they derive their meaning from a particularly established contrast rather than from some inherent or pure antithesis. Furthermore, according to Jacques Derrida, the interdependence is hierarchical with one term dominant or prior, the opposite term subordinate and secondary. The Western philosophical tradition, he argues, rests on binary oppositions: unity/diversity, identity/difference, presence/absence, and universality/specificity. The leading terms are accorded primacy; their partners are represented as weaker or derivative. Yet the first terms depend on and derive their meaning from the second to such an extent that the secondary terms can be seen as generative of the definition of the first terms.[4] If binary oppositions provide insight into the way meaning is constructed, and if they operate as Derrida suggests, then analyses of meaning cannot take binary oppositions at face value but rather must "deconstruct" them for the processes they embody.

Deconstruction. Although this term is used loosely among scholars – often to refer to a dismantling or destructive enterprise – it also has a precise definition in the work of Derrida and his followers. Deconstruction involves analyzing the operations of difference in texts, the ways in which meanings are made to work. The method consists of two related steps: the reversal and displacement of binary oppositions. This double process reveals the interdependence of seemingly dichotomous terms and their meaning relative to a particular history. It shows them to be not natural but constructed oppositions, constructed for particular purposes in particular contexts.[5] The literary critic Barbara Johnson describes deconstruction as crucially dependent on difference.

4. The Australian philosopher Elizabeth Gross puts it this way: "What Derrida attempts to show is that within these binary couples, the primary or dominant term derives its privilege from a curtailment or suppression of its opposite. Sameness or identity, presence, speech, the origin, mind, etc. are all privileged in relation to their opposites, which are regarded as debased, impure variants of the primary term. Difference, for example, is the lack of identity or sameness: absence is the lack of presence: writing is the supplement of speech, and so on." See her "Derrida, Irigaray, and Deconstruction." *Left-Right, Intervention* (Sydney, Australia): 20 (1986): 73. See also Jacques Derrida, *Of Grammatology* (Baltimore: Johns Hopkins University Press, 1976): and Jonathan Culler, *On Deconstruction: Theory and Criticism after Structuralism* (Ithaca: Cornell University Press, 1982).

5. Again, to cite Elizabeth Gross's formulation: "Taken together, reversal and its useful displacement show the necessary but unfounded function of these terms in Western thought. One must both reverse the dichotomy and the values attached to the two terms, as well as displace the excluded term, placing it

The starting point is often a binary different that is subsequently shown to be an illusion created by the working of differences much harder to pin down. The differences *between* entities . . . are shown to be based on a repression of differences *within* entities, ways in which an entity differs from itself. . . . The "deconstruction" of a binary opposition is thus not an annihilation of all values or differences; it is an attempt to follow the subtle, powerful effects of differences already at work within the illusion of a binary opposition.[6]

Deconstruction is, then, an important exercise, for it allows us to be critical of the way in which ideas we want to use are ordinarily expressed, exhibited in patterns of meaning that may undercut the ends we seek to attain. A case in point – of meaning expressed in a politically self-defeating way – is the "equality-versus-difference" debate among feminists. Here a binary opposition has been created to offer a choice to feminists, of either endorsing "equality" or its presumed antithesis "difference." In fact, the antithesis itself hides the interdependence of the two terms, for equality is not the elimination of difference, and difference does not preclude equality.

In the past few years, "equality-versus-difference" has been used as a shorthand to characterize conflicting feminist positions and political strategies.[7] Those who argue that sexual difference ought to be an irrelevant consideration in schools, employment, the courts, and the legislature are put in the equality category. Those who insist that appeals on behalf of women ought to be made in terms of the needs, interests, and characteristics common to women as a group are placed in the difference category. In the clashes over the superiority of one or another of these strategies, feminists have invoked history, philosophy, and morality and

beyond its oppositional role, as the internal condition of the dominant term. This move makes clear the violence of the hierarchy and the debt the dominant term owes to the subordinate one. It also demonstrates that there are other ways of conceiving these terms than dichotomously. If these terms were only or necessarily dichotomies, the process of displacement would not be possible. Although historically necessary, the terms are not logically necessary." See Gross, 74.

6. Barbara Johnson, *The Critical Difference: Essays in the Contemporary Rhetoric of Reading* (Baltimore: Johns Hopkins University Press, 1980): x–xi.
7. Most recently, attention has been focused on the issue of pregnancy benefits. See, for example, Lucinda M. Finley. "Transcending Equality Theory: A Way Out of the Maternity and the Workplace Debate," *Columbia Law Review* 86 (October 1986): 1118–83. See Sylvia A. Law, "Rethinking Sex and the Constitution, *University of Pennsylvania Law Review* 132 (June 1984): 955–1040.

have devised new classificatory labels: cultural feminism, liberal feminism, feminist separatism, and so on.[8] Most recently, the debate about equality and difference has been used to analyze the Sears case, the sex discrimination suit brought against the retailing giant by the Equal Employment Opportunities Commission (EEOC) in 1979, in which historians Alice Kessler-Harris and Rosalind Rosenberg testified on opposite sides.

There have been many articles written on the Sears case, among them a recent one by Ruth Milkman. Milkman insists that we attend to the political context of seemingly timeless principles: "We ignore the political dimensions of the equality-versus-difference debate at our peril, especially in a period of conservative resurgence like the present." She concludes:

> As long as this is the political context in which we find ourselves, feminist scholars must be aware of the real danger that arguments about "difference" or "women's culture" will be put to uses other than those for which they were originally developed. That does not mean we must abandon these arguments or the intellectual terrain they have opened up; it does mean that we must be self-conscious in our formulations, keeping firmly in view the ways in which our work can be exploited politically.[9]

Milkman's carefully nuanced formulation implies that equality is our safest course, but she is also reluctant to reject difference entirely. She feels a need to choose a side, but which side is the problem. Milkman's ambivalence is an example of what the legal theorist Martha Minow has labeled in another context "the difference dilemma." Ignoring difference in the case of subordinated groups, Minow points out, "leaves in place a faulty neutrality," but focusing on difference can underscore the stigma

8. Recently, historians have begun to cast feminist history in terms of the equality-versus-difference debate. Rather than accept it as an accurate characterization of antithetical positions, however, I think we need to look more closely at how feminists used these arguments. A close reading of nineteenth-century French feminist texts, for example, leads me to conclude that they are far less easily categorized into difference or equality positions than one would have supposed. I think it is a mistake for feminist historians to write this debate uncritically into history for it reifies an "antithesis" that may not actually have existed. We need instead to "deconstruct" feminist arguments and read them in their discursive contexts, all as explorations of "the difference dilemma."

9. Ruth Milkman, "Women's History and the Sears Case," *Feminist Studies* 12 (Summer 1986): 394–95. In my discussion of the Sears case, I have drawn heavily on this careful and intelligent article, the best so far of the many that have been written on the subject.

of deviance. "Both focusing on and ignoring difference risk recreating it. This is the dilemma of difference."[10] What is required, Minow suggests, is a new way of thinking about difference, and this involves rejecting the idea that equality-versus-difference constitutes an opposition. Instead of framing analyses and strategies as if such binary pairs were timeless and true, we need to ask how the dichotomous pairing of equality and difference itself works. Instead of remaining within the terms of existing political discourse, we need to subject those terms to critical examination. Until we understand how the concepts work to constrain and construct specific meanings, we cannot make them work for us.

A close look at the evidence in the Sears case suggests that equality-versus-difference may not accurately depict the opposing sides in the Sears case. During testimony, most of the arguments against equality and for difference were, in fact, made by the Sears lawyers or by Rosalind Rosenberg. They constructed an opponent against whom they asserted that women and men differed, that "fundamental differences" – the result of culture or long-standing patterns of socialization – led to women's presumed lack of interest in commission sales jobs. In order to make their own claim that sexual difference and not discrimination could explain the hiring patterns of Sears, the Sears defense attributed to EEOC an assumption that no one had made in those terms – that women and men had identical interests.[11] Alice Kessler-Harris did not argue that women were the same as men; instead, she used a variety of strategies to challenge Rosenberg's assertions. First, she argued that historical evidence suggested far more variety in the jobs women actually took than Rosenberg assumed. Second, she maintained that economic considerations usually offset the effects of socialization in women's attitudes to employment. And, third, she pointed out that, historically, job segregation by sex was the consequence of employer preferences, not employee choices. The question of women's choices could not be resolved, Kessler-Harris maintained, when the hiring process itself predetermined the outcome, imposing generalized gendered criteria that were not necessarily relevant to the work at hand. The debate joined then not around equality-versus-difference

10. Martha Minow, "Learning to Live with the Dilemma of Difference: Bilingual and Special Education," *Law and Contemporary Problems* 48, no. 2 (1984): 157–211; quotation is from p. 160; see also pp. 202–6.
11. There is a difference, it seems to me, between arguing that women and men have identical interests and arguing that one should presume such identity in all aspects of the hiring process. The second position is the only strategic way of not building into the hiring process prejudice or the wrong presumptions about differences of interest.

but around the relevance of general ideas of sexual difference in a specific context.[12]

To make the case for employer discrimination, EEOC lawyers cited obviously biased job applicant questionnaires and statements by personnel officers, but they had no individuals to testify that they had experienced discrimination. Kessler-Harris referred to past patterns of sexual segregation in the job market as the product of employer choices, but mostly she invoked history to break down Rosenberg's contention that women as a group differed consistently in the details of their behavior from men, instead insisting that variety characterized female job choices (as it did male job choices), that it made no sense in this case to talk about women as a uniform group. She defined equality to mean a presumption that women and men might have an equal interest in sales commission jobs. She did not claim that women and men, by definition, had such an equal interest. Rather, Kessler-Harris and the EEOC called into question the relevance for hiring decisions of generalizations about the necessarily antithetical behaviors of women and men. EEOC argued that Sears's hiring practices reflected inaccurate and inapplicable notions of sexual difference; Sears argued that "fundamental" differences between the sexes (and not its own actions) explained the gender imbalances in its labor force.

The Sears case was complicated by the fact that almost all the evidence offered was statistical. The testimony of the historians, therefore, could only be inferential at best. Each of them sought to explain small statistical disparities by reference to gross generalizations about the entire history of working women; furthermore, neither historian had much information about what had actually happened at Sears. They were forced, instead, to swear to the truth or falsehood of interpretive generalizations developed for purposes other than legal contestation, and they were forced to treat their interpretive premises as matters of fact. Reading the cross-examination of Kessler-Harris is revealing in this respect. Each of her carefully nuanced explanations of women's work history was forced into a reductive assertion by the Sears lawyers' insistence that she answer questions only by saying yes or no. Similarly, Rosalind Rosenberg's rebuttal to Alice Kessler-Harris eschewed the historian's subtle contextual reading of evidence and sought instead to impose a test of absolute consistency. She juxtaposed Kessler-Harris's testimony in the trial to her ear-

12. Rosenberg's "Offer of Proof" and Kessler-Harris's "Written Testimony" appeared in *Signs* 11 (Summer 1986): 757–79. The "Written Rebuttal Testimony of Dr. Rosalind Rosenberg" is part of the official transcript of the case, U.S. District Court for the Northern District of Illinois, Eastern Division. *EEOC vs Sears,* Civil Action No. 79-C-4373. (I am grateful to Sanford Levinson for sharing the trial documents with me and for our many conversations about them.)

lier published work (in which Kessler-Harris stressed differences between female and male workers in their approaches to work, arguing that women were more domestically oriented and less individualistic than men) in an effort to show that Kessler-Harris had misled the court.[13] Outside the courtroom, however, the disparities of the Kessler-Harris argument could also be explained in other ways. In relationship to a labor history that had typically excluded women, it might make sense to overgeneralize about women's experience, emphasizing difference in order to demonstrate that the universal term "worker" was really a male reference that could not account for all aspects of women's job experiences. In relationship to an employer who sought to justify discrimination by reference to sexual difference, it made more sense to deny the totalizing effects of difference by stressing instead the diversity and complexity of women's behavior and motivation. In the first case, difference served a positive function, unveiling the inequity hidden in a presumably neutral term; in the second case, difference served a negative purpose, justifying what Kessler-Harris believed to be unequal treatment. Although the inconsistency might have been avoided with a more self-conscious analysis of the "difference dilemma," Kessler-Harris's different positions were quite legitimately different emphases for different contexts; only in a courtroom could they be taken as proof of bad faith.[14]

The exacting demands of the courtroom for consistency and "truth" also point out the profound difficulties of arguing about difference. Although the testimony of the historians had to explain only a relatively small statistical disparity in the numbers of women and men hired for full-time commission sales jobs, the explanations that were preferred were totalizing and categorical.[15] In cross-examination, Kessler-Harris's multiple interpretations were found to be contradictory and confusing, although the judge praised Rosenberg for her coherence and lucidity.[16] In part, that was because Rosenberg held to a tight model that unproblematically linked socialization to individual choice; in part it was because her descriptions of gender differences accorded with prevailing normative views. In contrast, Kessler-Harris had trouble finding a simple model that

13. Appendix to the "Written Rebuttal Testimony of Dr. Rosalind Rosenberg," 1–12.
14. On the limits imposed by courtrooms and the pitfalls expert witnesses may encounter, see Nadine Taub, "Thinking about Testifying," *Perspectives* (American Historical Association Newsletter) 24 (November 1986): 10–11.
15. On this point, Taub asks a useful question: "Is there a danger in discrimination cases that historical or other expert testimony not grounded in the particular facts of the case will reinforce the idea that it is acceptable to make generalizations about particular groups?" (p. 11).
16. See the cross-examination of Kessler-Harris, *EEOC vs Sears* 16376–619.

would at once acknowledge difference *and* refuse it as an acceptable explanation for the employment pattern of Sears. So she fell into great difficulty maintaining her case in the face of hostile questioning. On the one hand, she was accused of assuming that economic opportunism equally affected women and men (and thus of believing that women and men were the same). How, then, could she explain the differences her own work had identified? On the other hand, she was tarred (by Rosenberg) with the brush of subversion, for implying that all employers might have some interest in sex typing the labor force, for deducing from her own (presumably Marxist) theory, a "conspiratorial" conclusion about the behavior of Sears.[17] If the patterns of discrimination that Kessler-Harris alluded to were real, after all, one of their effects might well be the kind of difference Rosenberg pointed out. Caught within the framework of Rosenberg's use of historical evidence, Kessler-Harris and her lawyers relied on an essentially negative strategy, offering details designed to complicate and undercut Rosenberg's assertions. Kessler-Harris did not directly challenge the theoretical shortcomings of Rosenberg's socialization model, nor did she offer an alternative model of her own. That would have required, I think, either fully developing the case for employer discrimination or insisting more completely on the "differences" line of argument by exposing the "equality-versus-difference" formulation as an illusion.

In the end, the most nuanced arguments of Kessler-Harris were rejected as contradictory or inapplicable, and the judge decided in Sears's favor, repeating the defense argument that an assumption of equal interest was "unfounded" because of the differences between women and men.[18] Not only was EEOC's position rejected, but the hiring policies of Sears were

17. The Rosenberg "Rebuttal" is particularly vehement on this question: "This assumption that all employers discriminate is prominent in her [Kessler-Harris's] work. . . . In a 1979 article, she wrote hopefully that women harbor values, attitudes, and behavior patterns potentially subversive to capitalism" (p. 11). "There are, of course, documented instances of employers limiting the opportunities of women. But the fact that some employers have discriminated does not prove that all do" (p. 19). The rebuttal raises another issue about the political and ideological limits of a courtroom or, perhaps it is better to say, about the way the courtroom reproduces dominant ideologies. The general notion that employers discriminate was unacceptable (but the general notion that women prefer certain jobs was not). This unacceptability was underscored by linking it to subversion and Marxism, positions intolerable in U.S. political discourse. Rosenberg's innuendos attempted to discredit Kessler-Harris on two counts – first, by suggesting that she was making a ridiculous generalization and, second, by suggesting that only people outside acceptable politics could even entertain that generalization.

18. Milkman, 391.

implicitly endorsed. According to the judge, because difference was real and fundamental, it could explain statistical variations in Sears's hiring. Discrimination was redefined as simply the recognition of "natural" difference (however culturally or historically produced), fitting in nicely with the logic of Reagan conservatism. Difference was substituted for inequality, the appropriate antithesis of equality, becoming inequality's explanation and legitimation. The judge's decision illustrates a process literary scholar Naomi Schor has described in another context: it "essentializes difference and naturalizes social inequity."[19]

The Sears case offers a sobering lesson in the operation of a discursive, that is a political field. Analysis of language here provides insight not only into the manipulation of concepts and definitions but also into the implementation and justification of institutional and political power. References to categorical differences between women and men set the terms within which Sears defended its policies *and* EEOC challenged them. Equality-versus-difference was the intellectual trap within which historians argued not about tiny disparities in Sears's employment practices, but about the normative behaviors of women and men. Although we might conclude that the balance of power was against EEOC by the time the case was heard and that, therefore, its outcome was inevitable (part of the Reagan plan to reverse affirmative action programs of the 1970s), we still need to articulate a critique of what happened that can inform the next round of political encounter. How should that position be conceptualized?

When equality and difference are paired dichotomously, they structure an impossible choice. If one opts for equality, one is forced to accept the notion that difference is antithetical to it. If one opts for difference, one admits that equality is unattainable. That, in a sense, is the dilemma apparent in Milkman's conclusion cited above. Feminists cannot give up "difference"; it has been our most creative analytic tool. We cannot give up equality, at least as long as we want to speak to the principles and values of our political system. But it makes no sense for the feminist movement to let its arguments be forced into preexisting categories and its political disputes to be characterized by a dichotomy we did not invent. How then do we recognize and use notions of sexual difference and yet make arguments for equality? The only response is a double one: the unmasking of the power relationship constructed by posing equality as the antithesis of difference and the refusal of its consequent dichotomous construction of political choices.

Equality-versus-difference cannot structure choices for feminist politics; the oppositional pairing misrepresents the relationship of both terms.

19. Naomi Schor, "Reading Double: Sand's Difference," in *The Poetics of Gender*, ed. Nancy K. Miller (New York: Columbia University Press, 1986), 256.

Equality, in the political theory of rights that lies behind the claims of excluded groups for justice, means the ignoring of differences between individuals for a particular purpose or in a particular context. Michael Walzer puts it this way: "The root meaning of equality is negative; egalitarianism in its origins is an abolitionist politics. It aims at eliminating not all differences, but a particular set of differences, and a different set in different times and places."[20] This presumes a social agreement to consider obviously different people as equivalent (not identical) for a stated purpose. In this usage, the opposite of equality is inequality or inequivalence, the noncommensurability of individuals or groups in certain circumstances, for certain purposes. Thus, for purposes of democratic citizenship, the measure of equivalence has been, at different times, independence or ownership of property or race or sex. The political notion of equality thus includes, indeed depends on, an acknowledgment of the existence of difference. Demands for equality have rested on implicit and usually unrecognized arguments from difference; if individuals or groups were identical or the same there would be no need to ask for equality. Equality might well be defined as deliberate indifference to specified differences.

The antithesis of difference in most usages is sameness or identity. But even here the contrast and the context must be specified. There is nothing self-evident or transcendent about difference, even if the fact of difference – sexual difference, for example – seems apparent to the naked eye. The questions always ought to be, What qualities or aspects are being compared? What is the nature of the comparison? How is the meaning of difference being constructed? Yet in the Sears testimony and in some debates among feminists (sexual) difference is assumed to be an immutable fact, its meaning inherent in the categories female and male. The lawyers for Sears put it this way: "The reasonableness of the EEOC's *a priori* assumptions of male/female sameness with respect to preferences, interests, and qualifications is . . . the crux of the issue."[21] The point of the EEOC challenge, however, was never sameness but the irrelevance of categorical differences.

The opposition men/women, as Rosenberg employed it, asserted the incomparability of the sexes, and although history and socialization were the explanatory factors, these resonated with categorical distinctions inferred from the facts of bodily difference. When the opposition men/women is invoked, as it was in the Sears case, it refers a specific issue (the small statistical discrepancy between women and men hired for commission sales jobs) back to a general principle (the "fundamental" differences between women and men). The differences within each group

20. Michael Walzer, *Spheres of Justice: A Defense of Pluralism and Equality* (New York: Basic Books, 1983), xii. See also Minow, 202–3.
21. Milkman, 384.

that might apply to this particular situation – the fact, for example, that some women might choose "aggressive" or "risk-taking" jobs or that some women might prefer high- to low-paying positions – were excluded by definition in the antithesis between the groups. The irony is, of course, that the statistical case required only a small percentage of women's behaviors to be explained. Yet the historical testimony argued categorically about "women." It thus became impossible to argue (as EEOC and Kessler-Harris tried to) that within the female category, women typically exhibit and participate in all sorts of "male" behaviors, that socialization is a complex process that does not yield uniform choices. To make the argument would have required a direct attack on categorical thinking about gender. For the generalized opposition male/female serves to obscure the differences among women in behavior, character, desire, subjectivity, sexuality, gender identification, and historical experience. In the light of Rosenberg's insistence on the primacy of sexual difference, Kessler-Harris's insistence on the specificity (and historically variable aspect) of women's actions could be dismissed as an unreasonable and trivial claim.

The alternative to the binary construction of sexual difference is not sameness, identity, or androgyny. By subsuming women into a general "human" identity, we lose the specificity of female diversity and women's experiences; we are back, in other words, to the days when "Man's" story was supposed to be everyone's story, when women were "hidden from history," when the feminine served as the negative counterpoint, the "Other," for the construction of positive masculine identity. It is not sameness *or* identity between women and men that we want to claim but a more complicated historically variable diversity than is permitted by the opposition male/female, a diversity that is also differently expressed for different purposes in different contexts. In effect, the duality this opposition creates draws one line of difference, invests it with biological explanations, and then treats each side of the opposition as a unitary phenomenon. Everything in each category (male/female) is assumed to be the same; hence, differences within either category are suppressed. In contrast, our goal is to see not only differences between the sexes but also the way these work to repress differences within gender groups. The sameness constructed on each side of the binary opposition hides the multiple play of differences and maintains their irrelevance and invisibility.

Placing equality and difference in antithetical relationship has, then, a double effect. It denies the way in which difference has long figured in political notions of equality and it suggests that sameness is the only ground on which equality can be claimed. It thus puts feminists in an impossible position, for as long as we argue within the terms of a discourse set up by this opposition we grant the current conservative premise that because women cannot be identical to men in all respects, we cannot expect to be equal to them. The only alternative, it seems to me, is to refuse to oppose equality to difference and insist continually on differences – differences as the condition of individual and collective identities, differences as the constant challenge to the fixing of those identities, history as the repeated illustration of the play of differences, differences as the very meaning of equality itself.

Alice Kessler-Harris's experience in the Sears case shows, however, that the assertion of differences in the face of gender categories is not a sufficient strategy. What is required in addition is an analysis of fixed gender categories as normative statements that organize cultural understandings of sexual difference. This means that we must open to scrutiny the terms women and men as they are used to define one another in particular contexts – workplaces, for example. The history of women's work needs to be retold from this perspective as part of the story of the creation of a gendered workforce. In the nineteenth century, for example, certain concepts of male skill rested on a contrast with female labor (by definition unskilled). The organization and reorganization of work processes was accomplished by reference to the gender attributes of workers, rather than to issues of training, education, or social class. And wage differentials between the sexes were attributed to fundamentally different family roles that preceded (rather than followed from) employment arrangements. In all these processes the meaning of "worker" was established through a contrast between the presumably natural qualities of women and men. If we write the history of women's work by gathering data that describes the activities, needs, interests, and culture of "women workers," we leave in place the naturalized contrast and reify a fixed categorical difference between women and men. We start the story, in other words, too late, by uncritically accepting a gendered category (the "woman worker") that itself needs investigation because its meaning is relative to its history.

If in our histories we relativize the categories woman and man, it means, of course, that we must also recognize the contingent and specific nature of our political claims. Political strategies then will rest on analyses of the utility of certain arguments in certain discursive contexts, without, however, invoking absolute qualities for women or men. There are moments when it makes sense for mothers to demand consideration for their social role, and contexts within which motherhood is irrelevant to women's behavior; but to maintain that womanhood is motherhood is to obscure the differences that make choice possible. There are moments when it makes sense to demand a reevaluation of the status of what has been socially constructed as women's work ("comparable worth" strategies are the current example) and contexts within which it makes much more sense to prepare women for entry into "nontraditional" jobs. But to maintain that feminity predisposes women to certain (nurturing) jobs or (collaborative) styles of work is to naturalize complex economic and social processes and, once again, to obscure the differences that have characterized women's occupational histories. An insistence on differences undercuts the tendency to absolutist, and in the case of sexual difference, essentialist categories. It does not deny the existence of gender difference, but it does suggest that its meanings are always relative to particular constructions in specified contexts. In contrast, absolutist categorizations of difference end up always enforcing normative rules.

It is surely not easy to formulate a "deconstructive" political strategy in the face of powerful tendencies that construct the world in binary terms. Yet there seems to me no other choice. Perhaps as we learn to think this way solutions will become more readily apparent. Perhaps the theoretical and historical work we do can prepare the ground. Certainly we can take heart from the history of feminism, which is full of illustrations of refusals of simple dichotomies and attempts instead to demonstrate that equality requires the recognition and inclusion of differences. Indeed, one way historians could contribute to a genuine rethinking of these concepts, is to stop writing the history of feminisms as a story of oscillations between demands for equality and affirmations of difference. This approach inadvertently strengthens the hold of the binary construction, establishing it as inevitable by giving it a long history. When looked at closely, in fact, the historical arguments of feminists do not usually fall into these neat compartments; they are instead attempts to reconcile theories of equal rights with cultural concepts of sexual difference, to question the validity of normative constructions of gender in the light of the existence of behaviors and qualities that contradict the rules, to point up rather than resolve conditions of contradiction, to articulate a political identity for women without conforming to existing stereotypes about them.

In histories of feminism and in feminist political strategies there needs to be at once attention to the operations of difference and an insistence on differences, but not a simple substitution of multiple for binary difference for it is not a happy pluralism we ought to invoke. The resolution of the "difference dilemma" comes neither from ignoring nor embracing difference as it is normatively constituted. Instead, it seems to me that the critical feminist position must always involve *two* moves. The first is the systematic criticism of the operations of categorical difference, the exposure of the kinds of exclusions and inclusions – the hierarchies – it constructs, and a refusal of their ultimate "truth." A refusal, however, not in the name of an equality that implies sameness or identity, but rather (and this is the second move) in the name of an equality that rests on differences – differences that confound, disrupt, and render ambiguous the meaning of any fixed binary opposition. To do anything else is to buy into the political argument that sameness is a requirement for equality, an untenable position for feminists (and historians) who know that power is constructed on and so must be challenged from the ground of difference.

16

The plague of discourse: Politics, literary theory, and AIDS

Lee Edelman

In an article titled "The Metaphor of AIDS," published for a popular audience in the Sunday magazine of the *Boston Globe,* Lee Grove, an instructor of creative writing and American literature at the University of Massachusetts, reflects on the ways in which the AIDS epidemic had altered his understanding of literary texts and his relation to the teaching of literature. Referring specifically to the Renaissance pun that brought together, at least linguistically, the experiences of orgasm and death, Grove writes:

> "To die," "to have sex" – that coupling has always been figurative, metaphorical, sophisticated wordplay, a literary conceit, one of those outrageous paradoxes dear to the heart of a racy divine like John Donne.
> Outrageous no longer. The coupling isn't figurative anymore. It's literal.[1]

I want to consider the highly charged relation between the literal and the figural as it informs the discussion of AIDS in America and to explore the political uses to which the ideological framing of that relationship has been put. Toward that end my subtitle locates "literary theory"

The earliest version of this essay was presented at a session on "The Literature of AIDS" at the 1987 MLA Convention. I would like to thank Michael Cadden and Elaine Showalter, the other panelists, for offering helpful suggestions. In revised form the essay was delivered at Bowdoin College and I am happy to thank those who sponsored me there, the Lesbian/Gay/Straight Alliance and the Bowdoin Literary Society. Finally I want to express my gratitude to Joseph Litvak for his invaluable assistance.
Lee Edelman, "The Plague of Discourse: Politics, Literary Theory and AIDS," *South Atlantic Quarterly,* 88:4, pp. 301–317. Copyright Duke University Press, 1989. Reprinted with permission of the publisher.

1. Lee Grove, "The Metaphor of AIDS," *Boston Globe Magazine,* 28 February 1988.

between the categories of "politics" and "AIDS" to indicate my belief that both of those categories produce, and are produced as, historical discourses susceptible to analysis by the critical methodologies associated with literary theory.

This is not to say that literary theory occupies some unproblematic or privileged position; to the contrary, literature, including that form of literature that is literary theory, is by no means distinct from political discourse, and thus from either the discourse on AIDS, or the politics that governs the discourse on AIDS. By the same token, politics and AIDS cannot be disentangled from their implication in the linguistic or the rhetorical. Indeed, one of the ideological oppositions I would call into question is that whereby the biological, associated with the literal or the "real," is counterposed against the literary, associated with the figural or the fictive. That opposition is already deeply and unavoidably political, which is to say, it bespeaks an ideologically determined hierarchy of values in which power – the power to speak seriously, to speak with authority, and thereby to influence policy – is very much at stake in the claim to be able to speak literally.

The AIDS epidemic, then, is not to be construed, as Grove asserts, in terms of its defiguralizing literality, but rather, and more dangerously, as the breeding ground for all sorts of figural associations whose virulence derives from their presentation under the aspect of literality. Indeed, one of the most disturbing features that characterizes the discourse on AIDS in America is the way in which the literal is recurrently and tendentiously produced as a figure whose figurality remains strategically occluded – a figure that thus has the potential to be used toward the most politically repressive ends. The often hysterical terms within which the Western discussion of AIDS has been conducted reflect an untenable, but politically manipulable, belief that we can separate biological science, and therefore the social policy based on that science, from the instability and duplicity that literary theory has increasingly identified as inherent in the operations of language.

Though my subject necessarily involves literature and AIDS, my focus falls not on those literary works wherein the urgency of AIDS achieves thematic inscription, but rather on the inevitable inscriptions of the literary that mark the discourse on AIDS. The text that provides the occasion for my analysis, the text on which my remarks will turn or trope, is a relatively brief one, "Silence=Death." This slogan has achieved wide currency, particularly – though by no means exclusively – within the gay community, both as a challenge to the murderously delayed and cynically inadequate official responses to AIDS and as a rallying cry for those who have borne the burden of death and suffering, calling upon them to defend themselves against the dangerous discourse of mastery produced by medical or legislative authorities in order to defend their *own* vested interests in the face of this epidemic. Significantly, issues of defense achieve an inevitable centrality in discussions of AIDS in ways that critically distinguish this epidemic from many others. Because the syndrome attacks the body's defensive mechanisms; because once it does so, science as yet can offer no defense against it; because in the West it has appeared primarily among groups already engaged in efforts to defend themselves against the intolerance of the dominant culture; because modern science and the national political institutions funding modern science feel called upon to defend their prestige against the assault on medical know-how represented by this disease; because individuals and groups, often irrationally, seek ways to defend themselves against contact with this disease; and because some politicians, in order to defend against political opposition, deploy the AIDS issue strategically to ensure their own political survival: for all of these reasons the question of defense is inextricably and distinctively inscribed in the discourse on AIDS. And as this preliminary formulation of the issues suggests, my focus is on the interrelations among the notions of discourse, defense, and disease – particularly as they intersect with the already activated ideologies of homosexuality and homophobia in the West to converge at the virulent site of discursive contention that is AIDS.

These last words seem to define AIDS in a way that few in the medical profession would recognize, so let me present a definition of AIDS at the outset that will seem more literal, or as students of rhetoric would say, more "proper." According to current scientific understanding, and I hasten to add that it is not my intention necessarily to endorse or validate that understanding, AIDS results from infection with some quantity of HIV or Human Immunodeficiency Virus, which attacks the cells of the immune system, particularly the T-helper or T-4 cells, and impairs the body's ability to defend itself against viral, fungal, and parasitic infections. Medical researchers would thus accept a characterization of AIDS as an infectious condition in which the stake is "literally" the possibility of defense. As David Black puts it simply in *The Plague Years,* his "chronicle" of AIDS, "the immune system is the body's complex and still imperfectly understood defense mechanism. Its job is to tell the difference between Self and Not-Self."[2] I will come back to the Emersonian implications of this description of the immune response, but for now I want to examine the notion of defense and its importance not only in the bio-logic articulated within the body by AIDS, but also in the reactive or defensive discourse embodied in the slogan Silence=Death. For if that slogan chal-

2. David Black, *The Plague Years: A Chronicle of AIDS, the Epidemic of Our Times* (New York, 1986), 80.

lenges those in the communities most affected by AIDS to defend themselves, it does so by appealing to defensive properties that it implicitly identifies as inherent in discourse. The slogan, after all, which most frequently appears in a graphic configuration that positions the letters of its text, in white, beneath a pink triangle on a field of black, alludes to the Nazi campaign against homosexuals (identified in the concentration camps by the pink triangle they were required to wear) in order to propose a gay equivalent to the post-Holocaust rallying cry of Jewish activists: "Never again." At the same time, Silence=Death can be read as a post-AIDS revision of a motto popular among gay militants not long ago – "Out of the closets and into the streets" – and as such it similarly implies that language, discourse, public manifestations are necessary weapons of defense in a contemporary strategy of gay survival. For if we assert that Silence=Death, then one corollary to this theorem in the geometry that governs the relationship among discourse, defense, and disease must be that Discourse=Defense, that language, articulation, the intervention of voice, is salutary, vivifying, since discourse can defend us against the death that must result from the continuation of our silence.

But to speak of mechanisms of defense, particularly in terms of linguistic operations, is necessarily to invoke the specter of Freud, who offered us a taxonomy of psychic defenses in his studies of the unconscious and its operations. And here, as always, Freud calls into question the basis for any naive optimism about the success of our defensive maneuvers. Here is a passage from H. D.'s memoir of her psychoanalysis by Freud that speaks to the relation between discourse and defense in a particularly telling way: only once, according to H.D., did Freud ever "lay down the law" and that was when he said "never – I mean, never at any time, in any circumstance, endeavor to defend me, if and when you hear abusive remarks made about me and my work." H.D. then goes on to recall: "He explained it carefully. He might have been giving a lesson in geometry or demonstrating the inevitable course of a disease once the virus has entered the system. At this point, he seemed to indicate (as if there were a chart of the fever patient, pinned on the wall before us), at the least suggestion that you may be about to begin a counterargument in my defense, the anger or frustration of the assailant will be driven deeper. You will do no good to the detractor by mistakenly beginning a logical defense. You will drive the hatred or the fear or the prejudice in deeper."[3] Defense of this sort is necessarily failed defense; far from being salubrious, it serves only to compromise further one's immunity and to stimulate greater virulence. Interestingly enough, this corresponds to the process whereby, according to some medical researchers, HIV moves from a state of latency in an in-

3. H. D., *Tribute to Freud* (Boston, 1974), 86.

fected cell to active reproduction. The defensive "stimulation of an immune response" seems to be one of "the conditions that activates the production of new" HIV that can then go on to infect other cells.[4] Since defensive maneuvers may have the unintended effect of disseminating or intensifying infection, the relationship between the two can be rearticulated in the formula: Defense=Disease.

Freud's argument in warning H. D. against engaging in defensive interventions significantly echoes the logic sounded centuries earlier by Plato in the *Timaeus*. Writing specifically about the wisdom of medical interventions to defend the body against the ravages of disease, Plato offers a cautionary note: "diseases unless they are very dangerous should not be irritated by medicines, since every form of disease is in a manner akin to the living being, whose complex frame has an appointed term of life. . . . And this holds also of the constitution of diseases; if any one regardless of the appointed time tries to subdue them by medicine, he only aggravates and multiplies them."[5] The word here translated as "medicine" derives, as Jacques Derrida argues in "Plato's Pharmacy," from the Greek word *pharmakon* signifying a drug or philter that occupies an ambiguous position as remedy and poison at once. Commenting on this passage from Plato, Derrida observes: "Just as health is auto-nomous and auto-matic, 'normal' disease demonstrates its autarky by confronting the pharmaceutical aggression with *metastatic* reactions which displace the site of the disease, with the eventual result that the points of resistance are reinforced and multiplied."[6] Thus for Plato, as for Freud, gestures of defense can aggravate rather than ameliorate one's condition. Freud, of course, is referring explicitly to language or discourse as a mechanism of defense against one's enemies or detractors; H. D.'s reference to the "course of a disease once the virus has entered the system" is clearly presented only as a figural embellishment. Plato, on the other hand, is referring explicitly to medical defenses against disease, but considerations of discourse are decisively at issue in his discussion as well.

In the long and complicated argument unfolded in "Plato's Pharmacy," Derrida shows how Plato identifies writing with the *pharmakon,* thus rendering its simultaneously a poison, a remedy, a fantastic or magical philter, and a rational medical technology. If writing as *pharmakon* is already, at the beginning of Western culture, producing an entanglement of

4. Johns Hopkins University, Population Information Program, "Issues in World Health," *Population Reports,* series 50, no. 14 (1986): 198.

5. Plato, "Timaeus," in *The Dialogues of Plato,* trans. Benjamin Jowett (Oxford, 1953), 3:89.

6. Jacques Derrida, "Plato's Pharmacy," in *Dissemination,* trans. Barbara Johnson (Chicago, 1981), 101.

literary and medical discourse, its antithesis, and true voice of speech, is identified by Plato in the *Phaedrus* with the vital force of *logos*. Thus Derrida characterizes Plato's notion of *logos* in the following words:

> *Logos* is a *zoon*. An animal that is born, grows, belongs to the *phusis*. Linguistics, logic, dialectics, and zoology are all in the same camp.

> In describing *logos* as a *zoon*, Plato is following certain rhetors and sophists before him who, as a contrast to the cadaverous rigidity of writing, had held up the living spoken word.[7]

Derrida's strategy in deconstructing the opposition between speech and writing is to show how the living word of speech is already informed by or predicated upon a form of writing or an *archi-écriture*. But of particular importance for my purposes is the way in which Derrida's reading of Plato insists upon the inextricability of the textual and the biological even as it uses rhetorical or literary techniques to subvert or dismantle the rational edifice of the Western philosophical tradition.

Consider again Derrida's gloss on Plato's wariness about the *pharmakon* in *Timaeus*: "Just as health is auto-nomous and auto-matic, 'normal' disease demonstrates its autarky by confronting the pharmaceutical aggression with *metastatic* reactions which displace the site of the disease, with the eventual result that the points of resistance are reinforced or multiplied." Bearing in mind that Derrida's reading of the *pharmakon* explicitly invokes the critical conjunction of discourse and biology informing the platonic opposition between writing as supplement and speech as living word, his gloss suggests that defensive strategies deployed – in the realm of discourse or disease – to combat agencies of virulence may themselves be informed by the virulence they are seeking to efface, informed by it in ways that do not produce the immunizing effect of a vaccine, but that serve, instead, to reinforce and even multiply the dangerous sites of infection. Derrida makes explicit this pathology of rhetoric when, elsewhere in "Plato's Pharmacy," he remarks that "metaphoricity is the contamination of logic and the logic of contamination."[8] In other words, Disease=Discourse. Derrida's diagnosis of metaphor as contamination makes clear that the rationalism of philosophical logic – a rationalism that provides the foundation for Western medical and scientific practice – is not untainted by the figurality that philosophy repudiates as literary, and, in consequence, as deceptive, inessential, and expendable. Both logic and contamination are very much at stake in the unfolding of these infectiously multiplying equations. Perhaps by returning to the germ

7. Ibid., 79.
8. Ibid., 149.

of these remarks it will be possible to see how the logic of equations distinctively contaminates the discourse on AIDS.

Against my initial text, Silence=Death, let me juxtapose a passage from an open letter written by Larry Kramer, AIDS activist and author of, among other things, *The Normal Heart,* a play about the difficulties of getting Americans – gay and straight alike – to pay serious attention to the AIDS epidemic. Outraged by dilatory and inadequate responses at the early stages of the medical crisis, Kramer is quoted as having addressed the following words to both the press and the leaders of the gay rights movement: "That all of you . . . continue to refuse to transmit to the public the facts and figures of what is happening *daily* makes you, in my mind, equal to murderers."[9] Beside Kramer's remark I would place a graffito that David Black describes as having been scrawled on a wall at New York University: "Gay Rights =AIDS."[10] A somewhat less overtly homophobic but no less insidious version of this notion is offered by Frances Fitzgerald in her analysis of the effects of AIDS on San Francisco's Castro Street community: "The gay carnival, with its leather masks and ball gowns, had thus been the twentieth-century equivalent of the Masque of the Red Death."[11] And finally, here is a quotation from a "26-year-old-never-married woman" cited by Masters and Johnson in *Newsweek* magazine's excerpt from their controversial book on AIDS: "No sex, no worries. No sex, no AIDS. It's really a very simple equation, isn't it?"[12] Even this brief list indicates that it is by no means a "simple equation," but rather a complex pattern of equations that must lead us to consider just what is at issue in this effort to translate differences (such as silence/death, leaders/murderers, gay rights/AIDS) into identities through a language that invokes the rhetorical form of mathematical or scientific inevitability (A=B), a language of equations that can be marshaled in the service of homophobic (Gay Rights=AIDS) or antihomophobic (Silence=Death) discourse.

In thinking about this we would do well to recall that it is precisely the question of equality, the post-Stonewall demand for equal rights for gays, that has mobilized in unprecedented ways both of these discursive fields. Indeed, the already complex matter of AIDS is exponentially complicated by the fact that the homophobic response to the demands for gay equality, long *before* the phenomenon of AIDS, was largely predicated on the equation of homosexuality with the unnatural, the irrational, and the dis-

9. Cited in Black, *Plague Years,* 17–18.
10. Ibid., 30.
11. Frances Fitzgerald, "The Castro – II," *New Yorker,* 28 July 1986, 50.12.
12. William H. Masters, Virginia E. Johnson, and Robert C. Kolodny, "Sex in the Age of AIDS," *Newsweek,* 14 March 1988, 48.

eased. The logic of homophobia thus rests upon the very same binary that enables Plato in the *Phaedrus* to value speech at the expense of writing – and lest this assertion seem too frivolous or far-fetched an association, let me cite another passage from Derrida's reading of Plato: "the conclusion of the *Phaedrus* is less a condemnation of writing in the name of present speech than a preference for one sort of writing over another, for the fertile trace over the sterile trace, for a seed that engenders because it is planted inside over a seed scattered wastefully outside: at the risk of *dissemination*."[13] If Derrida displaces the opposition between speech and writing by identifying speech itself as just another "sort of writing," he thereby calls into question the logic of the Western philosophical tradition that claims to be able to identify and distinguish the true from the false, the natural from the unnatural. In so doing he enacts the law of transgression that he sees as operative in "both the writing *and* the pederasty of a young man named Plato," a "transgression . . . not thinkable within the terms of classical logic but only within the graphics of the supplement or of the *pharmakon*."[14] Deconstruction, as a disseminative project, then, can be subsumed beneath the rubric of the homosexual and one can read, by contrast, in the emphatic equations cited earlier as politically antithetical responses to the AIDS epidemic, an insistence on the possibility of recuperating truth, of knowing absolutely, even mathematically, some literal identity unmarked by the logic of the supplement or the indeterminacy of the *pharmakon*. So homophobic and antihomophobic forces alike find themselves producing, as defensive reactions to the social and medical crisis of AIDS, discourses that reify and absolutize identities, discourses that make clear the extent to which both groups see the AIDS epidemic as threatening the social structures through which they have constituted their identities for themselves.

Of course heterosexual culture in the West has long interpreted homosexuality as a threat to the security or integrity of heterosexual identity. In our dauntingly inconsistent mythology of homosexuality, "the love that dared not speak its name" was long known as the crime "inter Christianos non nominandum," and it was so designated not only because it was seen as lurid, shameful, and repellent, but also, and contradictorally, because it was, and is, conceived of as being potentially so attractive that even to speak about it is to risk the possibility of tempting some innocent into a fate too horrible – and too seductive – to imagine. One corollary of this fear of seduction through nomination is the still pervasive homophobic misperception of gay sexuality as contagious – as something one can catch through contact with, for instance, a teacher who is lesbian or gay.

13. Derrida, "Plato's Pharmacy," 149.
14. Ibid., 153.

Thus even before the historical accident of the outbreak of AIDS in the gay communities of the West, homosexuality was conceived as a contagion, and the homosexual as parasitic upon the heterosexual community. One chilling instance that may synecdochically evoke the insidious logic behind this homophobic ideology was produced in 1977 in a dissent written by William Rehnquist, now chief justice of the United States, in response to the Court's refusal to grant certiorari in the case of *Gay Lib v. University of Missouri*. As an essay in the *Harvard Law Review* described the case, "the university had refused to recognize a gay students' organization on the ground that such recognition would encourage violation of Missouri's anti-sodomy statute. In support of the university's position, Justice Rehnquist argued that permitting the exercise of first amendment rights of speech and association in this instance would undercut a legitimate state interest, just as permitting people with the measles to associate freely with others would undercut the state's interest in imposing a quarantine."[15] Here, in 1977, the ideological configuration of both homosexuality and discourse in relation to disease, and the invocation, albeit in metaphor, of quarantine as an acceptable model for containment, is offered as an argument against the right to produce a nonhomophobic public discourse on homosexuality.

If such a context suggests the bitter urgency of the activists' assertion that Silence=Death, it does not suffice as a reading of the slogan or of the slogan's relation to the historically specific logic that governs the interimplication of discourse, defense, and disease. For what is striking about Silence=Death as the most widely publicized, gay-articulated language of response to the AIDS epidemic is its insistence upon the therapeutic property of discourse without specifying in any way what should or must be said. Indeed, as a text produced in response to a medical and political emergency, Silence =Death is stunningly self-reflexive. It takes the form of a rallying cry, but its call for resistance is no call to arms; rather, it calls for the production of discourse, the production of more text, as a mode of defense against the opportunism of medical and legislative responses to the epidemic. But what can be said beyond the need to speak? What discourse can this call to discourse desire? Just what *is* the discourse of defense that will immunize the gay body politic against the opportunistic infections of demagogic rhetoric?

An answer to this question can be discerned in Kramer's accusation: "That all of you . . . continue to refuse to transmit to the public the facts and figures of what is happening *daily* makes you, in my mind, equal to

15. "The Constitutional Status of Sexual Orientation: Homosexuality as a Suspect Classification," *Harvard Law Review* 98 (1985): 1294.

murderers." Kramer's charge explicitly demands the production of texts in order to defend against the transmission of disease. In so doing it makes clear that the defensive discourse is a discourse of "facts and figures," a discourse that resists the rhetoric of homophobic ideologues by articulating the truth that it casts in the form of mathematical or scientific data beyond the disputations of rhetoric. In a similar fashion, the textual prescription offered in Silence=Death takes the form of a formula that implies for it the status of a mathematical axiom, a given, a literal truth that is not susceptible to figural evasions and distortions. In this light, the pink triangle that appears above the slogan in the graphic representations of the text functions not only as an emblem of homosexual oppression, but also, and crucially, as a geometrical shape – a triangle *tout court* – that produces a sort of cognitive rhyme with the equation mark inscribed in the text, thus reinforcing semiotically the scientific or geometric inevitability of the textual equation.

At the same time, however, the very formula of mathematical discourse ($A=B$) that appeals to the prestige of scientific fact evokes the paradigmatic formulation or figure of metaphoric substitution. $A=B$, after all, is a wholly conventional way of representing a process whereby metaphor improperly designates one thing by employing the name of another. Though Silence=Death is case in the rhetorical form of geometric equation, and though it invokes, by means of that form, the necessity of articulating a truth of "facts and figures," the fact remains that the equation takes shape as a figure, that it enacts a metaphorical redefinition of "silence" as "death." What this means, then, is that the equations that appear to pronounce literal, scientifically verifiable truth cannot be distinguished from the disavowed literariness of the very figural language those equations undertake to repudiate or exclude. The truth of such equations can only pass for truth so long as we ignore that the literal must itself be produced by a figural sleight of hand.

The rhetorical form of Silence=Death thereby translates the mathematical into the poetic, the literal into the figural, by framing the call to discourse in terms that evoke the distinctive signature of metaphoric exchange. It would be useful in this context to recall for a moment Harold Bloom's identification of trope and defense and to cite yet one more equation, this one actually a series of equations proposed by Bloom in his essay "Freud and the Sublime": "Literal meaning equals anteriority equals an earlier state of meaning equals an earlier state of things equals death equals literal meaning."[16] Silence =Death, read in light of this, would gesture metaphorically toward the process of tropological substi-

---

16. Harold Bloom, "Freud and the Sublime," in *Agon: Towards a Theory of Revisionism* (New York, 1982), 107.

tution that resists or defends against the literality that Bloom, following Freud, identifies with death and sees as producing the reductive absolutism that informs the reality principle. Indeed, Silence=Death would seem to cast itself as that most heroic of all texts: a text whose metaphoric invocation of textuality, a text whose defensive appeal to discourse would have the power "literally" to counteract the agencies of death by exposing the duplicity inherent in the false equations that pass for "literal" truth and that make possible, as a result, such virulent formulations as Gay Rights=AIDS. In this case, for trope to operate as defense would involve, in part, the repudiation of what passes for the "literal truth" of AIDS by attending to the ideological investments that inform the scientific and political discourse about it and by articulating the inevitable construction of the disease within a massively overdetermined array of figural associations.

But such a defensive discourse can claim no immunity against contamination by the figural – a contamination that is nowhere more evident than in its defensive production of the figure of literality, the figure of mathematically precise calculation implicit in the equation Silence = Death. For the politics of language governing the claim of absolute identity in such a formula as Silence=Death aligns that formula, despite its explicitly antihomophobic import, with the logic of natural self-identity implicit in Plato's binary oppositions, a logic that provides the ideological support for the homophobic terrorism Plato himself endorsed in order to defend the "law of restricting procreative intercourse to its natural function by abstention from congress with our own sex, with its deliberate murder of the race and its wasting of the seed of life on a stony and rocky soil, where it will never take root and bear its natural fruit."[17]

The proliferating equations that mark the discourse on AIDS, then, suggest that in the face of the terrifying epistemological ambiguity provoked by this epidemic, in the face of so powerful a representation of the force of what we do not know, the figure of certainty, the figure of literality, is itself ideologically constructed and deployed as a defense, if not as a remedy. (Note one manifestation of this deployment of the figure of knowledge or certainty in the way that political debate about AIDS in America has been counterproductively fixated on proposals to divert millions of dollars from necessary research toward compulsory testing of various populations for the presence of HIV antibodies. Given the persistence of the identification in America of AIDS with the gay male community, it is hard not to see this fixation as part and parcel of the desire to combat uncertainty not only about who has been infected by the so-called "AIDS virus," but also, and perhaps more deeply and irrationally, about how it

17. Cited in Derrida, "Plato's Pharmacy," 152–53.

is possible to determine who is straight and who is gay.) Precisely because the defensive appeal to literality in a slogan like Silence =Death must produce the literal *as a figure* of the need and desire for the shelter of certain knowledge, such a discourse is always necessarily a dangerously contaminated defense – contaminated by the Derridean logic of metaphor so that its attempt to achieve a natural or literal discourse beyond rhetoricity must reproduce the suspect ideology of reified (and threatened) identity marking the reactionary medical and political discourse it would counteract. The discursive logic of Silence =Death thus contributes to the ideologically motivated confusion of the literal and the figural, the proper and the improper, the inside and the outside, and in the process it recalls the biology of the human immunodeficiency virus as it attacks the mechanism whereby the body is able, in David Black's words, to distinguish between "Self and Not-Self."

HIV, scientists tell us, is a retrovirus that reproduces by a method involving an enzyme called reverse transcriptase. This "allows the virus to copy its genetic information into a form that can be integrated into the host cell's own genetic code. Each time a host cell divides, viral copies are produced along with more host cells, each containing the viral code."[18] At issue in the progress of the disease, then, is the question of inscription and transcription, the question of reproduction and substitution. The virus endangers precisely because it produces a code, or speaks a language, that can usurp or substitute for the genetic discourse of certain cells in the human immune system. AIDS thus inscribes within the biology of the human organism the notion of parasitic transcription. And this metastatic or substitutive transcription of the cell is particularly difficult to counteract because HIV, like metaphor, operates to naturalize, or present as proper, that which is improper or alien or imported from without. Subsequent to the metonymy, the contiguous transmission, of infection, the virus establishes itself as part of the essence of essential material of the invaded cell through a version of metaphoric substitution. It changes the meaning of the cellular code so that each reproduction or articulation of the cell disseminates further the altered genetic message. Moreover, one of the properties of HIV is that it can change the "genetic structure of [the] external proteins" that constitute the outer coat by which the immune system that attempt to defend against what is alien or improper. Even worse, since HIV attacks the immune system itself, depleting the T-4 or T-helper cells, it prevents the immune system from being able to "recognize foreign substances (antigens) and . . . eliminate them from the body."[19] Even as it works its tropological wiles within the infected cells, HIV is subverting

18. Johns Hopkins University, "Issues in World Health," 198.
19. Ibid.

the capacity of the immune system to read the difference between what is proper to the body, what is "literally" its own, and what is figural or extrinsic.

But these metaphoric flights of fancy that are at work in the scientific discourse on AIDS, just as they are at work in my own metaphorizing discourse, the flights of fancy in which the failures of discourse as defense are already inscribed within disease, have no literal warrant in "nature." Reverse transcriptase and immune defense systems are metaphoric designations that determine the way we understand the operations of the body; they are readings that metastasize the metabolic by infecting it with a strain of metaphor that can appear to be so natural, so intrinsic to our way of thinking, that we mistake it for the literal truth of the body, as if our rhetorical immune system were no longer operating properly, or as if the virus that is metaphor had mutated so successfully as to evade the antibodies that would differentiate between the inside and the outside, between the proper and the improper. This once again brings to mind Derrida's analysis of the parasitic relation of writing to Plato's living word of speech: "In order to cure the latter of the *pharmakon* and rid it of the parasite, it is thus necessary to put the outside back in its place. To keep the outside out. This is the inaugural gesture of 'logic' itself, of good 'sense' insofar as it accords with the self-identity of *that which is:* being is what it is, the outside is outside and the inside inside."[20] But since, as Derrida says, "metaphoricity is the logic of contamination and the contamination of logic," no discourse can ever achieve the logic of self-identity, the logic of scientific equations, without the infection of metaphor that finds the enemy or alien always already within. As Emily Dickinson declared in anticipation of Derrida's reading of the *pharmakon,* "infection in the sentence breeds."[21] And in the case of AIDS, infection endlessly breeds sentences – sentences whose implication in a poisonous history of homophobic constructions assures that no matter what explicit ideology they serve, they will carry within them the virulent germ of the dominant cultural discourse.

If my conclusion presents the somber circularity of Discourse=Defense =Disease =Discourse, I cannot conclude without trying to locate the zone of infection within these remarks. What I have been suggesting is that any discourse on AIDS must inscribe itself in a volatile and uncontrollable field of metaphoric contention in which its language will necessarily find itself at once appropriating AIDS for its own tendentious purposes and becoming subject to appropriation by the contradictory

20. Derrida, "Plato's Pharmacy," 128.
21. Emily Dickinson, "A Word Dropped Careless on a Page," in *The Complete Poems of Emily Dickinson,* ed. Thomas H. Johnson (Boston, 1960), 553.

logic of homophobic ideology. This essay is not exempt from those necessities. As much as I would insist on the value and urgency of examining the figural inscriptions of AIDS, I am sufficiently susceptible to the gravity of the literal to feel uneasy, as a gay man, about producing a discourse in which the horrors experienced by my own community, along with other communities in America and abroad, become the material for intellectual arabesques that inscribe those horrors within the neutralizing conventions of literary criticism. Yet as painfully as my own investment in the figure of literality evokes for me the profound inhumanity implicit in this figural discourse on AIDS, I am also aware that any discourse on AIDS must inevitably reproduce that tendentious figurality. At the same time, I would argue that the appeal of the literal can be an equally dangerous seduction; it is, after all, the citation of the pressing literality of the epidemic with its allegedly "literal" identification of homosexuality and disease, that fuels the homophobic responses to AIDS and demands that we renounce what are blithely dismissed as figural embellishments upon the "real," material necessities of human survival – embellishments such as civil rights and equal protection under the law. We must be as wary, then, of the temptations of the literal as we are of the ideologies at work in the figural; for discourse, alas, is the only defense with which we can counteract discourse, and there is no available discourse on AIDS that is not itself diseased.